WITHDRAWN
Augsburg College
Library

Date Loaned

May 8 '46			

BETWEEN WAR AND PEACE

A HANDBOOK FOR PEACE WORKERS

BY
FLORENCE BREWER BOECKEL
EDUCATION DIRECTOR OF THE
NATIONAL COUNCIL FOR PREVENTION OF WAR

New York
THE MACMILLAN COMPANY
1928
All rights reserved

COPYRIGHT, 1928,
BY THE MACMILLAN COMPANY.

Set up and printed.
Published October, 1928.

SET UP BY BROWN BROTHERS LINOTYPERS
PRINTED IN THE UNITED STATES OF AMERICA
BY THE CORNWALL PRESS

"History is the record of the mitigation and decline of war, though the slow decline. For ages the human race has gone on under the tyranny of this first brutish form of their effort to be men, for ages showed so much of the nature of the lower animals, the tiger and the shark. But the eternal germination of the better has unfolded new powers, new instincts. The sublime question has startled one and another happy soul in different quarters of the globe—Cannot love be, as well as hate? Cannot peace be, as well as war? This thought has now become so distinct as to be a social thought. This having come, much more will follow. Revolutions go not backward.

"So it is not a great matter how long men refuse to believe the advent of peace; war is on its last legs; and a universal peace is as sure as is the prevalence of civilization over barbarism, of liberal governments over feudal forms. The question for us is only, how soon?"—EMERSON.

FOREWORD

The peace movement is a worldwide movement, effectively organized in many countries. In each it has its special problems and special methods of work. This handbook is an attempt to collect suggestions and material which will be of use to American peace workers, particularly to those who are out of touch with national organizations and in communities where research work is difficult. No one can be more keenly aware than the compiler of such a book of its incompleteness and of the opportunities for error in it. But only by an attempt at a general survey can an idea be given of the scope and resources of the peace movement, of the many opportunities for participation in it, and of the number and complexity of the problems involved in establishing peace with the consequent pressing need for intensive work and for effective organization.

Indebtedness to publishers, organizations and authors is so obvious that acknowledgment seems almost superfluous, but gratitude for favors granted by many individuals must be expressed. Special thanks are due Miss Lucy Swanton for her help in connection with the chapter on Young People and World Peace; to Miss Sybil Jane Moore, Mr. Joseph H. Baird, and Mr. Mark Eccles for special research, and to Mr. Joseph Hutchinson Smith for work on the bibliographies. The book as a whole has been made possible because of the information and material on the peace movement which, through the co-operation of people in all parts of the country, has steadily accumulated in the offices of the National Council for Prevention of War during the seven years of its existence.

CONTENTS

	PAGE
FOREWORD	vii

PART I
INTRODUCTION

CHAPTER		
I.	FOCUSING THE DEMAND FOR PEACE	3

PART II
MATERIAL OF INTEREST TO SPECIAL GROUPS

II.	EDUCATION AND PEACE	15
III.	THE CHURCH AND PEACE	71
IV.	WOMEN AND PEACE	106
V.	COMMERCE AND PEACE	124
VI.	LABOR AND PEACE	143
VII.	FARMERS AND PEACE	157
VIII.	WAR VETERANS AND PEACE	166
IX.	YOUNG PEOPLE AND PEACE	183

PART III
INTRODUCTION TO FURTHER STUDY OF INFLUENCES FOR AND AGAINST WORLD PEACE

X.	THE LEAGUE OF NATIONS AND INTERNATIONAL LABOR ORGANIZATION	197
XI.	THE WORLD COURT	217
XII.	THE OUTLAWRY OF WAR AND THE KELLOGG TREATY	231
XIII.	ARBITRATION OF INTERNATIONAL DISPUTES . .	241
XIV.	INTERNATIONAL LAW	265

CONTENTS

CHAPTER		PAGE
XV.	INTERNATIONAL COÖPERATION	277
XVI.	INTERNATIONAL REDUCTION OF ARMAMENTS	286
XVII.	PACIFISM AND THE ABSOLUTE PACIFIST POSITION	299
XVIII.	THE MILITARY POLICY OF THE UNITED STATES PAST AND PRESENT	309
XIX.	THE MONROE DOCTRINE	334
XX.	IMPERIALISM	342
XXI.	WORLD POPULATION AND THE IMMIGRATION POLICY OF THE UNITED STATES	358
XXII.	THE WAR-MAKING POWER IN THE UNITED STATES GOVERNMENT	373
XXIII.	WAR DEBTS AND REPARATIONS	380
XXIV.	WHAT WAR IS	391
XXV.	WHAT WAR COSTS	401

PART IV

MATERIALS FOR A WORKING PROGRAM

XXVI.	WHAT YOU CAN DO FOR PEACE	415
	LIST OF ORGANIZATIONS WORKING FOR PEACE	509
	BIBLIOGRAPHY	514
	APPENDIX:	
	COVENANT OF THE LEAGUE OF NATIONS	557
	TEXT OF THE MULTILATERAL TREATY FOR THE RENUNCIATION OF WAR	574
	INDEX	575

PART I
INTRODUCTION

BETWEEN WAR AND PEACE

CHAPTER I

FOCUSING THE DEMAND FOR PEACE

THE peace movement has apparently escaped from the red-herring theory that human nature is what needs to be changed and has definitely turned its attention upon governments as the agency responsible for war. In monarchical days it was well understood that it was kings who made the wars, and early pleas for peace were addressed directly to them. Under democracy it has been hard to place responsibility for war upon the government as something apart from the people. The World War, however, clearly revealed that there is a distinction between those who control the government and the people as a whole—a distinction which has, perhaps, never been more definitely stated than by Alanson B. Houghton, United States Ambassador to Great Britain, in a speech which he made before the Harvard Alumni in June, 1927:

"War does not originate from time to time simply in a sudden and uncontrollable impulse on the part of one great national mass to go out and slaughter another. War is possible, no doubt, because these masses are willing, under conditions, to fight, but these conditions are themselves an integral part of the problem. Before a war is conceivable there must be an issue. And that issue, broadly speaking, is the outcome of a series of maneuvers by which the masses concerned are brought into positions of opposition. Obviously, this maneuvering is not done by the masses themselves.

Collectively and as individuals they have little, if anything, to do with the subtle and gradual shifting of international relationships. Their interests are directed to the more humble and prosaic task of earning a living. The maneuvering is done by little groups of men called governments. These little groups seek constantly and naturally to gain supposed advantages of one sort and another for their own nationals. Out of their efforts to enlarge or to strengthen or to maintain the interests entrusted to their charge, the masses they represent are gradually maneuvered into positions which, to say the least, cannot easily be surrendered. If the process continues, sooner or later a situation arises in which an agreement between these small groups becomes impossible. Then, on the ground that their lives and families and property are somehow involved and endangered, these great masses of men and women, roused by every power of organized appeal and propaganda, are ordered under arms, and war follows. The entire process is in control of the smaller groups. They make the issue. They declare the war. . . . And the very men through whose instrumentality, consciously or unconsciously, this dreadful catastrophe has been brought about, explain it on the ground that, human nature being what it is, any other determination was impossible."

Once it is recognized that governments are the determining agency in issues of peace and war, it becomes obvious that the peace movement can achieve results only through political action. It has been slow to act politically not alone for the reason suggested above, but because, so far as support of a plan for the prevention of war goes, it has not been a united movement. Work in many different directions is needed to organize the world on a peace basis, and there are various methods for the peaceful settlement of international disputes, applicable to different situations. This being true, the peace movement can never have sufficient unity for effective political action if it conceives its function to be the proposal of a single peace plan. But it begins to conceive the part which it is to play in the establishment of peace rather differently. Social and economic forces quite outside the peace movement, which have been developing through the centuries, are converging to eliminate war. Peace is inevitable. The function of the peace movement is to protect the immediate future against war, to save the world the sacrifice of another generation to an outgrown custom, by building up a public opinion which will hasten this development by requiring governments to concentrate their attention upon the peace problem before all others.

Activities during the last year, notably the negotiation of a treaty renouncing war, indicate that governments are becoming increasingly aware of the demand of the people for peace. Public opinion should support every effort put forth looking toward peace, should make each such effort an opportunity for greater concentration of public attention upon the problem in general, should use each gain as a point of leverage for further advance, and should seek to close the gap between the principles to which governments give verbal adherence and their daily practice in the conduct of international affairs.

Already the peace forces in England and the United States, and in other countries as well, have learned to unite in times of crisis to demand as international disputes arise that governments find some way other than war to adjust them. In England they averted war with Russia and later with China. In this country measures that carried the threat of war have been successfully opposed, for example, in the modification of the government's policy toward Mexico and in the defeat of the big navy program which encouraged naval competition. United action in emergencies, however, is not enough, for issues of peace and war are determined by gradually developed policies. Ways must be found to focus the common demand for peace, day in and day out, upon men in control of government policies in order that as every significant decision is made, its effect upon the vitally important problem of the protection of the nation against the waste and interruption of war shall be taken into consideration.

"Most governments," according to Sir Arthur Salter, British economic expert, "will temper their action by considering any imminent risk of war which it may involve. What is necessary—and this is much more difficult—is that they shall deliberately guide their policy by considering whether it is likely ultimately to increase or diminish the world tendencies that make for peace."

Collier's in its issue of September 8, 1923, stated the situation bluntly:

"War is purely and entirely a governmental industry. . . . Peace also is a governmental product. The fact to get into your head is that every government day by day is either manufacturing peace or else manufacturing war."

To urge consideration of all questions from the point of view of peace is not to make it the chief end of government. Peace is merely the minimum. Only if international peace is established can the pressing problems of modern national life be solved. Woodrow Wilson once said:

"I call you to witness that our civilization is not satisfactory. It is an industrial civilization, and at the heart of it is an antagonism between those who labor with their hands and those who direct labor. You cannot compose those differences in the midst of war, and you cannot advance civilization unless you have a peace of which you make the fullest use in bringing these elements of civilization together into a common partnership. We have got to have leisure and freedom of mind to settle these things."

A statement in the *Japan Chronicle* may be taken as a further sign of the thought of responsible leaders on this question. Meeting an argument that the renunciation of war at present would mean the establishment of a status quo very favorable to the Anglo-Saxon races, it said:

"It is doubtful, even if we succeeded in destroying the status quo by force, whether the world re-created in that way would make a society more agreeable to the sense of justice. The fact is that peace and justice are very delicately interlocked. . . . In order to establish order based on justice in international society, it is essential to have security for peace as foundation work. International justice can be made sure only on the basis of consolidated order and in a society where brute force does not stalk about as the final arbiter but social relations are regulated by human wisdom and virtue. Even the development of domestic law has been a perpetual rational war for justice on peaceful foundations. International law and order must also develop in the same way."

The peace movement has, therefore, a second purpose. It must look beyond the abolition of war and prepare for the utilization of the opportunities a world at peace will offer for increased justice and happiness among men and for increased power through increased coöperation. Except as an opportunity, peace is meaningless.

No single government can establish peace; international action is required. But besides controlling its own policies in the interest of peace, an individual government can initiate international action for peace. The founders of the government of the United States looked to it to do exactly this. Samuel Adams, writing for the General Assembly of Massachusetts, sent a letter to the delegates of that state in the first Congress in which he said:

"You are hereby instructed and urged to move the United States in Congress assembled to take into their deep and most serious consideration whether any measures can by them be used, through their influence with such of the nations in Europe with whom they are united by treaties of amity or commerce, that national differences may be settled and determined without the necessity of war, in which the world has too long been deluged, to the destruction of human happiness and the disgrace of human reason and government."

Franklin sent a copy of the Constitution of the United States to friends in Europe with this message, "I send you enclos'd the propos'd new Federal Constitution for these States. If it succeeds, I do not see why you might not in Europe carry the Project of good Henry the 4th into Execution, by forming a Federal Union and One Grand Republick of all its different States & Kingdoms; by means of a like Convention; for we had many Interests to reconcile." Washington told the first United States commission sent abroad to negotiate treaties of commerce that his "first wish" was to see "war banished from the earth," and he was responsible as President for the first arbitration treaty in modern history.

The form of government set up in the United States, "a coöperative sovereignty," with a court representing this joint sovereignty, set an example for the peaceful organization of the world. This country continued to lead in the development of arbitration; in its early years it took the initiative in the establishment of the first unarmed boundary, between Canada and the United States; later it laid before the other nations plans for an international court which resulted in the Hague Tribunal; it established new precedents in international relations by returning the Chinese Boxer Indemnity and by withdrawing from Cuba; more recently it has been largely responsible for the establishment of the League of Na-

FOCUSING THE DEMAND FOR PEACE

tions and for the organization of the World Court, and it was the first to make official proposals for the outlawry of war.

It is obvious that in calling upon their government to bend its energies to establishing peace, until the whole complicated problem is solved and international peace assured, Americans today are not asking it to take up a new idea or to support a principle foreign to its traditions. No more are they asking it to do something which other governments are not being called upon to do. In England the Liberal Party has issued a manifesto expressing its support of arbitration treaties, reduction of armaments and the codification of international law. The position of the British Labor Party is well known, and the following amendment which it recently proposed to the Air Estimate Bill received 116 votes in Parliament:

"In view of the peril to civilization in air warfare, this House regrets that His Majesty's Government did not advocate bolder proposals for aerial disarmament at the meeting of the Preparatory Commission for the Disarmament Conference at Geneva, and urges them to take the initiative in putting forward a programme containing the abolition of military and naval air forces and the establishment of the international control of civil aviation."

In the treaties of Locarno, France and Germany by mutual concession have made one of the greatest contributions possible to the peace of the world. In every important country today an organized peace movement is demanding a solution of the peace problem and is beginning to judge government officials according to their efforts in this direction.

The chart which accompanies this chapter indicates the channels through which a public opinion sufficiently well informed to be articulate can be built up, and the channels through which that opinion can be effectively focused upon the men who control government policies. But all charts are too simple. Public opinion not only leads to government action, but government action, if by no more than the expression of official opinion, should be called upon to play its part in forming public opinion. In its issue of October 6, 1923, the *Saturday Evening Post* printed this remarkable editorial:

"Perhaps war is inevitable. It is rapidly being made so, but only because those whose duty it is to make it impossible are leading the world towards it through the stupidity of their policies. To cover insensate ambition, or greed, or blundering it is always possible, temporarily at least, to inflame the minds of the people, to make them believe that their lands and lives are in danger from a nation that they have been taught to hate; and then to lead them on to violent action. But it would be just as easy by the same methods to teach tolerance and goodwill for a neighbor. Then when disputes arose the people could be led to an international court instead of to a battlefield.

". . . What then shall we say of those leaders who play on the emotions of their people to their undoing? If they would iterate, and the parrots would reiterate, that war is unthinkable; that international as well as national differences can be settled without bloodshed, we should be in a fair way to get rid of all this stuff and nonsense about the 'inevitability of war.'"

When governments accept the secure establishment of peace as their first duty and undertake it wholeheartedly instead of with the hesitancy they now show in peace proposals, they will be quick to exercise their power to create a supporting public opinion. In the meantime, public opinion must precede government action. The only basis on which to build up an active and enduring public opinion is facts. The chief facts of the modern world call for

FOCUSING THE DEMAND FOR PEACE 11

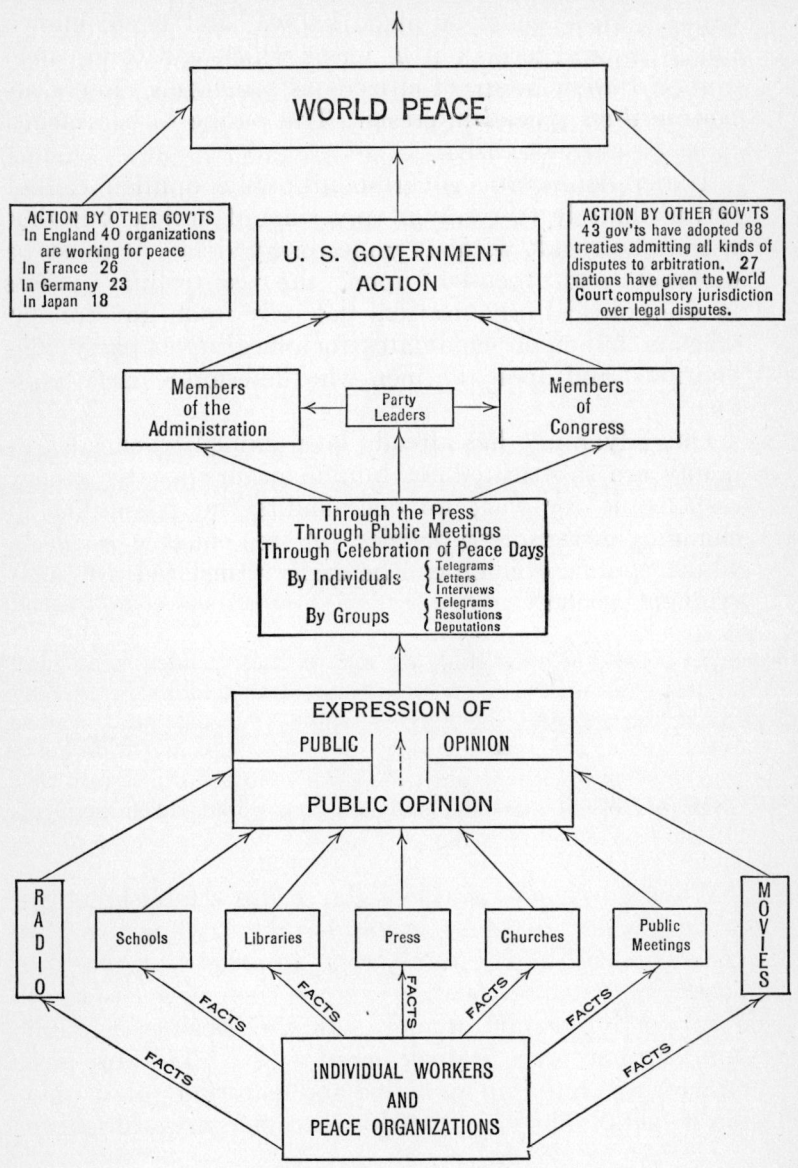

peace. These must be made known, and made known not in general terms but in terms which will bring them home to every group of citizens as something closely affecting their special interests. The public to be reached must be individualized.

Under democratic government public opinion cannot fail ultimately to result in government action, but that it may so result without unnecessary delay, it must be directed and focused upon the controlling points in the political organization, not only upon government officials, but upon candidates for office, upon party conventions, and upon the men who determine party platforms.

One advantage has already been gained when governments are substituted for human nature as the agency responsible for war; no one doubts the possibility of changing government policies. A free country is one in which "public opinion can be easily translated into government action."

PART II
MATERIAL OF INTEREST TO SPECIAL GROUPS

CHAPTER II

EDUCATION AND PEACE

THE difficulty with which educators today find themselves confronted might be compared to that of men and women who have grown up in a pioneer community and who, as it ceases to be the frontier and becomes an organized town, are called upon to train their young for a kind of life they themselves have not experienced. Mankind's pioneer days of exploring the earth and settling it are over. An organized world community is rapidly developing. The question is, Can the present generation train the one that is growing up for the kind of world that lies ahead of it?

The problem is not one of "education for peace," but of education for a way of life in harmony with new conditions. The individual's environment reaches today around the earth. Science has brought all parts of the world within his easy reach, and so interwoven its relationships that nothing anywhere is wholly remote or foreign to him.

What facts does he need to know and with what attitude ought he to approach life if he is to live successfully in such an environment? How is he to be given a knowledge of the facts and helped to acquire the attitude he needs? In every nation educators are trying to answer these questions.

The account in this chapter of what is already being accomplished has been made detailed and concrete in order that, although much of it may not be of interest to the general reader, its practical value to the teacher may be as great as possible. For the same reason, the chapter has been divided into sections dealing with international and national educational organizations, with schools of an international character, with the training of teachers, with academic and extra academic work in the universities, and with work in the elementary schools.

It is encouraging to remember that the activities described in this outline are merely examples of many methods for cultivating international understanding and goodwill that are being tried out today in the schools and colleges of the country. Clearly there exists an enlightened determination to win the race between education and catastrophe in which, according to H. G. Wells, we are engaged.

Studies in Attitude

In order that it may be known what attitude toward world problems is being cultivated in students by the present methods of education, several illuminating "studies in attitudes" have been made. One of these, "A Study of International Attitudes of High School Students" by Dr. George Bradford Neumann, was published in 1926 by Teachers College of Columbia University. Tests were given to 110 high school students nearing graduation. Among the twelve subjects on which the tests were based were racialism, nationalism, imperialism, militarism and humanitarianism. The responses of the students showed a strong tendency toward nationalism, fear for the welfare of their own nation and suspicion of other nations; a tendency away from imperialism with a conviction in favor of self-determination for weaker nations; and a general tendency in favor of military preparedness which, however, it was held should not be al-

EDUCATION AND PEACE 17

lowed to interfere with the ideals of the nation. Although the students showed strong humanitarian tendencies, when they faced a conflict between their concern for humanity and for their nation, their nationalism tended to lower their humanitarian impulses to within the area of indecision.

Dr. Neumann says of the data resulting from his study:

". . . it raises the serious question as to whether or not the international attitudes now being developed belong to a generation past or rapidly passing rather than to the generation to which the students belong. . . .

"But what are right attitudes? Certainly one answer is that they must be based upon facts so far as facts can be known rather than upon prejudices contrary to facts. The data resulting from this study show certain tendencies which appear to be based upon prejudices and therefore call for correction. . . .

"The tendency of each generation is to impose its own values on the succeeding generation, but if the new generation's needs differ from the old, can the old values adequately meet the new needs of the new generation? In international relations is the present generation right in inculcating attitudes based upon the old values of the present generation? Is there not rather a demand that the new generation be helped to discover ways and means of determining its own values to meet its own needs?"

An investigation of "Student Opinion on War" was carried on in 1925 and 1926 by Mr. Elliot Porter in connection with postgraduate work in the University of Chicago. One hundred and fifty statements about war and peace to be marked "certainly right," "probably right," "doubtful," "probably wrong," "certainly wrong," were sent to over a thousand students in eighteen colleges. The results showed in general that students "recognize the economic roots of war, vote fairly pacifist on abstract statements regarding preparedness, and have largely revised their ideas regarding responsibility for the recent war. . . . Most students agreed with all but the most extreme statements regarding the results of war. Scarcely any revealed a consistently romantic attitude toward it. Save a few pessimists, students voted in favor of all but the most extreme proposals to eliminate war. Surprisingly little pronounced nationalism appeared." A vote on the statement "My country right or wrong" was "certainly right," 186; "probably right," 128; "doubtful," 151; "probably wrong," 148; "certainly wrong," 387. Over 92% preferred the version "My country when right to be kept right, when wrong to be put right."

"The Measurement of Fair-Mindedness," by Professor Goodwin B. Watson, was published by Teachers College in 1925. Professor Watson has worked out methods of testing a student's "fair-open-scientific-mindedness." Of the need of such tests he says:

"There seems to be clear evidence that there is a need and demand for a type of education which shall bring about progress towards fair-mindedness. Such progress is at best uncertain until some instrument can be constructed which will measure the degree to which fair-mindedness, or freedom from bias, has been achieved."

The earliest study made in this field was conducted by James C. Manry at the University of Iowa in 1923 and published under the title "World Citizenship" in 1927. Through a series of carefully tested questionnaires submitted to freshman, sophomore, junior and senior classes of representative colleges and universities an attempt was made to answer two questions: To what extent are our institutions of higher learning bringing their students into effective contact with world affairs? What are the most practical lines of further advance in the development of world citizenship? The general conclusions drawn from the study as briefly stated by the author are: that colleges vary greatly in the degree to which they are promoting world-mindedness; orientation courses and travel are shown to be important factors influencing ability to score well on the test; the exchange of teachers and the migration of students should be encouraged; an initiatory course for the purpose of enabling students to orientate themselves with reference to a world point of view should be offered in the early part of all college courses. Although the test revealed astonishing ignorance on the part of students it did not show any deep-seated prejudices or antipathies, and the author concludes:

"Among American college students education does not have to combat age-old racial hatreds and animosities. The most common errors bear eloquent testimony that sheer ignorance, together with the democratic impulse to entertain opinions notwithstanding, is responsible for the most part for the purely emotional and verbal thinking about international affairs. This situation gives real ground for the hope that our colleges and universities can do much if they will in the development of world citizenship."

In the *Journal of Educational Psychology* for May, 1928, a report is published of an "Experimental Investigation of the Reaction of the School Children of Poland to Enemy Occupation During the World War, Designed to Determine Why Children Hate." The investigation, unique of its kind, was made by Dr. Francisca Baumgarten, Polish psychologist, in the schools of her country during 1918. It was necessary at the time to bury the papers embodying the results of this investigation, and they have only recently been recovered and not yet fully published. In the article describing them, written by Dr.

Daniel A. Prescott of Harvard University, the results of the investigation are declared to indicate that international or interracial hatred, so often said to be instinctive, a part of "human nature," and therefore impossible to change, is due rather to war experiences which teach hate and which, if not personal, are a part of social heredity and not of biological heredity.

Studies of Textbooks

A different approach to this problem of discovering what is actually being taught in the schools is to be seen in the various studies that are being made of school textbooks.

The most comprehensive study of history texts is that of the Carnegie Endowment for International Peace, which includes a detailed study of the textbooks of France, England, Germany, Belgium, Italy and Bulgaria. In it an attempt was made to answer these questions: "In what spirit do school histories present to their young readers the events of the five tragic years of the World War? What lesson is learned from the manner in which they recount the facts and comment upon them? Will the generation which is growing up in the schools learn from these books the horror of war, a sense of justice, a belief that a new era has begun for humanity, bought by the very excess of its faults and sufferings, or will these histories prolong the reactions of the war and give the impression that men will never cease to prey upon each other, and so, without hope, must continue to prepare themselves for more terrible conflicts?" The results of this study have so far been published only in French. They occupy two volumes and can be obtained through the Carnegie Endowment offices in New York City.

The American Historical Association has appointed a committee, of which Prof. A. C. Krey of the University

EDUCATION AND PEACE

of Minnesota is chairman, to carry on a five-year study of the teaching of history and social studies in the schools of America.

The Department of Political Science of the University of Chicago is conducting "a somewhat comprehensive study of comparative civic training—that is, of the methods by which citizens are produced in a number of foreign countries."

The American Association of University Women is now making, through its state associations, a detailed survey of history textbooks used in the United States.

The World Federation of Education Associations, through an international committee, plans a worldwide investigation of the present teaching of history and of history textbooks from the standpoint of international amity. According to the program adopted, the textbooks of each country will be examined by local committees and later compared in order to discover differences of statement and inaccuracies. The committee of the American Association of University Women, referred to above, has been made a joint committee with the local committee for the United States.

The Association for Peace Education of Chicago has published a careful study made by educational experts, of history textbooks, under the title, "The War Emphasis in the Histories in our Elementary Schools, and its Impress upon the Mind of the Child."

A briefer study of the thirty textbooks most widely used in the schools of the United States in 1923 was published under the title, "War and Peace in U. S. History Textbooks" by the National Council for Prevention of War. This revealed that no one of the texts recognized the significance of the efforts in the history of this country to promote peace. Discussions of William Penn's colony ignored its importance as an experiment in government based not on force but on justice and goodwill. Eight of the texts did not mention the effort of the United States to promote arbitration. Less than one-half of the books gave any account of the Hague Conferences and none gave more than a few paragraphs to them. Nineteen of the histories made no mention of the Pan American Conferences, and only two gave any account of the Bryan Conciliation Treaties. While the labor movement and woman's movement were treated at least briefly in practically all the histories, only six took any cognizance of the peace movement and several of these disposed of it in a phrase or sentence.

The International Committee on Intellectual Coöperation of the League of Nations adopted in July, 1925, what is known as the Casares proposal, providing for a method of correcting misstatements in textbooks. The plan which is to be carried out through the National Committees on Intellectual Coöperation is as follows:

(a) When a National Committee thinks it desirable that a foreign text concerning its country and intended for use in schools should be amended for the reasons indicated in the present resolution, it shall make a request to this effect to the National Committee of the country where the text is in use, at the same time submitting, if necessary, a draft emendation on the desired lines, together with a brief statement of the reasons.

(b) National Committees on receiving a request of this kind, shall decide in the first instance whether the request should be accepted and shall then determine what representations of a friendly and private nature, if any, should be made to the authors or publishers with a view to the proposed emendation.

(c) All the National Committees will at the same time be requested to specify the publications most suitable for giving foreigners a knowledge of the history, civilization and present position of their country.

What International Educational Organizations Are Doing

The extent of the interest of educators in the question of training their pupils as world citizens, as well as citizens of the country in which they live, is strikingly evident in the number and activities of the international organizations of teachers formed in most instances since the World War.

Shortly following the close of the War, the National Education Association of the United States proposed an international conference of teachers which was held in San Francisco in 1923 and resulted in the formation of the *World Federation of Education Associations*. The purposes of the Federation, as stated in its articles of incorporation, are:

"to promote the cause of education and to elevate the character of teaching throughout the world; to secure international coöperation in educational enterprises; to foster the dissemination of information concerning the progress of education in all its forms among nations and peoples; to advise and promote suitable and effective means to bring into closer coördination the various agencies in every civilized country which have to do with education; to cultivate international goodwill, and to promote the interests of worldwide peace."

The Federation is under the management of a board of directors, the members of which are geographically distributed, and of a board of trustees of from 15 to 21 persons, who direct the financial administration. Its president is Dr. Augustus O. Thomas, Commissioner of Education for Maine. The conferences of the Federation are biennial. The first was held in Edinburgh in 1925, the second in Toronto in 1927, and the third will be held in Geneva in 1929, at the invitation of the International Bureau of Education.

Full membership in the Federation is open to international and national educational organizations or associations of persons directly connected with education, and organizations of educators in a country not possessing a nationwide organization; also to delegates chosen by the associate representatives from individual universities and recognized institutions of higher learning of any country, who have the right to elect from among their number one delegate or more as may be provided in the by-laws; and to the associate representatives from the individual education authorities of any country, who have the right to elect one delegate from among their number. Associate membership is open to individual institutions or associations whose chief function is education, but which are ineligible to full membership. Associate members have full right of discussion in open assembly, but have no right to vote in the delegate assembly.

The organization of the World Federation, led Mr. Raphael Herman of Washington, D. C., to offer in 1923 a prize of $25,000 for the best educational plan calculated to promote world peace. Dr. David Starr Jordan, Chancellor Emeritus of Leland Stanford, Jr., University, was the author of the plan which received the award and which has been adopted by the World Federation as a program of work. Five "Herman-Jordan" Committees have been appointed to carry it out. They are in brief:

Committee No. 1. A world committee on education for international understanding and peace to coordinate the work of educational groups in this field and cooperate with organizations working along similar lines in all parts of the world.

Committee No. 2. A committee to investigate the present teaching of history and history textbooks, stressing the need that history, whether elementary or advanced, should be just and true so far as it goes; that it should not be perverted in the supposed interest of national honor or partisanship, and should promote patriotism built upon love of country rather than upon hatred of any people.

Committee No. 3. A committee to consider plans for promoting international understanding among students, especially through international athletic sports, and games involving cooperative action or team play as distinguished from individual competition; international correspondence among school children; the study of international civics; essay and oratorical contests; and exchange of students.

Committee No. 4. A committee to investigate the current arguments for war as a cosmic necessity, and both sides of the question of military training in school and college.

Committee No. 5. A committee to study the Hague Court and the present Permanent Court of International Justice, and the relation of these to world education; to determine, if possible, what international activities of this nature should furnish material for instruction within the schools, and how to approach the subject in a fair-minded and open manner.

At the first biennial meeting of the World Federation, which was held in Edinburgh in 1925, resolutions were adopted urging:

The universal celebration of Goodwill Day;

The teaching of "geography, history and training in citizenship, not only from a national point of view, but also from a modern sociological and international point of view;"

The encouragement of "movements and committees which establish international contacts among school children through correspondence, exchange of school work and interchange of pupils;"

The preparation of "textbooks for elementary schools descriptive of child life in all lands and setting forth in brief and simple form the best each nation has achieved;"

Special courses in teacher-training institutions and universities to develop an international outlook;

The development of plans for foreign travel and interchange of teachers.

At the second conference twenty-one associations were represented as full members, and twelve as associate members. Among the national organizations were the National Union of Teachers of England and Wales, the Japanese Education Association and the Bund Entschiedener Schulreformer of Germany. The chief emphasis of the meeting was upon the development of international understanding. The Federation has recently begun the publication of a monthly bulletin through the office of the Secretary, Mr. Charles Williams, at Columbia, Missouri.

The International Bureau of Education, which has headquarters in Geneva, was founded by the Jean Jacques Rousseau Institute in 1926 "to develop international relations in the teaching profession by establishing a link between teachers of all nations, and thus to assist in the advancement of education in general." The activities of the Bureau, which is under the direction of Professor Pierre Bovet, fall under three heads: information, scientific research, and coördination of organization activities. The Bureau, which is managed by a Council consisting of seventeen members representing nine nationalities, coöperates in the organization of international conferences on education, and was responsible for the international conference held at Prague in April, 1927, on "What the Schools Can Do for Peace." The resolutions adopted at this conference included recommendations for the development of contacts between students of all nations through correspondence, voyages and international camps, and for the development in all branches of education of better international understanding. The International Bureau, which has recently taken over the work of the Bureau of Moral Education of which the headquarters were at The Hague, is affiliated with the World Federation of Education Associations. It issues a quarterly bulletin and valuable reports, bibliographies and other publications. Individuals may belong to the Bureau and receive its publications by paying an annual fee of $5.00.

The International Federation of Associations of Teachers also was formed in 1926 when representatives of the General Association of German Teachers, with a membership of 150,000, met with representatives of the National Association of French Teachers, which has 78,000 members, and agreed to unite for two purposes: collaboration in the solution of professional problems and coöperation in the promotion of peace. A few months later, the National Union of Teachers in England with 121,000 members and similar organizations in Holland, Bulgaria, Sweden, Czechoslovakia, Switzerland and Latvia joined the Federation.

The International Federation differs from the World Federation of Education Associations in that it admits to membership only teachers and aims to limit its program somewhat more definitely in order to become immediately "a center of action." It affirms in the statement of its program that the necessary fundamental condition of a durable peace is an education for the children of all countries designed to create mutual understanding. It has established headquarters at the International Institute of Intellectual Coöperation at Paris. It is collecting information concerning the schools of all countries; developing a system of exchange of teachers, of pupils and of publications, and arranges international tours and exchange visits. It has begun the publication of a periodical in German, English and French, through which it hopes to coördinate activities carried on simultaneously in the various countries for the promotion of international goodwill.

The New Education Fellowship was established in 1921. Its fourth international conference in Locarno in August, 1927, was attended by 1,200 educational leaders from 42 countries, including 130 delegates from the United States. The Fellowship opposes "the old spirit of rule by force, of competition, of fear—engendering hate and war—and promotes the new spirit of coöperation, unity, psychological freedom, engendering love and a brotherhood of nations." Membership in the Fellowship may be held by individuals, and entitles them to information and advice as well as to the three official magazines published, one in England, one in France, and one in Germany. The address of the organization is 11 Tavistock Square, London, W. C. 1, England.

The Progressive Education Association, which was organized in 1919, has members in thirty-five countries. Its educational principles are similar to those of the New Education Fellowship. It seeks the promotion of the spirit of goodwill and coöperation between individuals, groups and nations as part of its educational program. The headquarters are in Washington, D. C.

The International Federation of Teachers Federations has recently been completed by the International Federation of Trade Unions at Amsterdam.

The *International Kindergarten Union,* with headquarters in Washington, carries on work for better international understanding through a committee on international relations.

In 1927, an *International Federation of Home and School* was formed to carry on internationally such work as is now being done by the National Congress of Parents and Teachers, and unites men and women of many nations in a common program for the welfare of children.

GOVERNMENTS INTERESTED IN INTERNATIONAL EDUCATION

In addition to what educational organizations are doing to create international understanding through the schools, governments acting individually and through the League of Nations are encouraging the adoption of educational programs of goodwill.

The new constitution of Germany calls for education "in the spirit of German national culture and of international conciliation."

In Japan chapters on recent developments in international coöperation have been introduced into all history textbooks, and an effort has been made not only to eliminate all unfriendly references to other countries, but to include in textbooks an account of the great men of all nations. A textbook on morals used in a majority of the secondary schools of Japan, and written by the professor of ethics of the Tokyo Higher Normal College, includes chapters on the preservation of world peace, internationalism, the League of Nations and international morality. A Japanese Association for International Education was organized in 1922 "to promote mutual understanding and justice between nations, to advance the cause of world culture and to work for the realization of enduring peace." It has joined the National Peace Council of Japan, which includes some ten national organizations, and is closely associated with the Imperial Education Association. The two organizations reach 200,000 teachers in the common schools.

In France following the suggestion of the Ministry of Education, French teachers adopted the following resolution:

"The 78,000 French teachers of both sexes, grouped in their national union, realizing their duties as educators and being convinced that the reconciliation and coöperation of the peoples who fought against each other during the war must be hastened by education at school, decide to make every effort to lead the younger generation to the knowledge and understanding of other peoples in order that it may thus contribute towards the organization of peace. They undertake to abstain in their teaching from any word which might be injurious to international understanding and to eschew all school books which advocate war and thus represent a danger for the organization of peace."

In England conferences of teachers and government officials have worked out programs of instruction and plans for textbooks designed to give children a knowledge of the League of Nations, and teach them the principles of international peace.

In Mexico the graduating classes of the primary schools are required to keep a moral score card under eleven main heads, self-control, health, kindness, sportsmanship, self-confidence, duty, good faith, truth, good workmanship, coöperation, and loyalty—to family, to school, to city, state, and country, to humanity and civilization. According to William English Walling in "Mexican Life," intolerance is sharply criticized by the teachers, on the ground that "any intolerance whatever disturbs the collective life."

In the Czechoslovakian schools ten commandments are taught of which the last two are:

Do not call anyone a patriot who hates other nations or despises them or desires war; war is a relic of barbarism.

Love your country and your nation, but work to the end that all men may one day live together as brethren in happiness and peace, and that no nation need be afraid of being attacked by another.

An idea of what is being done in the schools of the United States and by the educational organizations of this country may be gathered from the following pages. It is an interesting fact that in the constitution of at least one state, Massachusetts, there is a statute which imposes upon teachers the obligation of teaching the principles of "love of country, humanity and universal benevolence."

THE LEAGUE OF NATIONS AND INTELLECTUAL COÖPERATION

The League of Nations, believing that it was its task "to accelerate the exchange of ideas between nations," as well as to improve the exchange of material products, undertook in 1920 a consideration of what "practicable steps might be of aid in the international organization of intellectual work." The result was the appointment in 1922 of the International Committee on Intellectual Coöperation composed of men and women of different nations, individually best qualified to deal with matters of education and science. The members included such international figures as Henri Bergson, Mme. Curie, Albert Einstein and Gilbert Murray. In 1925, the International Institute of Intellectual Coöperation, to act as an executive body for the Committee, was created. Funds for the support of the Institute are appropriated by individual governments, the largest amount being contributed by France.

National committees coöperating with the International Committee have now been formed in thirty-two countries, including the United States. The American National Committee on International Intellectual Coöperation was organized in 1926 with headquarters in the building of the National Academy of Science in Washington. The Chairman is Dr. Robert A. Millikan and the Executive Secretary, Mr. J. David Thompson.

The fundamental object of the Committee has been said to be to accustom men's minds to coöperate. It seeks to bring about friendlier international relations and to improve the conditions of intellectual work by increasing coöperation and assistance among intellectual workers in different countries. In general the Committee acts as a clearing house of information; it coördinates activities in the various fields of intellectual endeavor; it provides headquarters for international associations and assists them in arranging conferences; it carries on investigations; it develops plans for the protection of intellectual property rights; it coördinates international bibliographical material; it studies the possibilities for the exchange of professors and students and for a system of mutual recognition of scholastic degrees; it encourages international student travel by inducing governments to grant special passport and visa privileges and in some instances to reduce rates on government-controlled railroads; it develops plans for the instruction of young people in the aims and purposes of the League of Nations and the ideals of international coöperation.

Among the investigations which the Committee is carrying on is one regarding the possibility of post-graduate scholarships and the assembling of post-graduate scholars in coöperative research centers according to their special subjects. Another question which it is studying is that of securing a wider translation of important works. It is also attempting to coördinate national centers of advanced international studies by inducing the interested institutions to establish contacts, exchange teachers and pupils and bring their programs as far as possible into line.

A carefully worked out plan for the instruction of youth in international relations, which is quoted below, has been submitted by the Committee to all governments belonging to the League of Nations and brought to the attention of the school authorities. Interesting reports on what is being done to carry it out in the different schools are being received by the Committee.

The publications of the Committee, which may be obtained in the United States from the World Peace Foundation of Boston, include a quarterly International Bulletin of Universal Relations; an International Bulletin of Scientific Relations; the *Mouseion* dealing with international topics of interest to museums; an annual list of notable books published in different countries; and a monthly bulletin of information.

The detailed work of the Committee is carried on through six sections: a University Relations Section concerned with the exchange of professorships and students and equivalence of degrees; an Artistic Relations Section which is arranging a Congress of Popular Arts; a Scientific Relations Section; a Literary Relations Section; a Section of Information and Reference; and a Legal Service Section which deals with questions of copyright and scientific property.

A Liaison or Coördination Committee of the Major International Associations has been formed by the International Committee on Intellectual Coöperation to coordinate work of peace organizations interested in the education and training of youth.

At the Sixth Pan American Conference a proposal was adopted to establish the *Intra-American Institute of Intellectual Coöperation*. The plan for the institute is to be formulated by the Pan American Union and submitted to a conference of university administrators and others interested in education who will be officially appointed by their governments.

NATIONAL ORGANIZATIONS

Besides these international organizations, national groups within each country are working for the same purposes. The trend of thought among educational leaders in the United States is indicated in these statements:

Dr. Augustus O. Thomas, President of the World Federation of Education Associations, said of citizenship at the World Conference on Education in San Francisco in 1923:

"Citizenship today must be broader than nationalism. There must be an international consciousness; there must be an 'international heart,' and a 'world mind.' This 'world mind' is largely an attitude or habit of thinking in the larger units of the world and the habit of regarding the nations as cooperating parts of the great whole. It is learning to measure other peoples by their own standards and getting their point of view. The question now is, Has the world progressed to such a point or will it ever come to such a point in the fundamental principles of morality that the nations can live together as sharers of the world's civilization?"

In a bulletin of the Federal Bureau of Education on "The Social Studies in Secondary Education" the "world community" is discussed and the following statements made concerning its relation to national life:

"Humanity is bigger than any of its divisions. The social studies should cultivate a sense of membership in the world community, with all the sympathies and sense of justice that this involves as among the different divisions of human society. The first step, however, toward a true 'neighborliness' among nations must be a realization of national ideals, national efficiency, national loyalty, national self-respect. . . . Nations are becoming more and more closely dependent upon each other. Common world interests need emphasis, world sympathies need cultivation. Such study should be concrete and based upon current events and problems. It offers a socially important line of development, and every available opportunity to this end should be seized upon."

As Commissioner of Education, Dr. J. J. Tigert, recently called attention to a report of the Commission on

EDUCATION AND PEACE 35

the Reorganization of Secondary Education made in 1918 to the National Education Association:

"Civics education should consider other nations also. As a people we should try to understand their aspirations and ideals that we may deal more sympathetically and intelligently with the immigrant coming to our shores, and have a basis for a wiser and more sympathetic approach to international problems. Our pupils should learn that each nation, at least potentially, has something of worth to contribute to civilization and humanity would be incomplete without that contribution. Such a study of dissimilar contributions in the light of the ideal of human brotherhood should help to establish a genuine internationalism, free from sentimentality, founded on fact, and actually operative in the affairs of nations."

Dr. Tigert has said further:

"We have here in the United States both the opportunities and the equipment for giving students intimate and correct knowledge of the peoples of other countries. We have now to determine as well as we can whether we are using them in the best way possible and what more we can do through education to promote friendly international relations."

A brief account of a few of the organizations working in this field suggests the extent of the effort devoted to a solution of the problems involved.

The Institute of International Education was founded in 1919 to develop international goodwill by means of educational agencies. It is directed by Dr. Stephen P. Duggan and has headquarters at 522 Fifth Avenue, New York City. The Institute which has recently taken over the activities of the Division of International Relations of the American Council of Education, and directs the work of the American University Union, acts as a clearing house of information between the educational institutions of Europe and America. It promotes the interchange of professors and of students between this and other countries. It administers a large number of international fellowships and is working toward the standardization of degrees. It arranges lecture tours for visiting professors and public men from other countries. Its publications deal with activities in international education and offer information of great value to foreign students in the United States, and to American students planning courses of study abroad, including very complete lists of fellowships for American students abroad and for foreign students in the United States.

The National Education Association coöperates through its Committee on International Relations with the World Federation of Education Associations, and encourages the teaching of international goodwill through its monthly publication, *The Journal of the National Education Association,* and through discussions at its annual conferences. Its offices are in Washington. At its 1927 convention, the Association passed the following resolution on world understanding:

"The Association reaffirms its oft-repeated pronouncement in favor of every legitimate means for promoting world peace and understanding among the peoples of the earth."

The American Federation of Teachers, which has offices at 327 S. La Salle St., Chicago, and is affiliated with the American Federation of Labor, opposes compulsory military training in schools and colleges, and at its annual convention in 1927 created a committee for the purpose of promoting international goodwill, adopting at the same time a platform which includes the following statements:

". . War not only militates against the development of the highest type of socially minded citizens, but is also

destructive of all that is best in mankind. War makes for the survival of the biologically unfit, for economic disorganization, for misery, and engenders hatreds." (The teachers of the world should tell.)
"tell the truth about war,—its cold-blooded butchery, its elimination of the biologically fit, its economic chaos, its debts, starvation, misery, and disease. Glorify the heroes of peace as symbolized by the physician who risks all to discover a cure for leprosy, or the idealist who holds fast to minority views which make man's progress possible.

"We should support measures which seek to prevent the use of Government funds for the support of compulsory military training in public schools and colleges.

The National Association of Secondary School Principals has adopted as its Eighth Objective:

"The development of a generation of young people who may seriously enter upon the program of the proposed development of international understanding, and of amity and goodwill between economic groups, races, and religions—in fact, in all realms of social intercourse, through a study of problems of worldwide significance."

Commenting upon this objective, the author, Mr. L. W. Brooks, principal of the high school in Wichita, Kansas, and formerly President of the National Association, said:

"This Eighth Objective should promote an understanding of problems of world import; a desire among students to understand racial, political, economic and social situations in various lands, to follow the true statesmen of the world in their efforts to bring about international understanding and ultimate peace; to build up into the consciousness of the nations a belief that the abolition of war is not only possible but necessary. It should ask that the horrors of war, unadorned by any gloss of romance or glory, be taught honestly to our boys and girls; that students be instructed in tolerance instead of hate, goodwill instead of suspicion, and international understanding."

SCHOOLS AND COLLEGES OF AN INTERNATIONAL CHARACTER

Since the World War there has been a notable development in international schools and colleges. At Geneva, Switzerland, several schools of an international character offer summer courses, which were attended in 1926 by over 30,000 students.

The Geneva School of International Studies, originated Dr. Alfred Zimmern as director, aims to train leaders in international affairs, and to promote an enlightened public opinion. It offers summer courses designed for those preparing for a teacher's career, for foreign service, for work in research institutes, or for positions on metropolitan newspapers, and for men in public life interested in foreign politics.

Professor Zimmern states in his book, "Learning and Leadership," that the final stage of education, after the student has been thoroughly grounded in national institutions, should consist in "a first-hand experience of foreign countries acquired under conditions which promote true international understanding." He maintains that for this purpose "schools of international contacts need to be developed—institutes at which university students in the later stages of their academic course are brought together from many countries to meet one another and a distinguished and equally international group of university teachers." He believes that this sort of school can be organized during the summer months.

In the winter the School continues its work by means of traveling secretaries who visit the universities and aid student groups in the discussion of international problems. A complete outline of courses and other information in regard to the School may be obtained from the New York Office, 366 Madison Avenue, New York City.

The Geneva Institute of International Relations is designed more especially to acquaint students and the general public with the purpose and methods of the League of Nations and with the historic development of international government which has made the League possible. It arranges an intensive course of one week during the summer, and its offices are open throughout the season to offer intelligent guidance to visitors to the League.

The *University Institute of Higher International Studies in Geneva* was organized in 1927 for postgraduate work in juridical, political, economic and social international problems of the present day but also admits undergraduates. Annual and half-yearly courses, seminars and discussion classes are conducted. Statesmen and men of science from many countries give lectures and short courses. The Institute coöperates closely with the University of Geneva, which offers summer courses on current international problems, and there are special opportunities for the study of international documents and for contacts with men immediately concerned with international affairs.

The International Committee on Intellectual Coöperation is developing a plan for the coördination of existing national institutions for higher political studies, which it is hoped will enable students to pursue their studies in one national center after another, and in this way have the benefit of observation of foreign political systems as well as of special educational advantages. Thus there will be developed, not an international university, but "an organism dispersed in different institutions throughout the world serving the needs of an international profession." Ultimately there may be a final course arranged at Geneva which would tend to coördinate and appraise the experience gained in the foreign capitals.

In addition to these schools of international affairs in Geneva, there is *The International Peoples College,* established in Denmark in 1921 by Dr. Peter Manniche. It is designed to bring men and women of all nations together for study and discussion under the leadership of trained scholars to prepare them to work actively for international peace. The school aims to reach across both national and class barriers and to sow the seeds of universal understanding and goodwill. The hope of the founders is that similar colleges will be established in other countries. Information may be obtained from Dr. S. A. Mathiasen, Pocono Peoples College, Henryville, Pennsylvania.

In America the experiment of traveling universities is being tried. The *College Cruise Around the World* for boys and young men (it is hoped later to establish one for women students) is described by its sponsors as a new method of education, the coördination of travel and study, Its educational director is Dr. James E. Lough, former dean of New York University. The cruise is arranged by the University Travel Association, 285 Madison Ave., New York City.

The *University Afloat,* under the direction of Mr. A. J. McIntosh, offers men and women students an around-the-world study cruise occupying eight months. Full information may be obtained from International University Cruise, Inc., 11 Broadway, New York City.

Teachers and World Peace

No complete account of what is being done in teacher-training institutions to develop an international outlook among teachers has been compiled. The work in individual institutions described in this chapter indicates a growing interest in this field, yet in "A Social Study" recently published by Teachers College, on the social beliefs and attitudes of American educators, it is stated that "with rare exceptions, American educators have done but little thinking on the more fundamental and pervasive phases of our more important social problems." Responsibility for this fact apparently rests on the training schools, since the author of the study, Dr. Manley H. Harper, proved by retesting certain groups that exceptionally stimulating graduate courses of six semester hours produce "a measure of growth in liberalism and in correlative qualities of reflective thinking equal to five times the growth in this direction produced in a year of thirty semester hours by the usual higher education of the country."

In 1923 the *International Institute of Teachers College* was established at Columbia University to give special attention to the needs of foreign students of education. The Institute promotes special educational investigations in foreign countries, and has established a unique library of textbooks and educational literature from all parts of the world. An Educational Yearbook makes a part of this information quickly available. Courses are offered dealing with foreign school systems and philosophical problems arising from their major differences. The Institute has also organized discussion groups for its foreign and American students, which have become a clearing house of educational problems and resulted in mutual understanding and good fellowship. Behind the Institute, a member of its staff states, lies the hope

"That a better international understanding may result; that both foreign and native students of Teachers College may return to their respective tasks with a clear purpose and a firm resolution to serve mankind in the true spirit of international goodwill."

The Foreign Education Section of the United States Bureau of Education, besides assisting educational institutions in evaluating the credentials of foreign students and aiding in the orientation of foreign students in this country, gathers and translates information about all phases of education in foreign countries and makes it available to teachers and any other persons for whom it may have interest or value. Mr. J. F. Abel, Chief of the Section, stated recently:

"Both the work of the Section and its opportunities for service have been greatly increased in recent years by the widened public knowledge and desire for knowledge of international affairs. This has been reflected in the field of education in the formation of international educational organizations, a growing exchange between countries of students and teachers, the frequent visits of foreign educators to the United States . . . and the relatively large number of students of education from this country that are making investigations abroad."

In an article in the *Educational Review* for March, 1921, William Heard Kilpatrick, of Teachers College, suggests certain facts to which the attention of teachers should be called. After emphasizing the point that propagandism is out of place in public schools, Mr. Kilpatrick goes on to say:

"If the teacher does not get the right point of view, does not see the social processes involved, we can have but little hope that the schools will play any part in abolishing war. What point of view may we expect our teachers to get as a result of impartial study?

"First, that wars are not inevitable. Rivalry is inherent, but not warfare.

"Next, I would have our teachers know more about social integration, and understand how it must inevitably increase if civilization shall but continue. . . . Men are brought together in ever greater and greater aggregates by a process which at the same time increases the number of respects in

EDUCATION AND PEACE

which each is dependent upon others. . . . Let the integration continue, and sooner or later the ties that bind will outgrow the forces that separate. . . .

"From this point of view it will come to be seen that the notion of a final absolute and exclusive national sovereignty is unworkable, manifesting itself in fact as truly a nuisance in the world of practical affairs as it is vicious in the moral world.

"We should further wish our teachers to see the utter fallacy and fatuity of competitive armaments. . . .

"We wish our school people, teachers and officials, to place at its right valuation military training in secondary schools; to understand that physically it is probably inferior to other types of exercise, that morally the military type of discipline is more likely to be bad than good, and that we cannot expect such virtues as respect for law to be developed by such obedience as the military man is likely to demand.

"A most important part of the teacher's equipment in the coming years will be to understand the Great War. How its deeper causes lay in a vicious world policy; how much the war cost, in treasure, in men, in misery, then and now and hereafter; how America was stirred and sustained by unselfish idealism; how we hoped and planned to stop wars. It is no warped or one-sided treatment that we ask, only the full facts, the really significant facts. Granted this, we believe that our teachers and leaders will burn, as America did at its best, to abolish war."

The World Federation of Education Associations adopted resolutions in 1925 and in 1927, urging courses in normal schools to give teachers the information and the point of view necessary to develop among children a spirit of international goodwill. At the meeting of the Federation in 1927 many concrete suggestions for such courses were made, among the most useful those prepared by Dr. H. L. Smith of Indiana University, which can be obtained from him in full in mimeographed form.

Briefly, the courses, materials and methods suggested by Dr. Smith were these:

1. Teachers should have a knowledge of the nature, work and publications of the various organizations for the promotion of international friendship.
2. A course in international relationships and social psychology should be offered in normal schools to develop a better understanding of world problems. The course in international relationships should stress international interdependence "and give a realizing sense of the horror of modern war and an understanding of the psychic and economic causes of war."
3. Teachers should become acquainted with racial backgrounds of school children in order that their pupils may learn to disregard such differences as those of dress, language and complexion and to find the essential human qualities.
4. Teachers should be trained in the use of newspapers, magazines and bulletins in order that they may judge the value of news stories and current articles.
5. International contacts among teachers should be developed through international correspondence and through foreign travel and study, for which there should be additional scholarships provided.
6. Cosmopolitan and world affairs clubs should be organized in teacher-training institutions.
7. Teachers should be encouraged to attend institutes of politics during the summer months.
8. Such attitudes and ideals should be cultivated among teachers as will lead to an understanding of the fact that education is the only sure and permanent method of change; that international friendship must be based on mutual knowledge; that, if children are to have freedom for self-development, prejudices in their minds must be broken down and they must be given in their place a passion for truth.
9. Teachers must themselves know, in order that their pupils may know, that love for one's own country no longer involves hatred of other countries; that, on the contrary, in

EDUCATION AND PEACE 45

the world today disloyalty to the whole involves disloyalty to every part.

10. American teachers should know that teachers in other countries are striving to instill ideas of international goodwill in the minds of the children.

In line with the suggestions of the World Federation of Education Associations, individual normal schools are working out concrete plans for the teaching of peace. A summer course on the literature of international goodwill has been inaugurated at the Michigan State Normal School by Miss Estelle Downing. The Teacher-Training Department of the Olivia, Minnesota, High School, under the direction of Mrs. Vesta Armstrong, presents at the graduation exercises each year a program setting forth the history and achievements of some foreign country, with pageantry, tableaux, and music. Interest among normal school students in international affairs is also stimulated by the annual World Essay Contest held under the auspices of the American School Citizenship League. The prizes for this contest are donated by Miss Mary and Miss Helen Seabury. The subject of the essay during the last year was "The Teacher, an Agent in International Goodwill."

Foreign travel for teachers is particularly recommended in the resolutions of all recent conferences on the subject of education for world peace. It has even been suggested that a year's residence or travel abroad should be required on the part of primary teachers during the first ten years of their teaching experience. In the summer of 1926 the Carnegie Endowment for International Peace invited 50 teachers of international relations in American colleges to be its guests at a European conference, in order to study the problems of international coöperation and to form direct contacts with the leading personalities engaged in the work of international coöperation.

The International Bureau for Educational Travel, the American representative of which is the Open Road, Inc., arranges European tours for teachers. The Travel Bureau of the National Union of Teachers of England, which is represented in the United States by Miss Langley Spence, 520 Lexington Avenue, New York City, assists teachers in making educational contacts in other countries and to travel at a materially lowered cost. Several European countries offer reduced rates to teachers on state railroads. Information on this subject can be obtained from the International Institute of Intellectual Coöperation, Paris.

Information as to the possibilities for an exchange of teaching posts can be obtained from the Institute of International Education, 522 Fifth Ave., the English Speaking Union, 19 West 44th St., New York City, and the Pan American Union, Washington, D. C. Through Pomona College exchanges of teachers with Mexico are arranged. The World Federation of Education Associations and the International Committee on Intellectual Coöperation are preparing complete reports on this subject.

In the Universities

In past centuries a few great universities were meeting places for men of all nations. Today each nation has its universities which are "centers of international knowledge," and through which the great body of human knowledge is revealed as the common product as well as the common heritage of all races and countries. An exchange of professors and students increases their international character. In "Europa," the Year-Book of Europe, for 1927, M. Luchaire, Director of the Institute of Intellectual Coöperation, makes this interesting statement in regard to European universities:

"Moreover the spirit of the universities is being slowly transformed to meet the intellectual needs of the modern world. . . . A determined effort is being made to provide future politicians, internationalists and diplomats with a training more thorough and more rational than has hitherto been given in the fields of history, law and geography. . . . The movement of students across the various frontiers is growing, and would be considerable if economic difficulties did not bar the way for so many. Exchanges of professors between the universities of various countries is becoming more and more common. Permanent educational missions and national institutes in foreign countries are growing from year to year. Finally, the entry of Germany into the League of Nations and the quite recent steps taken in various countries by important intellectuals in the Union of Russian Republics seem to warrant the hope that in a little time, at least as far as higher education is concerned, Europe will have no more watertight compartments, and will tend to establish one great organised unit for this end."

The neglect of an important aspect of the contribution which universities can make to the solution of modern world problems is indicated in a recent study made by Professor Frederic Ogg for the American Council of Learned Societies, under the title, "Research in the Humanistic and Social Sciences." Professor Ogg calls attention to the fact that crises in the future will have to do with problems of human conduct rather than the control of physical things, and that when these crises come our scholars in human relations will have to be better prepared to meet them than they were in 1917. The public has, however, he says, little appreciation of this fact and men of means are only beginning to perceive that economic and sociological investigations may be equally worthy of support with physical and biological. James Harvey Robinson is quoted as saying that the progress of men in scientific knowledge and regulation of human affairs has remained almost stationary for over two thousand years, and Raymond B. Fosdick is further quoted on this point to the effect that the well-being, if not the survival, of the race is conditioned on the rapid upbuilding of man's knowledge of his own motivations, interests, reactions, and relationships:

"With the allegiance of our age and generation so completely committed to the natural sciences we must face the fact that the social mechanism can be kept from cracking under the strain only as we develop the sciences that relate to man. Unless we can marshal behind such studies as economics, political science, and sociology the same enthusiasm, the same approach, and something of the same technique that characterize our treatment of physics and chemistry; unless the results of this research can be applied to human life as freely and boldly as we apply the natural sciences to modify our methods of living; unless we can free ourselves of prejudice and stale custom and harness intelligence to the task of straightening out the relations of man with his fellowmen and promoting an intercourse of harmony and fairness— unless, in brief, in our generation we can make some appreciable progress toward this goal of social control, the chances of our keeping the train on the track are exceedingly slight."

Johns Hopkins University proposes to establish a graduate school to be known as the Walter Hines Page School of International Relations for research and training in this field. It will endeavor to throw light upon the problem of "how the nations and the peoples of the world may better live together in prosperity and peace."

The courses offered will probably provide for some study and investigation abroad, and the results of the researches conducted will be published from time to time for the use of the public. Enlarging upon the idea that the school will do in its field what postgraduate schools have done for medicine and law—that is, provide a more systematic science of international relations and better trained men in the fields of education and public service —Mr. Owen D. Young, President of the Board of Trustees, said in 1925:

"We have what one might call an industry of foreign relations, but we have no art. We have a trade, but we have no science. . . . We have a desire for peace, but we have not established an agency whose exclusive duty it is to study how to get it. . . . We must supply a science, a systematic body of things known, if we desire to make our aspirations for peace effective. But someone will inquire whether research or science in the sense in which I am using them can be advantageously applied to this field. My answer is that facts can be applied in any field. Our curse is ignorance. Facts are our scarcest raw material. . . ."

A Bureau of International Research has already been established at Harvard University and Radcliffe College for "the development of research of an international character in the social sciences," and is endowed by the Laura Spellman Rockefeller Memorial for a period of years. At Columbia University, a professor of international relations has been appointed, and at Yale, an associate in international relations.

The number and variety of university courses in international relations is steadily increasing. Several institutions have received endowments for work in this field ranging from $100 a year for special lectures or books on international problems, to $1,500,000 given by James H. Causey to Denver University as an "endowment for goodwill." Fifteen years ago a member of the Board of Trustees of Northwestern University gave a fund amounting to $25,000 to the university, the income of which was to be used for the furtherance of "international peace and interdenominational comity." A Chair of Peace has recently been endowed at Kiel University, Germany.

The following courses in world affairs introduced recently in Pacific coast universities illustrate in general the new tendencies in this field.

In connection with the University of Southern California, there has been created an affiliated University of International Relations which offers courses in the various fields of foreign service. The coöperation of many foreign teachers is enlisted and special methods, including contacts made outside of the college under the direction of members of the faculty, are being developed to assist students in understanding the psychology of the people of the country in which they plan to work.

The University of Washington in 1927 announced a course on international relations in which the departments of anthropology, economics, history, philosophy, political science, psychology and sociology and the schools of law, journalism and business administration are coöperating. The aim of the University in offering this course is "to make its measure of contribution to the general movement of international coöperation." Eleven of 45 history courses relate directly to international affairs. Because of its situation on the Pacific Coast it has 17 courses in Oriental studies, 15 of them with a distinctly international bearing. Moreover, 10 of its courses in economics, 8 of those in political science, and 5 of those in sociology are devoted to world aspects of the subjects treated.

The University of California is offering through twelve of its departments fifty courses promoting international understanding with special emphasis on the problems of nations bordering on the Pacific.

Professor Parker Thomas Moon, Assistant Professor of History in Columbia University, has prepared at the request of the Institute of International Education, a very clear and comprehensive "Syllabus of International Relations" designed primarily for the use of college teachers desiring to give a one year course covering the history, as well as the economic, geographic and sociological aspects of international relations.

Besides such courses on general international relations, a number of colleges are introducing special courses in Latin American and Pan American problems. Professor William Whatley Pierson, Jr., of the University of North Carolina, has published in book form under the title "Hispanic American History" a comprehensive syllabus covering all aspects of Hispanic American life especially designed for classroom use. The Pan American Union, through its Division of Education, is also developing courses on "continental fraternity."

In addition to courses on international relations, a new type of course designed to create a new attitude of mind on international problems is being introduced in various colleges.

Professor Hornell Hart of Bryn Mawr College offers a comprehensive course on the "Science of Social Relations," which has been published in book form and adopted by many college classes and adult study groups.

Two unusual and stimulating courses are given by Professor E. L. Clarke of Minnesota University, one on "Prejudice," and its control, and the other on the "Sociology of Conflict." Outlines of these courses may be obtained from the National Council for Prevention of War.

At Oberlin College, Professor Oscar Jászi, of the Department of Political Science, offers a course entitled "Problems of Constructive Peace," in which he gives "a systematic survey of those economic, moral and intellectual realities which determine international relations, and stresses proposals and plans for the elimination of war and the history of pacific thought."

At Syracuse University during the summer session of 1927 the Political Science Department offered courses on international relations in which there was a discussion of "policies which result in the clash of national interests and of methods by which these clashes can be avoided and peace preserved."

At Wesleyan University the students have made a report to the president asking for an elective course on "War, Its Cause and Cure." The poll showed 63% of the students in favor of such a course, the object of which would be:

"To give a background of facts on the subject of war as a method of settling international disputes, so that educated men would be capable of recognizing the various factors making for conflict when they appear on the horizon of current events, and could more confidently take steps to eliminate them."

Extension Courses

In the extension work and correspondence courses of universities the study of international relations is beginning to be emphasized. At the University of Wisconsin a very interesting and thorough course is offered in the extension division by Professor Pitman B. Potter, called "American Diplomacy." The extension departments of many British universities offer courses of lectures on the historic background of international relations and present international organization.

Junior Year Abroad

Another plan recently initiated by certain of the colleges for the development of international understanding is known as "Junior Year Abroad." This experiment was begun by the University of Delaware in 1923 when it sent under the guidance of a member of its faculty, and after careful preliminary arrangements with French educational authorities, selected members of its junior class, ranking among the first one-third of their class in academic standing, for one year's study at the Sorbonne in Paris, in lieu of the regular work of the junior year. Preliminary to the scholastic year the students devoted three months in France to the intensive study of the French language. The University has since accepted among its group students from other institutions. Following much the same plan, Smith College in 1925 sent abroad a carefully selected group of 40 juniors. So valuable does this junior year abroad seem to the Institute of International Education that it recommends the establishment of fellowships, and offers to place its resources of information and advice at the disposal of colleges that wish to investigate the plan.

The College of William and Mary, in 1924, organized summer schools to afford American students an opportunity to travel and study in foreign countries. One school is located in Europe, the other in Mexico. The University of Toulouse and the National University of Mexico coöperate.

New York University, through its extension division, arranges, in coöperation with a group of European universities, residential travel tours during the summer months. The tours include a residence period of from three to four weeks in a university of the country selected.

Fellowships

Several hundred fellowships are available to American students who wish to study abroad, and to foreign students desiring to come to this country. The number increases every year. The Institute of International Education provides full information in regard to these opportunities for foreign study in its two publications, "Fellowships and Scholarships Open to American Students for Study in Foreign Countries" and "Fellowships and Scholarships Open to Foreign Students for Study in the United States."

One college, and it is possible that others will adopt the same plan, has recently sent a student as an envoy of friendship for a year's study in a foreign university. In September 1927, Earlham College in order that it might show not only its friendly feeling but its desire to learn from the Eastern world, sent a member of the Junior Class, Wilfred Jones, for a year's work in the universities of Japan.

Foreign Tours

The National Student Federation of America and the International Student Hospitality Association coöperate through the Open Road, Inc., their official travel representative, in arranging "sojourns in Europe" for American students. The offices of the Open Road are at 2 West 46th St., New York City. The National Student Federation is a member of the Confederation Internationale des Etudiants, which is an association of national student organizations founded in 1919 and represented in 28 countries. The Hospitality Association is a small group of Americans and Europeans interested in student international relations. From its headquarters in Paris it makes arrangements for American students to meet young people of the other nations and be entertained by them. A student in each country visited travels with the American group as guide and host. The National Student Federation publishes a "Handbook of Student

Travel through Europe" and a "Handbook of Foreign Study."

International Debates

The growing custom of holding international debates in the colleges, which was initiated by the Institute of International Education, has proved an excellent means of bringing students of different nations into profitable contact. Arrangements for such debates are now made through the National Student Federation of America.

Foreign Students in America

American and foreign students are also finding within this country many opportunities for international friendships. International House at 500 Riverside Drive, New York City, which is under the direction of Mr. and Mrs. Harry E. Edmonds, is the home of five hundred men and women students of different nations. These young people, and as many more who are connected with it, are developing mutual understanding through international debates, representations of the art of their native countries, and constant friendly association. The National Committee on Friendly Relations among Foreign Students, which has its headquarters at 347 Madison Avenue, New York City, is another outgrowth of the desire to utilize every opportunity to bring about a friendly understanding among the coming leaders in all nations.

International Clubs

The study of international questions has been greatly stimulated in the colleges by the formation of International Relations Clubs which now exist in one hundred and twenty-six colleges in thirty-four states. They are intellectually and financially aided by the Carnegie

Endowment for International Peace, which publishes an "International Relations Club Handbook" fully describing their organization and activities. In fifty universities, branches of the Corda Fratres Association Cosmopolitan Clubs exist through which world friendships are made possible.

At certain of the larger universities, the students themselves are forming international clubs not only for study but for definite work in the promotion of international goodwill.

At Harvard University an International Council has been formed with a membership of thirty students each representing a different nationality. The Council meets once a month, announcing in advance some international question for study and discussion. A vote is taken at the end of each meeting to register the decision of the group. At the State University of Montana an International Club has been formed. An International Council has been organized by the students of the State University of Iowa "to find out the attitude of students from other lands towards the foreign policies of the United States, to understand the difficulties of other countries, to create the international mind and work towards world peace." Meetings are open to students, faculty and public. At Stanford University an International Club of men of different races and nations has taken a house in order that the members may live together and know each other intimately. At Earlham College the students have organized peace teams and worked out a schedule for speeches before organizations and church bodies in the vicinity.

Model Assemblies of the League of Nations

Among the other methods devised for increasing an interest in international affairs are the "Model Assemblies" of the League of Nations which are being held by many colleges and in some instances by several colleges acting together. The New England colleges joined in holding a model assembly of 169 delegates at Amherst. A report of the organization of such an assembly can be obtained from Syracuse University where one of the first was organized, and full information can also be obtained from the League of Nations Non-Partisan Association, 6 East 39th Street, New York City.

What Schools Are Doing

Activity in the lower schools is fully as great as in the colleges. The variety of methods which are being developed by individual faculties and teachers is reflected in the following brief accounts of some recent experiments.

Mrs. Alice Wilson, a member of the faculty of the Girls High School of San Francisco, California, has recently published a plan for "International Education in High Schools," by which the efforts of various institutions to give young people a truer knowledge of other countries can be organized into a single system for international education directed by the schools. This outline follows in full:

"1. To organize in each high school in every country a group of juniors and seniors with a background of history and preferably a modern language, who show a strong interest in foreign countries and modern international questions.

"(a) To establish correspondence among these various groups—correspondence touching any possible subject—art, music, history, economics, science—according to the special inclination of individual students or groups of students.

"(b) To make an intensive study of those countries through reading, lectures, etc.

"2. To select those students who have shown special ability

in grasping and assimilating international ideas, and encourage them—helping them through scholarships if necessary,—to continue this field of work in college or the university.

"3. To urge each government to employ the best of these students in its department of foreign affairs, in the field best suited to their special abilities, in order that they might gain a practical knowledge of the international policies of their own countries.

"4. To send abroad these young men and women, in connection with embassies and consulates, to study in universities, to live and work among the people in order to understand their needs and ideals, their ways and customs. Here they would meet on common ground a group of men and women from all countries with whom they would be already acquainted through their clubs, and with whom they would work toward a common aim, mutual understanding. These men and women should form the Diplomatic Corps of every nation.

"Thus through a careful process of selection, the best of our students would eventually lead the nation in its international relations. The others, in business or professions, would have gained a better understanding of the people with whom they deal, and, as voters, would have an enlightened knowledge and world-wide tolerance."

The success of the club in San Francisco has led to the creation of the World League of International Education Associations with Dr. Ray Lyman Wilbur as its president. Besides the schools in all parts of the United States which are joining it, the League has secured some coöperation from educational organizations in England, France, Italy, Spain, Belgium, Greece, the Scandinavian countries, Austria, Germany, Canada, New Zealand, Japan and Latin American countries. The bond among the various clubs is a loose one, for the League "is based upon the principle of absolute freedom for each organization." A central office for communications has been opened in the Phelan Building, San Francisco.

A School World Friendship League has been originated and incorporated by Mrs. Helen S. Evans of Brawley, California. Its object is to promote true patriotism, international justice and world brotherhood by making each school class a unit of the League, providing for daily lessons on world friendship correlated with some regular study, semi-monthly appreciation lessons on foreign countries, and monthly programs of world friendship.

In the Woodbury High School, Woodbury, N. J., special programs in "Education for World Mindedness" have been presented by the students in the morning assembly periods on two or three days a week during the school years of 1926-27, and 1927-28. All teachers and classes in the school have coöperated in these programs under the direction of the "teacher in charge," Mrs. Rachel Davis-DuBois.

The main theme of the first year's program was the "contribution of various racial elements to our complex American life." The nation to be presented during any month was determined so far as possible according to the special day falling in that month, such as Columbus Day in October for Italy, Lincoln's Birthday in February for the negro, and December for Germany because of the German Christmas songs.

The theme chosen for the program for 1927-28 was "World Unity Through Education." Each Department was made responsible for one month's program, that of the first month, for instance, was "world unity through language," the general plan being to "divide the subject into four parts, show the origins of that subject, its present-day status, and how in the future that subject can help bring world unity, with a special speaker each month on the subject, if possible." The complete programs for both of the years have been printed by the New Jersey Branch of the Women's International League for Peace and Freedom, and may be obtained from that organization at 79 Halsey St., Newark, N. J., or from the National Council for Prevention of War.

A new social studies course has been introduced in the junior high schools of Cleveland, Ohio. It contains between thirty and forty units of study. The major unit in each semester has something to do with important problems in social coöperation. The first semester deals with sectionalism in the United States, the second with religious toleration, the third with race toleration, the fourth with capital and labor, the fifth with town and country, and the sixth with international relations. These units do not consume all of the time available, but are considered the important units.

The South Philadelphia High School for Girls, under the leadership of the principal, Miss Lucy L. W. Wilson, undertook a project in world peace which occupied an entire year and in which the departments of History, Science and English coöperated. An account of the project and outline of study can be obtained from the school or from the National Council for the Prevention of War.

The Commencement exercises of the high schools of Pasadena, California, were utilized in 1928 to direct the attention of the students to the world movement toward universal brotherhood and the opportunity which it offers young men and women for careers of adventure and daring. In a pageant, "America's Opportunity," this country was shown as the melting pot of the nations where, as nowhere else, the brotherhood of man could find expression. The members of the graduating class pledged themselves "to press forward to the goal of world peace."

The Principia, St. Louis, Missouri, an educational

institution for the children of Christian Scientists, has appointed a committee on international relations representing every branch of the school work in order that the school may act as a unit in developing sympathetic understanding of other nations. Lecturers and artists from foreign countries are brought to the school, and one lecture a week is given by a member of the faculty on a foreign country or on some problem existing between this country and another. The subject matter of the lectures is used as a basis for composition work. Special attention is paid to cultivating speaking ability in foreign languages. The school has gradually collected an international museum of pictures, objects of art, costume dolls representing all nations, and other material showing the achievements and customs of foreign nations. An anonymous gift known as the School of Nations Fund has been received by the school to enable it to develop its international program and assist students to spend a year abroad, and teachers to travel abroad during their vacations.

The Platoon Schools of Calais, Maine, have worked out a year's program for teaching the social sciences from the first to the sixth grade, one of the objects of which is to bring about better understanding among the people of the world. The program ends with a goodwill pageant. A full account can be obtained from Mr. W. H. Phinney, superintendent of schools.

The schools of Oregon have adopted a very forward-looking course in world history for the ninth grade which includes these aims: knowledge leading to understanding of recent and present world problems; attitude of seeing institutions as changing rather than as permanent; knowledge of social movements and tendencies; evaluation of opposing forces in the progress of civilization, for example, the conservative and the radical; intelligent view of the struggle for democracy and of the forces opposing it; significance of strong leaders; perception that no nation is isolated, and that world coöperation would lead to permanent peace; desire to incorporate into our own civilization the spiritual and cultural values of other peoples.

Junior high-school geography in West Virginia is designed to develop in the children the disposition and ability to understand the contribution which the industries of the United States make to the world, what other nations produce and with which nations we can trade most satisfactorily; the characteristics and customs of the people with whom we must trade; and that no nation can live alone but that a nation's destiny will depend upon its attitude and methods in dealing with other nations.

School Correspondence

The importance which educators put upon the interchange of correspondence between school children is evidenced in the appeal of the Conference on "What the Schools Can Do for Peace" to the League of Nations to recommend to all governments that they facilitate the interchange of correspondence, and its further appeal to the International Bureau of Education to make application to the International Postal Union for special facilities for such correspondence. The extent to which international friendship is already being promoted among children by this means can be realized from the reports of the American Junior Red Cross and other organizations. Hundreds of thousands of boys and girls either directly, or indirectly through their school classes, are in this way making contacts in all parts of the world.

An exchange of vacation visits between school children has recently become very popular in European countries, and, in an increasing number of instances, children in their early teens are being exchanged for the school year. It has been suggested that such visits could be arranged between students in the United States and Canada, and the United States and Latin American countries. Such an experiment has already been begun in this country by Dr. Sven V. Knudsen, a government supervisor of the schools of Denmark, who, in 1927 and 1928, arranged for one hundred American boys to be entertained during their vacations in Danish, Swedish and Norwegian homes. Dr. Knudsen's account of the visits which can be obtained from him at 248 Boylston St., Boston, indicates the great value of such expressions of international hospitality.

In so far as agreement has been reached among the educators who are experimenting in this field of training young people to live in an integrated world community, the importance is emphasized of cultivating three things, world-mindedness, a sense of the unity of the world, and independence of thought.

Cultivating World-Mindedness

The various methods for cultivating world-mindedness and a sense of world unity are completely and authoritatively presented in the Recommendations of the International Committee on Intellectual Coöperation of the League of Nations on "How to Make the League of Nations Known and to Develop the Spirit of International Coöperation." These have been submitted to all nations members of the League and are being gradually adopted in the schools. Among the recommendations, which may be obtained in full from the World Peace Foundation, Boston, are these:

"Civilization in all its principal manifestations is a record of coöperative effort from the family, the village and the workshop to the vastly more complex institutions of today. To imbue the child with a deep and lasting affection for its family and country remains today, as in former times, the first principle of sound education. But a true patriotism understands the patriotism of others; and a recognition of the necessity and omnipresence of coöperation, both within and without the State, must be emphasized in any education that is to fit young persons for modern life.

"The following methods of promoting indirect contact—mainly during school terms—should be employed where circumstances and the age of the young persons, render them suitable:

"Children's games, the exhibition of suitable pictures and films, lectures, displays of foreign handicrafts, visits to historical and artistic museums.

"Fêtes and pageants, performances of music; in fact, all appeals to the artistic sense that will encourage a mutual knowledge of different civilizations and peoples.

"Translation of suitable foreign masterpieces, including national folk-tales and their publication in juvenile periodicals.

"Juvenile periodicals. Valuable results might be obtained at a conference where editors of the more important of these periodicals could discuss the possibilities of encouraging these contacts.

"Studies of different civilizations and the scientific and comparative study of present-day events.

"The following methods of encouraging direct contacts between young people would be valuable:

"Interchange of individual children between families.

"International camps for children and international holiday colonies.

"Group excursions under competent leaders.

"Congresses and other gatherings, as may be appropriate.

"Interchange of pupils between schools of different countries.

"Vacation courses.

"Government and voluntary associations should apply themselves to the task of promoting direct contacts for the benefit of the student, young teacher and professor. These contacts might take the form of travel abroad, of attendance at vacation courses, residence at foreign universities or special institutions designed to provide training for international careers, or actual teaching work in other countries.

"Governments should be approached with a view to obtaining all possible travelling facilities, passports, reduced fares, and to ensuring that those concerned derive the utmost benefit from their visit to foreign countries. The different means of subsidizing these visits and exchanges should be studied."

Behind the coöperation of nations and men, science is revealing more and more clearly the fundamental unity of the universe. If a picture of the universe as modern science sees it—a universe in which there is no beginning or end, which is composed of the same elements throughout, in which all things are but variations of an identical force and in which nothing is unaffected by what affects any other thing—could be given children as a background for their thinking, world unity and brotherhood would not seem to be artificial ideals superimposed upon humanity, but natural expressions in human relations of universal laws.

Nationalism and Internationalism

Undoubtedly the most serious obstacle to developing a content and spirit of education along lines of world unity is a mistaken expression of the spirit of nationality which pervades many textbooks and some teaching. It was unfortunate that the rise of popular education and of the spirit of extreme nationalism should have been coincident. Self-conscious nations in the modern sense did not arise according to most interpreters of history until the late 18th century. The partitioning of Poland, the French Revolution, Napoleon's later attempt to combine a whole continent under one rule, the development of democratic theories of government were all factors in creating self-conscious nationalism. In so far as nationalism means love of country, pride in its achievements and a sense of responsibility for its progress, in so far as it encourages groups of people to preserve and develop their special gifts and experience, it is good and deserves to be cultivated in any system of education. A spirit of nationalism does harm only when it leads to a misrepresentation of fact or is based on ignorance of fact. In its false form it tends to create an idea of nations as separate entities, to give a nation a personified reality apart from the individuals who compose it, and maintains a theory of unlimited sovereignty, an assertion of the right, as Professor Harold J. Laski defines it, "to will acts of universal reference without being called to account for them."

Nations are not separate entities considered historically or in terms of their present activities. History should make clear, as Professor Ernest Barker in his book, "National Character," points out, that . . . "there lives, moves, and has its being among us, the past, which is not only the past of ourselves, but also that of other peoples." So far as the present relations of nations are concerned the interests of their people are no longer separated by their boundary lines, and the extent to which nations have developed forms of coöperation to meet this fact, accepting limitation of their sovereignty in the interest of their own citizens, should be taught.

Personification of a nation growing out of a false nationalism leads to failure to discriminate between the actions of small groups of individuals temporarily in control of a government and the character and intent of the people as a whole. Such confusion obscures the common humanity of the people of different nations and leads to an acceptance, on the ground that they are in the interest of something beyond the individual, of activities that, if admittedly carried on in the interest of individuals, could not be justified. The falseness of this conception can be offset in the teaching of history, if, instead of the repeated assertion that "France," "Spain" or "Italy" did so and so, the distinction between the officials who acted and the people at large is brought out.

In all this the question is not one of teaching internationalism as opposed to nationalism. The two things are not opposed but complementary. In an interdependent coöperative world, national loyalty and loyalty to humanity are in harmony. If patriotism is to be taught the basic fact of that teaching must be that "love for one's own country no longer involves the hatred of other countries, but on the contrary, disloyalty to the whole now involves disloyalty to every part." Dr. Harry Emerson Fosdick states vividly the relationship between nationalism and internationalism:

"No other nation can mean to us what our nation means. Here are the roots of our heritage, and here our central loyalties belong. But, just because we feel so deeply about our own land, we understand how other people feel about their lands, and, using our patriotism to interpret theirs, we grow, not in bitterness but in understanding and sympathy. So all fine internationalism must be rooted back in the noble significances of nationalism."

How to Teach Independence of Thought

For the development of independence of thought the following definite methods and plans have been suggested by various educational authorities:

In their study of foreign countries, encourage students

to use more than one book and to compare the statements; to consider, also, in connection with each book the date of its publication, the author's other books, connections, and so on.

Teach pupils to distinguish between statements that are based on facts that can be ascertained and statements that are based on individual opinion; and do not insist that they accept those based on opinion.

Train students to read newspapers and magazines with intelligent discrimination, comparing the headlines with the body of an article, considering the source of information, considering whether it is based on ascertained fact or rumor, and noting items for future reference and verification.

Insist upon a distinction between the individual and the group in all general statements.

Train students to protect themselves against their own prejudices, which limit their power of intelligent observation.

Have questions discussed rather than debated, in order that the object of intellectual intercourse may always be to arrive at truth.

Cultivate the ability to enter into other people's points of view: among young children by asking them, when they have quarreled, to play that they are each other and reverse the parts; among older pupils by having them impersonate people of foreign nationalities in the community and write letters "home." In an article, "Forming First Habits for Internationalism," published in *Progressive Education* in the spring quarter of 1925, Dr. Harry A. Overstreet said:

"Trying to understand the other party unquestionably is one of the most broadening of human experiences. Trying sincerely to make an adjustment between one's own views and views that are divergent is perhaps the most civilizing of human experiences. Internationalism stands or falls with our wish and our ability to do those two things. Hitherto our educational schemes—as likewise our political techniques—have made little provision for training along these lines. Even history has been studied not so much for the purpose of understanding other peoples as for the purpose of learning information about more or less external events in their lives."

Give students a knowledge of the fact that new ideas are always opposed, by describing the opposition to innovations such as artificial lighting of the streets which was attacked as "contrary to nature," the introduction of bathtubs, the use of baby carriages which it was said would "take women out of the home," and so on.

Point out that the majority is not always right, that no idea when it is new has the support of the majority.

"A few generations ago there were in America many old women who were accused of casting spells on their neighbors and bringing them bad luck and even death. These old women were called witches, and the vast majority believed that it was God's will to burn them at the stake; and thousands of them were put to death in that way. . . . A few decades ago slavery was a well-established institution in this country. . . . The majority long believed that slavery was justified."

Those handicapped by prejudices will not be able to solve the problems of a new age, nor will those who are without a belief in progress. In *The Historical Outlook* for October, 1923, Jessie C. Evans of the Simon Gratz High School, Philadelphia, says of this phase of education:

"Above all things, we must teach the meaning of progress, both for national and for world citizenship. An appreciation of the growth of ideas is the best preparation for an acceptance of growth and change in contemporary society. If we could only train up a generation who were expectant of change and who welcomed it when it is for the betterment of mankind, it would not matter what particular ideas we tried to inculcate. In their day, which will not be ours, world problems may have developed in a way entirely unforeseen by us. The important thing is that they should have open and sympathetic minds and should have acquired the habit of thinking internationally."

To sum up these many opinions, it is clear that educators realize the truth of Emerson's statement, "Goodwill makes intelligence," and are convinced that the end of education must be today "not life or living but living together." *

* Suggestions as to programs, sources of material and in regard to teaching individual subjects will be found in Chapter XXVI under the section, "Through the Schools."

CHAPTER III

THE CHURCH AND PEACE

As the suffering and helplessness of the peoples was prolonged by the World War, individuals everywhere sought eagerly for some source, outside of the conflict and chaos, to which they could turn for help. Their disappointment in the Christian Church, which in so many instances allowed itself to become a part of the war machine, found widespread expression. It was charged that the churches had declared a "moratorium on Christianity;" and it was frankly said that if they allowed another war to develop, "they had better close their doors." Since the war, the churches have taken up this challenge and are rapidly organizing in support of peace. The *Christian Century*, one of the leading church papers, has gone so far as to say:

"The very fact of war shouts the failure of Christianity; . . . the Church cannot bless war without surrendering its character as Christian. The Church's clear duty, therefore, is to excommunicate war, deliberately and solemnly to say, and so to inform the State, that the State may never again expect to receive the resources of the Church . . . as aids of any war in which it might ask its citizens to engage."

In the first two centuries after Christ, individual Christians took the position that they could not as Christians participate in war. Men and officers in the Roman army, when converted to Christianity, laid down their arms and refused further service, giving as their only reason, "I am a Christian." A church order issued early in the third century called upon magistrates and soldiers to abandon their calling before baptism, and excommunicated those who joined the army.

In "The Early Christian Attitude to War," C. J. Cadoux reports these facts and explains them:

"The early Christians took Jesus at his word, and understood his inculcations of gentleness and non-resistance in their literal sense. They closely identified their religion with peace; they strongly condemned war for the bloodshed which it involved; they appropriated to themselves the Old Testament prophecy which foretold the transformation of the weapons of war into the implements of agriculture; they declared that it was their policy to return good for evil and to conquer evil with good. With one or two possible exceptions no soldier joined the Church and remained a soldier until the time of Marcus Aurelius (161-180 A.D.). . . . While a general distrust of ambition and a horror of contamination by idolatry entered largely into the Christian aversion to military service, the sense of the utter contradiction between the work of imprisoning, torturing, wounding, and killing, on the one hand, and the Master's teaching on the other, constituted an equally fatal and conclusive objection."

The testimony of the early Church Fathers makes it clear that to them war was inconsistent with Christianity. Justin Martyr in his first "Apology" said:

"That these things have come to pass you may be readily convinced; for twelve men, destitute both of instruction and of eloquence, went forth from Jerusalem into the world and by the power of God gave evidence to every description of persons that they were sent by Christ to teach all men the divine word; and we, who were once slayers of one another, do not fight against our enemies."

THE CHURCH AND PEACE

Irenaeus declared:

"The followers of Jesus have abandoned the weapons of war and no longer know how to fight."

Tertullian answered a question with a question:

"You inquire whether a believer may enter the military service and whether soldiers are to be admitted into the Church? How will a Christian man war without a sword, which the Lord has taken away? In disarming Peter he unbelted every soldier."

In "De Corona" he said further:

"When Jesus said, 'He who uses the sword shall perish by the sword,' He made it unlawful for a Christian to use the sword at all; if a Christian cannot go to law, much less can he, as a son of peace, go to battle; if he is not allowed to avenge injuries done to himself, he cannot consistently take part in imprisoning or torturing or punishing his fellow-creatures."

Lactantius wrote, in the time of the persecution of Diocletian:

"To engage in war cannot be lawful for the righteous man, whose warfare is that of righteousness itself."

Eusebius gives numerous instances which prove that this was the position taken by the early church and that many of the early Christians sacrificed their fortunes and their lives in loyalty to it. In Numidia, as late as 295 A.D., the recruiting officer brought before the Proconsul a young man named Maximilian. As he was about to be measured, he said, "I cannot engage in military service; I am a Christian." He persisted, saying, "I am a Christian; I cannot fight." When they found it impossible to persuade him, he was put to death.

When Marcellus, a centurion in the Legion called Trajans, became a Christian, he declared that he could serve no longer. He was thrown into prison, but he still persisted, saying, "It is not lawful for a Christian to bear arms for any earthly considerations."

The religious orders of the Middle Ages, such as the Franciscans and Dominicans, likewise refused to take part in war.

Various reasons for the failure of the Church to live up to these early teachings are indicated in a recent study of "The Christian and War," made by a group of Canadian ministers, published as an appeal to all followers of Christ. When the Roman state became the protector of the Church, the Church tended to become the defender of the policies of the state. The struggle between the two theories can be traced through the Church writings of the early centuries. In the "Canons of Hippolytus," credited to the end of the fourth century, voluntary enlistment was forbidden and conscripted soldiers were not permitted to take their place at the Lord's table until they had done penance. But when the wars of Rome became defensive wars of a Christian state against barbarians, the Church rallied, with scarcely a dissenting voice, to its support, and the Church leaders began to go back to the teachings of the Old Testament in justification of participation in war. The conversion by force of barbarian tribes who adopted the new religion with mental reservations did not strengthen its peaceful character. It is said that the Saxons when they were baptized in a deep river held their right arms, with sword uplifted, out of the water!

During the Middle Ages the Church sought to restrain the custom of petty wars between feudal lords. It declared what was known as the "Truce of God," which prohibited fighting from Wednesday night to Monday

THE CHURCH AND PEACE

morning, and which required that such necessary pursuits as those of agriculture be protected against the destruction of war. Through these centuries the Pope frequently acted as arbitrator in disputes, and courts of arbitration were set up at the instigation of the Church by the bishops and the feudal lords.

The Humanists of the 16th century proclaimed the inconsistency of war and Christianity. Erasmus persistently worked for peace. In one of his essays against war, "The Complaint of Peace," he wrote:

"Every page of the Christian Scriptures speaks of little else but peace and concord; and yet the whole life of the greater portion of Christians is employed in nothing so much as the concerns of war. . . . It were best to lay aside the name of Christian at once, or else to give proof of the teaching of Christ by its only criterion, brotherly love. . . . 'Dare you' (he challenges the priests) 'describe Christ as a Reconciler, a Prince of Peace, and yet palliate or commend war with the same tongue? That in truth is nothing less than to sound the trumpet for Christ and Satan at the same time. Do you presume, reverend sir, in your hood and surplice, to stimulate the simple, inoffensive people to war, when they come to church expecting to hear from your mouth the Gospel of peace? . . .'"

The early Protestant sects did not make a stand against war because they felt that they needed the support of the state in order to survive. So they tended, as had the Church under Rome, to support the state in exchange for its protection. The theory of the divine right of kings, the idea that the established authorities were so established by the will of God naturally strongly affected the attitude of the Church toward the state. To quote from the "Christian and War," referred to above:

"Submission to the royal will was conceived to be a religious duty, and the Articles of Religion specified that 'It is lawful for Christian men, at the command of the Magistrate, to bear weapons, and serve in the wars.'

"The history of Protestantism, since those first generations when it was itself a revolt against authority, discloses a growing disposition to support existing authorities. As in England, through all the long Stuart tyranny, democracy was hampered by episcopal support of the 'divine right of kings,' so in America slavery was prolonged by religious support. So powerful was the support of slavery by the Church that William Lloyd Garrison declared 'American Christianity is the main pillar of American slavery'; and, looking back upon the bitter struggle, Parker Pillsbury said: 'We had almost to abolish the Church before we could reach the dreadful thing at all.' Social conservatism is a besetting sin of Protestantism. For very few great social advances has she, corporately, provided leadership. Political democracy has come without her, almost in spite of her. Social and industrial democracy, and the emancipation of women, have come in the same way. Is it to be so of international peace?"

But however great or small a part the organized Church may be thought to have played, institutions have gradually been modified in harmony with the principles of Christianity, so that those institutions which do not conform stand out in ever greater contrast and contradiction.

As to the lesson to be drawn from the Scriptures on the subject of war the same study asserts:

"Christianity is not a nomistic religion, but a religion of the spirit. The most diligent search therefore will not disclose a set of rules covering all human situations; it will disclose only a spirit in which all situations are to be faced, principles by which all conduct must be determined. . . .

"Most Christians have never made clear to themselves what loyalty to the Scriptures requires of them. There is to them no progress in the Scriptures, no development in their truth and spiritual authority. They have not understood the word,

THE CHURCH AND PEACE

'The law and the prophets were until John' but thenceforth 'the gospel of the kingdom of God is preached.'

"Our Lord sets His own spiritual authority definitely above that of the ancient Scriptures. . . .

"Because Christian society has never finally distinguished between what is Christian and what is not Christian in the Scriptures, it is unable either to think clearly or to achieve Christian unanimity in the face of the deadliest danger."

Certain passages in the records of the teachings of Christ himself are sometimes used in an attempt to prove that he sanctioned war. Wilbur K. Thomas, Secretary of the American Friends Service Committee, 20 South 12th St., Philadelphia, has published a full discussion of these texts in a pamphlet which can be obtained from the committee. Of the text, "Think not that I came to send peace on earth; I came not to send peace, but a sword," Mr. Thomas says, "Those who use this passage to prove that war is right do not read it in its context, for in the following verses Jesus says, 'For I came to set a man at variance against his father, and the daughter against her mother.' Does this mean that a man must prove his love for Jesus by killing father or mother if put to the test? Yet, that is what it means if the sword in verse 34 means a sword of steel. The sword referred to is not a sword of steel, but a sharp dividing line between good and evil."

Kirby Page in "International Relations in the Light of the Religion of Jesus" discusses the scene in the Temple when Jesus drove out the money changers, by moral, he insists, not physical force. He cites the reading of the passage in the American Revised Version, which is

"and he made a scourge of cords, and cast all out of the temple, both the sheep and the oxen, and he poured out the changers' money, and overthrew their tables."

Moffat's Translation, which Mr. Page also cites, reads:

"Making a scourge of cords, he drove them all, sheep and cattle together, out of the temple, scattered the coins of the brokers and upset their tables."

The early Christian ideal of peace has been preserved through recent centuries by such sects as the Society of Friends, the Mennonites and the Dunkards which have cherished the ideal of individual responsibility and whose tenets are discussed in a later chapter on "Pacifism."

The extent to which the question of war or peace is occupying the attention and efforts of the churches at present will be indicated by the following official statements of the organizations and denominations themselves.

In 1930, a Universal Religious Peace Conference, the first conference in history of all religious faiths, will be held to consider how the forces of religion of all nations can be mobilized in concerted action against war and that spirit and those things that make for war. This Conference is being arranged by the World Alliance for International Friendship Through the Churches. An effort will be made to secure agreement on these points:

". . . that emphasis on human brotherhood is essential to all religions, that world peace can be established only through the recognition of universal brotherhood, and that the religions of the world can coöperate by each working in its own sphere for the attainment of these ideals; and the adoption of general plans looking toward such coöperation."

That the great religions may in fact consistently unite on this principle of world brotherhood is brought out in an article by Alfred W. Martin of the Society for Ethical Culture, in *World Unity* for October, 1927. Each of the seven great religions urges, he says, the practice of the

THE CHURCH AND PEACE

Golden Rule, and he gives the Rule as it is variously expressed in them:

The Christian: "All things whatsoever ye would that men should do unto you, do ye so to them."
The Jewish: "Whatsoever you do not wish your neighbor to do to you, do not unto him."
The Hindu: "The true rule is to guard and do by the things of others as you do by your own."
The Buddhist: "One should seek for others the happiness one desires for oneself."
The Zoroastrian: "Do as you would be done by."
The Confucian: "What you do not wish done to yourself, do not to others."
The Mohammedan: "Let none of you treat your brother in a way he himself would dislike to be treated."

These strikingly similar texts inculcating goodwill are quoted in a preliminary announcement of the Universal Religious Peace Conference:

Christianity: "Blessed are the peace-makers, for they shall be called children of God."
Hinduism: "To you I declare this holy mystery: There is nothing nobler than humanity."
Buddhism: "Let one cultivate goodwill towards all the world,—a mind illimitable, unobstructed, without hatred, without enmity. This mode of living is the supreme good."
Confucianism: "Within the four seas all are brothers."
Islam: "To God belong the East and the West. Therefore whithersoever ye turn, is the face of God. Verily, God is all-pervading, all-knowing."
Jainism: "Establish the religion of the law which benefits all living beings in the whole universe! It will bring supreme benefit to all living beings in all the world!"
Judaism: "And they shall beat their swords into plowshares and their spears into pruning hooks; nation shall not lift up sword against nation, neither shall they learn war any more."

Shintoism: "I will halt here today, and, having purified myself, will go forth tomorrow; and worship at the temple of the Deity."

Taoism: "Weapons, even though successful, are unblessed implements, detestable to every creature. Therefore, he who has the Eternal, will not employ them."

Sikhism: "Churches, teachers, teachings, half a dozen! The Teacher of teachers is One; His forms, many. The sun is one; the seasons many. Innumerable are the manifestations of the Creator."

Zoroastrianism: "May we ourselves be they who help to make this world progress!"

The Federal Council of Churches

As early as 1911, an interdenominational peace committee was organized by the Federal Council of Churches of Christ in America, which represents the following Christian Protestant denominations:

Baptist Churches, North
Free Baptist Church
National Baptist Convention
Christian Church
Churches of God in N. A. (General Eldership)
Congregational Churches
Disciples of Christ
Evangelical Church
Evangelical Synod of N. A.
Friends
Methodist Episcopal Church
Methodist Episcopal Church, South
Methodist Protestant Church
Colored M. E. Church in America
African M. E. Church
African M. E. Zion Church
Moravian Church
National Council of the Protestant Episcopal Church (Coöperating Agency)
Presbyterian Church in the U. S. A.
Presbyterian Church in the U. S. (South)
Primitive Methodist Church
Reformed Church in America
Reformed Church in the U. S.
Reformed Episcopal Church
Seventh Day Baptist Church
United Brethren Church
United Lutheran Church (Consultative)
United Presbyterian Church

The peace committee, which is now known as the Commission on International Justice and Goodwill of the Federal Council, is "committed to unremitting activity until a peace system takes the place of competitive armaments and recurring war."

An important joint message to the churches was issued in 1925 by representatives of twenty-eight denominations meeting in a National Study Conference of the Churches on World Peace, held under the auspices of the Federal Council. This message set forth the "Ideals and Attitudes of the Christian Church in Regard to War" as follows:

"The teachings and spirit of Jesus clearly show that the effective force for the safeguarding of human rights, the harmonizing of differences and the overcoming of evil is the spirit of goodwill.

"The Church, the body of Christ all-inclusive—transcending race and national divisions, should henceforth oppose war, as a method of settling disputes, between nations and groups as contrary to the spirit and principles of Jesus Christ, and should declare that it will not as a Church sanction war.

"The Church should not only labor for the coming of the Kingdom of God in the hearts of men, but should give itself to constructive policies and measures for world justice and peace. It should fearlessly declare its distinctive message of goodwill. It should proclaim this message regardless of fluctuating opinion and political exigencies.

"The Church should teach patriotic support of the State, but should never become the agent of the Government in any activity alien to the spirit of Christ. The Church should look to the responsible statesmen of a Christian country to conduct the public business along those lines of justice and reason which will not lead to war.

"The Church should recognize the right and the duty of each individual to follow the guidance of his own conscience as to whether or not he shall participate in war."

In January, 1928, the Executive Committee of the Federal Council adopted and issued a declaration of principles the far-reaching character of which is shown in the following extracts:

"With startling clearness we now see that war, in its spirit and modern practice, is the negation of everything to which the gospel of Jesus bears witness. What, then, shall the Church of Christ do with this institution which degrades human personality, sets brother against brother and rejects the constructive power of love? The Church can be satisfied with nothing less than the complete abolition of war. The Federal Council of the Churches commits itself with utmost earnestness to this task. . . .

"We pledge our ardent support to President Coolidge and Secretary Kellogg in any efforts, consonant with a proper consideration of the mutual interests of all the nations concerned, to negotiate treaties which will secure the abolition of war by the nations and assure the peaceful settlement of all international disputes. . . .

"The effect on world peace of America's unprecedented economic expansion calls for thoughtful study. . . . The widespread assumption that military forces are to be called into action whenever and wherever foreign investments are placed in jeopardy through internal political turmoil tends to perpetuate the maintenance of vast armaments and increases the likelihood of war.

"We regret that the United States is not a member of the Permanent Court of International Justice. We believe that it is yet possible for the representatives of our own country and of the nations signatory to the Court Protocol to arrive at a basis of agreement that would result in making the United States a full member of that judicial body.

"The United States, we believe, should be brought into a relationship of more effective coöperation with the rest of the world. We therefore express our gratification with the increasing number of the Committees and Commissions of the League of Nations on which the United States has full, active membership.

"The disestablishment of war and the maintenance of peace depend, in the last analysis, on the development of the spirit of goodwill, brotherhood and coöperation between nations and races. Misunderstanding and fears must be removed. Hatred must be banished. There must be created the will to peace. This is peculiarly the province of the church, which has always regarded it as its mission to nourish more Christlike motives and attitudes in the hearts of men.

"We deprecate a great naval building program, not primarily because of the vast sums involved, grave as this objection is, but because it moves in the direction of international distrust rather than of international agreement. . . . We urge our Government to give its best energies to working out, in coöperation with other nations, a plan of universal and progressive reduction of armaments.

"We rejoice to know that 36 communions now have commissions on international relations and that 57 state and city councils of churches and other local inter-communion bodies have similar committees. We urge these communions and local church councils greatly to strengthen their educational program for peace and to provide their commissions and committees with budgets sufficient to enable them to operate more effectively. The Church must ever cherish the age-old and inalienable liberty of the prophets to interpret public policies and the institutions of the day in the light of the Christian gospel. . . . Efforts being made by a few individuals and groups to cast aspersions on the character and honesty of purpose of many of our ablest Christian leaders, falsely charging them with being consciously or unconsciously agents of subversive influences, should be outspokenly condemned."

The Church Peace Union

In 1914, the Church Peace Union was organized to unite the Protestant, Catholic, Jewish and Greek Orthodox Churches in work for peace. The Union was endowed by Andrew Carnegie with a sum of $2,000,000. It immediately formed the World Alliance for International Friendship through the Churches to carry out its program. There are branches of the World Alliance in thirty nations. It was responsible in 1919 for the first international conference of the churches to be held after the World War, and international goodwill congresses are being held now annually. The World Alliance takes the position that "war should no longer be used for the settlement of controversies between nations" and "that the time has come to make a combined and frontal attack for the overthrow of the institution of war by outlawing it and making war a crime under the law of nations":

"We recognize that the approaches to a warless world are varied. We are still in the process of finding the most feasible paths to peace. We do not desire to be dogmatic as to details of policy, but the danger of drifting into war situations is so obvious, the silent forces which lead to international crises are so subtle, the delay of constructive action is so disheartening that we summon the proponents of peace to a sympathetic understanding of differing programs and to a united advance on certain great essentials.

"We believe that the churches and other religious organizations have in the Peace Movement a most searching test of their own foundations and the most challenging opportunity of their history. Religious groups must translate their ideals of a warless world into effective action through intelligent understanding of the political, social and economic problems facing the nations, and through support of practical measures to ensure international coöperation and justice."

The American Branch of the Alliance welcomes the coöperation of all faiths, all political affiliations, all shades of opinion in making

"America 100% effective in coöperation with other nations

in preserving peace throughout the world and in developing permanent methods of international goodwill and security.

"The entire program is based upon the conviction that the greatest need of the present time is an aroused public sentiment, in view of the ominous threatenings of more wars as a result of continued national, sectional and racial hatred and misunderstandings, and of the reasonable possibilities of preserving peace."

The Catholic Association for International Peace

During the World War the responsibility felt by the Catholic Church for world peace was several times given expression in messages from the Pope, and in his repeated effort to bring about a cessation of hostilities. One of the notable pronouncements was this of Pius XI in his First Encyclical:

"The nations of to-day live in a state of armed peace which is scarcely better than war itself, a condition which tends to exhaust national finances, to waste the flower of youth, to muddy and poison the very fountain heads of life, physical, intellectual, religious and moral."

"The Church is the teacher and example of world goodwill, for she is able to inculcate and develop in mankind the 'true spirit of brotherly love.'"

"The Peace of Christ in the Kingdom of Christ. . . . With might and main we shall ever strive to bring about this peace. . . . We ask that all assist and coöperate with us in this Our mission."

To further the objects and purposes of world peace "in accord with the teachings of the Church," several conferences of members of the Catholic Church were held following the Eucharistic Congress in Chicago in 1926, and led to the formation in April, 1927, of the Catholic Association for International Peace.

The constitution of the Association declares its objects and purposes to be, "to study, disseminate, and apply the principles of natural law and Christian charity to international problems of the day; to consider the moral and legal aspects of any action which may be proposed or advocated in the international sphere; to examine and consider issues which bear upon international goodwill; to encourage the formation of conferences, lectures and study circles; to issue reports on questions of international importance; and to further, in coöperation with similar Catholic organizations in other countries, in accord with the teachings of the Church, the object and purposes of world peace and happiness." The Association brings together in committees persons acquainted with particular problems concerning peace. These committees prepare reports which are discussed in meetings of the organization, revised and made public. In February, 1928, a "Report on International Ethics—War, Intervention, Peace Treaties, Means of Avoiding War" was issued.

The Hebrew Congregations

Both the Central Conference of the American Rabbis and the Union of American Hebrew Congregations have been active in organized peace work since the war. The 29th Council of the Union of American Hebrew Congregations, held in 1926, adopted the following resolutions:

"Whereas, It is coming more and more to be realized that the best way of preventing war is by promoting international understanding through education and by creating concrete instrumentalities for peace; now therefore be it

"Resolved, That the Union of American Hebrew Congregations join with other religious denominations of our country in petitioning the United States Government to . . . adhere to the World Court; and in petitioning the President of the United States to take steps toward inviting international coöperation in a drastic reduction of armaments and control of traffic in arms; and be it further

"Resolved, That it is the sense of this convention that, in order actually and permanently to prevent war, the nations of the World must resolve to look upon war as a crime against humanity and against International Law, and we therefore petition our Government to take counsel with other nations on ways and means of bringing about the outlawry of war; and finally be it

"Resolved, That we recommend to the various congregations which we represent that special instruction be given to the children of our religious schools on the causes of international friction, and also of those principles of life and conduct, both personal and national, taught by the sages and prophets of Israel, that emphasize our common humanity and make for peace and understanding; and we further recommend the appointment by each of our congregations of a Standing Committee on International Justice and Peace, whose function it shall be to assist in the creation and strengthening of a public opinion in behalf of peace and to represent the congregation in all community efforts for the promotion of peace."

The Central Conference of American Rabbis in 1924 adopted a resolution on peace which included the following statements:

"Together with our brothers of other creeds we are eager to give whatever we can of our strength and devotion, in order that the curse of war shall be lifted from the world. . . .

"We urge upon our fellow-citizens and upon those who guide the destinies of our land that, being true to themselves, they adopt an uncompromising opposition to war. We believe that war is morally indefensible. War that crushes the young, that brutalizes and degrades, that destroys all that is most precious, must not be honored and glorified. It must be recognized for what it is and this must be taught to our children.

"In conclusion we would repeat the words of our prayer-book: 'Grant us peace, Thy most precious gift, O Thou Eternal Source of Peace, and enable Israel to be a messenger of peace unto the peoples of the earth.' Bless our country that it may ever be a stronghold of peace and its advocate in the council of nations."

By action of its Executive Board in 1927 the Central Conference, referring to the threat of war with Mexico, adopted the following resolution:

"We hold that where there is the will, every international issue can be adjusted without resort to armed force.
"We hold the sanctity of human life to be paramount to all considerations of the rights of property.
"We hold that these two principles are an integral part of historic American idealism, as reaffirmed by President Coolidge in his Omaha address in these words: 'Our Country has definitely relinquished the old standards of dealing with other countries by terror and force, and is definitely committed to the new standard of dealing with them through friendship and understanding. . . .' In the Mexican situation, we have a crucial issue in which these principles are being put to test. Therefore, we urge upon the Government of the United States of America to apply to the Mexican situation the principles of arbitration and conciliation, and to settle this international dispute without resorting to armed force."

In 1926 at Geneva an International Committee of Anti-Militarist Clergymen was founded by individual clergymen from Holland, Germany, Switzerland and America. Its purposes are stated to be:

"To unite the anti-militarist ministers of all churches and of all denominations and of all countries and if possible to create new groups and to prepare the way for an international congress to be held in Holland in 1928;
"To study thoroughly the question of war from the theological and philosophical standpoint;
"To demonstrate without delay, by word and deed in and

THE CHURCH AND PEACE

outside the churches, against war and the preparations for war."

RESOLUTIONS ON WORLD PEACE

Resolutions adopted since the war by the various Protestant denominations have in many instances gone even further in renunciation of war than those passed by inter-denominational bodies. Striking extracts only can be included in this chapter. The resolutions in full can be obtained from the church bodies or from the National Council for Prevention of War.

The Advent Christians General Conference of America (1924):

"In view of the fact that war does not settle problems, but often increases them, that it is un-Christian in spirit, and must be much more inhuman and cruel in time to come, this Conference takes its stand as unalterably opposed to war."

If these resolutions meant that every church member was living up to them war would undoubtedly be already abolished; they do mean, however, that the way has been opened and made easy for every individual member and local church to throw their energies into work for peace.

The Baptist World Alliance (1923):

"This Congress, representing millions of citizens belonging to different Governments, appeals to the Governments of the world to make the maintenance of peace their first aim, for the sake of each nation and people, and for the sake of the happiness and well-being of mankind. . . .

"The Congress urges the members of all churches throughout the world to pray for peace, to counter-work everything that is likely to provoke Governments to act against each other, to cleanse the educational books of all nations of all racial and national antagonisms."

The Northern Baptist Convention (1924):

"Whereas: The Christian conscience of the world is coming to recognize that war is neither inevitable nor necessary; that it is contrary to the spirit and teaching of Jesus Christ; that it is the most colossal and ruinous social sin that afflicts humanity today; that under modern conditions war has now become not only futile but suicidal; and that the recognition of this fact is necessary to the continuance of civilization; therefore be it

"Resolved, That the Northern Baptist Convention again declares its conviction that war is a wrong method of settling international disputes, and that because it is wrong, the church must not only condemn war and the things which make for war, but must take an active part in discovering and promoting the things which make for peace."

The resolution adopted in 1927 read:

"Resolved, That we reaffirm the conviction that a primary Christian interest is the advancement of peace on earth, goodwill to men, and as means to that end:

"First, we most heartily favor the idea expressed by the terms 'the outlawry of war';

"Second, we endorse all efforts looking toward the reduction of armaments;

"Third, we proclaim adherence to the ideal of fellowship among the nations, and commend as complete coöperation as may be in the work of the World Court and the League of Nations."

The Southern Baptist Convention (1926):

"War is the colossal crime of the ages. War must be banished. If it is banished, it must be banished by the active influence and effort of the great Christian bodies of the world. . . . It is the high privilege and duty of Christian men and of Christian bodies in the spirit of Christ to cultivate the spirit of peace and to do all within their power for the banishment of war."

The National Council of Congregational Churches (1927):

"Whereas compulsory military training in our schools and colleges fosters a general attitude of mind conducive to militarism and sole reliance on force, and gives ground for other nations to question the peaceful purposes of the United States, therefore be it

"Resolved, That the National Council of Congregational Churches assembled in Omaha condemn both in theory and practice any compulsory military training in public schools, or in tax supported or land grant institutions of higher learning.

"Resolved, That we protest the giving of high school or any other academic credit for attendance at the Citizen's Military Training Camps, and be it further

"Resolved, That we urge congressional action to release all instructors in courses in military science from the direct control of the War Department to the regularly constituted local academic authorities, thus effectually freeing our educational system from the control or influence of the War Department."

The Commission on International Justice of the National Council of Congregational Churches has drawn up the following principles for adoption by the churches of this denomination:

"That the churches in all their departments endeavor to inculcate in the minds of their constituents, and especially the youth, a knowledge of the folly and inhumanity of war and to foster and extend the will to peace based upon the doctrine of equal rights and just treatment for all nations; and that Christian homes throughout our congregations be open to the foreign students within our gates, that they may return to their respective countries with an exalted sense of the power of Christianity in the home and a new conception of Christian fraternity;

"That the denomination stand for the new diplomacy which

repudiates threats and violence as a means of settling international difficulties and advocates instead resort to conferences, courts and arbitration;

"That the denomination condemn as vicious and unchristian all propaganda of hate, and stand against the employment of the churches for the support of war."

The General Convention of the Christian Church (1926):

"A false and foolish patriotism may be the very germ of another and a hundred times worse world war than the one we have passed through. The Christian Church should speak in no uncertain way for the outlawry of war, and all lands should come to understand that the Church of Christ brands international strife and bloodshed with all its accompanying hatred and destruction as crime between the nations, as murder is crime between man and man.

"The church and the world should have learned its lesson by this time, but there still arises a demand for militarism, under the guise of patriotism and national defense, which seeks to make military service practically compulsory in our schools. The church should stand unalterably opposed to such a movement and should be on guard in every local community and in the national counsels of the nation to raise its voice and to give its influence against such a perilous step toward militarism."

The International Convention of the Disciples of Christ in 1926 adopted resolutions calling for the celebration of Armistice Day and for the enactment of a law designating that day as Peace Day. It opposed military training in the following resolution:

"Whereas, our people are committed to the principle of no conscription in times of peace,

"Be it resolved, That we oppose all compulsory military training in the colleges, universities and high schools of this country."

THE CHURCH AND PEACE

The General Convention of the Protestant Episcopal Church (1925):

"We believe that a warless world is a possibility; that life based on the spirit and principles of the Prince of Peace, so far from being visionary, contains the only practical method of security for the future. We regard this work not only as a corporate responsibility of the whole Church, but as the individual duty of every Christian citizen. The American Ambassador to England, himself a communicant of this Church, said in one of his first public utterances, 'The Foreign Office of the United States is in the American home.' In this true and striking statement he reminds every one of us of the part each must play in this work which transcends all others in importance.

"We reaffirm the conviction stated by the General Convention of 1922 that the nations of the world must adopt a peace system. It is fundamental to such a system that it be built on the conviction that war is unchristian in principle and suicidal in practice."

The Evangelical Synod of North America (1925):

"We declare our conviction that international warfare is incompatible with the Gospel of love and brotherhood which we profess to believe. The methods used and the passions aroused by war both outrage Christ's conception of a Kingdom of God in which men shall trust, love and forgive one another. We therefore pledge ourselves to support every movement which looks toward an organization of the nations for the elimination and outlawry of war; and to use every means to create the spirit of international goodwill among our people. We furthermore declare that we will not, as a Christian Church, ever bless or sanction war. We make this declaration of abstention as a Christian communion and do not intend it to bind individuals unless and until they accept it personally. We do mean it to commit our Church to the fundamental proposition that to support war is to deny the Gospel we profess to believe."

The United Lutheran Church in America (1924):

"We believe that the time has come when it is necessary to stress the fact that nationalism and internationalism are not mutually exclusive terms, that patriotism and the love of other nations and races are complementary, that the processes employed by and within the nation to secure justice, peace and stability must be employed in an ever-increasing measure in the intercourse between nations, that the arbitrament of arms must yield in an ever larger degree to the arbitrament of reason, of law and of Christian love, and that to this end Christian citizens are pledged as such to exert every effort, through the establishment of some effective agency, to further justice and goodwill in their own country and in the commonwealth of nations. We believe that the Lutheran World Convention can contribute materially to the furtherance of world peace and petition it to consider this problem.

"Holding these fundamental principles we recognize the fact that sin is still in the world and that nations might be unwarrantably incited to attack and invade our nation and therefore we believe that in accordance with the teaching of Article XVI of the Augsburg Confession and Article I of the Constitution of the United States, Christians may engage in just war and act as soldiers."

The New York and New England Synod of the United Lutheran Church in America (1924):

"The record of human progress reveals that we arrive at certain stages when the Christian conscience, enlightened by the Word of God, demands the sloughing off of evils which can be endured no longer. That hour, we believe, has arrived for the horrible practice of war. . . .

"If the existing desire for peace is expressed and spread still further and intensified, it will become a dominant issue in our political life and a determined citizenry will substitute law for military force. Governments will find a way to accomplish what the people demand.

"We petition the United Lutheran Church to recommend to the next Lutheran World Conference to adopt a program of education and action so that the 80,000,000 Lutherans throughout the world may be enlisted and led in a campaign against war."

The General Conference of the Methodist Episcopal Church (1928):

"Whereas, the Honorable Frank B. Kellogg, Secretary of State of the United States, has taken a heroic, earnest and unprecedented stand in favor of the outlawry of war, and is persistently endeavoring to bring the same to pass;

"Therefore, Be It Resolved, that we instruct the Secretary of this General Conference to express to Secretary Kellogg our appreciation of his efforts and to assure him that the General Conference of the Methodist Episcopal Church in session at Kansas City wishes to coöperate with him in every possible way.

. . . .

"We rejoice in the efforts now being made by the United States and other governments to enter into compacts with other nations for the outlawry of war. We are convinced that war has become the supreme enemy of mankind. Its continuance is the suicide of civilization. We would utterly repudiate our professed faith in our Lord Jesus Christ, the Prince of Peace, if we held that war is inevitable. War is not inevitable. Disputes between nations, like disputes between individuals, may be settled by judicial processes. We believe, therefore, that war should be made a public crime under the law of nations.

"We recognize the need of an army and navy sufficient to serve as a police power for the protection of life and property on land and sea. But as a Christian body we 'renounce war as an instrument of national policy,' and set ourselves to create the will to peace. The agencies of our Church shall not be used in preparation for war. They shall be used in preparation for peace. We must do our full share to mould the present youth of all races into a peace-loving generation. To this end we recommend that the Board of Bishops appoint a commission on peace and world fellowship, consisting of seven ministers and eight laymen, and that this commission be empowered to employ an executive secretary and to secure from the General Conference Expense Fund a sufficient sum to finance its operation.

"Preparation for war leads to war. We therefore urge the President of the United States to prepare for another Conference of Nations to secure a more drastic reduction of armaments of every kind. We adhere to the principle that diplomacy should be used instead of military intervention in our relations with other nations. The rights of the smallest nation must be held as sacred as those of the strongest.

"We call upon our members as citizens to exert themselves to the utmost to secure the participation of their respective governments in a World Court which shall have affirmative jurisdiction over all international disputes, and shall develop and administer international law upon the basic principle that war is a crime. We urge upon our members their duty as citizens to secure the participation of their respective governments in an effective association of nations which shall undertake to remove the causes of war and to lead the world into the ways of peace.

. . . .

"We record our appreciation of the efforts being made by the government of the United States of America looking toward world peace. There are, however, certain policies now in vogue which tend to weaken these efforts, and against which we protest.

"We are opposed to compulsory military training in high schools, colleges and universities.

"We are opposed to the advertising of military training camps by government postmarks on mail matter, the distribution of which in this and foreign countries tends to create a wrong impression regarding the attitude of the United States toward the spirit of universal peace.

. . . .

"In accord with the desire for world peace by understanding as often expressed by the Methodist Episcopal Church, be it Resolved, That we as a General Conference request the Congress and the President of the United States to withhold their support of the naval bill now before the Senate looking to the laying down of more cruisers beyond the fiscal year ending June, 1929, and to any clause in such a bill which would restrict the President in his power to suspend construction of cruisers authorized in the event of the calling of an international conference for further reduction of naval armaments.

"The secretary is instructed to wire this petition to the President and to the Senate of the United States."

The General Assembly of the Presbyterian Church (1924):

"The Presbyterian Church in the U. S. A. pledges all its energies to the outlawry of war and to the hastening of the day when nations shall learn war no more. We refuse to believe that the wholesale slaughter of human beings upon the battlefield is morally necessary to man's highest development any more than is killing by individuals. We see in war's cruelties, made more terrible by modern invention, not only a menace to civilization but also a definite challenge to the followers of the Prince of Peace."

The Eastern Synod of the Reformed Church in the United States of America (1924):

"We avow our sincere patriotism and our unquestioned loyalty to the nation that we love, but we claim for ourselves the right and the liberty to speak at any time contrary to those who may temporarily be in control of the government, if loyalty to the Spirit of Jesus Christ, as we apprehend it, demands such action.

"Recognizing the moral and spiritual attainments of the race to be what they are, we do not cherish the illusion that a nation attacked would refuse to defend itself. We, therefore, believe that international agencies and instrumentalities must be created that will insure justice and protection to all nations, great and small, strong and weak.

"We refuse to believe that such agencies cannot be created but are of the firm conviction that if the government would set itself aggressively to the pursuit of peace, and would expend the equivalent of time, thought, energy and money in devising peaceful means for the settlement of disputes that it now spends in preparing for war, the peace of the world would be more assured than it is at this time.

"But we are likewise convinced that no organization of government and no international agencies can in themselves be depended on to insure the peace of the world and we, therefore, call on all our pastors and churches to be instant in season and out of season to create the spirit of goodwill and brotherliness in all human relationships and to bring the life of Christ and the powers of the gospel to bear on the spirit of the age."

The General Conference of the Seventh Day Baptist Church (1926):

"War is un-Christian. For twenty centuries, two diametrically opposed systems of philosophy have grown up together in this world. One is based upon love and goodwill toward God and fellow man. It exalts the value of the individual life and soul. The other is based on hate and organized slaughter. It exalts the value of force and counts life as nothing except as it contributes to the military strength of the State. . . . The time is here when we must decide which of these traditions shall prevail—whether the Cross or the sword shall be our symbol; whether we will worship Christ or Mars, for both cannot prevail together."

The Universalist General Convention (1925):

"Whereas, a cardinal principle of the Universalist church is that of allegiance to 'the Spiritual Authority and Leadership of Jesus,' to be interpreted by its members as their conscience may direct; and whereas, there are those among its members who interpret this authority as a complete condemnation and renunciation of violence between nations as well as between individuals, operative even in time of war itself.

"Therefore, be it resolved that the fifty-fifth convention of the Universalist church recognizes as being in accord with our fundamental principles the right of members of this church to refuse on conscientious grounds to participate in any warfare."

The Universalist General Convention (1927) sent a memorial to the President and Senate of the United States urging acceptance of the Briand proposal for a treaty renouncing war and declaring:

"That war should never again be resorted to by civilized nations as the means for settling disputes or enforcing claims.

"That war should be declared by the nations to be an international crime.

"That the renunciation of war by treaties and solemn engagements should be undertaken between all the principal nations.

"And that the settlement of every threatening dispute, whatever its nature, should be sought only by pacific means."

The American Unitarian Association in 1925 pledged itself to support all efforts to bring about better understanding among nations and to organize the nations on a basis of international coöperation and law.

The religious groups which have from the beginning made non-participation in war a fundamental part of their faith—the Brethren, the Moravians, the Mennonites and the Quakers—pass few resolutions on this subject, although there is an occasional reiteration of their position.

The Church of the Brethren in 1928 adopted a resolution as follows:

Be it resolved:

That we believe the Church of Christ is a holy institution, founded on love, peace and brotherhood, and therefore cannot bless warfare, or endorse the killing of our fellowman.

That every effort be made to foster the altruistic spirit among the nations and peoples of the world; that all propaganda tending to mislead peoples and create prejudice and misunderstanding be discouraged; that selfish economic imperialism by individuals or corporations be condemned as unrighteous and out of harmony with the Christian spirit which has been a cardinal principle of our American life; that military armament and preparations for war be abolished by the outlawry of war through peace treaties, and that only such forces be maintained as may be needed for police protection; that we advocate the settlement of all international differences by peace conferences and arbitration; that compulsory military training in universities, colleges and high schools, being un-American and un-Christian, be discontinued.

The Eastern District Conference of Mennonites in 1927 stated:

"The Mennonite Church has for more than four centuries held the Bible as the one valid and true rule of life. One of the Biblical principles emphasized by our forefathers, which we sincerely believe to be essential for the highest type of life, is that which directs us to affirm that international differences should be settled by arbitration and not by armies, according to the New Testament teaching concerning peace. We therefore reaffirm our solemn conviction that peace ought to be striven for in the lives of individuals and the lives of nations."

The Mennonite General Conference in 1917 issued a statement which said:

"As a Christian people we have always endeavored to support the government under which we lived in every capacity consistent with the teaching of the Gospel as we understand it, and will continue to do so; but according to this teaching we cannot participate in war in any form; that is, to aid or abet war, whether in combatant or non-combatant capacity."

At the *Conference of All Friends* held in England in 1920, a new statement of the Quaker position on war was adopted, in the foreword of which the following paragraphs are found:

"The whole redemptive process, which reveals the nature of God intimately bound up with a true experience of the life of God, has at the same time made clear, as nothing else ever has, the infinite worth of personal life seen in the light of that love that suffers long and is kind. Love is no accident of a creation struggling to survive and to propagate life; it is the expression of the deepest nature of things; it is the energy by which the spiritual world is formed and built.

"It is because in some real sense we see the truth of the nature of God and man that we cannot have any part in the way and method and spirit of war, either for the settlement of international differences or as a solution of the social and industrial problems which beset our age. It belongs to the very essence and fiber of our religious faith to take Christ's way of life as a program to be practiced and to regard His estimate of the worth of man as the true one. We have no illusion as to the cost and the difficulty of such a venture. But we cannot do otherwise. We know of no other way to preserve our loyalty to the highest or to bring in the Kingdom for which Christ lived and died."

The Moravian Church adopted through its Provincial Synod in June, 1925, a resolution which said in part:

"Whereas, The Moravian Church, in view of its history and ideals, should be among the foremost of those who carry on this 'war against war'. . . .

"Resolved, That it is our conviction, that when such vast

sums are being spent in preparation for possible war, the Government should stand ready to spend liberal sums in the cultivation of peace, in the holding of Disarmament Conferences, in the maintenance of a World Court and in the prosecution of other enterprises having the same end in view."

In some instances church groups have not made it their practice to pass resolutions. Nevertheless, the promotion of peace is a fundamental part of their belief.

The Corresponding Secretary of the *Christian Science Board of Directors* recently made the following statement:

"The Discoverer and Founder of Christian Science, Mary Baker Eddy, was a lifelong advocate of conciliation, arbitration, and peace. In a letter to an editor, she said 'I am absolutely and religiously opposed to war' ("The First Church of Christ, Scientist, and Miscellany," page 284). One of the By-Laws which she wrote for the Church she founded reads in part as follows: 'It shall be the duty of the members of The Mother Church and of its branches to promote peace on earth and goodwill toward men' ("Church Manual," page 45). Accordingly, all Christian Scientists are actively interested in practical measures for the prevention of war. The international character of our Church contributes to goodwill between nations, but much of what is being done by Christian Scientists for the abolition of war is being done through our international newspaper, *The Christian Science Monitor*. One of the aims of this newspaper is to be an active and vigilant agency for international peace."

In the Bahá'í faith the unity of mankind and world peace are basic principles. The writings of 'Abdu'l-Bahá are filled with teachings and prophecies in regard to peace. The following statement occurs in the Discourses of 'Abdu'l-Bahá, delivered during his visit to the United States in 1912, which have been published in two volumes under the title, "The Promulgation of Universal Peace":

"All the divine manifestations have proclaimed the oneness of God and the unity of mankind. They have taught that men should love and mutually help each other in order that they might progress. Now if this conception of religion be true, its essential principle is the oneness of humanity. The fundamental truth of the manifestations is peace. This underlies all religion, all justice."

The Theosophical Society carries on active educational work for peace through an International Order of Service with a director of peace work in each city where the Order exists. One of the objects of this Order of Service is to develop a World Prayer Week from November 4th to November 11th. In the belief that "fine thoughts and prayers are energies that stream forth from the mind" it seeks to have as many people as possible in all parts of the world during the two minutes of the Great Silence observed at noon on November 11th, unite in prayer for peace. It urges also that at noon each day throughout the year individuals everywhere think peace and pray for peace.

The desire of the churches to promote world peace is by nothing better attested than by the recent change in the attitude of various denominations toward the work of missionaries. The underlying theory of foreign mission work is changing from one of carrying salvation to the heathen to one of conducting a joint search with the men and women of other nations for the principle of divine goodness. This line of development is even leading to missionaries working under the native Christian churches rather than their home church. Of more immediate bearing upon issues of war and peace are recent pronouncements in regard to the military protection of missions by the home government.

The following cablegram was sent in May, 1927, to all missionaries appointed by the Baptist board:

"Please inform our own missionaries and Chinese Christian leaders that the policy of the board is as follows: Equal and reciprocal treaties with China as soon as possible, the United States negotiating independently if necessary. No armed intervention by foreign powers. We support the United States Government in its policy of non-intervention. We are in favor of the rapid tranfer of administrative responsibilities to Chinese Christians and the reoccupation as soon as practicable of stations by missionaries urgently needed and desired, who understand that no call must be made for protection by foreign armed forces and that there must be no personal participation in Chinese political movements. The United States Government recognizes that the final decision concerning missionaries leaving their station rests with the missionaries themselves. We are notifying the United States Government of our position."

The China Inland Mission on October 28, 1925, made the following official statement:

"As an international organization having home centres in Great Britain, North America, Australasia, and the Continent of Europe, the China Inland Mission in London, without the delay for consultation which would be necessary if a new declaration were to be made, is glad to reaffirm that from the Mission's foundation, its principles and practice have been not to rely upon Government protection, not to make demands for rights or restitution, but rather to accept as a privilege what may be offered by its own and the Chinese Government, to avoid appeals to Consuls and Chinese officials, to show honour to all in authority whether Chinese or their own Government officials, as required by the Word of God, and to recognize practically that the weapons of its warfare are spiritual and moral, not carnal."

The International Missionary Council, meeting in 1928 in Jerusalem, placed on record its "conviction that the protection of missionaries should only be by such methods as will promote goodwill in personal and official relations," and urged upon all missionary societies that they make "no claim on their governments for the armed defense of their missionaries or their property."

Here and there fear has been expressed that the churches are taking too active a part in political life and should devote themselves to the spiritual life of the individual. A different point of view is taken by Dr. Reinhold Niebuhr, member of the Executive Board of the Federal Council of Churches, who agrees that the churches may be "too politically minded," but holds that they are not taking an active enough part in influencing the policies of states:

"Is it not true that in everything that the Church has been doing since it has achieved an interest in politics it has been too politically-minded? Not that the Church should have less interest in politics. It should have more, but we cannot afford to be politically-minded when we are settling political questions. We must be prophetic. If we cannot stand for some principle that is higher than that politicians are willing to accept, we show that we have not sufficient moral vision to guide our nation spiritually. If all we can do is to make a pronouncement that sounds like the platform of a political party, where is the uniqueness of our ethical insight? . . . As a Church we must challenge the nations to a mutual trust, to the building up of a new kind of international system. We must go far beyond anything the nations are willing to do today. As Christians we must divest ourselves a little bit of 'statesmanship,' with its compromises—become more prophetic. We are still being dragged at the chariot wheels of the state. We will have to be more heroic."

CHAPTER IV

WOMEN AND PEACE

FIFTY years ago the only women's organizations working for peace were a dozen groups in Europe called "Olive Leaf Circles" which had been organized by men as Ladies' Auxiliaries to the Universal Brotherhood of Man. Today women's organizations having a total membership of several millions have undertaken to study the problem of how war can be abolished and to work for its abolition.

When the first peace organizations were formed early in the 19th century, women were not allowed to speak at their meetings. Julia Ward Howe was denied permission to speak at a national convention of the English Peace Society as late as 1878 on the ground that women never had spoken at these meetings. In the same year she went as a delegate to an international peace congress in Paris, but when she asked permission to speak, she was told she might talk with the officers of the Society when the public meeting had adjourned.

The peculiar antagonism of women to war and their special responsibility for peace have nevertheless always been taken for granted. Among certain primitive tribes it was left to the judgment of the women to decide when fighting had gone on long enough and to command the chiefs to make peace, which the chiefs then did without loss of their reputation for bravery. In the literature of the Greeks there are two famous dramas, written by men, expressing women's antipathy to war, "The Trojan Women," which voices their lament, and "Lysistrata," which depicts their rebellion. To Virgil, war was that which is "hateful-to-mothers."

In modern as well as ancient literature, the dramatic conflict between the creative impulses of women and the destructive nature of war finds repeated expression, most vivid, perhaps, in a modern French romance, also written by a man, which pictures the women of Paris stopping the outbreak of another conflict by breaking through the guards at the stations where troops are entraining, and throwing themselves with the wild passion of a mob against the locomotives, so that the trains can proceed only over their bodies.

Modern psychologists show this conviction that women are by nature enemies of war to be well founded. They declare further that it is only through the expression of women's instinctive opposition to war that war will be abolished. Among the points they make are these, which were emphasized in the address of Dr. Beatrice Hinkle before the Conference on the Cause and Cure of War in 1925:

"War is the product of the irrational (that is to say, unrational) impulses of men toward self-assertion and power; reason is not yet strong enough to control such impulses; they can be controlled only by other and stronger irrational impulses; the impulses of women are toward creation and preservation of life; and because they have been less suppressed and modified than those of men, they are stronger and will be able to overcome them if given full play."

Benjamin Kidd in his "Science and Power" declares that civilization depends upon the control of the present in the interest of the future; that men are led by the impulse of the fight to seek power in the present; but that to women the future is greater than the present and the race greater than the individual. It is upon women, therefore, that the carrying forward of civilization depends.

If this claim of the psychologists, that the overthrow of war depends upon the expression of the special impulses of women is true, the organized, voting women of today face this problem: How can they express their impulse for peace in practical political terms, that is, use for its expression the methods and the tools of men, without destroying the vital force of the impulse itself?

Dr. Hinkle indicates the necessary conditions for success. Women must learn to accept themselves and to value themselves "as beings possessing a worth at least equal to that of men"; they must not unthinkingly accept standards based on masculine psychology; they must realize that their own development does not "involve imitation of men or repudiation of their own instincts." To quote Dr. Hinkle directly:

"If women can be emotionally aroused to the danger knocking at their door, and, with minds firmly set to 'War shall not be,' will act true to their own instincts, giving them free play without argument or reason, one generation will be sufficient to banish the mass crime of humanity and force men to find new ways and means of solving the problems of civilization."

Ellen Key writes in "War, Peace and the Future":

"But if we wish to create a new world without continuing in the old circle where women bear and bring up children to be destroyed on the field of battle, women must arise and hold together in the will to make an end of this state of affairs that has for century after century made the goal of their mother love and mother labors so meaningless. It is madness to try, in times of peace, to produce a more and more virile race only to let it be buried in the graves of the battlefields. . . .

"The characteristics that are now scornfully called feminine—as the apostles of might are ashamed to call them Christian in the same breath that they denounce them—were in the springtime of Christianity active in the suppression of violence. If these assets are again to hold violence at bay, it will be only through the power of women to make them living again, living not only in the souls of men but in the growth and intergrowth of the communities. . . .

"Until the majority of women in the world can say with our Selma Lagerlof:

"'As long as my tongue can utter a word,
As long as blood flows in my veins,
I shall work for the sake of peace,
Though it cost me my life and happiness,'

humanity is still far from peace."

The first attempt in modern times to give practical expression to women's will to peace was made by Julia Ward Howe. Roused by the suffering caused by the American Civil War and by the Franco-Prussian War which closely followed it, she determined to organize a "women's peace crusade." She says in her "Reminiscences" that the question forced itself upon her: "Why do not the mothers of mankind interfere in these matters to prevent the waste of that human life of which they alone bear and know the cost?" The "august dignity of motherhood and its terrible responsibility" appeared to her in a new aspect, and she immediately drew up an appeal to the womanhood of the world, which she had translated into all the European languages and distributed far and wide. Although Mrs. Howe succeeded in arranging a large public meeting in London, she was not able to rouse women to the crusade she had hoped. She continued, however, to work for peace herself throughout the rest of her life, and to do everything she could to increase women's public and political power, in the belief that they would use this power for peace.

During the World War another American woman, Mrs. Clara Guthrie d'Arcis, living in Geneva, again attempted to unite all women upon the "common basis of womanly compassion" in an attack on war, and established the World Union of Women for International Concord. In a speech before the members of this World Union of Women, the appeal to women's emotions against war was put very vividly by the President of the International Council of Women, the Marchioness of Aberdeen and Temair:

"If the wild deer knows how to protect its young against the eagle hovering around, by sheltering it under an overshadowing rock—if a savage mother knows how to hide her babe from the vendetta of a rival tribe, cannot the mothers of today devise plans for an international understanding among themselves, whereby, inspired by an all-conquering love and strong in the faith which removes mountains, they will be able to protect the children of the human race from the calamities which threaten their very existence?"

But in general, organized women today are approaching the problem of establishing world peace from the scientific and intellectual rather than from the emotional point of view, and with the obvious intent of bringing their new political power to bear upon it.

Before the World War and before their attainment of political power, there were no national or international women's groups organized solely for the promotion of peace. The International Council of Women, however, as early as 1888, at the instigation of Mrs. May Wright Sewall, whose life was devoted to peace work, included world peace among its objectives and called an International Conference of Women which met in this country at the time of the World's Fair. At about the same period other women's organizations, formed for various purposes, notably the Woman's Christian Temperance Union under the leadership of Frances E. Willard, created special committees to work for world peace, while frequent international conferences of women and the formation of the International Woman Suffrage Alliance tended to bring to consciousness the fact that women in their needs and purposes are united across border lines. During the last quarter of the last century, individual women in practically every country of the world were to be found working for peace. Many of the suffrage pioneers worked also for peace, among them Lucretia Mott, who is said to have been the first to urge upon President Lincoln that the "Alabama" dispute be submitted to arbitration. The best known of the women peace workers was Baroness Bertha von Suttner of Austria, who inspired Alfred Nobel to include in his world prizes one for those who had promoted peace. She was herself awarded this prize in 1905 for her book, "Lay Down Your Arms," and is the only woman ever to have received it.

In 1915, stirred by the suffering of the nations at war, Jane Addams and Mrs. Carrie Chapman Catt issued a call for a convention of women, out of which grew the first national organization of women designed solely to promote peace, the Woman's Peace Party. This same year saw the creation of a Women's International Committee for Permanent Peace, as the result of an international congress of women called at The Hague by Dutch, British, German, and Belgian women. The Woman's Peace Party sent 47 delegates to this congress, and its president, Jane Addams, presided. Twelve countries were represented. The Congress appointed committees of women to visit the governments of all neutral and belligerent nations in an attempt to secure the formation and acceptance of a neutral international body which should be empowered to carry on continuous mediation. These committees were received by the highest government officials and their plan listened to with attention and expressions of approval.

Nothing could indicate more clearly the peculiar relation of women to war than this congress held in the midst of war, at which women from enemy nations sat side by side on a platform dedicated to "a passionate human sympathy not inconsistent with patriotism but transcending it." Not only did the delegates to this congress, who braved ridicule, ostracism, and imprisonment to attend it, prove that women are capable of putting humanity above any single nation, but they showed that it is possible for women to play a part in the service of peace which it would be quite impossible under present conditions for men to undertake.

After America entered the war, the activities of women's organizations interested in peace practically ceased. A very large proportion of their members took up some form of war work. The Woman's Peace Party held its fourth annual meeting in the Friends Meeting House in Philadelphia in 1917. Several of the members reported that they were making speeches on such subjects as "After the War, What?" and "The New Preparedness," designed to promote a peace that should be permanent. Others were lecturing on the conservation of food, including Miss Addams, who has since stated that she felt at the time that the effort to ward off starvation united women the world over in their own ancient task of feeding humanity. In one or two instances state branches continued to carry on educational work for permanent world peace, as independent organizations, notably the League for Permanent Peace, in Massachusetts, of which Mrs. J. Malcolm Forbes was president.

WOMEN AND PEACE 113

Following the announcement of the Armistice, a second international congress of women, agreed upon at the Hague conference, was called to meet simultaneously with the Peace Conference. This meeting of women protested against the Treaty of Versailles as violating the principles upon which alone a just and lasting peace could be based, and was instrumental in securing in the provisions of the League of Nations a clause declaring all positions under the League open to women as well as to men. The name of the organization was at this time changed to the Women's International League for Peace and Freedom. This remains the only international organization of women working exclusively for peace. It now has branches in 24 countries and connections in 12 others.

Work for peace was not undertaken by other women's organizations to any great extent in the years immediately following the war, but in 1921 at a national convention of the League of Women Voters, Mrs. Carrie Chapman Catt, throwing aside a speech on other subjects, roused the women by a magnificent outcry against war, appealing to them to prevent another war and ending with the challenge, "The women in this room can do this thing! The women in this room can do this thing!" This speech may be considered the starting point of a campaign of organized women for peace, in which the greatest women's organizations in the country are participating.

Shortly before Mrs. Catt's speech, a group of women in Washington had formed the Women's Committee for World Disarmament in the hope of reviving interest in a proposal made by Senator Borah for an international disarmament conference at Washington. Mrs. Catt's speech and the mass meeting arranged by this Women's Committee, at which Senator Borah renewed his demand that this government call a disarmament conference, were recognized as effective forces, along with the work of the organized churches, in securing the actual calling of the Washington Conference.

Preceding the opening of the Disarmament Conference, a joint committee of the outstanding women's organizations in Washington arranged a second large mass meeting which gave effective expression to the public desire that the Conference should be thoroughgoing and that it should not end without definite results.

Discussion caused by the Disarmament Conference further stimulated peace work in women's organizations. Today there are committees on peace or international relations in the National League of Women Voters, the American Association of University Women, the General Federation of Women's Clubs, the National Council of Jewish Women, the Woman's Christian Temperance Union, the National Council of Women, the Woman's Missionary Union of Friends in America, the National Women's Trade Union League. Other organizations support work for peace by study groups, by resolutions, or by promoting, through their international membership, understanding and friendship. Among these organizations are the Council of Women for Home Missions, the Y. W. C. A., the National Federation of Temple Sisterhoods, and the International Federation of Soroptimists Clubs.

In addition to the American section of the Women's International League for Peace and Freedom, there are in the United States two other national women's organizations which are devoted solely to work for world peace—the Women's Peace Union and the Women's Peace Society. These two women's organizations courageously occupy the extreme left wing of the peace movement, standing against all participation in war on

WOMEN AND PEACE 115

the ground that human life should be held sacred and inviolable under all circumstances. The Women's Peace Union has secured the introduction in Congress of an amendment to the Constitution making it illegal to prepare for, declare, or carry on war.

The two most effective activities for peace which organizations of women, not primarily formed for peace work, have undertaken since the Disarmament Conference, are the legislative campaign of the Women's World Court Committee and the calling of three national Conferences on the Cause and Cure of War.

Seventeen organizations were represented on the Women's World Court Committee: the American Association of University Women, American Federation of Teachers, American Home Economics Association, American Nurses' Association, Council of Women for Home Missions, General Federation of Women's Clubs, National Board of Young Women's Christian Associations, National Congress of Parents and Teachers, National Council of Friendly Societies in America, National Council of Jewish Women, National Council of Women, National Education Association, National Federation of Colored Women, National League of Women Voters, National Service Star Legion, National Woman's Christian Temperance Union, Medical Women's National Association. This committee of women was the only organized group working constantly at the Capitol for the two years preceding the passage of the World Court resolution, and it is given credit by members of the Senate for the passage of that resolution.

Under the leadership of Mrs. Catt, the first Conference on the Cause and Cure of War was called in December, 1925, the second in December, 1926, and the third in January, 1928. Nine organizations participated, the American Association of University Women, the Council of

116 BETWEEN WAR AND PEACE

Women for Home Missions, the Federation of Woman's Boards of Foreign Missions of North America, the General Federation of Women's Clubs, the National Board of the Young Women's Christian Associations, the National Council of Jewish Women, the National League of Women Voters, the National Woman's Christian Temperance Union, and the National Women's Trade Union League.

The reasons for calling the Conferences were declared to be these:

"The futility of war as a means of settling difficulties between nations becomes increasingly apparent as science is demonstrating the danger of destroying our civilization by the character of modern warfare.

"The women's organizations of this country which have been working, through their respective programs, for an ordered human society, feel deeply their responsibility in this realm of war and peace. They believe it is time for their organizations to unite in taking steps to study the causes and cures of war."

In opening the first Conference Mrs. Catt made this statement:

"Men have been taught that physical courage is man's chief virtue. Every man hates to be called a coward, and when a man pleads that physical conflict is no longer an effective institution in our time, someone is sure to call him a coward. We women have no such obstacle in our way. If we fail, it will be because we lack moral courage."

The Third Conference on the Cause and Cure of War agreed to support the renunciation of war as an instrument of national policy; the use of existing and the creation of needed international machinery to care for the common concerns of nations and for the peaceful settlement of international disputes; the development of a foreign policy by the United States which shall promote peace and mutual goodwill; Secretary Kellogg's proposals for the negotiation of treaties to renounce war as an instrument of national policy; efforts to clear up the difficulties which are now hindering our adherence to the World Court; the Burton resolution (or similar resolutions) prohibiting the shipment of arms to any nation at war; the movement to keep our current navy building program within such bounds as shall be consonant with our efforts and those of other countries to promote the use of peaceful methods for the settlement of international disputes; and revision of the "unequal treaties" between the United States and China. The Conference decided upon a continuous study of the relations of the United States with the Latin American countries "to the end that an intelligent public opinion may encourage our government in such policies as will carry a maximum of inter-American support." It further agreed to confer with those groups of women who question the efficacy or wisdom of the peace program, with a view to promoting common understanding of the problems of peace and war, and of differing methods of work. In conclusion it recognized that women of other countries are deeply concerned in the building of world peace, and resolved:

"That the National Committee on the Cause and Cure of War communicate with the leading women's groups in other countries, particularly those enumerated in the proposal of the State Department, informing them of our purpose; and further, that we express our hope that together we may be a strong influence in the development of international public opinion for support of the use of peaceful methods as a substitute for force which may enable all civilized nations to renounce war as an instrument of their national policy; and in addition we ask their continued support of concrete methods for the peaceful settlement of international disputes."

Such Conferences as these and the study programs of their organizations, show a thoroughgoing effort on the part of women to understand world problems and to learn how to use their political power to secure such a solution of those problems as will promote peace. But if women are to influence the conduct of international affairs, it is important to recognize the fact that in world affairs women are still exerting only an "influence," even though it is an influence expressed in votes. They are not playing a direct part; decisions involving issues of peace and war are made by men, not women, and once a decision is made, opposition to it is looked upon as an "attack on the government." This situation is being made the most of by militaristic organizations to make women feel that anything they do or advocate for the promotion of peace which goes beyond the announced policies of the men who form the existing administration is disloyal. Here and there, there have been indications that women realize that the answer is to vote for candidates on the basis of their position on problems affecting peace and war, that is to take the advice of William James and "put peace men in power," while at the same time they seek for themselves equal power with men in the responsible direction of international affairs.

The International Woman Suffrage Alliance, now called the International Alliance of Women for Suffrage and Equal Citizenship, which for many years has sought greater political power for the women of all countries, in 1926 created a special committee to work directly for world peace. This International Committee for Peace and the League of Nations held the first of a proposed series of study conferences on peace problems at Amsterdam in 1927, at which Mrs. Corbett Ashby, of England, speaking to the conference as President of the Alliance, urged the delegates to take up the question of peace "not sentimentally, but as voting citizens" prepared to develop public opinion in their countries and to use their votes "to take the next practical step toward peace."

Organized women appeared this year before the national conventions of political parties in this country, to urge inclusion in their platforms of planks promoting world peace. It is perhaps even more significant that they are beginning to send questionnaires to candidates for Congress asking their position on measures affecting the establishment of world peace.

The National League of Women Voters appeared before the platform committees of the 1928 conventions and proposed the adoption of the following plank on "International Coöperation":

We endorse the effort to secure by one uniform agreement with many nations the renunciation of war as between themselves, and we support the substitution of arbitration for war as an instrument of public policy in the settlement of international differences. We further reiterate our support of the entry of the United States into the Permanent Court of International Justice.

The Women's International League for Peace and Freedom proposed to the 1928 conventions planks supporting the outlawry of war, opposing intervention as unethical in principle and ultimately unsound in practice, recommending the demilitarization of the Mexican border under a treaty similar to that between the United States and Canada, declaring in favor of the greatest possible reduction of naval armaments by international agreement and the abandonment of any program for the increase of the naval establishment of this country. The questions which this organization is putting to candidates for elective political offices in the 1928 campaign ask their position in regard to the entry of the United

States into the World Court, the ratification of the treaty renouncing war, the abandonment of a program for an increase in the naval establishment, the reduction of arms by international agreement, the establishment of an international claims commission to deal with property rights of citizens abroad, the demilitarization of the Mexican border, the independence of the Philippines, and the appropriation of funds for military training in schools and colleges.

It is obvious that the peace movement and the woman's movement are closely interwoven; fundamentally, indeed, they are the same, for both protest against rule by force and assert the value of the individual. It has even been claimed that the reason American women enjoy so large a degree of power and freedom is due to the fact that the military tradition has never been strong in this country. The abolition of war when women have won an equal share in the control of government was prophesied by Olive Schreiner in "Woman and Labor":

"War will pass when intellectual culture and activity have made possible to the female an equal share in the control and governance of modern national life; it will probably not pass away much sooner; its extinction will not be delayed much longer."

It is easy, therefore, to see how it happens that the one-time bitter opponents of woman suffrage are found today among the most bitter opponents of the peace movement.

One old argument of the military-minded against suffrage, which was that women took no part in war and therefore had no right to vote, cannot, however, be used in the attempt to keep women from using their votes to promote peace. Women were shown in the last war to be indispensable to the successful prosecution of war under modern conditions, and in the next war it is an accepted fact that munition workers and those engaged in the production and distribution of food to say nothing of civilians in general will be subject to as deadly attack as the armies in the field. The effort of the military authorities to introduce rifle practice and military drill into women's schools and colleges, the proposal of citizen training camps for women to be conducted under the War Department, and official recognition in one form or another of the older women leaders of the various groups serve two purposes: to prepare women for participation in war activities and to break down their psychological opposition to war.

The New York Federation of Progressive Women admits in one of its publications:

"It is not to the credit of women's intelligence that, with less excuse, they have been almost as completely deceived as men by the propaganda of warmakers. They have fallen victims to popular opinion, to the incredible vanity of wanting a vicarious hero in the family, and have permitted themselves to be proud of the abandonment of their first duty, the protection of the younger generation from the passions and jealousies of their elders."

H. G. Wells has recently emphasized, in a bitter attack on the superficiality of women's effort to abolish war, the dangers involved in the new relationship of women to the war machine:

"For most women and girls war is as good as a richly sentimental film that moves them to tears and pity. While it converts great multitudes of men into a muddy mixture of rags of flesh and uniform, it greatly enhances the economic importance of women and their value as nurses, war-wives, and the inspirers of heroic sacrifices."

Is there a possibility that such influences as these will make women deny their own natures and fail to do what they can to ward off war? If such a possibility does exist, it is because women do not realize what war is. Not long ago a soldier wrote this letter to "those who have never been in a battle," that is to say, to all women:

"You, who have never seen a man disappear, literally blown to atoms, on being struck by a shell; who have never heard the shrieks of wounded human beings; who have never heard the hysterical laughter of a man as he gazes at the stump where his hand was a moment ago; who have never heard the cries, the groans, the swearing, the praying of men with festering wounds, lying in a first-aid station, waiting too long and in vain for ambulances; who have never witnessed the terror of those men when the station is gassed and there are no gas masks; who have never seen convalescents, totally blind and with both hands amputated above the wrists; can you say that we should stop at anything in order to prevent this frightfulness, this savagery, this horror from occurring again?"

Dr. Charles R. Jefferson points to the same truth:

"Nobody knows what war is unless he has been in it. Nobody can tell you what it is. You cannot catch the sound of pain in books. You cannot hear the sighing of a boy whose life is ebbing away, and who keeps on saying, 'Mother, Mother,' until his heart stops beating. You cannot hear the groan of a man whose legs have been blown off, or the shriek of a man whose every breath is an agony. You cannot hear the death rattle in a single throat, much less in a thousand throats. These things are not to be found in books. Nor can you get the sights of war in books. You cannot see the twitching of a nerve, the spasm of a muscle, the contortion of a body twisted into terrible shapes by a torture that cannot be expressed. Nobody knows what war is who has not been in war."

If women, who today have no longer the excuse that they are compelled to accept passively the acts of government, knew war in its brutality and agony, it is incredible that they would listen with complacence to statesmen and generals who praise them for their vicarious "heroism" in sending their sons, not only to endure, but to inflict that agony.

Here and there a woman who has realized what war is, is calling upon women to rise against it. Kathleen Norris in a widely syndicated article asks, "You mothers of sons, where are you, that we do not hear your voices?" *The Woman's Home Companion* in an editorial in its issue for November, 1927, makes the same plea, "Will mothers keep on doing nothing to save their sons?"

Organization resolutions, conferences of leaders are not enough. There must be behind these the determined demand and action of individual women everywhere.

CHAPTER V

COMMERCE AND PEACE

In a widely published advertisement of an international investment company of New York and Chicago, one line reads:

"Capital recognizes war as its arch enemy and destroyer."

The truth of that assertion has been well supported by the declaration of the International Chamber of Commerce that "the chief responsibility of government is to find a better means than yet exists for promoting security and removing fear of war." The reiteration of this conviction in the resolutions of business conferences shows that it is beginning to be generally recognized that under modern conditions of economic interdependence, war and the threat of war are obstacles to normal business development and prosperity.

The extent of international economic interdependence under modern industrial conditions is indicated by the imports of the United States which, it is well known, is of all nations the most nearly self-sufficient. Bass and Moulton in their book, "America and the Balance Sheet of Europe," quote a report of the Guaranty Trust Company of New York as follows:

"We must obtain manganese for our steel mills from Russia and South America. Our automobile tire industry must obtain crude rubber from Brazil; our machine shops, rail mills, armored-plate works, and wire-rope factories must have nickel from Canada and New Caledonia; our tinplate manufacturers must import their tin from the Malay Straits and from Bolivia; our silk factories must get their raw product from China and Japan; our clothing wools must be imported from Australia and Argentina; our manufacturers of twines, canvas, linens and laces must get their flax from Russia and Belgium; our burlap makers must get their jute from India; the sisal which is used to make our binder twine, which is so essential in the harvesting of our crops, must come from Yucatan. We must also import large quantities of cocoanut oil and other vegetable oils from the Dutch East Indies and from the Pacific Isles; coffee from Brazil; tea from China, India, Japan and Java; cocoa from Venezuela; sugar from Cuba; rice from the Far East; spices from the East Indies; platinum from Colombia; and vanadium from Peru."

Former Secretary of Commerce Redfield says in his book, "Dependent America," that:

"If we excluded imported goods we should have to abandon all or part of many things in constant use, such as telephones, electric light, radio, phonographs, carpets, linoleum, newspapers, railways, automobiles, brushes, bagging linen, woolen and silk clothing, shoes, and the doormats on which our shoes are wiped. These things and many more are made by securing from other countries essential elements that we either are unable to supply or cannot supply in sufficient quantity or proper quality. . . .

"It is an interesting speculation to think what would happen to one of our fellow citizens if each element of his clothing and of the articles commonly used by him at home were given a voice and spoke in its native dialect. The result would be such as is written of the Tower of Babel. His hat would talk in several tongues, his shoes would break out in polyglot speech, and his clothing would unite the languages of Europe to that of our own land, all languages bearing witness to the common interests of men, and to the fact that we are engaged in a common task, a mutual labor, save when it is ruptured to the hurt of all by the brutal hand of war."

Commerce is today dependent also on an interchange of goods, for rapid transportation has led to greater and greater specialization in production, which means production in excess of domestic demand along certain lines, making the maintenance of markets as important as the securing of raw materials for production.

On this point, Bass and Moulton in "America and the Balance Sheet of Europe" say:

"If the power of European nations to produce commodities required by the United States is seriously impaired, this will carry with it not merely a reduction in European ability to buy goods from us, but it will in many cases seriously hamper American industries as well. Run back over the list of commodities that must be imported by the United States, and you will find that the maintenance of imports is quite as essential to American prosperity as the maintenance of exports. The maintenance of trade, whereby the modern system of specialized production is made possible, is the vitally important requirement. . . . The modern world is an economic unit, and no part of it can prosper when other important portions are in decadence."

Foreign markets and the free flow of trade are obstructed not only by war, but by the nationalistic policies which are encouraged by the war system, while the normal development of specialized industries is definitely obstructed by preparation for war. The need, because of the possibility of war, to be self-sustaining, causes nations to carry on industries for which they are not suited or are less well suited than other countries. This means that the volume of goods produced of the kind which the country is best fitted to produce is less than it should be. Both facts tend to raise prices and restrict trade.

COMMERCE AND PEACE

A leader in one of the small European governments, regretting the necessity, because of the threat of war, for an uneconomic industrial development, said recently:

"We could succeed if we could make full use of our own opportunities, which are chiefly those of agriculture. We have the population, the land, and the right climatic conditions. If we could confine our major efforts to agriculture we could export a large surplus, could stabilize our money, pay our debts, and become prosperous."

Industrial prosperity demands more than the avoidance of war, it requires active coöperation among nations, and national policies based upon a consideration of the interests of all the countries concerned. It has been convincingly demonstrated in post-war years that business depression in one part of the world affects all other parts. The inability of the people of Russia to buy tea depresses the tea industry in India, with the result that the people of India have less money with which to buy the cotton goods produced in England, and this in turn means great unemployment in the cotton-manufacturing centers of England and a falling off in the demand for the cotton raised in the United States with a consequent decrease in the prosperity of the cotton growers of this country. Studies made in preparation for the World Economic Conference held under the auspices of the League of Nations in 1927, emphasized the fact that prosperity, if it is to exist at all, must be general:

"During the great war, the nations were driven temporarily to live to a quite abnormal extent on their own resources, but this condition of self-sufficiency—incomplete though it was—was only attained at the cost of hardships which tended rapidly to become almost intolerable. The attempts after the war to seek prosperity by a policy of economic isolation have, after an experience of nearly nine years, proved a failure. The opinion of the world is beginning to understand that prosperity is not something which can be enjoyed in small compartments."

In the "Great Illusion" Norman Angell sets forth the actual situation:

"When the prosperity of an average German factory is distributed pretty evenly over some such factors as these: the capacity of a peasant in Provençe who sells his olives in New York to subscribe to a South American loan, in order that a dock might be built on the Amazon to enable the manufacturer in Manchester to sell furniture in Baku to a merchant whose wealth is due to the development of petrol consumption in an automobile trade created in Paris,—in a world where business is done under such conditions as these, we are told that the limits of commercial or industrial activity are determined by the limits of political influence, and that there exists some direct relation between political power and economic advantage! And we are still told it even when the prosperity of lesser states with no political power give it daily the lie. The whole thing is one vast mystification, the most colossal illusion of the modern world."

Another phase of the interest which the people of one country have today in the prosperity of other countries is represented in the large number of small foreign investments. According to a statement of Jerome D. Greene of Lee, Higginson and Company, made at the Institute of Pacific Relations Conference July 28, 1927, there were before the war less than half a million buyers of foreign securities in the United States and the average individual sale was more than $10,000; while today the number of investors reaches into the millions and the average subscription is about $3,000. Between 1914 and 1927 the foreign investments of American citizens increased from $2,500,000,000 to $14,500,000,000.

In an effort to bring about the coöperation which modern economic conditions call for, the business leaders of Europe and America in 1921 organized the International Chamber of Commerce, of which the United States Chamber of Commerce is a member. Permanent headquarters were established in Paris with a resident administrative commissioner for each country. The first purpose of the International Chamber of Commerce is to promote "peace and progress." The importance it places on the maintenance of peace is shown in the following resolution in which it declares that the chief responsibility of governments is to maintain peace:

"Business men may do their part to promote better understanding and increase goodwill. It remains for governments, however, representing the authority of the people, to find better means than yet exist for promoting security and removing fear of war. The chief responsibility of government is the solution of this problem."

One of the significant features of the International Chamber is its own Court of Arbitration, which for the first time places at the disposal of business men a universal procedure for the settlement of commercial differences through arbitration rather than through litigation. The acceptance of the decisions of the representatives is obligatory. If one party refuses to present his case an award by default may be made. If a party refuses to accept a decision, the local chamber of commerce to which the member belongs is called upon to take disciplinary measures and the name of the defaulting member, with the facts in the case, is published. This publicity feature is declared to be effective in bringing about the acceptance of arbitral awards.

Business men are also attempting to meet the fact of a world market by the organization of international cartels through which, by combining to regulate production, markets and prices, in the light of the world situation, they hope to counteract the effects of the war upon commerce and trade and to supply remedies where governments have failed to do so. Cartels existed before the World War but their operations have been increased and their numbers greatly expanded since the war. Besides certain basic products such as zinc, white lead, sulphur, the commodities involved in these cartels include cement, copper, dye stuffs, electric lamps, enamel ware, glass bottles, matches, oleomargerine, paper, pipes, rayon and steel rails. The recently formed cartels control a larger proportion of the world's trade than the pre-war cartels, as, for instance, the copper cartel which controls 90% of the output and the rayon cartel which controls four-fifths. The ultimate effect of these international combinations of producers is uncertain, but they are an unmistakable indication of the fact that national boundaries are no longer economic realities.

In 1925 the Assembly of the League of Nations adopted a resolution for a World Economic Conference, which should approach the problem of the inter-relation of peace and commerce from the point of view of the responsibility of business leaders to modify their policies in the interest of world peace, rather than from the point of view that governments should maintain peace in the interest of business prosperity. The resolution read:

"The Assembly, firmly resolved to seek all possible means of establishing peace throughout the world; convinced that economic peace will largely contribute to security among the nations; persuaded of the necessity of investigating the economic difficulties which stand in the way of the revival of general prosperity and of ascertaining the best means of overcoming these difficulties and of preventing disputes; invites the Council to consider at the earliest possible moment the expediency of constituting on a wide basis a preparatory committee which, with the assistance of the technical organizations of the League and the International Labor Office, will prepare the work for an international economic conference."

The conference proposed in this resolution was held in 1927. Its discussions recognized the interdependence of the problems of commerce with labor and agriculture. The International Chamber of Commerce, the International Labor Organization, and the International Institute of Agriculture coöperated closely in its work. Although unofficial in its character, the importance of this conference was widely recognized. Of the value of such international business coöperation as it represented the *Baltimore Sun* said editorially:

"International business coöperation, which on analysis is what this conference sought, can in many ways give pointers to those who seek the more difficult end of harmonious political relations between nations. That the nationalistic passion of post-war years has injured the prosperity of many who have indulged most fiercely in forwarding the 'each for himself' doctrine is no longer open to question. That all the leading powers should have agreed to consider the doctrine of mutuality instead is a real advance, even though no overnight change results."

Among the general resolutions adopted by the conference were the following:

"Recognizing that the maintenance of world peace depends largely upon the principles on which the economic policies of nations are framed and executed, the Conference

"Recommends that the governments and peoples of the countries here represented should together give continuous attention to this aspect of the economic problem and look forward to the establishment of recognized principles designed to eliminate those economic difficulties which cause friction and misunderstanding in a world which has everything to gain from peace and harmonious progress.

"Whereas the world as a whole still devotes considerable sums to armaments and to preparations for war, which reduce the savings available for the development of industry, commerce and agriculture, and are a heavy burden upon the finances of the different States, entailing heavy taxation which reacts upon their whole economic life and lowers their standard of living, the Conference

"Expresses the earnest hope that all efforts to effect, by agreements between States, limitation and reduction of armaments, and particularly those under the auspices of the League of Nations, will have successful results and thus alleviate the burdens described above."

The outstanding action taken by the World Economic Conference was on the subject of tariffs, the conclusion reached being summarized in the final report as follows:

"The essential conclusion which emerges from the discussion in this field is that the Conference declares that 'the time has come to put an end to the increase in tariffs and to move in the opposite direction.'

"A fact that may be taken as marking a considerable step in the evolution of ideas in customs tariffs is that this question, notwithstanding its fundamental importance in the economy of each State, has now come to be considered as no longer being exclusively within the domain of national sovereignty but as falling within the scope of problems for which parallel or concerted action among the different nations is possible and desirable. Each nation will then know that the concession it is asked to make will be balanced by corresponding sacrifices on the part of the other nations."

In order that the coöperation begun by the conference might be continued, the Assembly of the League voted at its 1927 meeting to set up an Economic Organization, which is composed of a committee dealing particularly with the economic relations between states and their international economic policies; subcommittees of experts

COMMERCE AND PEACE

for the study of the various phases of problems involved; and an advisory committee on which specially qualified individuals from any nation may serve as members. Two places are reserved for nationals from the United States.

At the fourth biennial session of the International Chamber of Commerce, which met shortly after the World Economic Conference, the problem of tariff barriers again occupied a large part of the discussion. Among the resolutions adopted on this point was the following:

"The Congress wishes most particularly to affirm the emphatic adhesion of the business world to the declarations of the Geneva Conference regarding those tariff walls and policies which are unduly hampering trade directly or indirectly. It especially associates itself with this statement:

" 'The Conference declares that the time has come to put an end to the increase in tariffs and to move in the opposite direction.' "

In the introduction to its resolution on trade barriers, the Congress included, at the suggestion of the American group, the following statement:

"Trade is not an end in itself. It is only a means to an end. The general economic welfare is its goal. It is in such a sense, and with a view to the welfare of all sections of the community in all countries that the Congress desires its conclusions to be interpreted."

Owen D. Young, chairman of the American delegation, enlarged upon this statement as to the importance of general economic welfare as follows:

"The most significant pronouncement of the Congress was its declaration that the object to be sought was the largest and most economical production and distribution of goods and services to all peoples—that trade was not an end in itself, but only a means to enable people to produce more and buy more, and thereby raise their standards of living. All barriers to trade are to be examined in the light of this principle. The test is not whether they are a bar to the trader, but whether they restrict unnecessarily economic development. International business at last places itself squarely on the foundation that in the long run its own best interest is served through improved economic conditions rather than by an attempt to obtain, here or there, temporary advantages for the trader himself."

This emphasis on the need for tariff reform is directly traceable to the post-war policies of European nations which sought unsuccessfully to recover a part of the economic loss of the war years by the imposition of high duties. As early as 1926 the bankers of 16 nations, including the United States, which was represented by various financiers, among them J. Pierpont Morgan, issued a manifesto appealing for lowered tariff barriers. The manifesto contained these paragraphs:

"Too many states in pursuit of false ideals of national interest, have imperiled their own welfare and lost sight of the common interests of the world by basing their commercial relations on the economic folly which treats all trading as a form of war.

"Happily there are signs that opinion in all countries is awakening at last to the dangers ahead. The League of Nations and the International Chamber of Commerce have been laboring to reduce to a minimum all formalities, prohibitions and restrictions, to remove inequalities of treatment in other matters than tariffs, to facilitate the transport of passengers and goods. In some countries powerful voices are pleading for the suspension of tariffs altogether. Others have suggested the conclusion for long periods of commercial agreements embodying in every case the most-favored-nation clause.

"On the valuable political results which might flow from

such a policy, of the substitution of goodwill for ill will, of coöperation for exclusiveness, we will not dwell. But we wish to place on record our conviction that the establishment of economic freedom is the best hope of restoring the commerce and the credit of the world."

Immediately upon the issuance of this Bankers' Manifesto, the Secretary of the Treasury, Mr. Mellon, issued a statement that the Manifesto was concerned only with Europe. President Coolidge on several occasions also emphasized this point. It is, nevertheless, the policy which the United States has followed within its own boundaries that business leaders are urging Europe to imitate, for when the United States was founded, it broke entirely with the economic policy of the mercantilists, under which high protective tariffs had been developed during the 17th and 18th centuries, and established free trade among the states of the Union.

Besides the obstacle of high import tariffs, the normal flow of trade has been interfered with in recent years by attempted governmental control of the export of raw materials. Dr. E. Dana Durand, Chief of the Division of Statistical Research in the Bureau of Foreign and Domestic Commerce of the Department of Commerce, says of this practice:

"Government control of raw materials is likely to lead to very serious abuses and injustices. . . . No doubt most of those favoring such plans have contemplated at the outset only such a moderate advance in prices as would prevent loss. But once such a policy is entered upon and some success achieved in advancing prices, producers and government authorities are all too likely to become greedy and to push the limitation of output and the advance in prices to wholly inordinate lengths.

"There is grave danger that further extension of the recent tendency toward the establishment of government control of exportation of raw materials will go contrary to all the hopes and aims of those who are seeking world peace, economic and political. Discriminatory measures breed retaliation, and interferences with the normal laws of economics tend, once started, to pile up like a rolling snowball and to pile up at the same time international ill will."

In spite of the widespread recognition on the part of business leaders that war is no longer compatible with prosperity, the question remains whether a large enough portion of the financial interests of the world and of the governments which come under their influence, have reached the point where they are willing to pay the price of assured peace by the modification of certain current economic policies. Perhaps nothing illustrates more clearly the fact that we are at a turning point in civilization than this conflict between the recognition of business leaders that prosperity demands peace and the continuation of certain customary methods of business which tend toward war.

Besides the danger involved in excessive tariff barriers, the various policies grouped under the term imperialism, in which financial and political interests are closely associated, are recognized as a constant threat to world peace. It is also true that, although business interests in general suffer severely from war and the maintenance of the war system, manufacturers of munitions and of other supplies, needed in large quantity by an army, directly profit from war and war scares.

By its policy of "mobilizing" industry, that is, placing contracts ready to go into effect upon the declaration of war in the hands of manufacturers, the War Department necessarily calls attention to a possibility of profit in war. Although it is incredible that many business men would be willing to encourage war for the sake of personal gain, there is little doubt that individuals in this group

COMMERCE AND PEACE

have exerted an influence against the passage of legislative measures designed for the restriction or abolition of war, and have encouraged war talk and war "preparedness" programs.

Professor Raymond Leslie Buell, in "International Relations," says of the pro-war influence of munitions manufacturers:

"As the size of the armaments depends upon the fear that war is imminent, unscrupulous men may go so far as to stimulate international animosity. If the armament interests worked in the open, their purpose would be defeated. Consequently they frequently make use of 'patriotic' organizations and support 'preparedness' campaigns, really in the interest of business profits. Before the World War, the executive committee of the British National Service League was composed of nine men who were at the same time officers in armament firms.

"Armament firms may also make use of distorted information to create war scares. The Dreadnaught panic of 1909 in England was caused by the false report that the German fleet would outdistance the British fleet in 1912 by 9 dreadnaughts. This information was innocently given to Parliament by Lord Balfour from a 'secret' source which later proved to be an armament firm. Although the information was false, this fact was not established until Parliament had passed the desired appropriations."

In 1913, a member of the German Reichstag disclosed, in a speech before that body, practices of certain private German munition firms in whose behalf on the plea that their productiveness must be maintained in the interest of war organization, the government was restricting production by state-owned plants. Conclusive evidence was produced to show that orders for arms were being stimulated by such methods as securing the publication in a French paper of the statement that France intended to double her orders for machine guns. The following letter, sent by the Waffen-Und-Munitions-Fabrik to its agent in Paris, was among the documents discovered:

"We should like to have inserted in the most widely read French newspaper, if possible in the *Figaro,* an article containing the following passage: 'The French War Office has decided considerably to hasten the re-arming of the army with machine guns, and to order twice the number that was at first intended.'

"We request you to take all steps to have an article of the kind indicated accepted."

Commenting on these revelations, the *Evening Post* of New York said, on April 21, 1913:

"Well, these Berlin revelations will help a little. . . . They ought to open the eyes of many who have been blinded heretofore by the familiar cant and humbuggery of the imperialist —manifest destiny, race entity, preserving peace by arming for war, paying merely insurance on a nation's welfare, etc. All these and other stereotyped phrases have befuddled the taxpayers. But the time is coming when the people will insist that their Prime Ministers and Presidents are hired primarily to insure peace by their conduct of national affairs, and will decline to dance further to the tune of the gun-making piper. There is really no adequate penalty for such offences against the peace of the nation as are now revealed in Germany."

On December 15, 1915, in the House of Representatives of the United States, the Hon. Clyde H. Tavenner of Illinois, in a long and carefully documented speech, declared the identity in some instances and close associations in others, of the founders of the Navy League which had been conducting an agitation for an increased preparedness program and the great munition manufacturers of this country. Mr. Tavenner said in the course of his speech:

"I have carefully compiled a list of the directors of the Navy League for every year from the day it was organized down to date. Always a predominant number on the board of directors are war traffickers or persons connected, through interlocking directorates, with the war-trust manufacturers. The interests that are back of the Navy League are exactly the same interests that are back of the war-trafficking firms."

The profits of the firms whose officers were on the board of directors of the Navy League were listed by Mr. Tavenner and their increase in business in time of war. He also gave the figures showing that had the armor plate which had been purchased from these firms been manufactured in a government factory some $35,000,000 would have been saved. Coöperation among the armament interests of different nations was likewise disclosed —a situation to which attention had been previously called by Josephus Daniels, as Secretary of the Navy, who stated before a congressional committee in 1914:

"When we came to the armor we rejected all the bids, and were then absolutely in a situation from which it appeared there was no relief. Though you can not establish it in black and white, there is no doubt of an Armor Plate Trust all over the world. That is to say, the people abroad who make armor plate will not come here and submit bids, because they know if they do our manufacturers will go abroad and submit bids. They have divided the world, like Gaul, into three parts."

Two types of legislation have been proposed to remove the danger of agitation for war on the part of individual manufacturers, first, government manufacture of munitions, and, secondly, various plans for the conscription of capital and labor. The plans so far proposed to achieve this last object have been unsatisfactory because of their unfairness to labor and their ineffectiveness so far as controlling capital was concerned.

It is, perhaps, not too much to hope that the growing recognition of the disastrous effects of war today upon business in general may in the future lead the rank and file of business men to curb any militaristic activities of the few who profit by war and war propaganda. *The Nation's Business*, in its issue for October 1921, published an article by Pierre du Pont on "War—a Disaster Even to the Maker of Munitions," which shows these manufacturers already on the defensive.

The attitude of the general run of business men and business interests is perhaps best reflected in the pronouncements of Rotary International, which in 1927 had a membership of 2,627 clubs in 40 countries. As its Sixth Object, Rotary International has undertaken:

"To encourage and foster the advancement of understanding, goodwill and international peace through a world fellowship of business and professional men united in the ideal of service."

At the 18th annual convention of Rotary International, meeting at Ostend in 1927, there was constant reference to the responsibility and power of Rotary International for world peace, while in a Rotary Club publication, designed to promote the Sixth Object, there occurs this statement:

"The world has become one close community with specialized production and a universal market. . . . Both industry and commerce are built upon interdependence and coöperation. The greatest need of the age, then, is goodwill, confidence and peace. . . . Peace will not be brought about by mere wishing or dreaming. Peace must be a direct object of our civilization, not a by-product. If our civilization is to endure, a definite, positive, immediate program of education for peace must be inaugurated."

One of the encouraging signs of the times is the fact that the principles of economic internationalism calcu-

COMMERCE AND PEACE

lated to prevent international friction are gradually being developed in commercial treaties negotiated between individual states. These treaties include provisions for most-favored-nation treatment, which means that no discrimination will be practised against the trade of one foreign nation in favor of that of another; the principle of "national treatment," which means there shall be no discrimination between foreigners and citizens; the principle of "freedom of transit," which means freedom to ship goods across one country to a third. Recent commercial treaties also embody the principle of free access to the sea and freedom of navigation on important rivers and canals. Under its Covenant the governments belonging to the League of Nations agree "to secure and maintain freedom of communications and of transit and equitable treatment for the commerce of all Members of the League."

In the early days of this country when lack of political organization interfered with economic development, business interests demanded the unification of the colonies which made possible the country's later development and prosperity. Today, business faces much the same conditions in the world as a whole.

Professor Charles Hodges recently called attention to this analogy:

"If the American financier, trader, or captain of industry would recall his history, he would remember how like the contentious nations of Europe the thirteen separate and individual states of America were when the Revolutionary War closed. By the Treaty of 1783 Britain recognized the sovereign existence not of the United States but of each individual state. During the critical years under the Confederation, the forebears of present leaders of American business carried on a precarious life, the states in which they lived being as thirteen independent countries engaging in trade restrictions, commercial discriminations, and retaliatory legislation directed against their neighbors. The policy of New York, endeavoring to build herself up through hostile activities threatening the economic life of the adjacent states, almost provoked hostilities with New Jersey and Connecticut."

From the economic point of view, war between nations today would be as much civil war as a war would have been between the original thirteen American states.

CHAPTER VI

LABOR AND PEACE

THERE is a current impression that organized American labor profited by the World War. It is even charged that labor was a "war profiteer." All the facts assembled go to prove these statements false. A thoroughgoing research into the effect of the war on labor as a whole would be a valuable contribution to the cause of labor and to the cause of peace.

It is true that the prestige of labor unions was temporarily increased during the war because their leaders were taken into close association by high government officials and shown the most careful consideration so long as hostilities lasted. The general recognition of an eight-hour standard, also counted as a war gain, was probably at most only accelerated by the war. Of the supposedly large wartime increases in wages, Hanna and Lauck in their book, "Wages and War," say:

"There was an increase in money wages in all branches though no uniformity in the degree of increase. The great advances have taken place in those lines of industry for the products of which war has created a special demand, e.g., iron and steel industry, coal mining, and ship building. In some industries, such as printing, the war made no special demand; in still others, such as building, the war had a depressing effect."

Paul H. Douglas states of wages in relation to purchasing power:

"It is probable that labor gained ground upon the cost of living in 1919 and the early part of 1920. . . . Whether this was sufficient to bring it back to the pre-war basis is not certain. . . . All the evidence seems to indicate that at the termination of the great war the return in commodities which the American workers received for an equal length of time worked (one hour) was less than it was before 1915. American labor, as a whole, therefore, can not legitimately be charged with having profiteered during the war."

Erville B. Woods in the *Annals of the American Academy* for May, 1920, declares that organized workers were able merely to hold their own under war conditions:

"Wages have advanced throughout the field of employment. Occupations which felt least the impulse of war prosperity have lagged behind while other occupations or industries which were urgently needed to arm and equip our military forces prospered out of proportion to the rising cost of living. By the fall of 1919, weekly earnings overtook the retail price of food. At the beginning of 1920 real wages appear on the average to have risen to their 1914 level. In conclusion, it may be said that American labor has prospered during the past five years in a negative sense, in that, in spite of high prices, it emerged at the end of 1919 no worse off on the average than in 1914."

The railway employees in particular were supposed to have received noteworthy advances, but hearings before the United States Railroad Labor Board show that the increase in their pay was based upon living costs in 1917, that these costs continued to rise and that demands in 1919 for wage increases to meet this rise were not granted, the President urging the employees to refrain from pressing their demands pending a better opportunity to estimate the permanence of high living costs. The United States Railroad Labor Board later found that in this country under wartime government control, railway wages

LABOR AND PEACE 145

were in general below the pre-war standard of living of the employees.

In maintaining labor standards and protective labor laws, labor was even less successful than in maintaining its standard of wages. There was a general movement in all warring countries in 1914 to set aside laws and regulations protecting labor, on the assumption that production would thereby be increased. In the British munition factories the trade unions agreed to the suspension of their regulations with the result that hours were lengthened, Sunday rest abolished, child labor standards broken down and health regulations abolished. These facts led to the appointment of a committee for the protection of the health of the munition workers, which stated in its report:

"Taking the country as a whole the Committee are bound to record their impressions that the munition workers in general have been allowed to reach a state of reduced efficiency and lowered health which might have been avoided, without the reduction of output, by attention to details of daily and weekly rest. Conditions have been accepted without question which will be ultimately disastrous to health. It is for the nation to safeguard the devotion of its workers lest irreparable harm be done to body and mind both in this generation and the next."

Having followed the results of the setting aside of protective regulations in Europe, American labor was in a somewhat better position to check the tendency. In spite of this, various states, Vermont, Minnesota, New Hampshire, and Connecticut, enacted laws empowering the governor to suspend labor laws. Other states considered such legislation. New York passed a drastic bill along these lines which the Governor vetoed. On June 4, 1917, President Wilson found it necessary to issue a statement, made originally in a letter to Governor Brumbaugh of Pennsylvania, that it would be most unfortunate to relax protective labor laws and that there was no necessity for doing so. Standards in regard to child labor were seriously affected. Boys and girls left school in greatly increased numbers as soon as they reached 14, and had little difficulty in obtaining work papers at an earlier age.

These results reveal clearly the fact that war and the toleration of the war system, by their cheapening of human life, contradict in principle everything for which labor contends. The most direct step toward the fulfillment of labor's own program would be successful opposition to war.

Aside from this contradiction in principle, war and preparation for war limit the resources and waste the effort which should be devoted to the social improvements which labor more than any group needs. The *Saturday Evening Post* pointed this moral in its issue of February 26, 1921:

"Until we stop producing so much for war and begin to produce more for peace there can be no peace, no real prosperity. Workmen all around the world are marching and countermarching endlessly, producing nothing, wasting much; other armies are toiling ceaselessly at prodigious tasks—building battleships, guns, forts, and heaping up vast stores to be wasted and destroyed. Until they are demobilized they must be carried on the backs, supported out of the savings of those engaged in useful industry. Then, too, past and half-forgotten wars still hold the world in mortmain; this century is still paying the war bills of long-dead kings and statesmen. . . ."

The French labor leader, Jouhaux, proclaimed, "The social transformation desired by the workers can only be realized when the peace of the world is assured." Norman Angell in "War and the Workers" elaborates the facts behind this statement:

"If during the last fifty years we had been training something like five millions of our young men, annually, to equip themselves for the real battle of life, and if every man in Europe had been practically trained to know and deal with the real problems of civilization; if $400,000,000 annually were devoted to the systematic struggle with poverty, destitution, preventable disease; if national service meant for our wealthy young men not going into the Guards, but systematic and scientific help in the improvement of the people; if the main object of governments had been a cordial coöperation one with the other for these purposes; if all the interest and emotion that has gone into our wars had been devoted to this other war with poverty, ignorance and wild nature—if in short, these lives, this time, money and emotion had gone to improving the world instead of preparing for the destruction of the people living in it, do you really think that such rudimentary things as finding actual food and clothing and housing for millions would still be unsolved?"

The need of labor is for more than peace, it is for international coöperation and action in the adoption of uniform labor standards. No nation wishes to adopt protective labor legislation in advance of that of other nations because of the fear of handicapping national industries. Labor had begun to recognize its common interests and to unite across national boundaries before the war, and the plight to which the war reduced the working people in all European countries greatly strengthened this tendency to international organization.

The significance of the establishment of the International Labor Organization in connection with the League of Nations has hardly begun to be appreciated. The provision of the treaty of Versailles under which it was created emphasizes the importance of improving the conditions of labor throughout the world and of making them uniform, as factors in bringing about international peace. American labor leaders were influential in securing the establishment of the International Labor Organization, but although nations which are not members of the League of Nations may participate in the work of the Labor Organization, there has been no sustained effort on the part of American labor to secure such participation by the United States.

The International Federation of Trade Unions with headquarters at Amsterdam which has reached since the war a membership of over 20,000,000, devotes a large part of its activity to educational and legislative efforts against war. In 1922, the International Federation called a peace conference of labor and peace organizations at which 600 delegates representing 24 nations were present. In summoning the workers to a war for peace, the Secretary of the International Federation said:

"The trade unions regard the struggle for world peace and war against war as one of their most sacred tasks. . . . War is a crime against humanity. It does not merely take its ghastly toll of life; it also destroys completely at one blow all the achievements gained by labor at great sacrifices through years of strenuous fighting. . . . The working classes take very seriously their campaign against war and militarism. . . . An appeal to their international solidarity in the interests of the whole of mankind will only meet with whole-hearted response when the working classes are not merely filled with a horror of war but have realized clearly that every war is bound to bring ruin upon them, when they feel coöperation in all war to be as despicable as black-legging in a strike. . . . Workers are now aware that in every preceding war they have been duped and led out to murder each other, not in order to defend civilization but in order that the capitalist groups of their respective countries might acquire greater economic power. . . . No war but this war for peace is worthy of honor."

The American Federation of Labor has so far not become affiliated with the International Federation at Amsterdam.

That labor may exert a decisive influence on issues of war and peace has more than once been clearly demonstrated. On August 9, 1920, when British participation in the war between Russia and Poland was threatened, a joint conference representing the various labor groups of England notified the Government "that the whole industrial power of the organized workers will be used to defeat this war," and that they had agreed "that the Executive Committee of affiliated organizations be summoned to hold themselves ready to proceed immediately to London for a National Conference; that they be advised to instruct their members to 'down tools' on instructions from that National Conference; and that a Council of Action be immediately constituted to take such steps as may be necessary to carry the above decisions into effect."

In September, 1922, when war again threatened—this time in the Near East—British Labor sent a deputation to the Prime Minister, and "stop-the-war" demonstrations were held in London, Manchester and other cities in England. A manifesto was issued stating that if hostilities increased, the British Government would bear the greatest part of the responsibility and that if the League of Nations could not be used, a conference should be called, including representatives of Russia, Bulgaria and Germany. The Municipal Employees Association, in National Convention, September 18, 1922, protested against sending troops to Constantinople and pledged, as far as they were concerned, "not a man or ship or ammunition shall leave England in support of that war." The Trades and Labor Congress of Canada adopted a declaration at this time:

"The Government's decision to obtain the sanction of Parliament before committing Canada to a policy of war is one in which organized labor fully concurs. The time has passed when this country should be swept into war on the declaration of a single individual or the Cabinet, without full investigation and approval of Parliament."

The All-Australian Trade Union Congress also established a Council of Action to resist this threatened war in 1922. In a manifesto, the Council pointed out that

"60,000 Australians have sacrificed their lives, 166,000 suffered mutilation, and 330,000 risked life and limb, under the solemn promise that the recent European war was the last that would afflict mankind."

In 1925 the Miners' Federation of Great Britain passed unanimously the following resolution:

"Believing wars are the result of the present system in its mad rush for new markets, and that the workers are used as pawns in the game, this Conference calls upon the Federation to give a mandate to the Miners' International to declare a strike in the mines of the world in the event of a situation arising whereby any of the nations may become involved in war."

When the British Labor Party came into power in 1924, its Prime Minister, Ramsay MacDonald, devoted his chief effort to bringing about a more friendly understanding with France, thereby making possible a resumption of friendlier relations throughout Europe. In his victory speech, January 8, 1924, he said:

"The first great duty we put our hands to is to establish peace and create the conditions of peace. . . . It would be a great thing today . . . to establish with . . . all peoples of the nations, an understanding not of rival military forces, but an understanding of human men and women who have no cause for war, no cause for enmity."

In his first letter to Premier Poincaré, discussing public opinion in France and England, he wrote:

"The security which we want is security against war."

When difficulty again threatened between England and Russia and between England and China in 1926 and 1927, the attitude of British labor was likewise a strong influence for peace.

Perhaps the most definite contribution of American labor to the cause of world peace since the war is the organization of the Pan American Federation of Labor on November 16, 1918. Its influence was emphatically and courageously brought to bear during the dispute between the United States and Mexico in 1926 and 1927 and was undoubtedly an influential factor in bringing about a peaceful adjustment.

When President Green of the American Federation accepted the chairmanship of the Pan American Federation at its 1927 convention, he said:

"I cannot believe that there can be resort to the sword in the settlement of any disputes that arise between the Latin American countries and the United States so long as we maintain this economic force strong and powerful. . . . Our motto should be that there should never be any war between the Latin American republics and the United States of America."

A resolution passed at this convention of the Pan American Federation of Labor in regard to the activities of the United States marines in Nicaragua was noteworthy, although not effective in modifying the policy of the United States:

"Resolved, That the Executive Committee of the Pan-American Federation of Labor address the government of the United States, expressing regret for the events having occurred recently in Nicaragua; that it likewise address a respectful but emphatic petition to withdraw immediately the United States forces on land and sea and air in Nicaragua, and to terminate its intervention in the interest of that nation so that the people of Nicaragua may fully and freely work out their own problems, both for the present as well as in the coming election of a President for Nicaragua, and without any interference on the part of a foreign nation, it being the opinion of this congress that interference on the part of a foreign nation will only make more difficult the solution of Nicaragua's problem."

The official resolutions of the American Federation of Labor, which, though not including all organized groups, represents a cross section of labor groups in this country, have from the beginning been vigorous in their support of peace measures and afford ground for an active peace program on the part of local labor organizations. At the first convention in 1887, this resolution was adopted:

"The demands of the working people will never be fully heard in all their strength and nobility of aspiration until the nations of the world mutually agree to refrain from the fratricidal strife that has so often brought misery and desolation into many millions of happy homes. The working class, the class that always has to bear the brunt of war, has the most profound interest in the establishment and maintenance of peace."

In the conventions of 1904, 1905 and 1908 the same ideas were reiterated. The following resolutions, adopted by the 1912 and 1914 conventions, represent the trend of labor sentiment throughout this period:

"Organized labor recognizes the identity of the interests of the wage workers and the brotherhood of man over all the

LABOR AND PEACE

world, and realizes the duty which devolves upon the organized labor movement of all civilized countries to carry on an educational propaganda having for its purpose the awakening of the hearts and consciences of all mankind to the enormous waste and cruelty of war; therefore be it

"Resolved, That the American Federation of Labor emphatically reaffirms its previous declaration for the settlement of all international differences through arbitration, looking toward the final establishment of universal international peace among the peoples of the civilized world."—*Adopted by 1912 Convention.*

"Militarism and competitive armament must be abolished and tribunals for awarding justice and agencies for enforcing decisions must be instituted. International interests and issues exist. Political institutions should be established corresponding to political developments.

"Those most interested should lead in the demands for world federation and the rule of reason between nations. The working people of all lands bear the brunt of war. They do the fighting, pay the war taxes, suffer most from the disorganization of industry and commerce which results from war.

"The national labor movements can promote the cause of international peace by two complementary lines of action: by creating and stimulating within their own nations a public sentiment that will not tolerate waste of human life, and by establishing international relations, understanding and agencies that will constitute an impassable barrier to policies of force and destruction."—*Adopted by 1914 Convention.*

The Federation strongly supported the Hague Conferences, all efforts to develop arbitration, and more recently the Washington Conference on the Limitation of Armaments. In regard to the League of Nations its resolution in 1918 was:

"We are of the opinion that no permanent peace can be made nor should be made until democracy supplants autocracy and until a league of nations is established for the purpose of maintaining a just peace and for the protection of small nations."

In 1919 and 1920 the League was again endorsed, but following the Senate's vote against America's participation in the League the Federation dropped it from its platform. It continued until 1925 to support the World Court but has since refused to take any stand, always referring the question to its Executive Council.

The Federation recognized the danger of the development of a spirit of militarism following the war, and has reiterated its opposition to military training, adopting a resolution in 1926, recommending:

"Greatest vigilance to prevent the passage of legislation providing for compulsory military training. Labor is unalterably opposed to both the principle of compulsion and to militarism."

At the 1927 Convention the committee on legislation recommended continued opposition by the Federation to what the Council considered "obnoxious measures," among them the Capper-Johnson bill for conscription of labor and fixation of wages and prices in time of war.

"One of the forms of 'preparedness' propaganda that is the aftermath of the late war are legislative proposals to authorize plans for future mobilization of materials and men in event of other wars. Your committee recommends that we commend the Executive Council for its opposition to the Capper-Johnson Bill.

"Your committee believes that such measures involve serious dangers in that they would provide machinery that could be diverted to purposes of repression and recommends that the Executive Council continue its opposition to all such measures embracing the dangers herein indicated."

LABOR AND PEACE

The concluding paragraph of the report of the Federation's foreign relations committee in 1927 contained this statement on the subject of military protection of American citizens and interests in foreign countries:

"As to the general subject of foreign relations, we express the hope that the United States will again adopt the policy which in the main it adhered to during the first century of our national life, a policy based upon the proposition that Americans and so-called American interests in foreign countries must abide by and accept the consequences of the laws of such countries just as foreigners and foreign interests within our borders must abide by and accept the consequences of American law."

From the point of view of labor, whose interests demand both the protection of high standards of living and the development of international goodwill for the maintenance of world peace, a solution of the immigration problem to meet both these requirements is one of the most important phases of the complicated peace problem. Organized labor's own position in regard to immigration has so far been vigorous advocacy of restrictive legislation, including reiterated insistence upon the Japanese Exclusion Act.

The resolutions cited above leave no doubt that the leaders of American labor understand the vital importance of the abolition of war. The thing that seems to be necessary is a program to educate the rank and file of the labor movement as to the basic importance of acting upon these resolutions. President Green in a recent speech discussed at length the importance of individual action for peace.

"Safety against war," he said, "must rest with the individual. He must think in terms of peace. His desire for peace must approximate a passion for peace. He must be so well grounded and firmly settled in his thinking about peace and his desire for peace that at no time will he be swept away by a warlike spirit or feelings of revenge and hatred toward any nation or any people throughout the world.

"The thoughts and general attitude of the individual standing alone might not affect governments or those in authority, but the mobilized thoughts and attitude of the individuals who make up the governments will prevent war and preserve peace. There can be no war if the people, individually and collectively, resolve in favor of peace and the peaceful settlement of disputes between nations."

CHAPTER VII

FARMERS AND PEACE

EACH year since the World War the number of international meetings of agricultural leaders has increased. This tendency on the part of those engaged in agricultural pursuits to think and act internationally is one of the notable developments of recent years and can be traced directly to the effect of the World War upon agricultural interests.

The war made it clear to all those who grow staple farm products that their prosperity depends upon two conditions, which can be assured only in times of peace: access to the markets of the world, and a steady demand for their products since these products cannot be increased or decreased over night. When the war broke out, American farmers as a whole were better off than they had ever been for any extended period in the history of this country. Everything indicated that the United States was approaching an agricultural-industrial balance with supplies abundant enough to make a prosperous industry and trade, and farm prices high enough to make a prosperous agriculture. The cotton growers, who as a group have long recognized their dependence on international trade, as their support of low tariffs indicated, were the first to feel the disastrous effects of the interruption of trade.

With the outbreak of the war, Europe greatly decreased its production of all farm products. Other sources of supply were more remote, and a large part of the European demand came upon the farmers of this country with the result that they tended more and more to turn their attention from general farming to the production of a few important staples, the prices for which were abnormally high, for, in five years, farm prices as a whole advanced 108%.

As the war went on, food became scarcer. The farmers were urged to cultivate more and more land. They went heavily in debt to buy land and the machinery for farming it, the prices of both being high, with the result that the total farm debt of 1920 was estimated at $13,000,000,-000, the largest part of it having been incurred during war years.

At the end of the war there inevitably followed a period of great deflation, and it has become an axiom in economics, according to Senator Capper of Kansas, that "farmers always suffer more from the post-war deflation than any other class." The surplus of agricultural products, the restriction of domestic demand as a result of industrial depression, the renewal of competition from other countries, broke prices to a disastrously low level.

The average income of the American farm family dropped after the war from $1,774 to $917, of which $420 was required to meet interest charges and taxes. In 1923 the Federal Reserve Bank of Minneapolis reported that 17.7% of the farmers of Montana had gone into bankruptcy; 10.5% in North Dakota; 7.3% in South Dakota; and 3.7% in Minnesota. Because of the abandonment of farm life, the farm population was reduced by 3.6% during the years immediately preceding 1922, and it was estimated that a million people left the farms in 1923. The farmers also recovered from post-war deflation more slowly than any other group. In 1927 the farmer's dollar was still worth only eighty-five cents as compared with the five-year period preceding the war.

FARMERS AND PEACE

The report of the World Economic Conference, which met in Geneva in 1927, stated that the documents and facts gathered in preparation for the conference showed that agricultural prices were low, not because of an abnormal increase in the production of food-stuffs, but because of a decrease in demand due to the post-war poverty of the manufacturing communities of Europe.

If this was the effect of the last war, that of any war in the future will be even more disastrous, for according to Will Irwin, in "The Next War":

". . . the bill will probably show a larger item for destroyed fields—agricultural wealth. The struggle just finished was the first in history where any considerable area of land was ruined for cultivation. Now it is a property of the new poison gas that it sterilizes—not only kills cells but prevents the growth of cells. Concerning one successor of Lewisite gas an expert has said: 'You burst a container carrying a minute quantity of the substance which makes the gas, at the foot of a tree. You do not see the fumes rise; it is invisible. But within a few seconds you can see the leaves begin to shrivel. While we are not quite certain, we estimate that land on which this gas has fallen will grow nothing for about seven years.' In the next war, unless we discover meantime some still more effective method of killing—clouds of such gas will sweep over hundreds of square miles, not only eliminating all unprotected life, animal and vegetable, but sterilizing the soil—'for about seven years.' What were farms, orchards and gardens will become in a breath deserts. The power of its soil to produce food is the first, vital item in the wealth of a nation."

The failure of farmers after the war to secure adequate aid from the government made clear that not only war but the preparation for war costs them dearly. When more than 80% of the national income goes to pay war costs, appropriations for agricultural purposes, and for such public works as irrigation, drainage, development of water transport, scientific experimentation, are difficult to obtain. Farmers have also had an opportunity since the war to realize that the preservation of the goodwill of other nations is a matter in which they have a close interest, for as Mr. Wilbur Carr, of the Department of State, observes:

"The prices of our farmers' crops are fixed not alone by the conditions in this country over which we have control, but by events thousands of miles away in foreign lands. Misinformation about the United States and its policies may almost overnight give rise to conditions resulting in the loss of a market worth many millions of dollars."

Aside from the effects of war, the nature of the farmers' calling, which requires steady uninterrupted labor over long periods and settled life in one locality, has tended through the centuries to make farmers less predisposed to war than any other group. In a statement issued by the Cosmos Newspaper Syndicate, January 2, 1927, Senator Capper said:

"Out of all the classes of people who make up the population of the United States, it seems to me that peace is dearer to the rural folks than any other group. Dealing, as they are, day by day with the physical forces of life, they perhaps come to appreciate, better than the men and women in most other lines at least, the importance of making these forces function for the benefit of humanity, rather than for its destruction."

The largest of the farm organizations in the United States, the National Grange, which was organized shortly after the Civil War by a northern farmer who recognized the need of coöperation among the farmers of the whole country, has from the beginning, constantly emphasized the importance of substituting arbitration for war.

FARMERS AND PEACE

In a declaration of principles adopted in 1921, "after long and careful consideration," the Grange stated:

"As so often reiterated in *The Grange,* the Order does now and always has stood for the principle of arbitration in American affairs, and in those which affect both American and foreign countries. . . .

"We are opposed to militarism, universal military training and a large standing army. We deplore any effort to develop in America a caste of authority which has its sole excuse in a shoulder-strap, and any tendency in thought which would substitute armed force for moral ideals. The invincible character of a citizen army when equipped with justice and Americanism has again been demonstrated. We favor the preparedness of right, rather than the preparedness of might."

The 1927 annual session of the Grange included in its legislative program the following resolution:

"Resolved, That the National Grange believes in outlawing war and that we favor the United States Government taking the lead in the movement which will place war outside and beyond the protection of law."

It is an interesting fact that in Canada, where farmers have come into political power, they are using that power to oppose war. The United Farmers of Alberta have made a fundamental attack upon the problem and called upon their Provincial government to teach children in the schools the truth about war. After the resolution given below had been received by the government it was announced that an effort would be made to have the courses of study revised and textbooks used in which less attention would be paid to war, and the ideal of peace held before the minds of the children:

"Whereas, there seems to be evident in the minds of the young more or less glory in the mention of, and the teachings of war, in our schools, and

"Whereas, it has been proven and demonstrated that war is degrading and uncivilized, and a great loss to life and property,

"Therefore be it resolved, that we, the United Farmers of Alberta in convention assembled do hereby request, instruct and demand our farmers' government to enact legislation necessary to have a textbook placed in our public schools that will explain the horrors of war past, present and future, as well as the loss of lives and property and influence of legalized murder on the human mind."

The need of the farmer today is not only for the abolition of war, but for the development of active international coöperation. As long ago as 1905, David Lubin, an American farmer, realized the need for a world organization to guide the farmer in the production and marketing of his crops, and, with the aid of the King of Italy, who saw more clearly than any other ruler the far-reaching effects of his proposal, established the International Institute of Agriculture with headquarters at Rome. Although the diplomats who controlled the international conference at which the Institute was established, failed to give it the administrative powers which Lubin had planned for it, and restricted it largely to an agency for the collection and distribution of information, farmers may point to it with pride as a forerunner of the international bodies which are now being formed. It collects, studies and publishes information concerning farming; provides protection against the spread of plant diseases; studies questions of agricultural coöperation, insurance and credit, and suggests measures for the protection of the common interests of farmers and the improvement of their condition. The strength of the mutual interests and the desire to coöperate in goodwill among the farming interests was shown by the fact that three months after the outbreak of the World War, the Permanent Committee of the Institute held a meeting in Rome. It was attended by representatives of thirty-six nations, including the Allied Nations and the enemy countries, Germany and Hungary. The president of the committee said on this occasion:

"Nothing could be more contrary to the purposes of our International Institute (than the World War), but we shall have from now on a noble and a difficult task—that of aiding the nations to replace, when the war is over, the wealth which has been destroyed by the war. . . . This is the first time that official representatives of so many nations engaged in a war have met with the representatives of neutral states during hostilities to carry on a piece of work of an entirely civil character. This fact testifies to the solidarity of mankind, even while events which strike the mind with horror seem to deny its existence."

Immediately following the war in 1919 the World Agricultural Society was created and now represents 50 countries. It is an informal fellowship of individuals and organizations who believe that a sympathetic understanding between the peoples of the world, and between town and country dwellers is essential both for solving the food and fibre problems of the world and for permanent world peace. As president of the World Agriculture Society, Dr. Kenyon L. Butterfield, in discussing the need for a new education of rural youth, has said:

"We are entering upon an era when racial conflicts and national competitions, more particularly in the economic field, are more serious than ever before, largely because communication has crowded races and nations together and revealed all sorts of prejudices and competing ambitions. The only way out of this sharpened conflict is coöperation. Unquestionably, the farmers of America will be obliged to organize more effectively and may even be compelled to maintain a political farm bloc, which is often deprecated, yet may be necessary for class protection. But it would be a pitiful situation if that were the end. The apparent antagonism between labor and agriculture, between consumers and producers, between urban and rural, must melt into deeper understanding and closer affiliation. It is vital that rural youth be wisely and fairly taught with respect to such problems as the economic adjustments between classes and nations, the proper relationships between rural and urban interests, and the terms on which people can better live together in a crowded world. All depends upon attitude, spirit, point of view, and these can be imparted to rural youth."

In 1927, ten international meetings of agricultural leaders were held. In addition to the organizations already mentioned, the agricultural interests of twenty-six nations are united in the International Commission of Agriculture, which is studying the problem of a world market for cereals, meat and milk. An International Council of Agricultural Organizations also meets annually.

How important international organization is to the progress and prosperity of farmers is emphasized by Dr. Paul Reinsch, who says in "Public International Unions":

"Agriculture is by no means an activity that can be fully protected upon a national basis. International protection is demanded against the importation of plant and animal diseases. In order that agricultural operations may be effectively adjusted to atmospheric and climatic conditions, the meteorological service ought to be organized upon an international basis. To determine accurately the status of the market for agricultural products, world-wide determinations of the conditions of supply and demand are necessary: and agricultural labor, in fully as great a measure as that employed in the industries, is dominated by international conditions and population movements."

In the World Economic Conference which met at Geneva in 1927 under the auspices of the League of Nations, and at which the United States and Russia, as well as the members of the League, were represented, one of the three main committees was devoted to international problems affecting agriculture. The Agricultural Committee in its final report laid special emphasis on developing all forms of coöperation, including trade between Consumers' Coöperative Societies "both within and across national frontiers."

The Consumers' Coöperative Societies, it should be noted, numbering hundreds of thousands of members and organized internationally, which are in themselves a strong influence for world peace, find their greatest support in the United States among the farmers.

The Pan American Union, to promote coöperation in the study of the agricultural problems of the American continents, has recently undertaken the publication of a special series of monthly pamphlets on the subject, which will be widely distributed among those interested in agriculture in the different countries belonging to the Union.

In order that American farmers might share more fully in the international contacts which are being developed, the American Farm Bureau Federation in the summer of 1927 arranged for five hundred American farmers to visit Europe and travel in small groups from country to country and from farm to farm. Such direct consultation and personal acquaintance must lead to a recognition of common problems and common interests which will prove a strong influence against international conflict.

Through international association it will become clear that the farm interests of no country can be protected against the disruption of world trade and world markets which inevitably accompanies war, except by the abolition of war. The old prophecy, "swords shall be turned into plowshares," expresses an antagonism that is fundamental between war and the work of the farmer.

CHAPTER VIII

WAR VETERANS AND WORLD PEACE

AT its convention in 1925, the American Legion adopted a peace program which closes with this paragraph:

"In conclusion, we urge that each recurring Armistice Day should be used as an occasion for reckoning the progress made by America in the promotion of world peace as the great objective of the World War."

That the men of the American army fought the World War in the belief they were fighting a war to end war, and came back to this country expecting the job to be carried through to completion, is asserted repeatedly in widely representative statements made by officers of the army and by Legion conventions and spokesmen.

In the *American Legion Weekly* of November 24, 1922, Major General John F. O'Ryan, who held a higher rank than any other member of the National Guard in the war, said:

"As I estimated the point of view of the average soldier of our war army—and I had an intimate acquaintance with the habits and thoughts of many of them—I came to believe that he recognized the inconsistency of Christians doing the things that war impels men to do, but that he justified his participation in the war because of the conviction that the success of the Allies was a step toward the realization of the fundamental teaching of Christianity. By the fundamental teachings of Christianity is meant, of course, those general rules of proper human relations that are subscribed to alike by the teachers of all religions. The general idea was expressed in the phrase so often heard, 'A war to end war.'"

On another occasion, speaking before the Southern Commercial Congress at Chicago, November, 1922, Major General O'Ryan said:

"When the combat divisions of the American army returned home, I think many of the officers who had seen something of the cruelty and waste of war were surprised at the apparent apathy of our own people in relation to the possibility of a recurrence of war. Not that the people did not continue to express their aversion for war, not that there was lacking the hope that war would not recur, but it seemed that they were reconciled to let the future rest upon the insecure foundation of hope. It seemed astonishing that a people so practical as ourselves, so gifted and experienced in the field of organized effort, should not translate their hopes and their goodwill into something practical. It seemed remarkable that the high state of exaltation which held the people when we left them to go across,—a spirit of unselfishness and of determination to meet any sacrifice for the common good that was quite without precedent,—should have largely disappeared, and that in its place there had developed a reaction so marked that most men and women seemed concerned only with their own affairs."

On Armistice Day, 1923, John R. Quinn, as National Commander of the American Legion, issued the following message:

"Five years ago the war ended—officially. However, it has not really ended, nor can it end until the principles for which our soldiers fought have been fulfilled to the utmost.

"To do your part today in this repledging to principle, pause for a moment and recall the principles for which our men went willingly to the chance of death—many to die.

"You remember the phrase on their lips and in their hearts: 'a war to end war.' Yet wars are not ended. They went beyond the seas into a hell of death and destruction that their sons and daughters might be spared a like horror. Yet today there is no guaranty, no certainty that another war will not be forced upon this nation, or any nation.

"The American Legion pledged itself at its last annual convention to strive unceasingly for peace. This does not mean that we have joined the ranks of those so-called pacifists of war-time memory. Far from it. As long as conditions make war necessary to protect our nation from aggression or oppression, we stand ready, nay anxious, to answer the call to arms.

"But we strive toward an era when our nation and all nations may live and fulfill their destinies without injustice, oppression or the necessity to protect themselves from such by force.

"The American Legion pledged itself to no one plan to end war. Neither does it ask that you do so.

"But we do ask that you, upon this Armistice Day, take solemn resolve that you will leave no act undone or word unsaid that may advance, even in the smallest degree, the era of perpetual peace. You may not have the opportunity of speaking from a platform, but this does not excuse you. If you have one neighbor, one friend, whom you can convert to the cause of peace and fail to do so, then you have not kept faith with those who 'sleep in Flanders fields.'

"I ask that now you solemnly enlist in this greatest cause of all time, the ending of war. Thus, and thus only, can you keep faith with those who kept faith with you in the time of your greatest need."

In 1920, the soldiers of the allied armies formed, for the promotion of world peace, an interallied federation of veterans, popularly known as "Fidac" from the initial letters of its name, "Federation Interalliee des Anciens Combattants." The American Legion is the American branch of this group, which now numbers more than 6,000,000 veterans from 32 associations in ten countries.

WAR VETERANS AND PEACE

At its meeting in the United States in 1922, Fidac adopted a declaration of principles, which was unanimously approved by the American Legion representatives and which included a resolution that:

"An international court be established to outlaw war and when the decrees of such court become operative (except for machinery necessary to maintain them and the minimum police forces) to entirely disarm and disband our land, sea and air forces and destroy the implements of warfare."

In 1926 Fidac invited the veterans of the ex-enemy countries to meet with the allied veterans in an international conference, "in order to discover the best means of collaboration in the interests of world peace."

The international conference was held in Luxembourg on July 10, 1927, with 4,500,000 German and Austrian ex-service men belonging to eight different associations represented. In opening the Conference, the President of Fidac, Marcel Heraud, said:

"What force our action will take if you say together with us, in the face of the world, that in so far as it depends on us, we do not want the sufferings our generation has gone through, to be again borne by our children."

In answering this speech, the German representative replied:

"The sacrifices of the war can only have a meaning if its result is to kill all future wars and to give victory to the idea of peace. . . ."

The resolutions as finally adopted read as follows:

"Convinced that the task of war veterans is to make clear to all people the horrors of war and to aid in preventing a return of these horrors by all the means in their power, the International Congress of War Veterans meeting at Luxembourg on the 9th and 10th of July, and including the veteran associations of countries which were at war from 1914 to 1918—associations equally loyal to their countries and having nothing to do with politics—

"Declare that international relations must be founded upon respect for treaties and condemn all attempts to employ arms for aggressive purposes.

"Considering the fact that in the course of committee discussions the most delicate questions have been examined by former enemies without friction because these questions have been approached with frankness and debated with precision, this Congress is thoroughly convinced that if methods of frankness and mutual understanding were always practiced in international relations, sentiments of hatred would disappear and many disasters be avoided.

"In consequence, it urges the veteran associations which hold the same opinion to keep in close touch, in order to inform themselves directly about incidents which may disturb public opinion, and to make sure that they have the facts concerning events which may prove the cause of armed conflict.

"The Congress invites war veterans, who have never failed to give proof of their patriotism and of their loyalty, to teach young people that whoever loves his country must apply himself to the task of maintaining peace among all nations—a peace in harmony with the self-respect of all."

At this 1927 Congress two minority groups of veterans' associations of Germany and Austria were not represented. Extreme nationalist associations refused to participate so long as the Treaty of Versailles, putting the entire responsibility for the World War upon Germany and its allies, remained unaltered, and certain communist associations were not invited because of their attitude toward class war.

The results of this first meeting of veterans who had been enemies led to plans for a second similar conference

WAR VETERANS AND PEACE 171

scheduled to assemble at Luxembourg in September, 1928. An international mixed commission of ex-service men representing 56 organizations in 14 countries met in Paris the 31st of March to organize this second congress. A dispatch from the Paris bureau of the *New York World* dated April 7, 1928, in discussing this conference cited two important instances in which already Fidac has lived up to its resolution to keep the people on both sides of an international boundary informed of the actual facts in any given controversy. The dispatch says:

"The first was at the time of the Communist riots in Vienna last summer. Into Vienna, tense with excitement, came a shower of false rumors. One that made a deep impression and almost threw Austria into a panic was that the Italians were rushing troops into the Tyrol and were about to seize all upper Austria. One of the war veteran associations of Vienna wired to another in Germany to learn the truth. The latter wired Paris—the headquarters of their association, which got in touch with the chief of the biggest war veteran association in Italy. This man went directly to Premier Mussolini, who gave him a message of reassurance that was sent to Vienna. All Austria, including the government, was calmed.

"The other delicate situation concerned Italy and Jugo-Slavia. Worried by the friction between their Governments, the heads of the war veteran associations of the two countries, who were personally acquainted, got into correspondence and decided between them that there was no occasion for, and would not be, any hostile acts.

"These men can talk to each other because they in many cases fought each other in the trenches and the peace they have made is a real one. Not one of them has the slightest intention of breaking it."

The American Legion, in addition to its participation in the work of Fidac, authorized in 1924 the creation of a special world peace committee. The resolution creating this committee follows:

"That the national commander be authorized and directed to appoint an American Legion world peace committee, composed of ten members, which committee shall report to the national convention of the Legion in 1925 the most practical plan whereby the influence and power of the Legion may be most effectively utilized for securing permanent world peace."

The Committee's report to the 1925 Convention, as amended and adopted by the Convention, spoke of the duty which Legion members owe not only to their children, but "to those who died in the belief which America pledged to them that our war was to end war, and not otherwise may we keep faith with them," and reads in part:

"A better method than war must be found for settling international disputes.
"Such disputes are of two general classes:
"1. Controversies legal in character, and, therefore, properly justiciable, and
"2. Contested claims having political aspects which require for solution at least quasi-legislative processes.
"For the first class, judicial tribunals or courts, properly constituted and regulated by law, should be available, to which disputants should be encouraged to resort, while for the second class some further means are required to bring to bear the forces of world opinion upon those tempted to break its peace.
"General declarations of purposes and principles, however high, fall short of the present need.
"International coöperation to prevent war must displace international competition in war itself.
"Your committee, therefore, recommends to the Legion the adoption of the following peace program:

"1. The maintenance of adequate forces for internal and external national defense.

"2. The prompt enactment into law of the principle of the universal draft.

"3. The immediate adherence by the United States to a permanent court of international justice.

"This should be the chief objective of Legion peace activities, and every influence and power of the Legion should be exerted to press the matter to a favorable vote in the United States Senate at the earliest practicable date.

"4. The committee makes no recommendations for or against the entry by the United States into the League of Nations. We do, however, recommend that our nation continue its coöperation in such of the activities of the League as may, from time to time, be approved by our government. We further recommend the maintenance of an official observer at the seat of the League without uniting in its covenants. Full publicity should be given to the reports of the observer as to its sessions, conferences and activities.

"5. The endorsement of the holding of international conferences to promote world security, disarmament, the codification of international law and the arbitral settlement of disputes, with the respectful suggestion to the President of the United States to secure the inclusion in the agenda of the next such conference to be called by or to be attended by the United States, the consideration of the problem of effectively outlawing a nation waging a war of aggression.

"6. The maintenance and strengthening of the fraternal bonds between The American Legion and the Fidac, in the common cause of promoting a better understanding among the nations of the earth, and close coöperation with the Fidac in carrying out its educational program adopted at its recent convention in Rome for the purpose of educating the youths of the nation to understand, sympathize and coöperate with those of other countries.

"7. We urge writers and teachers of the youth of our land to inculcate in their pupils an appreciation, not only of our own national virtues, but also of those of other nations and races, and an understanding with and sympathy for their glories and ideals. We advocate an exchange, on a large scale, of pupils and teachers with foreign countries in our schools and universities. International sports should be encouraged. We advocate the truthful exposition of the facts of history to the end that the causes of wars may be recognized and determined. Those charged with the responsibility of teaching the young are urged and requested to study how best to educate mankind in international goodwill. The national commander is urged to refer to the proper committee of the Legion the study of the same problem, with instructions to report at the 1926 convention.

"News-gathering and disseminating agencies are urged to guard against the dissemination of inflammatory dispatches from and to foreign countries which represent the sentiments of only a small minority of a country's citizens. Attention is called to the Walter Hines Page School of International Relations at Johns Hopkins University, the first school of its kind in America or Europe.

"8. We recommend that the work of this committee and of the permanent foreign relations commission shall be merged and carried on hereafter by that commission; that the name of that commission should be changed to the commission on world peace and foreign relations, and that three more persons shall be added to the commission, who shall, together with such other members of the commission as the commander may designate, constitute a sub-committee charged with the consideration of questions affecting world peace. The commission, during the coming year, shall study the question of the proper relation of the United States to the League of Nations, and shall report to the 1926 convention. We suggest to departments and posts that this question shall constitute a special order of the coming year. We further suggest to departments and posts the advisability of their appointing world peace committees.

"In conclusion, we urge that each recurring Armistice Day should be used as an occasion for reckoning the progress made by America in the promotion of world peace as the great objective of the World War."

At the 1926 convention which was held in Philadelphia, the Legion ignored its program of work for peace and concentrated its attention on a program of national defense, which supported "the fundamental principles" of the National Defense Act of 1920, called for an increase in the National Guard to 250,000 men by 1936, a regular army of 12,000 officers and 125,000 enlisted men, endorsed military training in the high schools, colleges and universities and condemned those who endeavor to stop such training. The resolutions in support of the Reserve Officers' Training Corps and the Citizens' Military Training Camps were as follows:

"Whereas, propagandists have organized and disseminated reports discouraging and opposing Military Training in high schools, colleges and universities; and
"Whereas, This seems to be one of the most desirable agencies to assist in making young men physically fit and educationally qualified to defend our country in case of war;
"Therefore Be It Resolved, By the Eighth National American Legion Convention assembled, that we not only use our efforts for the continuation of the C.M.T.C. and the R.O.T.C. in high schools, colleges and universities, but that we also condemn as unwise and un-American the propaganda spread against this training."

These two sets of Legion resolutions, on peace and on preparedness for war, indicate the conflict in policy which the present effort to change the organization of the world from a war to a peace basis involves. It is a conflict which is reflected, not alone in Legion opinion, but in such inconsistency of governmental policy as was evident in the contradictory efforts of the State Department and the War and Navy Departments for and against ratification of the poison gas protocol in 1927. Conflict is inevitable since there is involved the replacement of old institutions by new, and farsighted national leadership is needed in order that the common purpose, rather than the divergent theories as to how it is to be achieved, shall be kept uppermost.

The professional military men who say that the military organization must be maintained because we have not yet devised methods for preventing war, and who at the same time, on the ground that they interfere with the maintenance of military forces, oppose all efforts to organize the world for peace, contribute little to a solution of the world's chief problem. The peace forces would contribute little more if they concentrated on an attack upon the military establishment instead of building up agencies of peace.

The American Legion, whose members are citizens with an experience of war, would seem to be the group best fitted to bring about understanding between the forces preparing for war and the forces preparing for peace. So far the Legion has devoted a large part of its activity to the promotion of its military preparedness resolutions, and very little to its preparedness for peace resolutions. In repeated instances, its members and a few posts have attacked men and women and organizations representing thousands of American citizens who were seeking to carry out the principles of the Legion's own resolutions. But these attacks upon peace workers have not had the support of the Legion as a whole. Writing on this point in *The Nation* of September 7, 1927, Sylvanus Cook, who describes himself as a friend of leaders in the Legion, says:

". . . There was almost as much indignation in the Legion over the action of General Fries in attacking Professor Flury [whom he sought to have removed from the school system of Washington because of a definition of Socialism which he had written in a magazine contest] as there was among the readers of *The Nation*. The General just missed a public reprimand.

"It is natural to inquire why the temperate element in the Legion permits itself to be advertised by die-hard extremists of the Fries-Watkins type without objecting. The reason is twofold. First, temperateness is seldom controversial. The temperate Legionnaire may feel totally out of sympathy with an act or pronouncement masquerading under Legion authority, but because he is temperate he will say nothing about it save to his more intimate associates. Second, absurd as it may seem, the Legion as a whole is rather fearful of its swashbuckling minority . . . for the minority presents a unified front while the temperate or liberal majority is no support whatsoever. . . ."

One explanation of the hesitancy of the Legion actively to promote its peace program is offered in the following statement contained in a letter from a Legion member, Joseph P. Milgram, published in *The Nation* of September 28, 1927:

"Ninety per cent of the Legion, I judge, believe in adequate preparedness—but not in over-preparedness. . . . The Legion has among its members nearly every army officer who served in the war. These officers are men of experience and it is not strange that their opinions often prevail over those of other Legionnaires who have not the military mind. In the large cities the Legion often avails itself of the hospitality of commanders of armories for meetings and social affairs. As a result, when favors are sought by army or navy officers, they are difficult of refusal. As long as the Legion accepts favors from professional army and navy boosters, it will be criticised for its militarism. As a whole, the Legion has no love for conflict, having tasted of it in the raw."

That the Legion is coming to recognize its own special

and independent position in the struggle between the die-hards of the old order and the new activities of peace, is indicated by the publication in the July, 1927, issue of the *American Legion Monthly* of an article by Rupert Hughes condemning vigorously repressive measures. After making it clear that he is "as bitter against pacifism as anybody" and that he believes the "next war" is inevitable and "abhors" many doctrines advocated by peace speakers, Mr. Hughes says:

"In the meanwhile, we have peace—or what we call peace. One of the most striking things about the peace is that great numbers of our fellow-citizens have made war on speakers whose doctrines they disapprove of; they have invaded halls and driven out the audiences; they have prevented auditoriums from being rented to speakers. . . .

"The institutions of our nation are magnificent in their ideas and ideals. It is proper to defend them from foreign attack or internal rebellion. But it is horrible to punish men for expressing their honest opinions or suggesting changes.

"If this nation is never to grow, never to be allowed to improve itself, and advance to newer and greater heights of liberty, it is dead already. And the people who have killed it are those who are loudest in its defense.

"The duty of organized American veterandom is plain. The opportunity superb. Let no patriotic organization longer be turned into an instrument of tyranny and the oppression and the suppression of free speech, by a few of its zealots. Let it fight in peace the fight it fought in war, for the same American ideal, freedom and equality. Let it stand always and more and more for absolute liberty. . . .

"There is only one liberty that deserves the name, and that is the liberty that grants even to its enemies every privilege it claims for itself. So long as we hold to that creed we cannot fear time or eternity. No other Americanism is American."

Aside from seeing to it that peace work is not interfered with, the soldiers who fought in the last war have one contribution to make to the peace movement which no one else can make. They and they alone can make known the truth about war as it is fought today. Fidac has repeatedly urged the importance of telling young people the truth about war and has pointed out among the inherent advantages which members of Fidac possess in carrying on peace education their "first-hand knowledge of the tragedy of war."

There seem to be two reasons why soldiers have not oftener spoken out. One is that non-combatants do not understand the soldiers' point of view. The other is the desire of the soldier to forget.

Dr. Harry Emerson Fosdick, in a sermon preached at the First Presbyterian Church, New York, on June 5, 1921, told this incident:

"One of our young men came back from France and like many others, would not talk. One day his father took him apart and rebuked him for his silence. 'Just one thing I will tell you,' he answered. 'One night I was on patrol in No Man's Land and suddenly I came face to face with a German boy about my own age. It was a question of his life or mine. We fought like wild beasts. When I came back that night, I was covered from head to foot with the blood and brains of that young German boy. We had nothing personally against each other. He did not want to kill me any more than I wanted to kill him. That is war. I did my duty in it, but for God's sake do not ask me to talk about it. I want to forget it.'"

The unwillingness of the soldier who fought to make known the truth about war as he saw it is the theme of a book, "The Inexcusable Lie," by Harold R. Peat, who entered the war as a volunteer and was decorated with the Victoria Cross. For several years after his return home, Mr. Peat refused to speak of his experiences. One day, however, he was sitting in a public square which was ornamented with a statue of a famous soldier. A group of little children began marching around it, playing war, waving flags and shouting. He was overcome, he says, by a sense of guilt when he realized how false a picture of war was in these children's minds. From that day he began to write and to lecture on war as he knew it.

"If a war started tomorrow," he asks, "would we of 1914 be as enthusiastic in going again? I know we wouldn't be, we couldn't be. It isn't the danger, it isn't that war is lacking in adventure, but because we now know that it isn't glorious. We were told in school it was.

"We know now that for every Victoria Cross won, there must be 10,000 wooden crosses won—we were not told so much about the wooden cross at school. We know that men excel themselves in war—but now we also know that to excel is to kill. In 1914, we saw and knew statues of heroes of our glorious tradition, but now as fathers of our boys, we, the super-patriots of 1914, pray our governments of England, France, Germany, Russia, America and humanity, that our sons be told and taught the truth of war. A little more of the wooden cross and a little less of the glory cross. Teach them young, so that as statesmen they may know that war is too filthy a way for civilized men to settle their differences. War is filth!"

The soldier feels, too, that his experiences would not be understood. A young officer quoted by Kirby Page in his book, "The Sword or the Cross," adds this picture to the truth about war:

"It is hideously exasperating to hear people talk the glib commonplaces about the war and distribute cheap sympathy to its victims. Perhaps you are tempted to give them a picture of a leprous earth, scattered with the swollen and blackening corpses of hundreds of young men. The appalling

WAR VETERANS AND PEACE

stench of rotting carrion, mingled with the sickening smell of exploded lyddite and ammonal. Mud like porridge, trenches like shallow and sloping cracks in the porridge—porridge that stinks in the sun. Swarms of flies and bluebottles clustering on pits of offal. Wounded men lying in the shell holes among the decaying corpses, helpless under the scorching sun and bitter nights, under repeated shelling. Men with bowels dropped out, lungs shot away, with blinded, smashed faces, or limbs blown into space. Men screaming and gibbering, wounded men hanging in agony on the barbed wire, until a friendly spout of liquid fire shrivels them up like a fly in the candle."

The plays, the books, the moving pictures which the men who fought the war have been producing in the last few years indicate that many of them are overcoming the desire to forget and are facing the past again for the sake of the future.

The *Boston Herald* printed the lines below in its editorial column, June 19, 1927, with the following note: "We have received on brown paper from a man who signs himself R. W. Stewart, and describes himself as a private in the United States Army, some verses which he begs us to 'put some place,' and not on any account to 'tear it up.' He asked that we print them under the heading, 'Remember Again!'"

REMEMBER AGAIN

Rain in the blackness. Stabs of flame in the blackness.
Whines and groans in the blackness.
    Remember?
    Remember again.

Rockets at dawn. Shells, come and gone.
   Mists in the dawn.
Cheers in the dawn.
    Remember?
    Remember again.

Stillness at noon. Curses in the stillness of noon.
Writhing bodies at noon. Still bodies at noon.
  Remember?
  Remember again.

Flashing shovels at twilight. Prayers at twilight.
Dry-eyed men at twilight. Soul-twisted men at twilight.
  Remember?
  Remember again.

Time will pass. Crises will rise.
  Remember?
  Remember again.

There is every reason to believe that the great majority of the men who actually fought in the American army in the World War agree with the statement of the president of Fidac:

"In so far as it depends on us, we do not want the sufferings our generation has gone through to be again borne by our children."

CHAPTER IX

YOUNG PEOPLE AND WORLD PEACE

Young people—the phrase means officially those "under thirty"—are forming independent groups in every country to discuss the problems of modern life and to arrive at their own conclusions as to what ought to be done about them.

A breaking away of the younger generation from the older was bound to occur at a time of such tremendous change as the present. It had begun before the war; the war made the break a conscious determined movement. It was the accepted sign that there was no time to be lost in working out a new scheme of life to meet new world conditions and that the older generation could not be entrusted with doing it. "If there's one way that's been proved wrong, it's your way! If we live exactly as you lived, it will all happen over again." Those are the words in which Youth in a modern drama condemns its elders.

If there had been no World War, young people determined to express life in terms of today might have seen as clearly as they do that there is no longer a place for war in the world. But as it is, war and the results of war are not something that they merely speculate about. Thousands actually fought in the war. Thousands of others lived through the war as cold and hungry children. It is not to be wondered at that in group after group and in conference after conference young people of today insist that war be abolished.

In order to unite their efforts in the promotion of peace, five hundred young men and women from Europe, America, Africa and Asia, representing every kind of young people's organization, are meeting in Eerde, Holland, from August 17 to 26, 1928, to hold the first World Youth Peace Congress and to form a World Federation of Youth for Peace. The announcement of the conference explained why young people feel they must work together for peace independently of the older generation.

"The Twenty-fifth International Peace Congress, held at Geneva at the beginning of September (1926) and representing the official Peace societies of many countries, was as strong evidence as could well have been asked for the necessity of a vigorous Youth Peace Movement. It represented almost entirely the older generation, people who, we readily admit, rendered yeoman service to the International Peace Movement of last century and the beginning of this century but who seemed incapable of adapting themselves to the very different conditions of these post-war years. Hesitant of passing resolutions which might be thought extreme in governmental circles or of making recommendations which statesmen would not be willing almost immediately to carry out, they failed utterly to give a lead to the peace thought of the world or to suggest a vigorous constructive policy. Peace needs courage and the spirit of adventure quite as much as does war."

The same idea is expressed in this letter from a young German who fought in the war:

"We must build up a new world, a new temple. Every step that brings us nearer to the completion of this temple is illuminated by the flame of life which sprang from the eyes and lips of our dying comrades into our souls in the war. It is impossible that all the anguish they endured should

YOUNG PEOPLE AND PEACE 185

have been in vain. Let us set out on the journey that will lead us to the fulfillment of the visions we had in those trenches in France. Else our life would be useless."

In England, Sir James Barrie, in a speech before the students of Edinburgh University, spoke for Youth rather than to Youth when he urged work for peace in memory of the young men killed in the war:

"They want to know if you have learned from what befell them; if you have, they will be braced in the feeling that they did not die in vain. Some of them think they did. They won't take our word for it that they didn't. . . . They call to you to find out in time the truth about this great game, which your elders play for stakes and youth for life. . . .

"You have more in common with the youth of other lands than Youth and Age can ever have with each other. You ought to have a League of Youth as your practical beginning."

The main purposes of the World Youth Peace Congress, which may lead to the fulfillment of Barrie's hope for a World League of Youth, are:

"To stimulate and promote the study of the basic causes of war and their elimination.

"To focus the enthusiasm and power of the Youth of the world upon the development of methods and agencies for dealing with the problem of war."

The helplessness of youth in the World War, the fact that they had had no part in bringing about the conditions which led to the war and had none in determining the policies by which it was conducted, but were, nevertheless, depended on to carry it to victory, increased youth's self-consciousness. The sense which many young people had of having been led into the war without knowing what it was all about or having any control over it, is dramatically expressed in an open letter to Dr.

David Starr Jordan written in December, 1926, by Carter Osborn, Jr., who led an antipeace riot in Baltimore shortly before America's entrance into the war and broke up a meeting which was being addressed by Dr. Jordan:

"On the first Sunday in April, 1917, you were standing on the stage of the Academy of Music in Baltimore, Maryland, making—before the Baltimore Open Forum—a protest against the impending participation of this country in the European War. You were interrupted and the meeting broken up by the sudden violent entrance of a mob which had burst through the cordon of police outside the theatre. I was the leader of this mob which succeeded in rendering your appeal unavailing.

"This event took place nearly ten years ago. I was at that time twenty years old. I have tried to recall what motivated my action on this occasion. At twenty, one is mature and presumably motivated by reason.

"Much has happened during those ten years. I spent part of them overseas and saw something of the actuality of war. And now I find it impossible to recall my definite thought which motivated me in leading that excited horde through the police and down the aisle of the Academy of Music.

"With the best possible will to reconstruct the episode I can recall no reasoned conviction individually held by me. . . .

"I acted after the fashion of an animal. The propaganda surrounding me on every side had affected me precisely as the tom-tom beating of a tribe in an African jungle affects the youths whom their chiefs and medicine men desire to stir to battle.

"I see now with what little use of his intelligence a man can go from birth to death through modern civilization—his way made always easy for him by the forces profiting by using him as a pawn.

"You were not successful in your appeal. Seventy thousand youths were killed in the struggle which came despite your endeavors. I saw many of those youths die. By sea and on land I saw their agonies, their miseries, their racked and mangled bodies. I happened to escape their fate.

"One learns much and quickly when the veneer of class and city and state and nation are ruthlessly torn away and the stark reality of life and war are seen without glamour or illusion. I learned that before I am any particular kind of man, I am first of all a man with sympathies which should embrace all mankind; an ephemeral cell in the social organism of humanity as a continuing whole. I learned that the essential characteristic of man is intelligence and that the greatest treason of which a man can be guilty is to fail to use this essential characteristic, to surrender his will to anything whatever outside himself and to let himself be made as I was made, the unreasoning tool of folkway passion.

. . . .

"In a democratic nation assuredly argument should always be met with argument. Argument should never be stifled by force. It would, at least, have been possible for those differing from you to meet your arguments with more convincing arguments on the other side. They chose instead to use me and similar befuddled youths to prevent you from being heard. . . .

"I do not apologize to you, Sir. No apology is possible for such an act. I assure you only, that experience and maturity have brought me the poignant realization that on that Sunday evening so long ago, you were motivated by the principles of civilization, while I was motivated by the passions of barbarism."

The effect of the war was, of course, much more severely felt by the youth of Europe than by the youth of America. The suffering and poverty among students, particularly in the Central European countries, led to an International Student Aid movement which did much to bring young people into close touch. Immediately after the war, a young woman, Ruth Rouse, traveling as a secretary of the World Christian Student Federation, was so shocked by the suffering that she saw among students that she appealed to the young people of the nations where the suffering was less severe to form the European Student Relief Organization. The gifts of students to students in the first ten years equalled nearly $2,500,000. When there was no longer need for relief, the students were unwilling to give up their friendships and contacts, and the European Student Relief became the International Student Service. Three international conferences have been held. The nations that received help have begun to repay their debts, so that the money may be used to carry abroad the work of the International Student Service, and the spirit of its declaration of faith which says:

"We believe that the task of spreading fellowship is essentially spiritual; that it is an expression of the real nature of the world and of that power which, without distinction of creed, we believe to be working for the fulfillment of the destiny of mankind. . . . We seek a world partnership of fully developed communities in which every individual is able to achieve his highest development in the fellowship and service of mankind. We do not seek uniformity. We seek a unity which is expressed in many different ways."

From one of these international student conferences a young Canadian delegate wrote home:

"For the first time in my life I met students from lands which had until then been but 'colored spots on a map.' And I discovered that, in spite of differences of color, language and environment, these foreign students were much like myself, with similar aspirations and ideals. No longer can I think of their countries as inhabited by strange 'foreign' beings whom I know by group-names, German, Hungarian, Russian or Czech. These 'colored spots' on the map of the world are now the homes of my friends."

Because the conditions of life which they had to meet were a severer challenge, the young people of Europe are also more definitely organized and articulate than the young people of America. Yet even in Europe where international meetings are held with considerable regularity there is little formality, for organization contradicts the spirit of experiment in which young people are carrying on their new world adventure. After a spring and summer spent abroad a young American, James Waterman Wise, in *The Century Magazine* for January, 1928, says this of what he saw and felt:

"Of primary importance is what I would term the 'youth consciousness' existing abroad. . . . It takes many forms and finds diverse outlets, but it grows out of one almost universally accepted insight. That insight is of the inability of the older generation, the war generation, to maintain or to create an order of life that shall be secure and stable, let alone just and righteous altogether. . . .

"Out of that insight and that realization grow the more positive feeling that youth must consciously as youth take upon itself much of the task and shoulder a large part of the responsibility of creating a new world; that youth cannot allow the heavy burden of maintaining civilization to devolve upon it so gradually that ultimately it will go on in the old ineffective bungling way, but that now, while it is still hopeful and young and strong, it must consciously prepare to meet the dark and danger-fraught years ahead.

"This consciousness is not always articulate, nor is it well ordered, nor of a piece. There is no apparent unity to give it force, nor clear direction to point its purpose. Yet it is in some ways the most important outcome of the war, a new and vital factor in the socio-political complex of European life."

Of the internationalism which he found among the young people of Europe, Mr. Wise says:

"The new internationalism of the younger generation stands out perhaps as the surest sign of the consciousness of youth of its own power and responsibility, and of the ability to organize and develop that power. . . .

"It is . . . so intense in its earnestness that it must be reckoned with as a serious factor in international relationship. Another great war will find bitter and powerful opponents in great numbers of young people in all lands. And statesmen and governments are beginning to take note of the fact."

In the United States an organized effort for peace was begun among college students in 1921, when a conference of 40 eastern colleges met at Princeton University in support of the Washington Conference for the Limitations of Armaments. The following resolution was adopted:

"Whereas, the recent World War has demonstrated that future war would be a calamity whose consequences are beyond all calculation; and

"Whereas, the costs of vast armaments prevent the diverting into constructive channels of money and energy, sorely needed for the solution of the problems of peace; and . . .

"Whereas, the college men who speak have proved their devotion and loyalty in the past war and whereas the present generations would in all probability bear the brunt of a future war; therefore

"Be It Resolved, That we, the representatives of 40 colleges and universities in conference assembled, do hereby express to the Government of the United States our unqualified approval of the course it has taken in summoning the Washington Conference and our entire sympathy with the purpose of the conference, pledging our faithful support to the United States delegates in their efforts to alleviate the burden of war and preparation for war, through mutual understanding and through world reduction and limitation of armaments; and that we do hereby urge upon all delegates that their effort shall not cease until some solution be found whereby the

YOUNG PEOPLE AND PEACE 191

possibility of war may be minimized, and whereby at least a considerable portion of the vast amount of energy and money expended by the nations for armament may be released for the development rather than the destruction of civilization and the human race."

A second conference was held in Princeton in 1925 in the interest of the World Court. Two hundred and fifty colleges and universities were represented. Following this conference the National Student Federation of America was formed by the students of 175 colleges and universities. The Federation does everything possible to increase first-hand contacts among the younger generation in different countries through travel tours and in the United States through association with foreign students.

But it is not only in academic groups that the interest of young people in peace is evident; in religious organizations also they are turning their attention chiefly to this problem and more than this are urging the churches to be more active in the movement to end war. In 1925 an interdenominational conference of 900 young people was held at Evanston, Illinois, to consider the position of the churches in regard to world problems. Since then the young people of various denominations, including the Methodists, Baptists, Congregationalists and Friends, have urged more definite work for peace on the part of their churches. Student missionary groups also, at their 1926 convention attended by 7,000 delegates, made world peace the chief topic of discussion. The National Council of Christian Associations at its convention in 1927 took a formal vote on the question of participation in war. Three hundred and twenty-seven declared that they would not support any war; 740 said they were ready to support some wars, but not others; 95 said they would support any war which their government entered upon; and 356 did not vote. The World Student Christian

Federation in which 23 national Christian student movements are represented, at its last international meeting declared:

"We, representing Christian students from all parts of the world, believe in the fundamental equality of all the races and nations of mankind and consider it as part of our Christian vocation to express this reality in all our relationships.

"We consider it our absolute duty to do all in our power to fight the causes leading to war, and war itself as a means of settling international disputes.

"As a result of our discussion at the Peking Conference we declare frankly that we have not succeeded in reaching an agreement as to what our individual attitude ought to be in the event of war. Some are convinced that under no circumstances can they as Christians engage in war; others, that under certain circumstances they ought to take their share in the struggle."

In these verses, quoted recently by the Chief of Chaplains in the course of a sermon, there is reflected the effort youth is making to bring religion and life into unity:

"My father prayed as he drew a bead on the greycoats
  Back in those blazing years when the house was divided.
Bless his old heart! There never was truer or kinder,
  Yet he prayed and hoped that the ball from his clumsy old
      musket
Would thud to the body of some hot-eyed young Southerner
And tumble him limp in the mud of the Vicksburg trenches.
Could I put my prayers behind a slim Springfield bullet?
Hardly . . . except to mutter: 'Jesus, we part here!
Do you see those humans herded and driven against me?
Turn away, Jesus!—I've got to kill them.'
My father could mix his prayers and his shooting,
And he was a rare, true man in his generation.
Yet if I should pray as he did, I'd spoil it by laughing.
What is the matter?"

In the United States young people who have definitely renounced war have organized the Fellowship of Youth for Peace as the Youth Section of the Fellowship of Reconciliation. The members make no definite pledge in regard to participation in war. The statement of purpose says:

"To our generation comes the challenge to abolish war. In rising to meet this challenge young men and women the world over are finding common ground.

"The Fellowship of Youth for Peace is a part of the worldwide movement of the youth of all classes, nations, and races who recognize the unity of the human family and wish to live in this spirit of friendship."

The fact that Youth feels it necessary to separate itself from the older generation in its struggle to abolish war and to build a world in which men and women can turn their energies to enriching life instead of destroying it, is, of course, a heavy indictment of the older generation. Yet it is true that a growing number of older people desire "to help Youth fulfill its will" along these lines. The hope with which the older generation looks to the younger is well expressed in a New Year's greeting to Youth which appeared in the New York *Times* in 1924:

"It is upon such a new age that the doors of this new year open for youth. It is the young men of our day—millions of them—who by the heroic adventure of their lives were largely responsible for saving the world from something worse than it is, and it will be those who are left of that vast company of youth, who can alone make it much better than it is. Age has its wisdoms, but it has antipathies, hatreds, fears which it cannot easily overcome and memories which unconsciously color its counsels for the future. By the international commingling which is now increasingly possible, through the intellectual exchanges which are multiplying, by the aid of moving pictures which are bringing the hidden parts of the earth and its strange peoples to the sight and acquaintance of everybody, by the voices which are heard across continents and seas, and by all the forces that are bringing the ends of the earth together and making the world an economic interdependent unit, the youth of the world will find increasingly that they have more and more in common.

"American youth, with a further reach for their voices, with mightier facilities for locomotion at their feet, with greater power at their elbows, with more wealth at their command, ought to take the lead in trying to bring the youth of all nations into an understanding which will overcome the stupidness and jealousies that may even now, as Barrie said, be leading us 'doddering down some brimstone path.' The earth needs the charity of youth to heal it, the ardor of youth to stir it, the faith of youth to lead it on. . . ."

PART III
INTRODUCTION TO FURTHER STUDY OF INFLUENCES FOR AND AGAINST WORLD PEACE

ORGANIZING THE WORLD FOR PEACE
(Chapters X to XVII)

NATIONAL POLICIES AFFECTING PEACE
(Chapters XVIII to XXIII)

WAR TODAY
(Chapters XXIV to XXV)

CHAPTER X

THE LEAGUE OF NATIONS AND THE INTERNATIONAL LABOR ORGANIZATION

EACH year an increasing number of well-informed Americans are among the distinguished men and women from all parts of the world who attend the meeting of the Assembly of the League of Nations, yet to a majority of the people in this country the League of Nations remains a phrase on paper, with a blurred picture behind it, and holding little suggestion of activity.

This is remarkable since in more than one respect the League is the kind of undertaking that traditionally interests the American mind. It is new, it is an experiment, it is one of those things that "can't be done." It is a tremendous undertaking, reaching out across the world, and far ahead into the future, and requiring for its successful operation great organizing ability.

From the time of Dante, who urged the necessity for a world state governed by a uniform system of law, intellectual leaders, century by century, have attempted the task of working out a plan of world organization. Gradually their ideas have influenced men's thinking and are finding expression in fact. As early as 1306 a Frenchman, Pierre Dubois, proposed a plan which included a council of nations and an arbitration tribunal very similar to the tribunal finally established at The Hague at the end of the 19th century. In the fourteen hundreds an international parliament of nations was proposed by

Podiebrad, King of Bohemia. Erasmus devoted much of his life to urging the substitution of arbitration for war. In 1625, Emeric Crucé, of France, published the first detailed plan for an international organization of both Christian and non-Christian nations, which included a permanent court of arbitration whose decisions were to be enforced by public opinion.

In 1635 the "Grand Design" of Henry IV of France, published by his minister Sully, advocated a general council of nations in continuous session with minor councils meeting in various cities, and the control of the military forces of the member nations by the central council. In 1682, William Penn laid before the various governments a plan for a general parliament of Europe to meet every three years, which should settle all differences between states. His suggestion that the parliament meet in a round room with a separate door for each nation so that no question of precedence might arise, calls attention to one of the difficulties which stood in the way of world organization.

In 1710 a proposal was made by another Quaker, John Bellers, for a parliament supported by an international army. Europe was to be divided into one hundred provinces, each province to send one representative for every one thousand soldiers raised. In 1712 Saint Pierre, a statesman of France, published a "Plan for Perpetual Peace," which included compulsory arbitration and an international army. Saint Pierre was persecuted for his peace proposal, expelled from the French Academy, and narrowly escaped the Bastille.

By the group of philosophers who preceded the American and French revolutions, it was clearly seen that war and monarchical government go hand in hand, and that peace and democratic government are allied in principle. Immanuel Kant declared that world federation must be based upon republican principles, that the federation must be voluntary and the states composing it must have a representative form of government.

In the organization of the United States of America many of the problems which early statesmen had encountered in their schemes for world organization were faced and solved.

Four principles applicable to the development of international government were illustrated in the Constitution. It created a new type of double citizenship by which Americans are both Pennsylvanians or Texans, and Americans; it made the central government dependent upon the individual citizens instead of the States; it forbade the individual States to keep armies or navies; and it created a Supreme Court for settling disputes between the sovereign States.

But the century when new continents were being settled, and new nations developing, was obviously not the time for the organization of a union of nations. And though the establishment of democratic government was the greatest single step toward the organization of the world on a basis of reason rather than force, there were other developments that had to be worked out before a league of nations, planned through so many centuries, could actually be set up.

One of these, the development of arbitration as a means of settling international disputes, was promptly inaugurated by the new democracy when in 1794, John Jay, as special representative of President Washington, negotiated with England the first modern treaty of arbitration.

A second event, in the 19th century, preparing the way for international organization was the creation of the Hague Court of Arbitration.

A third development making easier the way of a league of nations was the growth in international coöperation evidenced in international unions and commissions for the joint administration of such international undertakings as the postal, telegraph and cable services; and for the joint control of world conditions such as those affecting health.

By the time of the World War, close-knit economic relations had made world organization imperative, and there arose in the European countries and in the United States a new demand and new plans for a league of nations. Plans were outlined not only in the United States but in England, France and Germany, and urgent support for the idea came from all neutral countries, but that the League of Nations actually emerged at this time from theory into fact was finally due to the perseverance and prestige of Woodrow Wilson, as President of the United States.

The opening statement of the Covenant or constitution of the League of Nations as it was created by the Allied nations at the Peace Conference declared the reasons for establishing it to be

"To promote international coöperation and to achieve international peace and security."

It was proposed to do these two things

"By the acceptance of obligations not to resort to war,
"By the prescription of open, just and honorable relations between nations,
"By the firm establishment of the understandings of international law as the actual rule of conduct among Governments, and
"By the maintenance of justice and a scrupulous respect for all treaty obligations in the dealings of organized peoples with one another."

It was agreed that the League should consist of a large body, known as the Assembly, in which every nation should have one vote and which should control the finances; a small body, known as the Council, in which the larger nations should have permanent seats, and which should serve as the executive branch; and a permanent secretarial staff or secretariat under a Secretary General appointed by the Council.

The amount of intellectual effort that has gone into the making of the League as it is today can best be appreciated from a knowledge of the early days of its organization, after the plan for it had been worked out on paper, and it became necessary to decide how it should do the things it had been created to do. The Peace Conference appointed Sir Eric Drummond to act as Secretary General of the League, and named a committee to assist him. One of the men chosen by Sir Eric to act as undersecretary-general was an American, Raymond B. Fosdick. Mr. Fosdick's account of how this preliminary group set to work to meet the problem that faced them, is quoted by Burr Price in "The World Talks It Over":

"In June, 1919, three of us—representing the first three officials of the League—met together to decide how we would organize. There were Sir Eric Drummond, an Englishman, Jean Monet, a Frenchman, and myself. We had no program, no personnel, and no money. There were no precedents of any kind to guide us. It was all an untrodden wilderness without paths or sign-posts. The Covenant spoke of certain duties and we wrote them down on a sheet of paper as representing probable sections of the new organization.

"Little by little, too, the questions of personnel were settled. Mantoux, a Frenchman, was made Director of the Political Section; Van Hamell, a Dutchman, Director of the Legal Section; George Beers, an American, Director of the Mandate Section; and Sir Arthur Salter, an Englishman, Director of the Economic and Financial Section. . . . At first we had no money with which even to pay any salaries and we paid the stenographic force out of our own pockets. The outstanding problem that caused us infinite worry was when and where the first Assembly should meet and what it should do."

Such was the beginning of the first organized attempt to consider world problems as a whole, and in relation to each other, and to direct and control them from a world point of view. The Secretary General and his staff opened temporary offices in London in July, 1919, and permanent offices in Geneva, the city agreed upon for the headquarters of the League, in November of that year. The first meeting of the Council, called according to agreement by President Wilson, was held in Paris on January 16, 1920. The first meeting of the Assembly, also called by President Wilson, was held in Geneva November 15, 1920, with delegates from 41 nations present. In the meantime the Secretariat had decided "what the Assembly should do" by sending a questionnaire to all the nations belonging to the League asking them what they thought the Assembly ought to do, and working out an agenda on the basis of the answers.

Today the League and its activities have made of Geneva an international city, a common meeting ground for men who control the destinies of nations. From the three puzzled men who met in London in 1919 and paid their stenographers out of their own pockets, the secretarial staff has grown to include nearly 500 men and women from more than 40 nations, financed by all the nations belonging to the League. Day in and day out, this staff works at Geneva collecting facts on which national policies may be based and in the light of which international problems may be met. For the first time there is thus being created a body of common knowledge available to all nations alike, knowledge which it would be impractical, for financial reasons if for no other, for a single nation to gather. For the first time there is an official body whose members have "a definite professional interest in getting disputes settled, to whom it is a disgrace if a dispute goes on, and a triumph if they can get it settled."

Five times a year the Council, which is now composed of representatives of fourteen states, five from the larger nations having permanent seats, and nine from the smaller nations elected for brief terms, holds regular meetings in Geneva. It may meet more frequently and at any convenient point in case of an international emergency. Representatives of nations other than those elected to the Council, even of nations not members of the League, may sit with the Council when questions in which they have special interest are up for discussion.

The Council is in general the executive organ of the League. It is competent under the Covenant to "deal with any matter within the sphere of action of the League or affecting the peace of the world." All reports of disputes are laid before the Council, and through committees and the secretariat it provides for carrying out in detail the work outlined by the Assembly. Action must be by unanimous vote. To assist it in carrying on the different kinds of work for which it is responsible, and some of which are of a very technical nature, the Council calls in experts from all over the world to form permanent and temporary advisory and technical committees, known in general as auxiliary committees. The permanent advisory committees deal with the suppression of traffic in opium and dangerous drugs, with the protection of children and young people, with problems of intellectual coöperation and with questions concerning the mandated territories. Under the mandates system created by Article 22 of the Covenant of the League, which recognizes that "the well-being and development" of backward peoples form "a sacred trust" of civilization, "advanced" nations are entrusted with the tutelage of the colonies and territories taken from Germany and Turkey which are inhabited by peoples "not yet able to stand by themselves under the strenuous conditions of the modern world." The protection of religious and racial minority groups within various nations is a responsibility of members of the League assumed under certain treaties of which the League stands as guarantor, and any problems arising in this connection are handled directly by the Council. The principal technical committees, known as technical organizations, deal with problems of communications and transit, with economic and financial problems, and with problems of health.

In addition to the auxiliary committees, international conferences are arranged by the League, at which nations other than the members of the League are represented, in order to discuss and promote the solution of problems affecting the peace of the world. Representative men and women from the United States and other countries not belonging to the League of Nations serve on many of the special conference committees, and also attend the conferences as official or unofficial representatives appointed by their governments. Through the League's committees of experts, mankind is pooling its knowledge for the solution of the world problems upon which its progress and its welfare depend. In 1927 thirteen official delegates from the United States, in some instances with large staffs of advisers, participated in seven major conferences and committees, and twenty-nine unofficial delegates were sent by this government to represent it in lesser undertakings.

At "stated intervals"—according to the present custom, once a year—the members of the Assembly of the League meet in Geneva to hear the report of the work accomplished during the preceding year and to outline new work for the year ahead. Like the Council, the Assembly is empowered to "deal with any matter within the sphere of action of the League or affecting the peace of the world." The fact that identical authority is given both bodies leaves to the future the decision as to whether either will become supreme. A certain control of League activities is however in the hands of the Assembly, which controls the finances of the League and to which the Council must report. The Assembly also controls the admission of new members to the League, and has power to amend the Covenant by a majority vote, provided that the majority includes the votes of all the members of the Council represented at the meeting and that the amendments are ratified by the corresponding national legislative bodies. Action on other matters must be by unanimous vote, except on matters of procedure when a majority is sufficient, and for the admission of new members when a two-thirds vote is required. Although each nation has only one vote in the Assembly it is entitled to send three delegates. Among these delegates are a steadily increasing number of prime ministers and foreign ministers, demonstrating by their presence the importance and value of the League's work. One such official recently declared he "could do more business at Geneva in a day than he could do at home in a month."

When the Assembly meets, Geneva becomes the political center of the world, in which policies may be developed and from which influences may radiate which will affect all future history. There is, consequently, about even a routine Assembly meeting a noticeable dramatic tension, which is keenly felt by the hundreds of journalists who join for the occasion the large corps of newspaper men regularly stationed at the League headquarters. The sessions of the Assembly are open to the public and the galleries are crowded with visitors and students and representatives of national and international organizations from every country and of all races.

In the Assembly meetings, delegates sit at long desks marked with the names of the countries in alphabetical order. The President of the Council presides at the opening meeting of the Assembly. As the roll of the nations is called the delegates one by one walk to the platform and, exchanging greetings with the Secretary General, cast a ballot for the President of the Assembly. The Council's report of the past year's work is already in the hands of the delegates, having been sent in advance to the various nations. The delegates are therefore ready with speeches of criticism or agreement, or of suggestions for the future. Every nation has an equal opportunity to make known its point of view.

The Assembly aims to conclude its work within a period of three weeks and promptly divides into six committees, which recommend action to the Assembly. On each committee every nation has one representative. These committees deal with legal questions and questions concerning the Constitution; with the work of the technical organizations in connection with transit, health, and economic and financial questions; with the reduction of armaments; with questions of the budget and internal administration; with humanitarian and social questions; and with political questions.

To get a true picture of the League it is necessary to see it against a background of the world situation which conditions its activities. The facts of international life, of which the League of Nations must take account, are, as outlined by Professor C. Delisle Burns, of the University of London, such as the following:

(*a*) Political. There are about seventy "sovereign" Governments, each with jurisdiction over very different numbers of diverse peoples. The States so formed are all armed.

(b) Economic. Nearly all peoples are dependent for food and clothing upon other peoples living under alien Governments. Roughly, there is a distinction between agricultural and industrial peoples.

(c) Cultural. The world today is united by a common knowledge (History and Science) and a common intellectual attitude among educated men and women, comparable to the common religious attitude of the Middle Ages in Europe. There are about three powerful international religions—Christianity, Mohammedanism and Buddhism—and two chief types of culture—"Western" and "Eastern."

The League is not something outside and apart from these varied and conflicting elements indicated in this picture. It is rather, as has been said, a "method of promoting agreement," "a new way of doing business" made necessary by new conditions of life. It provides an opportunity for personal acquaintance, for periodic meetings and for continuous conference among the statesmen of the world.

In carrying out both parts of its purpose—the promotion of international coöperation and the achievement of international peace and security—the new method of doing business which the League is developing is of primary importance. The continuous conference which is carried on through the advisory committees of the League and in connection with the work of the Secretariat, and the joint action which results from committee recommendations and from the findings of the international conferences are leading to a recognition of international coöperation as "the normal method of conducting world affairs."

The provisions of the Covenant under which the League carries on its work for world peace put special emphasis on the value of conference and of publicity. Under Article 18 publicity for all treaties is secured by the provision that no treaty is binding until registered with the League Secretariat by which it must be published.

Under Article 11, when war or any threat of war arises in any part of the world, whether it affects members of the League or not, the League is to take any action which it deems wise and effectual for safeguarding the peace of the world. It is declared to be the friendly right of any member of the League to bring to its attention any circumstance affecting international relations which threatens to disturb international peace.

Under Articles 12, 13 and 15, members of the League agree to submit any dispute whatever, which is likely to lead to war, to arbitration or judicial settlement, or to the Council for mediation, and not to resort to war for three months after the conclusion of these proceedings. If a dispute which is recognized as suitable for arbitration or judicial decision arises between them, the members of the League agree to seek its settlement through these methods. Any member of the League involved in a dispute, not submitted to arbitration or judicial settlement, may secure its investigation by the Council by calling it to the attention of the Secretary General. Under Article 17, when a dispute arises between a member of the League and a nation which is not a member, the latter is to be invited to accept temporary membership in the League for the time such dispute is under discussion. If the nations involved in the dispute refuse to submit it to the procedure of the League for settlement, the Council may take whatever measures will prevent hostilities and result in a settlement.

If in regard to a dispute between members of the League, the Council fails to reach unanimous agreement except for one or more of the parties to the dispute, or if the Assembly, to which the Council may refer the dispute, fails to agree upon a report concurred in by all the states members of the Council and a majority of the rest, exclusive of the parties to the dispute, the members of the League have the right to take such action as they consider "necessary for the maintenance of right and justice." If a unanimous agreement is reached, an attack upon a nation abiding by the decision constitutes an act of war against all the members of the League. In case a dispute between members of the League arises out of a matter agreed to be within the domestic jurisdiction of one of the nations involved, the Council has no power to make a recommendation as to its settlement. Three months after a report by the Council has been made, the disputants may go to war without violating the Covenant.

It is these provisions which leave open what has come to be known as "the gap" in the protection which the League affords against war. Although consideration is constantly being given by League members to the problem of closing this gap, certain groups, such as the supporters of the outlawry of war plan and some extreme pacifists, have refused to support the League on the ground that it fails to disestablish the war system. The Kellogg treaty for the "renunciation of war as an instrument of national policy," it is anticipated, will help to remedy this weakness.

Under Article 19, the Assembly is given power to advise the members of the League to reconsider any treaty and to give consideration to any international condition which it believes may endanger the peace of the world.

It is a question whether the obligation to use force to compel observance of the provisions of the covenant—in carrying out, that is, the so-called "sanctions"—is definite enough to be binding, but the right to use force is proclaimed in Articles 10, 15 and 16. Under these articles, members of the League undertake to respect and preserve the territorial integrity and political independence of all members, and the Council is given power to advise what means shall be used to carry out this obligation. If any member of the League resorts to war in disregard of its agreement under the Covenant of the League, it is to be held to have committed an act of war against all the members, and the Council is to recommend what armed forces, in addition to the severance of economic relations, the members of the League are to contribute for the protection of the League Covenant.

In its efforts to carry out the provisions of the Covenant for the reduction of armaments, the application of methods of arbitration and the establishment of national security, the League has found that the three questions, arbitration, security and disarmament, are closely linked together. By some nations—England, for example—it is held that disarmament must be a preliminary step toward security and the outlawry of war. By others, such as France, the establishment of security is held to be necessary before plans for disarmament can be undertaken. The danger that plans for peace may be caught in a closed circle is evident. The treaties of Locarno, described in the chapter on Arbitration, are so far the outstanding answer which the League has found to this difficulty. In the technical provisions and machinery of the League there is no complete safeguard against war, but the existence of the League and the habit of continuous conference and of coöperation on international problems, which it is building up, may be found to provide one. Dr. Stresemann, German Foreign Minister and President of the Council of the League in 1927, said in an interview appearing in the *New York Times* for March 10, 1927:

"The great importance lies in the possibility of taking great questions from the atmosphere of written notes and bringing them into the realm of personal contacts. If before the war there had been reunions of Foreign Ministers such as have been realized by the League—if these personal contacts had existed—perhaps it would have been possible to avoid the misunderstandings which came to trouble the reality of things."

A handicap upon the League's power to bring about world peace is also found in the Treaty of Versailles. The Treaty, drawn up as it was while war sentiment was at its height, is calculated to create ill will rather than goodwill. It was signed by Germany under protest, due not only to the terms of the treaty, but to the fact that Germany had been excluded from all deliberations leading to its formulation, and there is a prevalent feeling in that country that its terms are not in accordance with the armistice or with the principles of the League of Nations. It contains provisions designed as punitive measures, which have since been recognized as unjust and as damaging to the victors as well as the vanquished. One such provision, which has, of course, an important bearing on the question of reparations, is the enforced assumption by Germany of exclusive responsibility for the outbreak of the war. The territorial arrangements under the treaty likewise have led to great dissatisfaction and constitute an unstable factor in international relations. As a result, those nations which wish to preserve the *status quo,* insist upon the maintenance of large military forces and seek to enlist the influence of the League. But the entrance of Germany into the League and her policy as a member have done much to allay the fears of those who regarded the Versailles Treaty as an insurmountable obstacle to the establishment of peace.

Many who originally refused their support to the League have now withdrawn their opposition because they recognize that the Treaty is steadily being modified by such agreements as the Dawes Plan and the treaties of Locarno.

Under the provisions of the Covenant referred to above, the League of Nations has taken part in the settlement of some twenty-eight political disputes between nations, notably disputes between Poland and Lithuania, between Albania and Czechoslovakia, and between Greece and Bulgaria, which carried a threat of immediate war. The League also took effective, if indirect, action in connection with the Corfu incident between Italy and Greece. This incident afforded an opportunity to witness the effect of adverse criticism publicly expressed in the League Assembly, of the policy of any one nation; it was found, in this instance at least, that the representatives of a nation subjected to such criticism were quick to use their influence to change the policy of their country.

The fact has been emphasized that in bringing about settlements of disputes between the smaller nations, the League may well have prevented another world war. Had it been in existence in 1914, it would have been called into action when Austria presented its ultimatum to Serbia; if it had then brought about a settlement of the differences between those countries, it would to all appearances have prevented merely another Balkan disturbance. Elihu Root has declared that "The League in the political field and the Court in the judicial field have been rendering the best service in the cause of peace known to the history of civilization; incomparably the best."

It is further pointed out by supporters of the League that whether or not it is as yet able to prevent the outbreak of hostilities between the larger nations, it is steadily educating public opinion to the fact that war is an activity in which the world as a whole can no longer afford to permit individual nations to engage. It is unquestionably true that men and women in Europe who are working for peace, especially the younger men and women, look toward Geneva and to the steps for peace which the existence of the League of Nations makes possible, as the chief hope of future protection against war.

INTERNATIONAL LABOR ORGANIZATION

The International Labor Organization, although it has not effected great changes in law, embodies a principle, a new method of international action, and an opportunity for the education of public opinion, that are most significant.

The Organization is an integral part of the League of Nations, since membership in the League includes membership in the Labor Organization and the League controls its finances, but it is nevertheless an autonomous body. It was created by a separate provision of the Treaty of Versailles, entirely distinct from the Covenant of the League. Nations not belonging to the League may belong to the Labor Organization. The reasons for its creation are set forth in the following paragraphs of the Treaty:

"Whereas, the League of Nations has for its object the establishment of universal peace, and such a peace can be established only if it is based upon social justice;

"And, whereas, conditions of labor exist involving such injustice, hardship and privation to large numbers of people as to produce unrest so great that the peace and harmony of the world are imperiled; and an improvement of those conditions is urgently required; as, for example, by the regulation of the hours of work, including the establishment of a maximum working day and week, the regulation of the labor supply, the prevention of unemployment, the provision of an adequate living wage, the protection of the worker against sickness, disease and injury arising out of his employment, the protection of children, young persons and women, provision for old age and injury, protection of the interests of workers when employed in countries other than their own, recognition of the principle of freedom of association, the organization of vocational and technical education and other measures;

"Whereas, also, the failure of any nation to adopt humane conditions of labor is an obstacle in the way of other nations which desire to improve the conditions in their own countries;

"The High Contracting Parties, moved by sentiments of justice and humanity as well as by the desire to secure the permanent peace of the world, agree to the following: ..."

The two reasons given for setting up the Labor Organization are both noteworthy. The first, based on the difficulty of raising the standards of labor in one country unless they are raised simultaneously in others, recognizes the economic, industrial and social interdependence of the modern world. The second points to human welfare as the object of government, and the importance of social and international peace in achieving it.

The machinery of the Labor Organization consists of a General Conference, to which some thirty million workers send representatives, which is required to meet at least once a year; a governing body of twenty-four members; and a Labor Office or secretarial staff, consisting of 350 men and women, one of the important duties of which is to act as an international research body.

The most striking feature in connection with the Organization is its method of representation. Every nation belonging to the League appoints four delegates, one representing the workers' group, one the employment group, and two the government. These delegates do not vote by nations but according to the points of view they represent. To this extent, the International Labor Organization is what many desire the League of Nations to become—a "League of Peoples."

The Labor Organization drafts conventions, or international treaties, covering measures which it desires to have embodied in national laws. The member governments are under agreement to bring before their national legislative bodies within a year any draft convention adopted by a two-thirds majority of the General Conference. Although governments need not press the adoption of the conventions, neither can they pigeonhole them, and whether adopted or not, they serve the purpose of educating public opinion. The interest of every nation in the labor standards of all other nations is further emphasized by the provision that when a convention is adopted, annual reports on the measures taken to secure its enforcement must be made each year to the General Conference.

The ratification of the draft conventions has so far proceeded more slowly than it was hoped, although at the 1927 conference 229 ratifications by different countries of the various conventions were reported. The value of the work of the Labor Organization in furthering mutual understanding of national industrial problems and coöperation in their just solution reaches far beyond the enactment of these legislative measures. To be fully appreciated it needs to be followed in the current reports and publications which can be secured from the organizations indicated at the beginning of this chapter.

The preceding chapter deals briefly with certain points of view and facts regarding the League of Nations that are of especial interest to American readers. Complete information in regard to the organization and activities of the League can readily be obtained from the League of Nations Non-Partisan Association, 6 East 39th St., New York City. All publications issued by the League of Nations, by the International Labor Organization and by the Committee on Intellectual Coöperation are distributed in the United States through the World Peace Foundation, 40 Mt. Vernon St., Boston, Mass. Detailed reports of the work of the Committee on Intellectual Coöperation of the League of Nations may be secured from Mr. J. David Thompson, Secretary of the American National Committee on Intellectual Coöperation, 2101 B Street, N. W., Washington, D. C. The International Labor Organization has an American office for the distribution of information at 15th and L Sts., Washington, D. C., of which the director is Mr. Leifur Magnusson.

CHAPTER XI

THE WORLD COURT

In 1922 it became possible, following the establishment of the League of Nations, to overcome certain obstacles which had previously prevented the organization of a permanent judicial court for the settlement of international disputes, and the Permanent Court of International Justice was established at The Hague. Although closely associated with the League of Nations, the Court is, so far as its judgments are concerned, an independent body. It was created by the nations acting as individual units. The judges of the Court represent no nation, and are completely free in rendering their opinions and subject to removal only by their colleagues.

The Court has had its own separate and distinct historical development which can be traced back through centuries. In international as in individual affairs, as is pointed out in the writings of Dr. James Brown Scott, arbitration has preceded judicial settlement and, while itself persisting as a method of settlement, has led to the creation of courts of justice. Arbitration, perhaps growing out of the friendly intervention of a third person, very early replaced personal combat as the recognized method of settling individual disputes. The contestants at first chose special arbiters, private individuals, for each dispute; later the state appointed a panel of arbiters from among whom the contestants made their choice. The next step was the selection of the arbiters by the state, and the enforcement of their judgment by the state. The arbiter then became a judge, the state took charge of the administration of justice, and courts were established.

In the history of the United States, a fact to which Dr. Scott calls attention, methods of arbitration preceded judicial settlements. Under the Articles of Confederation, the Colonies agreed to submit their controversies to the arbitration of a body in which all of the Colonies were represented. At the time of the adoption of the Constitution the question as to whether disputes between the States should be settled by arbitration or by judicial proceedings was debated, but decided in favor of the establishment of the Supreme Court.

Today the process of development from arbitration to judicial settlement may be observed in the international field, and the United States may justly claim that in this development it has pointed and led the way. During the 19th century proposals were made, as they had been earlier by statesmen and philosophers of various nations, for an international court. One of these, put forth by William Ladd of Massachusetts in 1840 in "An Essay on a Congress of Nations," was distributed by its author "to the crowned heads and leading men of Christendom," and influenced later developments in this field. It proposed a Congress composed of one ambassador from each nation "to settle the principles of international law," and a court composed of the most able civilians "to arbitrate or judge such cases as should be brought before it by the mutual consent of two or more contending nations." This idea was vigorously advocated for half a century by peace associations, church and women's societies, and by the members of the bar.

When the first Peace Conference was called to meet at The Hague in 1899, "with the purpose of preventing

THE WORLD COURT

armed conflicts between nations," the United States instructed its delegates to suggest the establishment of a permanent international court, organized along lines of judicial procedure, and the court as outlined was very similar to that suggested by Ladd. No agreement could be reached at the time for the creation of what so nearly approximated a court of law, and the proposals of the American delegation were modified to form what came to be known as the Permanent Court of Arbitration, which consisted in reality of a panel of jurists from among whom arbitrators could be chosen for each dispute. This Court has continued in existence to the present time and has not been superceded, as is sometimes supposed, by the World Court.

At the second Hague Peace Conference in 1907, the American delegates were again instructed to urge the establishment of a court of law. The chief obstacle to the creation of the court in 1907 was the inability of the large and small nations to agree as to how the judges should be chosen.

Later in the same year an International Court of Law, such as had been proposed at The Hague, was actually created by the Central American Peace Conference which was held in Washington under the auspices of Mexico and the United States. The Court, known as the Central American Court of Justice, was composed of one judge from each of the five member states, Costa Rica, Guatemala, Honduras, Nicaragua, and Salvador. These member nations agreed to submit to the Court

"All controversies or questions which may arise among them, of whatsoever nature and no matter what their origin may be, in case the respective departments of foreign affairs should not have been able to reach an understanding."

In 1913 Costa Rica and Salvador brought cases before

the Court, complaining that Nicaragua, in granting the United States exclusive right to the Nicaragua Canal route, had violated their rights. The Court decided in 1917 that the claims were just. The United States, however, made no effort to adjust the matter with the Central American states. This fact was held to have destroyed the prestige of the Court and it was permitted to expire in 1918 at the end of ten years.

In 1910, following the failure of the Second Hague Conference to establish a court of justice, France, Great Britain and the United States agreed to establish a permanent court of a limited number of powers, which could be used by other powers. In 1914 these nations were joined by Japan, Germany, Italy, Russia, Austria-Hungary and the Netherlands in a similar proposal. In both cases each of the contracting powers was to appoint a judge, and controversies between any two of the powers would be submitted to judges chosen by the seven disinterested members of the court. Any outside powers submitting disputes to the court were permitted to appoint temporary judges—a suggestion which was utilized later in the formation of the World Court. Although neither of these plans went into effect, they are interesting in connection with the general development of international courts.

The various steps by which the present World Court or Permanent Court of International of Justice came into actual existence in the years following the World War, were these:

The Peace Conference, in Article 14 of the Covenant of the League of Nations, called upon the Council to submit a plan to the members of the League for the establishment of a permanent court of international justice; and declared that the court should be competent to decide any international dispute submitted to it, and to give an advisory opinion on any question which the Council or the Assembly of the League referred to it.

At its second session in February, 1920, the Council discussed the problem of organizing such a court and invited an international committee of jurists to draw up a plan. Elihu Root was the American representative on this committee. The other principles of an international court having been largely worked out in the Hague Peace Conference in 1907, the chief difficulty before the committee of jurists proved to be the old one of devising a method satisfactory to both the small and large nations for the election of judges. Upon the proposal of Mr. Root it was agreed that the members of the court should be nominated by the national groups in the Hague Tribunal, or in the case of nations not represented in that Tribunal, by groups similarly chosen; and that they should be elected by majority votes of the members of the Council and of the Assembly of the League, which, in fulfilling this function, act independently of one another, not as bodies representing the League of Nations but as representative groups, in one of which the great powers predominate and in the other the lesser powers.

The plan of the Committee of Jurists, in the form of a Statute or law for the Court, was submitted to the Council and to the first meeting of the Assembly of the League in November, 1920. After minor modifications, the Assembly transmitted it to the members of the League for ratification. A Protocol, or agreement, expressing acceptance of the terms of the Statute, was attached to it for the signatures of the representatives of the nations desiring to join. When a majority of the nations which were members of the League had signed, the judges were duly elected and the Court opened in 1922, a quarter of a century after the American Government had first proposed such a court to the nations assembled at The Hague.

The Court consists of fifteen members, eleven judges and four deputy-judges, nominated by the national groups in the Hague Tribunal "regardless of their nationality from among persons of high moral character, who possess the qualifications required in their respective countries for appointment to the highest judicial offices, or are jurisconsults of recognized competence in international law." In making their nominations the national groups may propose four persons, "not more than two of whom shall be of their own nationality"; and it is stipulated that in every election it shall be borne in mind that "not only should all the persons appointed as members of the Court possess the qualifications required, but the whole body also should represent the main forms of civilization and the principal legal systems of the world." The members of the Court are elected for nine years and may be re-elected. A member of the Court cannot be dismissed "unless in the unanimous opinion of the other members he has ceased to fulfill required conditions."

The Court is required to meet at least once a year and may hold as many special sessions as necessary. Its sessions are held in the Peace Palace at The Hague. Any nation, whether or not it is a member of the Court, may bring a case before it, but cases can be brought only by governments.

According to the statute, the decisions of the Court are by majority vote and the reasons upon which a decision is based must be made public. Since there is, at present, no code of international law, the Court is guided by treaties, conventions, international customs, and general principles of law recognized by civilized nations. The fact that the judges form an independent and continuing body, not only safeguards the impartiality of the decisions of the Court but makes it possible to build up a body of international law and opinion. During the first six years of its existence, the Court has handed down eleven judgments and fourteen advisory opinions.

No means of enforcing the decisions of the Court other than through public opinion are provided. It is interesting to recall in this connection that, although the Supreme Court of the United States has decided that its judgment can be enforced by Congress, at the time the Court was created no provision was made for the enforcement of its decisions as between States of the Union, on the ground that force cannot be used against a State without inflicting punishment upon the innocent as well as the guilty.

Provision is made for the nations belonging to the Court to sign separately what is known as the "optional clause." By signing this clause nations agree in advance to submit to the Court all disputes of a legal nature, which, by definition, means those concerning the interpretation of a treaty, any point of international law, the existence of any fact which if established would constitute a breach of international obligation, and the nature and extent of the reparation to be made for such a breach. During the first five years of the Court's existence, twenty-six nations signed the optional clause,—twenty-seven with France, which signed with a condition that has not yet been met. Germany signed it in 1927, the first of the great powers to do so unconditionally.

It is generally admitted that if the World Court is to meet the full requirements of a court of law, a code of international law must be developed, and that ultimately the Court must be given affirmative jurisdiction, that is, power to summon a nation before it.

The Committee of Jurists, in the plan for the establishment of the World Court, recommended that the

League of Nations call an international conference to supply the Court with a definite body of law. In 1924, the Council of the League appointed an international committee of jurists to take preliminary steps toward the creation of an international code of law. The work of this committee is described in the chapter on International Law.

The United States is not at present a member of the World Court, since it has not as yet reached an agreement with the member nations in regard to the conditions upon which it voted to adhere. The following facts seem clearly to indicate, however, that such an agreement may be arrived at.

On February 24, 1923, President Harding sent a message to the Senate urging favorable action on membership in the Court, and the question was immediately referred under Senate procedure to the Foreign Relations Committee. This Committee delayed holding public hearings for over a year. In December, 1924, President Coolidge in a message to Congress again recommended favorable action. In the meantime both political party platforms had endorsed adherence. The House of Representatives, on March 3, 1925, approved American membership in the Court, by a vote of 301 to 28. On January 27, 1926, the Senate voted to join the Court by a vote of 76 to 17, provided that these five reservations were accepted by the member nations acting individually:

"1. That such adherence shall not be taken to involve any legal relation on the part of the United States to the League of Nations or the assumption of any obligations by the United States under the Treaty of Versailles.

"2. That the United States shall be permitted to participate through representatives designated for the purpose and upon an equality with the other states, members, respectively, of the Council and Assembly of the League of Nations in any and all proceedings of either the Council or the Assembly for the election of judges or deputy judges of the Permanent Court of International Justice or for the filling of vacancies.

"3. That the United States will pay a fair share of the expenses of the Court as determined and appropriated from time to time by the Congress of the United States.

"4. That the United States may at any time withdraw its adherence to the said Protocol, and that the Statute for the Permanent Court of International Justice adjoined to the Protocol shall not be amended without the consent of the United States.

"5. That the Court shall not render any advisory opinion except publicly after due notice to all states adhering to the Court and to all interested states and after public hearing or opportunity for hearing given to any state concerned; nor shall it, without the consent of the United States, entertain any request for an advisory opinion touching any dispute or question in which the United States has or claims an interest.

"The signature of the United States to the said Protocol shall not be affixed until the powers signatory to such Protocol shall have indicated through an exchange of notes, their acceptance of the foregoing reservations and understandings as a part and a condition of adherence by the United States to the said Protocol.

"Resolved further, As a part of this act of ratification that the United States approve the Protocol and Statute hereinabove mentioned, with the understanding that recourse to the Permanent Court of International Justice for the settlement of differences between the United States and any other state or states can be had only by agreement thereto through general or special treaties concluded between the parties in dispute; and—Resolved further, That adherence to the said Protocol and Statute hereby approved shall not be so construed as to require the United States to depart from its traditional policy of not intruding upon, interfering with, or entangling itself in the political questions of policy or internal administration of any foreign state; nor shall adherence to the said Protocol and Statute be construed to imply a relinquishment by the United States of its traditional attitude toward purely American questions.

The first three reservations protecting the United States against any responsibility in connection with the Treaty of Versailles or with the League of Nations, and arranging for its participation in the election and payment of judges, were readily accepted. The fourth and fifth reservations gave rise to certain questions which the members of the Court felt must be discussed and settled before the reservations could be accepted. They made it clear that they were perfectly willing that the United States should stand in the same relation to the Court as members of the League, but they wished to accomplish this result without injury to the effectiveness and usefulness of the Court.

In September, 1926, the nations belonging to the Court held a conference in Geneva for the purpose of discussing the Senate's reservations. They invited the United States to send a representative to this conference, but it refused to do so, saying that the reservations spoke for themselves and that the executive branch of this government could not interpret resolutions passed by the Senate. The following discussion of the points brought out at this conference in connection with the fourth and fifth reservations is taken from a statement by the American Foundation:

"The Court Statute contains no provision for withdrawal. The question is whether the signatories of a treaty which is for an indefinite term and which contains no provision for denunciation may simply denounce it at any time. Very contradictory opinions on this point were expressed at the Conference. The final result, however, was to accept unconditionally our demand to be allowed to withdraw at any time. . . .

"The Conference hesitated on the second part of the fourth reservation (providing that the Statute of the Court shall not be amended without the consent of the United States).

"The Court Statute has never yet been amended and the point as to how it may be amended has not come up. There is no provision covering this in the Statute. Some of the delegates to the Conference took the view that an amendment of the Court Statute, as of any treaty, requires the consent of all the signatory powers. If this view is taken, then this second part of the fourth reservation claims for the United States only the right automatically possessed by every signatory.

"But if the Statute can be amended by a three-quarters or a two-thirds vote, or anything less than a unanimous vote, then the United States reservation is asking a special power or privilege for the United States.

"Finally the Conference evidently inclined to the view that a unanimous vote should be necessary for amending, and was willing to accept this second part of the fourth reservation if the same right were assured to all the signatories. . . .

"So far as the first part of the fifth reservation is concerned, requiring that advisory opinions shall be rendered publicly after hearings, etc., the Conference suggested including in the special agreement between the signatory nations and the United States the following article:

> "'The Court shall render advisory opinions in public session.'

"It seems to meet in full the requirements of the American reservation.

"The real trouble-maker among the reservations is the second part of the fifth, asking for the United States the right to veto any request for an advisory opinion touching any question in which the United States 'has or claims' an interest. . . .

"The Conference readily agreed that if the United States

were a party to a dispute, it should have a right to veto the rendering of an advisory opinion upon that dispute. It further pointed out that the Court, not explicitly in any document but implicitly in its operation to date, has recognized the right of either of the nations party to a dispute to prevent the giving of an advisory opinion.

"But suppose the United States, though not a party to a dispute, 'claims' an interest in it, and demands the right to veto the giving of an advisory opinion upon it. Does this right of veto secure a privileged position for the United States?

"That depends upon an unsettled point—i.e., whether a majority vote or a unanimous vote is necessary in the Council or the Assembly of the League, in voting to request an advisory opinion. . . .

"The Conference saw a further source of grave difficulty in the lack of certain knowledge as to just what the procedure would be for applying the second part of the fifth reservation. . . . The Conference did not know whether, under the Constitution of the United States, it would be the duty of the Executive to state whether the United States had or claimed an interest in a dispute, and agreed to or objected to the giving of an advisory opinion, or whether such action could be taken by the Executive only by and with the advice and consent of the Senate; if the latter, and if Congress were not in session, what could be done? Under the wording of the reservation, the Court cannot even 'entertain a request' for an advisory opinion in such a case; and since the real use of the advisory function is to give an opinion on a specific point of law in an actually existing controversy, the delay in waiting for an expression of opinion from the United States might make it impossible to obtain the opinion in time to prevent the controversy from becoming acute. . . .

"The Conference made it repeatedly clear that it wished on every point to assure the United States an equal vote, but on no point a determining power of veto not possessed by the other signatories. . . .

"If the position of the United States is that it desires entire equality, and if the position of the other powers is that they desire to accord to the United States entire equality, these two positions are certainly not far apart.

"They are reconcilable."

The importance of the power of the World Court to render advisory opinions is explained in the following statement by Hon. George W. Wickersham:

"The most important power confided to courts and judges is the power to investigate and decide disputes. The principal objections to the practice of a court rendering an opinion at the instance of the executive or legislative branch of a government always has been that in effect it was a decision of an unargued case. The World Court, very wisely at the outset, adopted rules to the effect that when an application was made to it for an opinion, it would give notice to all states members of the League or mentioned in the Annex to the Covenant, and to all other bodies which seemed to have an interest in the question, of the request and that the Court would hear argument at the bar by any one of those parties claiming to be interested in the subject and render a decision only after the fullest argument pro and con. This in effect has turned the procedure of the application for an opinion into what, in modern practice, is known as an application for a declaratory judgment. It has enabled the Court to settle principles of law after full consideration of all sides of the question; and by settling the rules of law applicable to the controversy, in more than one instance, it has made possible the adjustment of an international complication which might otherwise have been incapable of peaceful solution."

It is obvious that the United States must make the next move. So far it has failed to answer either the communications sent it embodying the results of the conference of the member states, or the letters received from various individual member nations regarding the reservations.

On February 6, 1928, Representative Gillett of Massachusetts introduced the following resolution:

"Whereas the Senate on January 27, 1926, by a vote of seventy-six to seventeen gave its advice and consent to the adherence of the United States to the Permanent Court of International Justice, upon certain conditions and with certain reservations; and

"Whereas the signatory States in transmitting their replies referred to 'such further exchange of views as the Government of the United States may think useful': Therefore be it

"Resolved, That the Senate of the United States respectfully suggests to the President the advisability of a further exchange of views with the signatory States in order to establish whether the differences between the United States and the signatory States can be satisfactorily adjusted."

The Foreign Relations Committee of the Senate to which this resolution was referred, on May 23 voted in executive session to defer action on it until December when the short session of Congress opens. The passage of the Gillett Resolution would effectively break the deadlock in which the United States and the members of the World Court, contrary apparently to the desires of both, now find themselves.

Detailed information in regard to the World Court can be secured from the League of Nations Non-Partisan Association, 6 East 39th St.; the American Foundation, 565 Fifth Ave.; the Foreign Policy Association, 18 East 41st St., New York City. Official publications and documents in regard to the World Court are distributed in the United States by the World Peace Foundation, 40 Mt. Vernon St., Boston, Mass.

CHAPTER XII

THE OUTLAWRY OF WAR AND THE KELLOGG TREATY

The most boldly conceived of modern proposals for the prevention of war is the plan to "outlaw" war. This plan, originated by Mr. Salmon O. Levinson, a Chicago lawyer of wide repute, and elaborated into a complete scheme for the maintenance of world peace, is before the Senate of the United States in the form of a resolution, first introduced by Senator Borah in 1923, and since reintroduced at each session.

The plan in brief outline is this: The nations of the world are to meet in conference and declare war outlawed, delegalized, deprived of its protection as a recognized institution, a crime under the law of nations. This international conference will provide for a meeting of the leading jurists of the world and other competent persons to draw up a code of the international laws of peace, at the same time providing for an international court of law whose jurisdiction will be defined by the code. The scope of the court's jurisdiction and the laws determining its decisions will thus be known in advance to any nation accepting its authority. The code will be referred to the governments for ratification by the legislature or by a popular referendum. The decisions of the court, which is to be an absolutely independent institution and to have no power to render advisory opinions, are to rest for their enforcement entirely upon public opinion, which, strengthened by the treaty declaration of the nations that they will not resort to war, will, it is held, be sufficient guarantee that they will be accepted.

All disputes lying outside the jurisdiction of the Court would be settled out of court by the good offices of the other nations or by any conciliatory process, or left for time and for changed conditions to adjust.

The only force provided for in the outlawry plan, is the force to be employed by a nation against individual citizens who foment war in violation of the treaty. In his authoritative book, "The Outlawry of War," Dr. Charles Clayton Morrison says on this point:

"The outlawry proposal rests its whole structure on the foundation of the honor and good faith of the peoples of the world. . . . The outlawrist says that the philosophy of peace by force is fallacious, and that a world organized for peace can rest only upon the plighted word of the nations. He speaks not as a pacifist but as a pragmatist, not as a perfectionist but as a practical realist."

One of the great values of this plan is held to be that, when war is no longer recognized as a legitimate activity of governments, it will be possible to combine national loyalty with a "full and abundant release" of the desire to build up friendship and coöperation among nations. Professor John Dewey has said of this aspect of the plan:

"Nothing is more serious than conditions which compel masses of men to split into two antagonistic parts their moral beliefs and allegiances. There are a few persons who solve the difficulty by standing out against war on moral or religious grounds under all circumstances whatever. I have no word of reproach for them. But the masses of men never have been, and in my judgment, going by experience, never will be of this mould. We are nourished in the bosom of our own country; we owe to it indirectly if not directly our protection, security and opportunities for development. It is no easy matter in time of war to break ties and to put ourselves in opposition to the expressed will of one's mother country. For these reasons millions of persons who live in the spirit of peace in the time of peace feel bound to support their own country in time of war. Law is on one side, domestic law and international law, and that law sanctions war and demands some degree of active participation in war; ordinary everyday conscience is against war, against organized killing and organized hatred. This dualism reaches deep and extends far and wide. There is one obvious remedy. Place law on the side of conscience. At present the lover of peace becomes the criminal, the outlaw, in time of war if he ventures to hold out for peace. Outlaw war, and the law is on the side of peace and moral conviction. The criminal, the man who sets himself in opposition to the law of his country and of nations will then be the man who foments and instigates war."

Although the method of procedure proposed in this plan has failed to receive wide support, the idea upon which it is based of "outlawing" war has undoubtedly caught the imagination of the world and has exerted a powerful influence on the development of peace plans. The Geneva Protocol, resolutions passed at the Sixth Pan American Conference in 1928 and at the Eighth Assembly of the League of Nations, show its influence. It remained, however, for the United States to take the initiative in officially proposing in the Multilateral Treaty for the Renunciation of War, a general treaty which is a direct outgrowth of the outlawry idea.

In April, 1927, the French Minister of Foreign Affairs, M. Briand, made a public statement that France would be willing to subscribe to any mutual agreement with the United States tending to outlaw war,—"to use an American expression"—as between the two countries, and later submitted to the United States a draft treaty embodying this proposal. The diplomatic notes exchanged, as a result of this action by France, between the United

States and other powers have been published by the State Department and form not only an extremely interesting document but one which offers an opportunity to gain an insight into the complexity of international problems and the instability of present international relations.[1]

These notes show that the United States, after considering the French proposal for six months, suggested that, instead of a bilateral declaration, France and the United States attempt to obtain the adherence of all the principal powers of the world to a declaration renouncing war as an instrument of national policy.

France in reply limited the application of the treaty to wars of aggression on the ground, as was brought out in later diplomatic exchanges, that if not so limited, the treaty would interfere with previous commitments under the League Covenant and the Locarno and other treaties providing for military action against an "aggressor" nation. The United States refused to accept this limitation, expressed itself as "reluctant to believe that the provisions of the Covenant of the League of Nations really stand in the way of the coöperation of the United States and members of the League of Nations in common efforts to abolish the institution of war," and suggested that the correspondence in regard to the treaty be submitted to the British, Italian, German and Japanese Governments for their consideration and comment. The French Government agreed to this plan, demanding at the same time the participation in the treaty of all other governments, since "the treaty contemplated could not operate in respect to one power which is a party thereto unless the other states exposed to the possibility of grave contro-

---

[1] The publication is called "Notes Exchanged between the United States and Other Powers on the Subject of a Multilateral Treaty for the Renunciation of War" and may be purchased from the Government Printing Office, Washington, for 10c.

versies with that party were also signatories thereof." The French Government in its reply also emphasized the point that if the treaty were violated by one nation the other signatories should be released from their engagement with respect to the offending state, and further that the treaty "would not deprive the signatories of the right of legitimate defense."

The idea underlying what came to be commonly known as the Kellogg outlawry of war treaty was received with unexpected enthusiasm by the people of Europe, notably the liberal groups. The suggestion, originally put forward by Senator Borah, that if a treaty is broken by one party all of the others are released from its terms and recover their freedom of action, proved helpful in overcoming objections on the ground of interference with treaties providing for military support of nations attacked. The opinion, in fact, became prevalent that the proposed treaty by fortifying the efforts of the League of Nations to establish world peace would strengthen the League, and that, furthermore, if a nation violated treaties under the League it would thereby violate the outlawry of war treaty and the United States would not, in such a case, lend support to the offending nation. Senator Borah in an interview with Kirby Page, as published in the *New York Times,* March 25, 1928, emphasizing the fact that the United States must always decide for itself whether or not the treaty had been violated and what coercive measures it should take, stated:

"Another important result of such a treaty would be to enlist the support of the United States in coöperative action against any nation which is guilty of a flagrant violation of this outlawry agreement. Of course, the Government of the United States must reserve the right to decide, in the first place, whether or not the treaty has been violated, and second, what coercive measures it feels obliged to take. But it is quite inconceivable that this country would stand idly by in case of a grave breach of a multilateral treaty to which it is a party."

Mr. Kellogg discussed the proposed treaty for the renunciation of war before the Council on Foreign Relations in New York on March 15, 1928. Among the important statements which he made in this speech were these:

"I concluded my note (to France) with the unequivocal statement that the Government of the United States desires to see the institution of war abolished and stands ready to conclude with the French, British, Italian, German and Japanese Governments a single multilateral treaty open to subsequent adhesion by any and all other governments binding the parties thereto not to resort to war with one another. This is the position of the Government of the United States, and this is the object which we are seeking to attain.

"I cannot believe that such a treaty would violate the terms of the League Covenant or conflict with the obligations of the members of the League. Even Article 10 of the Covenant has been construed to mean that League members are not inescapably bound thereby to employ their military forces. According to a recent statement by the British Government, many members of the League accept as a proper interpretation of Article 10 a resolution submitted to the Fourth Assembly but not formally adopted owing to one adverse vote. That resolution states explicitly:

'It is for the constitutional authorities of each member to decide, in reference to the obligation of preserving the independence and the integrity of the territory of members, in what degree the member is bound to assure the execution of this obligation by employment of its military forces.'

"Since, however, the purpose of the United States is so far as possible to eliminate war as a factor in international relations, I cannot state too emphatically that it will not become

THE OUTLAWRY OF WAR

a party to any agreement which directly or indirectly, expressly or by implication, is a military alliance. The United States cannot obligate itself in advance to use its armed forces against any other nation of the world. It does not believe that the peace of the world or of Europe depends upon or can be assured by treaties of military alliance. The futility of such as guarantors of peace is repeatedly demonstrated in the pages of history. . . .

"I am not so blind as to believe that the millennium has arrived, but I do believe that the world is making great strides toward the pacific adjustment of international disputes and that the common people are of one mind in their desire to see the abolition of war as an institution. Certainly the United States should not be backward in promoting this new movement for world peace, and both personally and officially as Secretary of State, I shall always support and advocate the conclusion of appropriate treaties for arbitration, for conciliation, and for the renunciation of war."

Except in the case of Great Britain, the replies received from the various governments while emphasizing the importance of recognizing that the treaty would not affect the right of self-defense and that its violation by one nation would release other signatories from obligations assumed under it, made no other suggestions in regard to its terms or interpretation. The reply from Great Britain contained, however, this statement:

". . . there are certain regions of the world the welfare and integrity of which constitute a special and vital interest for our peace and safety. His Majesty's Government have been at pains to make it clear in the past that interference with these regions cannot be suffered. Their protection against attack is to the British Empire a measure of self-defense. It must be clearly understood that His Majesty's Government in Great Britain accept the new treaty upon the distinct understanding that it does not prejudice their freedom of action in this respect. The Government of the United States have comparable interests any disregard of which by a foreign power they have declared that they would regard as an unfriendly act. His Majesty's Government believe, therefore, that in defining their position they are expressing the intention and meaning of the United States Government."

On the 23rd of June, the United States Government submitted a revised treaty to fourteen governments, including the signatories to the Locarno treaties, with a note explaining the construction placed by the United States upon the treaty in regard to the various points raised, by quoting from a speech made by the Secretary of State, on April 28th, before the American Society of International Law. The statement as to the relation of the treaty to the League Covenant followed the lines of the earlier speech by the Secretary of State quoted above. The comment in regard to the right of self-defense was as follows:

"There is nothing in the American draft of an antiwar treaty which restricts or impairs in any way the right of self-defense. That right is inherent in every sovereign state and is implicit in every treaty. Every nation is free at all times and regardless of treaty provisions to defend its territory from attack or invasion and it alone is competent to decide whether circumstances require recourse to war in self-defense. If it has a good case, the world will applaud and not condemn its action."

In regard to the relations of the signatories with a treaty-breaking state it was stated:

". . . there can be no question as a matter of law that violation of a multilateral antiwar treaty through resort to war by one party thereto would automatically release the other parties from their obligations to the treaty-breaking state."

This idea was embodied in the revised preamble. The treaty itself was not altered, nor was any reference made to the British reservation in regard to "certain regions of the world," or any opinion expressed as to the possible effect of the treaty upon the Monroe Doctrine.

The vital articles of the treaty, which is given in full in the appendix, are these:

"The High Contracting Parties solemnly declare in the names of their respective peoples that they condemn recourse to war for the solution of international controversies, and renounce it as an instrument of national policy in their relations with one another.

"The High Contracting Parties agree that the settlement or solution of all disputes or conflicts of whatever nature or of whatever origin they may be, which may arise among them, shall never be sought except by pacific means."

On August 27th, the following fifteen nations affixed their signatures: Australia, Belgium, Canada, Czechoslovakia, France, Germany, Great Britain, India, the Irish Free State, Italy, Japan, New Zealand, Poland, South Africa and the United States. The treaty is now subject to ratification by these governments, and is open for adherence "by all the other powers of the world."

The treaty will, according to its terms, come into effect upon its ratification by the fifteen signatory nations which in addition to the powers originally consulted by the United States included the Dominions of the British Commonwealth and nations which had signed earlier treaties with France. The indefinite delay which would have resulted had the French proposal that ratification by all nations be required, been accepted, is thus avoided.

The Multilateral Treaty, while not in complete accord with the outlawry idea, is looked upon by the adherents of the outlawry plan as a first step of vital importance. By one group, the Committee on Educational Publicity, of which Samuel Colcord is chairman and George Gordon Battle secretary, the proposal has been made that a treaty now be negotiated to make the prohibition of war a basic principle of international law, thus insuring permanency to the idea, for an international law cannot be annulled by the action of one nation.

The Multilateral Treaty implies a fundamental frontal attack upon the war system. It establishes the fact that the problem is not one of eliminating conflicts of interests between nations, or the so-called "causes" of war, but of abandoning war as a method of dealing with these conflicts. By recognizing that war has been an "instrument of policy," it brings it clearly within the control of governments, and it bases opposition to war upon the rational ground of failure to obtain the ends that governments seek.

The fact that the treaty leaves many points undetermined—What shall it be decided constitutes war? What action will now be possible toward the international reduction of armaments?—gives large discretionary power to future governments and therefore decisive influence and responsibility to public opinion. In connection with the ratification of the treaty, there will be opportunity for the people of the world to give overwhelming expression to their demand that they be freed from war. Following ratification, it will remain for public opinion to give content to the new treaty by demanding that international policies and practices be made consistent with its terms and with its spirit.

Information in regard to the plan for the Outlawry of War can be obtained from the American Committee for the Outlawry of War, 134 South LaSalle St., Chicago, Ill.

CHAPTER XIII

THE ARBITRATION OF INTERNATIONAL DISPUTES

FROM even a superficial survey of the history of arbitration an impression can be gained of the process by which a steadily developing peace system is crowding war out of the world picture and creating a new basis for international life. Two detailed studies of the development of arbitration in modern times have recently been published. One, "Arbitration in the United States," by Denys P. Myers, is issued by the World Peace Foundation, and the other, "The United States and Treaties for the Avoidance of War," by Philip C. Jessup, by the Carnegie Endowment for International Peace. This chapter does no more than touch upon the rapid extension in the last century of the method of arbitration, essentially a legal process, and the simultaneous development of conciliation, conference and other methods of pacific settlement, and the part which the United States is playing in this effort toward the development of a peace system.

The obligation of civilized states to submit disputes to arbitration was recognized in ancient as well as modern times. In "Greek Life and Thought," Sir John P. Mahaffy says:

"Arbitration was an old fashion among the Greek states, so much so that it was considered decent when threatening war to offer a settlement by referring the dispute to a neutral power."

As early as 1291, the principle of compulsory arbitration was recognized in the Letters of Union adopted by the Swiss Federation. Yet, as Benjamin F. Trueblood in his studies of the question points out, no real development in arbitration was possible in modern times until nations had become quite definitely established, and efforts toward the conquest and subjection of other peoples had been curbed, for arbitration [1] "implies independent and mutually respecting parties standing over against each other . . .; it further implies confidence in the fairness of one's fellow men."

With the establishment of democratic governments in the Western Hemisphere, a definite effort, never since abandoned, was begun to devise methods and machinery for the peaceful settlement of the differences bound to arise between states.

The first modern arbitration treaty, the Jay Treaty, was negotiated in 1794 during Washington's administration, by the United States and England. It provided for the adjustment of boundary claims and questions of debts and neutral rights. In 1814, the Treaty of Ghent between the same countries set up three commissions for the arbitration of various boundary questions. In both

---

[1] Arbitration is a general term used to cover an increasing variety of procedures, besides the ordinary one of diplomatic negotiations, for the settlement of international disputes. In the Convention for Pacific Settlements adopted by the Hague Conference of 1907 the following methods are defined:

Arbitration has for its object "the settlement of disputes between states by judges of their own choice and on the basis of respect for law." Recourse to arbitration implies an undertaking to submit in good faith to the award.

Conciliation by inquiry is to "facilitate the solution of disputes by elucidating the facts by means of an impartial and conscientious investigation."

Mediation is "reconciling the opposing claims and appeasing the feelings of resentment which may have arisen between states at variance." The opinion rendered is not of binding force but only in the form of advice.

Good offices are the friendly and unofficial proceedings whereby a third power gives suggestions or advice for the amicable settlement of a difficulty. And beyond these methods of pacific settlement there are the further possibilities of direct conference, and of leaving disputes which cannot be adjusted by any method, to time to settle.

of these cases arbitration was accepted for the settlement of disputes which had already arisen.

An important step in advance was made by the Republics of South America, under the leadership of Bolivar, who, like the founders of the Government of the United States, constantly urged the substitution of peaceful settlement for war. In treaties between Argentina and Brazil in 1828 which provided for mediation before any declaration of war, and in treaties signed by Colombia and Peru in 1829, and by Colombia and Venezuela in 1842, pacific methods of adjustment were accepted in advance for any future disputes which might arise. In 1848 the United States and Mexico signed the Treaty of Guadelupe Hidalgo, a general treaty of peace and friendship, calling for "pacific negotiations" in the event of any disagreement. It attracted a great deal of attention at the time and is still in force.

During the first quarter of the nineteenth century a strong public demand arose in this country for action by the government to promote arbitration, which found expression as early as 1815 in the organization of local and state peace societies, and in 1828 in the formation of the first national body, the American Peace Society. It was officially voiced in resolutions of state legislatures and of Congress. In 1832, the Senate of Massachusetts adopted a resolution expressing the opinion that "some mode should be established for the amicable and final adjustment of international disputes, instead of resort to war." Five years later, both bodies of the Massachusetts Legislature adopted a resolution to the effect "that a congress of nations for the purpose of forming a code of international law and establishing a high court of arbitration . . . is a scheme worthy the careful attention of all enlightened governments." In 1844, the Legislature of Vermont also commended this suggestion.

The Senate Committee on Foreign Relations in 1851 reported out a resolution that "in the judgment of this body it would be proper and desirable for the Government of these United States whenever practicable to secure in its treaties with other nations a provision for referring to the decision of umpires all future misunderstandings that cannot be satisfactorily adjusted by amicable negotiation in the first instance, before a resort to hostilities shall be had."

Two years later in 1853 the same committee reported a resolution of advice to the President suggesting a stipulation in all treaties "hereafter entered into with other nations referring the adjustment of misunderstandings or controversy to the decision of disinterested and impartial arbitrators to be mutually chosen." Speeches made in connection with the introduction of these resolutions contained statements emphasizing the special responsibility of the United States for the establishment of world peace. The preamble to the resolution of 1851 declared:

". . . more especially the genius of our own government, the habits of our people, and the highest prosperity of our Republic . . . require the adoption of every feasible measure to prevent war."

The committee report submitting this resolution said:

". . . the United States, of all others, is the proper country to propose this policy to the nations of the earth. We have shown in our past history a capacity for war. The love of military glory is a passion as strong with us as any other people, if not stronger. . . . Our young men rush to battle with the full assurance that the highest civil honors often reward the toils and dangers of the triumphant soldier. Our institutions, therefore, tend to make us a military people. We are rapidly growing in power. Our progress is without a parallel. Under such circumstances, in proposing a policy of peace, it cannot be supposed that we are influenced by any other motives than those which spring from the purest philanthropy. The policy proposed is adverse to aggression. It respects the rights of all nations."

The settlement by arbitration in 1872 of the conflict between the United States and England over the claims resulting from the activities of the warship "Alabama" greatly strengthened the sentiment for arbitration. The "Alabama" had been built and fitted out in England and manned by Confederate officers and crew for preying on the commerce of the United States during the Civil War. The British Government long persisted in refusing to arbitrate, declaring it could not admit that it had acted with bad faith in regard to the neutrality it professed. The United States persisted in demanding arbitration and finally, after a change of ministry in England, a treaty was signed on May 8, 1871, which provided for the arbitration of the questions at issue by a tribunal of five arbitrators. The persistence of the United States government and its final success in having the "Alabama" claims case arbitrated led to greatly increased interest in arbitration. According to the pamphlet on "Arbitration and the United States" referred to above,

"There was no popular movement in favor of pacific settlement in continental Europe until the 'Alabama' claims arbitration in 1872. All governments were seriously impressed by the spectacle of the submission of the important questions involved in the 'Alabama' claims to the Geneva tribunal and the prompt acceptance of the award by Great Britain."

As a result of the successful outcome of this case both houses of Congress passed resolutions in 1874, expressive of sentiment—but without the force of law—in favor of arbitration. The House of Representatives adopted the following resolution:

"That the people of the United States, being devoted to the policy of peace with all mankind, enjoying its blessings and hoping for its permanence and its universal adoption, hereby through their representatives in Congress recommend arbitration as a rational substitute for war, and they further recommend to the treaty-making power [1] of the Government to provide if practicable that hereafter in treaties made between the United States and foreign powers war shall not be declared by either of the contracting parties against the other until efforts shall have been made to adjust all alleged causes of difference by impartial arbitration."

The Senate at this time adopted a resolution as follows:

"That the United States, having at heart the cause of peace everywhere, and hoping to help its permanent establishment between nations, hereby recommend the adoption of arbitration as a just and practical method for the determination of international differences, to be maintained sincerely and in good faith, so that war may cease to be regarded as a proper form of trial between nations."

Toward the end of the century Congress took the initiative in a new effort to secure treaties for the arbitration of "any dispute." Yet the Senate refused to ratify the first such treaty submitted to it.

In 1890 both the Senate and House adopted a resolution calling upon the President "to invite, from time to time as fit occasions may arise, negotiations with any Government with which the United States has or may have diplomatic relations, to the end that any differences

---

[1] The treaty-making power of the United States Government rests in the President and the Senate. Under the Constitution treaties are to be negotiated by the Executive with the advice and consent of the Senate. The usual plan is for the executive branch of the Government to carry on treaty negotiations with foreign countries, and when an agreement has been reached, to submit the proposal to the Senate for approval. A two-thirds vote of the Senate is required for ratification.

or disputes arising between the two Governments which cannot be adjusted by diplomatic agency may be referred to arbitration, and be peaceably adjusted by such means."

The English House of Commons responded in a resolution expressing the hope that her Majesty's Government would coöperate with the Government of the United States in its proposal. The French Chamber of Deputies unanimously invited the Government "to negotiate, as soon as possible, a permanent treaty of arbitration between the French Republic and the Republic of the United States of America."

In 1895 the Governments of England and the United States began the negotiation of a general arbitration treaty, but in 1897, after prolonged debates and amendments which excluded many questions from its provisions, the United States Senate rejected the treaty.

The greatest advance during this period toward development of a general system of arbitration was made by the Hague Conferences. The First Conference, called in 1899 by the Czar of Russia and attended by 126 delegates from 26 nations including all of the first-class powers, was originally designed to consider the reduction of military forces, but devoted the greater part of its attention to a discussion of pacific methods for the settlement of international disputes. The American delegates were instructed by the State Department to propose the establishment of a permanent international tribunal. In his remarkable "Instructions" to the delegates John Hay, Secretary of State, said:

"The duty of sovereign states to promote international justice by all wise and effective means is only secondary to the fundamental necessity of preserving their own existence. Next in importance to their independence is the great fact of their interdependence. Nothing can secure for human government and for the authority of law which it represents so deep a respect and so firm a loyalty as the spectacle of sovereign and independent states, whose duty it is to prescribe the rules of justice and impose penalties upon the lawless, bowing with reverence before the august supremacy of those principles of right which give to law its eternal foundation."

Considerably modified, this so-called "American Plan" became the Permanent Court of Arbitration. The court is in reality a panel of arbiters to which each nation appoints four representatives, chosen for a period of six years. From this panel states desiring to submit disputes to arbitration select five judges, only one of whom can be a citizen of either of the contending nations.

Under Roosevelt's administration an attempt was made by John Hay as Secretary of State to extend the system of arbitration by the negotiation of treaties submitting all disputes of a "legal nature," not including questions involving "national honor" or "vital interests," to the Hague Tribunal. In 1905 an arbitration treaty with France was submitted to the Senate as the first of a series. The treaty was ratified by the Senate but with an amendment which called in each case for the negotiation of a treaty subject to the approval of the Senate, instead of the usual foreign office agreement, defining the matter in dispute before its submission to arbitration. Because of this amendment, President Roosevelt failed to press for ratification of the other treaties. In a letter to Senator Lodge he said:

"I think this amendment makes the treaties shams, and my present impression is that we had better abandon the whole business rather than give the impression of trickiness and insincerity which would be produced by solemnly promulgating a sham. The amendment, in effect, is to make any one of these so-called arbitration treaties solemnly enact that there shall be another arbitration treaty whenever the two governments decide that there shall be one."

In 1908, twenty-five similar arbitration treaties embodying the Senate's amendment to the treaty with France were negotiated by Elihu Root, then Secretary of State. Twenty-two of these treaties were ratified for periods of five years.

In 1910, President Taft attempted to secure arbitration treaties of a wider scope, which should include all justiciable disputes, even those involving "vital interests" and "national honor." The effort met with approval in France and Great Britain and treaties were signed with these countries in 1911, which provided that either country before the submission of a dispute to an arbitral tribunal could request the formation of a joint high commission to investigate facts and make recommendations; the formation of this commission was, if either nation so desired, to be delayed one year after the request for it was made, in order to allow for an effort at adjustment through diplomatic discussions. In regard to these treaties President Taft said:

"If now we can negotiate and put through private agreements with some other nation to abide the adjudication of International Arbitration Courts in every issue which cannot be settled by negotiation, no matter what it involves, whether honor, territory or money, we shall have made a long step forward by demonstrating that it is possible for two nations at least to establish between them the same system which, through the process of law, has existed between individuals under government."

The Taft treaties were drawn in conformity with the previous Senate requirements by providing that the question in dispute in each case, previous to its submission to arbitration, should be formulated "by and with the consent of the Senate." The Senate, however, refused to accept a provision included in the treaties that the question of whether or not the subject matter of a dispute was justiciable should be decided by a commission of inquiry. It further excluded as subjects suitable for arbitration, questions concerning

"the admission of aliens into the United States or the admission of aliens to the educational institutions of the several states, or the territorial integrity of the several states, or of the United States, or concerning the question of the alleged indebtedness or monied obligation of any states of the United States, or any question which depends upon or involves the maintenance of the traditional attitude of the United States concerning American questions, commonly described as the Monroe Doctrine, or other purely governmental policy."

Because of the restrictions made by the Senate the treaties were never signed by President Taft.

The reasons given by the Senate for its amendments to these pre-war treaties are of interest and importance since they continue to affect seriously the ratification of arbitration treaties at the present time.

The more fundamental reasons have to do with the constitutional power of the Senate, and with the Monroe Doctrine. A third, which it is hard to believe can remain an insuperable obstacle to the acceptance by the United States of a general system of arbitration, concerns the repudiated debts of certain States of the United States.

The Senate's insistence upon its constitutional power was expressed vigorously in a minority report to the Senate in connection with the Roosevelt treaties:

"The firm grasp upon our relations with foreign governments, placed in the hands of a minority of one-third of the Senate by the Constitution, whereby entangling alliances and wars have been often prevented, is being relaxed and the people are losing that power of self-protection. It is silently passing from the hands of their representatives . . . into the sole and exclusive power of the President.

"Such is the effect that must result from the conventions

now before the Senate and, so far as can be seen, that is one of the real intents and purposes intended to be accomplished by their ratification. . . .

"This fatal door in these conventions, through which the rightful powers of the Senate will pass into the hands of the Executive, should be closed so that a mere diplomatic agreement concluded by the President cannot bind the Government of the United States and all the states and all the people to obey it as the supreme law of the United States. Our Government will become a true autocracy when the President is invested with this power."

The power of an opposition minority in the Senate to defeat any treaty negotiated by the Executive, and the difficulty of securing harmonious action between the two branches of the treaty-making power when they are in the control of opposing parties, are giving rise to serious consideration of the possibility of some new adjustment, guarding against obstructionist tactics in the Senate or providing for an earlier expression of opinion by that body.

As to the Monroe Doctrine, which is briefly considered in a later chapter, the United States Government maintains that this is a unilateral doctrine, and it has so far consistently refused to discuss with any foreign power questions concerning either its interpretation or application.

The difficulties growing out of the repudiated debts of certain States involve several important points in connection with the relation of the States to the Federal government. Because a two-thirds majority is required for the ratification of treaties, Senators representing these States are able effectively to oppose and delay ratification, and it is important that the situation be understood and met.

John Hay, on the day following the Senate's amendments to the treaties which as Secretary of State he had negotiated, made an entry in his diary which places side by side with the question of the Senate's constitutional prerogative the part played by the question of the repudiated debts.

"The Southerners felt their repudiated debts could not trouble them if the amendments were carried. There was a loud clamor that the rights of the Senate were invaded—but every individual Senator felt that his precious privilege of casting two votes in opposition to every treaty must be safeguarded."

The total debt, with accrued interest, owed in large part to British bond holders, amounts to approximately $250,000,000. A small number of repudiated bonds are held by the Government of the United States. The States which have repudiated certain debts are Alabama, Arkansas, Florida, Georgia, Louisiana, Mississippi, North Carolina and South Carolina. In nearly all cases the indebtedness arose out of responsibility assumed by the States for bank, railroad, and other development bonds. The following statement of the causes of repudiation and of remedies proposed for the situation is condensed from an analysis in "Editorial Research Reports," dated, Washington, May 22, 1925:

"The legal reasons given for repudiation fall under three heads:

> Certain of the bonds were not authorized by law.
> Certain of the bonds were authorized by legislative enactments which conflicted with state constitutions.
> In the issue of other bonds the provisions of the laws by which they were authorized were not strictly complied with.

"Back of the legal reasons for repudiation were economic conditions which explain, if they do not justify, the action of the repudiating states.

ARBITRATION

"The taxable basis of the repudiating states was greatly reduced by the Civil War and their debts were largely increased under 'carpet bagger' rule during the period of reconstruction. The per cent of decrease reached as high as 64% and averaged over 50%.

"The overburdened taxpayers, saddled with an increasing bonded indebtedness by the extravagance and dishonesty of 'carpet baggers,' seized upon any expedient having the color of legality to lighten their load. Furthermore the Fourteenth Amendment [1] forced the Southern states to repudiate the debts contracted in what they regarded as a righteous struggle, brought upon them through no fault of their own, and it was not easy for them to distinguish between these and their other debts. It was, on the whole, easier for them to repudiate the latter than the former, since some of the non-war debts were owed to Northern capitalists, and the desire for revenge upon the North was strong.

"The Constitution as originally adopted contained a clause whereunder a defaulting state could be brought before the bar of the Supreme Court by a defaulted creditor. But the Eleventh Amendment provides that 'The judicial power of the United States shall not be construed to extend to any suit in law or equity commenced or prosecuted against one of the United States by citizens of another state, or by citizens or subjects of any foreign state.'

"In 1883 a resolution was offered in the House by Representative Moore of Tennessee to repeal the Eleventh Amendment and to grant Congress power 'to provide by appropriate legislation for the legal enforcement of contracts entered into, by any of the states of the Union.' No action was ever taken by Congress on this proposal.

"Following repudiation by Mississippi, it was proposed that the defaulting states be deprived of their representation in Congress.

"The assumption by the federal government of the debts

[1] ". . . Neither the United States nor any state shall assume or pay any debt or obligation incurred in aid of insurrection or rebellion against the United States: but all such debts . . . shall be held illegal or void."

of the states was proposed in 1843, following an announcement by President Tyler that negotiations for a small loan to the federal government had failed because of the damage to the nation's credit resulting from the defaults of the states.

"The principal arguments against this proposed remedy were (1) The assumption of the state debts would bring no benefit to the non-indebted states, but would rather injure them by making them bear a portion of the debts of the others; (2) States intrusted with federal bonds for this purpose might apply them to other uses; (3) If the States were relieved of their current difficulties, they would speedily become indebted again; (4) Assumption of state debts would embarrass the federal government."

Until some final agreement can be reached as to the proper disposition of these debts they will continue to interfere with this country's acceptance of any form of compulsory arbitration.

William Jennings Bryan as Secretary of State in 1913 made a new approach to the problem of pacific settlement of disputes through the negotiation of treaties involving processes of investigation and delay. These treaties call for a permanent commission of five members to which "all disputes of every nature whatsoever which diplomacy shall fail to adjust shall be submitted for investigation and report." The report must be made within one year, and the parties to the treaties agree "not to declare war or begin hostilities during investigation and report," but "retain the right to act individually on the subject matter of the dispute after the report of the commission shall have been submitted."

Twenty-one of the Bryan treaties were signed with the following countries: Bolivia, Brazil, Chile, China, Costa Rica, Denmark, Ecuador, France, Great Britain, Guatemala, Honduras, Italy, Norway, Paraguay, Peru, Portugal, Russia, Spain, Sweden, Uruguay, Venezuela.

They mark an important advance for, for the first time, a method of procedure for pacific settlement was proposed which was applicable to any dispute whatsoever. In 1916, Congress, in connection with the adoption of the naval appropriation bill, declared it "to be the policy of the United States to adjust and settle its international disputes through mediation or arbitration, to the end that war may be honorably avoided." This government, nevertheless, continued until the renewal of the Root treaties in 1928 to demand the exclusion from arbitration treaties of questions affecting "vital interests, independence or national honor." In the new Root treaties the several questions which this earlier clause was designed to exclude from arbitration were somewhat more clearly defined as those involving "the Monroe Doctrine, domestic issues or a third nation." The new treaties likewise included a provision borrowed from the Bryan treaties for the submission of all disputes to a process of conciliation. In commenting upon these treaties Secretary Kellogg stated before the Council on Foreign Relations:

"In my opinion any government can well afford to submit to inquiry any question which may threaten to involve it in the horrors of war, particularly when, as in the Bryan treaties, the findings of the Commission have no binding force and to be effective must be voluntarily accepted."

In the agreement reached with the Latin American Republics at the Sixth Pan American Congress, this Government has gone one step further, at least in its implications as to the future. Following the action of the Conference condemning war as an instrument of national policy, an agreement was reached:

"That the Republics of America will meet in Washington within a period of one year in a conference of conciliation and arbitration to draw up a convention for the realization of this principle, with the minimum exceptions which they consider indispensable to safeguard the independence and the sovereignty of the states, as well as its exercise in matters within their domestic jurisdiction, and also excluding matters involving the interests or relating to the action of a state not a party to the convention.

"That the convention or conventions of conciliation and arbitration which they succeed in drawing up should leave open a protocol of progressive arbitration which will permit the development of this beneficial institution to the greatest possible extent."

This proposed arbitration conference, which is now scheduled to meet in December, 1928, is a part of a long effort in the development of methods of pacific settlement between the American Republics. In 1889 an International American Conference met in Washington at the invitation of the Government of the United States. Five conferences of the American states have since been held, and at all but one of them action has been taken in support of arbitration. At the Second Conference, in 1902, a treaty of arbitration for pecuniary claims was adopted, and a compulsory arbitration treaty was signed by nine Latin American states. In 1907 a Central American Court of Justice was set up to which the member states agreed to submit "all controversies of whatsoever nature." Because of the attitude of the United States, which ignored a decision of this court, it was allowed to expire at the end of ten years. In 1923 a Central American Tribunal was created to take its place, which consists of a panel of jurists, and to which all disputes not involving "national honor and independence" are to be submitted. At the Fifth Pan American Conference in 1923, the Santiago treaty, calling for a commission of inquiry in the case of any dispute not settled through diplomatic channels or by arbitration, was

ARBITRATION

adopted and has already been ratified by the United States and several other nations.

Throughout this period Latin America has made its own contribution to arbitration. Of 33 treaties in force in 1913 which provided for unlimited arbitration all were Latin American, Spain being the other party to seven. Of the four constitutions in the world which provide for arbitration before appeal to arms, three are those of South American republics: the Brazilian constitution of February 4, 1891, which authorizes a declaration of war only "when arbitration has failed or cannot take place"; the Dominican constitution of June 13, 1924, which provides that "the powers instituted by this Constitution shall not declare war without first proposing arbitration"; and the Venezuelan constitution of April 27, 1904, calling for the insertion of the clause in all international treaties that "all differences between the contracting parties shall be decided by arbitration without appeal to war." The Portuguese constitution of 1911 requires an effort to arbitrate before a declaration of war.

The International Joint Commission

As between the United States and Canada a different and so far unique instrument for the adjustment of controversies has been created, the success of which has recently led to a consideration of its wider adoption.

In 1896 the Government of Canada took up the question of the establishment of an international commission with the Government of the United States primarily to prevent and settle disputes regarding the use of boundary waters. This government, however, delayed acting until 1902, at which time the International Waterways Commission was created. This was purely an investigating body, but in its recommendations it urged the creation of a Joint Commission having power to decide disputes, and in 1909 the International Joint Commission was set up.

The Commission is composed of six members, three from each country, appointed by the President of the United States and by the King of Great Britain on the recommendation of the Governor of Canada. It holds regular sessions each year at Washington and Ottawa and special meetings at whatever place in the United States or Canada affords the best opportunity for collecting all the evidence in any given case. The Commission sits as one judicial body and the members are pledged to use the utmost impartiality in the settlement of the questions that come before them. At the organization meeting of the commission the following statement was quoted by one of the Commissioners, in illustration of the attitude with which he took up his work:

"Although I am a citizen of but one nation, I am constituted a judge for both. Each nation has the same, and no greater right to demand of me fidelity and diligence in the examination, exactness, and justice of the decision."

Questions are brought before the Commission by either one or both of the governments and through their respective governments by private and corporate interests in either country. Its decisions are final and binding. In the twenty and more cases so far decided, which have affected the interests of millions of people and involved the expenditure of millions of dollars, the decisions of the Commission have without exception been unanimous.

"Its jurisdiction is not altogether that of a court of law, nor of an umpire, nor of an investigatory body, but it combines some of the characteristics and a good deal of the spirit of all three. It is a final court of appeal for certain classes of cases involving the use or diversion of boundary waters. Subject to certain constitutional limitations, it may be used by the two countries for the final settlement of any matter at issue between them. And it is also available to investigate and report upon matters affecting the two nations whose final settlement is left to their Governments."

Arbitration Since the World War

The establishment of the League of Nations and the Permanent Court of International Justice following the World War greatly advanced the general development of methods for the pacific settlement of international disputes. The Covenant of the League provides for judicial settlement, arbitration, inquiry and mediation. In Articles 12, 13 and 15 of the Covenant, the members agree to submit to arbitration, to judicial settlement or to investigation by the Council, all differences and controversies arising between them, and agree in no case to resort to war until three months after the decision is known. This latter provision introduces the principle of delay for which the Bryan treaties were responsible.

One of the most important contributions of the League of Nations in this field has been the development of the new method of periodic conference by which responsible statesmen have frequent and easy opportunity for face to face discussion of their common problems. Differences that have seemed incapable of solution, such as those between France and Germany, have been reduced to manageable proportions by this method. The more formal conference has also under the League come to be an important method for the gradual solution of international problems which threaten the progress or security of international life. The working out of a technique of conference is declared by Dr. James T. Shotwell, a recognized authority in this field, to be a pressing problem of modern statesmanship.

There has likewise been evolved under the encouragement of the League a new procedure of conciliation. The early suggestions made by the different governments in regard to the method of procedure to be followed under the League for the settlement of disputes, included a proposal made by the Scandinavian countries for an International Council to serve as a central agency of investigation. The Norwegian government in 1920 suggested an amendment to the Covenant by which permanent commissions of arbitration and conciliation, one for every state, for the examination of the differences between that state and any other should be set up. Discussion of these proposals led to the adoption by the Assembly of the League, in 1922, of the following resolution:

"With a view to promoting the development of the procedure of conciliation in the case of international disputes, in accordance with the spirit of the Covenant, the Assembly recommends the Members of the League, subject to the rights and obligations mentioned in Article 15 of the Covenant, to conclude conventions with the object of laying their disputes before Conciliation Commissions formed by themselves."

This resolution led to the rapid development of a system of treaties and bilateral conventions of conciliation between groups of states. In certain of the European treaties of this period conciliation was proposed not only for questions not suitable for submission to arbitration, but as a preliminary approach to the settlement of any question, preceding resort to arbitration or submission to a court. The conciliation procedure thus tends to assume a more important part than arbitration since it is accepted as capable of being applied to all disputes and as obligatory.

Of the importance of combining arbitration with conciliation and occasionally with judicial decision, Mr. Myers in his study on "Arbitration and the United States" says:

"A limited arbitration treaty together with a conciliation treaty may have the effect of affording a neutral forum for all disputes that may arise."

All efforts since the war to develop an effective system of treaties for the pacific settlement of disputes have encountered the problem of providing at the same time for security which in turn has been held by certain powers to depend upon disarmament. There has come to be in Europe a general agreement that the development of any one of these three must depend upon the development of the other two, but one group led by England emphasizes disarmament as the first necessity, while France, on the other hand, desires that before the adoption of disarmament plans, security, based on military guarantees, be assured.

In 1925 the League of Nations drew up a Protocol of Pacific Settlement known as the Geneva Protocol which was the first attempt to solve these interdependent problems. It declared aggressive war a "crime" in that it is a violation of the recognized solidarity of the international community. It provided for the submission of every dispute to arbitration or to the World Court, and for the acceptance of the decisions arrived at. It granted the Council of the League power to decide when a nation was guilty of aggression and what measures should be taken against it. It undertook to define what should be regarded as constituting aggression, and declared a state which refused to submit a dispute to the procedure for pacific settlement as agreed, or to comply with a judicial decision or arbitral award, to be an "aggressor." [1]

The provisions of the Protocol were to take effect only after a disarmament conference had adopted some prac-

[1] The definition of an aggressor nation has since been simplified to read "one which, having agreed to submit international differences to conciliation, arbitration or judicial settlement, begins hostilities without having done so."

tical plan for the general reduction of armaments; thus arbitration, security and disarmament were linked together as three interdependent factors of a peace system. The Geneva Protocol was not, however, accepted by a sufficient number of states to be put into effect. Following its rejection, regional treaties affecting the states of Central Europe and making similar provisions for compulsory arbitration and mutual guarantees were signed at Locarno. In accordance with these treaties Great Britain and Italy in case of conflict between Germany and France, or Germany and Belgium, are pledged to take up arms against the aggressor, and France agrees to come to the aid of Poland or Czechoslovakia should Germany, contrary to her arbitration treaties with these countries, make an armed attack upon them. In connection with these treaties an agreement was reached that Germany should join the League and be given a permanent seat on the Council.

The Locarno Treaties of Arbitration provide that all justiciable questions which cannot be settled by diplomatic procedure may be referred to the Permanent Commission of Conciliation provided for in each treaty, and, failing settlement by that, to an arbitral tribunal or to the Court of International Justice. If the parties cannot agree to the terms of the question to be submitted, either one may bring the dispute before the Permanent Court of International Justice. This latter provision is a distinct step in advance, since heretofore treaties have commonly called for preliminary agreement upon the terms of the questions to be submitted—an agreement technically known as a *compromis*.

The Eighth Assembly of the League, meeting in 1927, created an Arbitration and Security Commission to work in connection with the Preparatory Committee for a Disarmament Conference, plans for which the Assembly urged should be hastened. In response to a demand that the principles underlying the Geneva Protocol be reconsidered, the Assembly declared:

"That all wars of aggression are and shall always be prohibited; that every pacific means must be employed to settle disputes of every description which may arise between states."

There are now in existence 88 treaties, which admit all questions whatsoever to one method or another of pacific settlement. The signatories to these treaties include forty-three nations, among them France, Germany, Italy, and Great Britain.

A general summary of progress in pacific settlement as shown in this succession of treaties is given in a Pan American Union compilation of arbitration treaties. It indicates the general lines of development in this way:

"Combinations, every day better thought out, of methods of conciliation, arbitration and recourse to judicial proceedings, tend to include under their provisions for peaceful settlements, all differences which might cause conflicts, and to close other avenues of procedure, so as to ultimately permit none but peaceful settlements. . . . The multiple variations in, and combinations of, reservations, such as those involving points of honor, independence, sovereignty, and vital interests, common in the older arbitration treaties, have disappeared from the modern type of arbitration and conciliation treaty. . . .

"The progress made indicates plainly a radical transformation in the bases, the structure and the objects of the present methods for the organization of peace. The significance of these changes becomes clearer when the system followed in the conventions of the two Hague Conferences is compared with the system which has developed from 1920 to 1927. The Conference of 1907 added little to what had been achieved in 1899, and the sum total of results of the two seem today meagre and mediocre when compared with the generous conception of international justice, with the deep and intense study, the sacrifice of national prejudices, and the amplitude of the field for peaceful action, which had their beginnings in 1919 and culminated in the treaties of Locarno in 1924 and 1925, and which are still developing, gaining in organic perfection, meriting the adhesion of governments and winning prestige and power in the minds of peoples."

Even this brief and superficial review of the steady advance in the practice of pacific settlement points convincingly to the ultimate acceptance, as a matter of course, of one form or another of rational adjustment of all disputes. The question remains to what degree this development can be accelerated by public interest, understanding and insistence.

CHAPTER XIV

INTERNATIONAL LAW

The codification of international law—or the clear statement of the rules of conduct accepted by nations in so far as their activities affect other nations—is recognized as an essential part of the organization of the world for peace. The importance of codification has long been stressed by statesmen of this country. President Coolidge in his second annual message to Congress said:

"Our country should support efforts which are being made toward codification of international law. . . . Expert professional studies are going on in certain quarters and should have our constant encouragement and approval."

As to how codification is to be achieved there is a difference of opinion. Some jurists urge that an international conference be called to draw up a code of laws which nations shall agree to follow in the interest of peace and justice. It is proposed by one group that such a code be based on the outlawry of war, and it is maintained that if the situation is simplified by thus delegalizing war, a statement of the laws of peace could be drawn up in one or two years.

To the majority of jurists, codification involves an entirely different process. It means a careful statement, upon which there can be general agreement, of the rules of conduct which have gradually evolved in the intercourse of states, and which governments now recognize.

An approach to codification in this latter sense is being

made under the auspices of the League of Nations. The governments of North and South America, through the Pan American Conferences, are also attempting to codify international law as it affects the countries of this hemisphere. In addition, there are at present before Congress two proposals looking toward codification. Both have been introduced by Senator Borah of Idaho. The first is for an international conference to prepare an ideal code of law based on the outlawry of war. The second is for a restatement of maritime law. The importance of the second proposal lies in the fact that the present assertion of the right of belligerents to interfere with neutral shipping in time of war, a claim which has always been combatted by the United States, is an obstacle to the reduction of naval armaments. The Borah resolution, which was especially designed to facilitate action by the second meeting of the League of Nations Disarmament Conference, reads in part:

"Whereas the present chaotic state of maritime law—leaving the seas subject to no definite rules save that of force, and commerce to no ultimate protection save that of battle fleets —constitutes an incentive for great naval armaments;

"Resolved, That the Senate of the United States believes:

"First: That there should be a restatement and recodification of the rules of law governing the conduct of belligerents and neutrals in war at sea.

"Second: That the leading maritime powers of the world owe it to the cause of the limitation of armaments and of peace to bring about such restatement and recodification of maritime law."

Although long study and research are necessary for more than a very superficial understanding of the subject of international law, it is important that the average person should have some comprehension of what it implies, in order that its development, which depends at various points upon political action, may not be delayed or obstructed.

International law is divided into public and private law. Private international law has to do with the conflicts that occur when a citizen of one country is involved in a legal difficulty in another country, and the laws of the two countries do not agree. Private international law is important from the point of view of international peace for, if there is doubt as to whether the nationals of one country have received justice in the courts of another, it may result in ill feeling, protest or intervention.

Public international law has to do with the practice of states in their conduct toward each other. It has not been enacted by any law-making body, as has the statutory law of the various nations, nor has it, like English common law, grown up out of the decisions of judges. It consists of rules of conduct resting upon common practice, or agreed to in treaties, in international congresses which are sometimes described as quasi-legislative bodies, in conventions establishing international administrative unions, such as the Postal Union, and in other international agreements. Recently decisions of the World Court and the Conventions of the League of Nations and of the International Labor Organization, in so far as they have been ratified, have increased the body of international law. The principles embodied in a treaty between two nations are international law as between them, but are generally considered international law only when agreed to by a number of nations (some states claim unanimity is necessary), or when it is recognized that their general observance can be enforced. Principles and lines of conduct which have been followed and enforced by the more powerful states are frequently regarded as international law.

Mr. Dwight W. Morrow, in his book, "The Society of

Free States," defines international law as "those rules of conduct which regulate the dealings of civilized states and which depend for their sanction upon the general approval of mankind. These rules are found in the solemn conventions and declarations made by civilized states in their separate treaties and at international conferences, in the works of great textwriters, and, what is most important of all, in that actual usage which furnishes the confirmation of written rules and agreements."

A primary distinction between international and national law is that there is no common agency for the enforcement of international law. Its enforcement depends upon the power of a nation or nations to compel its observance, or upon the existence of a public opinion so strong that no nation wishes to defy it. In a speech before the American Society of International Law in 1925, the opinion was advanced by Charles Evans Hughes that

"It may not be regarded as a defect or a misfortune that we escape the notion of the imposition of force in the field of international law. It makes for peace because it is accepted and is farthest removed from arbitrariness. Its gradual extension marks a gain that is not merely temporary or illusory, but genuine progress, and hence the effort to promote the reign of law, as accepted, not imposed, may be after all the most important contribution to permanent peace."

Codification, or a clear statement of what the law is, should enable public opinion to be more effective in securing its observance and in initiating changes. The right of intervention is now considered a part of international law as the right to secure territory by conquest was once so considered. A change in public opinion, leading to a change in the practice of nations, means a change in international law. In the speech referred to, Mr. Hughes said further:

INTERNATIONAL LAW

"Close attention to the reports of the conscience of nations, the effort to record its judgments, the endeavor to secure discussion of the principles and rules demanded by the sense of justice in the international sphere, may well be the sort of training which the world needs most. . . .

"Would it not be helpful, not merely in the interest of clarification and formal arrangement, but in educating peoples, now under prevalent democratic institutions more largely interested in foreign relations, with respect to the extent of their reciprocal obligations, and in cultivating the sense of responsibility, if the representatives of the nations could assemble and reassert the principles and rules of the law considered to be binding . . . ?"

Various efforts to determine the law of nations have been made, beginning with the "Laws of Peace and War," published by Hugo Grotius in 1625. Grotius held that dealings between nations should be regulated by the same principles that regulated the dealings between men, and made this first attempt to compile a body of rules based upon the usages of nations because he saw

" . . . prevailing throughout the Christian world a license in making war of which even barbarous nations would have been ashamed. Recourse was had to arms for slight reasons or no reasons; and when arms were once taken up, all reverence for divine and human law was thrown away, just as if men were henceforth authorized to commit all crimes without restraint."

During the Civil War "Instructions for the Government of the Armies of the United States in the Field" were drawn up by Francis Lieber at the request of President Lincoln. These instructions were translated into German, and published in 1878 by Bluntschli under the title, "Modern International Law of Civilized States."

Lieber later worked over a plan by which an authoritative statement on international law might be drawn up by an international group of jurists. His proposals led to a meeting of jurists in Ghent in 1873 at which the Institute of International Law was created as "an organ for the legal consciousness of the civilized world." Its principal purpose was "to be able by the free action of a limited group of eminent jurists to state in as precise a manner as possible the juridical opinion of the civilized world and to give to this opinion an expression so clear and so exact as to have it accepted by the various states as a rule of conduct for their foreign relations."

In 1893 The Netherlands invited all European governments to a conference to draw up conventions affecting private international law, and this first conference has been followed at regular intervals by others.

The First Hague Peace Conference in 1899 drafted three conventions, one dealing with pacific settlement of international disputes, the other two with rules of warfare. The conventions of the Second Hague Conference in 1907 dealt largely with the laws of war. At the Second Conference, a third was proposed for 1914 which, it was anticipated, would add to the formulated "principles of equity and right on which are based the security of states and the welfare of peoples." The plans for this third conference were interrupted by the World War. Following the War a proposal for international conferences similar to the Hague Conferences but called for the sole purpose of codifying international law was laid before the League of Nations by the Committee of Jurists which drew up the plans for the Permanent Court of International Justice. The suggestion originated with Elihu Root, the American member of the Committee.

This proposal was not accepted by the League of Nations. It was rejected on the ground that at the time there was not sufficient calmness of the public mind to

INTERNATIONAL LAW

undertake such a step without "very serious results to the future of international law." Commenting on the League's decision not to undertake codification at that time, Dr. Manley O. Hudson, Bemis Professor of International Law at Harvard University, has said:

"Any attempt at that time to restate the laws of war or to formulate the modifications made necessary by the World War, must almost certainly have tended to vindicate the views then prevailing among the governments of those countries which considered themselves victors in the war. It would have been difficult at that time to have had any collaboration from Germany or Russia or Turkey, and without the collaboration of Germany, at any rate, a restatement of the laws of war would probably have produced few desirable results. . . . In addition, the uncertainty of international relations in 1920, the precarious stage of the new experiment in international organization, and the extreme difficulty of effecting the necessary reconciliation between various states, rendered the time most inopportune for such an attempt as the Advisory Committee envisaged."

In 1924, the Assembly of the League of Nations, owing in part to the development of a large number of agreements which its member states had entered into during the post-war period, reconsidered the question of codification. The result was the appointment by the Council of the League of an international Committee of Experts for the Progressive Codification of International Law. The Committee consists of seventeen jurists, representing the various legal systems of the world. Mr. George W. Wickersham is the American member. After intensive study by sub-committees, consultation with authoritative bodies, and the submission of questionnaires to various governments, including the United States, the Committee of Experts in 1927 recommended seven topics to the Assembly of the League as "sufficiently ripe" for consideration by an international conference. The seven topics were these:

The conflict of laws regarding nationality;
Problems connected with territorial waters including jurisdiction of a State over foreign commercial vessels;
Diplomatic privileges and immunities;
Responsibility of States for damage done in their territory to the person or property of foreigners;
Piracy;
The procedure of international conferences and procedure of conclusion and drafting of treaties;
Exploitation of the products of the sea.

Consideration of the questions of the nationality of commercial corporations and of the recognition of the legal personality of foreign commercial corporations, would have been included in this list except for the fact that they were to be considered at the next Hague Conference on Private International Law.

The Assembly agreed upon the calling of a conference to be held, it is now planned, in 1929, and selected the first, second and fourth topics for consideration. The fourth topic, perhaps the most far-reaching, as stated in full is:

"Whether, and in what cases, a state may be liable for injury on its territory to the person or property of foreigners; and whether, if such liability exists, it would be possible to consider an international convention providing a method of ascertaining the facts that might involve liability on the part of the state, and forbidding the use of measures of coercion before means of pacific settlement have been exhausted."

In the desire to contribute to the success of the conference in 1929, and in the belief that independent cooperative research by American scholars and jurists might aid in the advancement of sound codification of international law, the Faculty of the Harvard Law School has organized a group of men actively working in this field to carry on research work, on the three topics to be discussed. An advisory Committee of 34 members has been formed with Mr. George W. Wickersham as Chairman and Dr. Manley O. Hudson as Director of research.

Separate codification of international law for the American continents, suggested as early as 1826 by the Congress of Panama, has been recommended repeatedly by the Pan American Conferences. Charles Evans Hughes said in regard to this proposal in a speech before the Pan American Union in 1925:

"It is natural that the law to be applied by the American Republics should, in addition to the law universal, contain not a few rules of American origin and adapted to American exigencies, and that the old and the new taken together should constitute what may be called American international law."

Resolutions were adopted by the Conferences of 1902 and 1906 for the appointment of a Commission of Jurists to prepare codes of public international law and of private international law. The actual formation of this Commission was delayed until the Conference of 1923. Following this conference a Commission composed of two representatives from each country was created. The American Institute of International Law, which was founded in 1912 and is composed of five members from each of the American republics, was requested by the Pan American Union to prepare a series of projects for the consideration of this Commission of Jurists. Individual jurists of several of the Latin American states also drafted projects for laws on special subjects. Thirty projects were accepted for consideration by the Commission. An additional one on the recognition of belligerency was rejected on the ground that war should not be encouraged by conventions on this subject.

The Commission adopted twelve projects of public international law and a code of private international law consisting of some 439 articles. The twelve projects of public international law dealt with the fundamental bases of international law; states, their existence, equality and recognition; status of aliens; treaties; exchange of publications; interchange of professors and students; diplomatic agents; consuls; maritime neutrality; the right of asylum; duties of states in case of civil war; pacific solution of international conflicts.

At the Sixth Pan American Conference to which these projects were submitted those dealing with the pacific solution of international conflicts, with maritime neutrality, with the status of aliens, with the right of asylum, with the duties of states in case of civil war, and with the rights and duties of neutrals were, in amended form, embodied in treaties and accepted for submission to the various governments. The United States entered a reservation to the clause of the Convention on Maritime Neutrality forbidding the arming of merchant men for defense in the time of war. On the subject of pacific solution of international conflicts, a resolution was adopted condemning war as an instrument of national policy and calling a conference to meet in Washington within a year to draft treaties for obligatory arbitration and conciliation. For the further consideration of the codification of international law for the American continents, a Permanent Committee was authorized, to which the Governments will appoint members chosen from the national Societies of International Law in each country. Projects drawn up by this Committee will be submitted to the International Commission of Jurists which will put them in final form and in turn submit them to the Seventh Pan American Conference.

The subject of the fundamental bases of international law, that is, of the rights and duties of nations, which it was asserted must be considered together, was referred to the Seventh Conference. In connection with it and in all probability in connection with the conference on obligatory arbitration, the project on intervention, which aroused heated discussion at the Sixth Conference but about which because of the insistence of the United States no action was taken, will again come up.

These attempts to achieve a separate codification of international law for the Americas are severely criticized by certain jurists for reasons indicated in the following statement by Dr. Manley O. Hudson:

"The day has passed," Dr. Hudson declares, "when international law can be continentalized in any part of the world, and with the currents of international trade and politics crossing all oceans as they do today, it would seem a very backward step to attempt to confine them in any way to a single hemisphere. . . . I fear that only unfortunate consequences would flow from an attempt to localize the law of nations."

The importance of making "the statement of our law of nations," as Dr. Hudson has said, "conform to the facts of our present-day world," is, however, stressed by jurists, statesmen and those interested primarily in world peace. The French jurist, M. de Laveleye, notes that although men of today are "infinitely less inclined than their ancestors to make war, on the other hand, their relations are more intimate and more constant and can lead more frequently to conflicts if they are not regulated by international law."

Dr. James Brown Scott, Director of the Division of

International Law of the Carnegie Endowment for International Peace, and long active in support of efforts toward codification, is very hopeful of present tendencies and declares that "It is evident that the codification of international law is in full blast. . . . The seed scattered to the wind by Lieber is bearing ample fruit in the old world of his birth, and in the new world of his choice."

The contribution which the general public can make is to recognize the necessity for persistent effort in this field and to support any government action encouraging it.

CHAPTER XV

INTERNATIONAL COÖPERATION

THE present extent of organized coöperation among governments and the success of international administrative undertakings bear out the statement that "international coöperation must be regarded not as a rare exception, but as the normal method for the present conduct of the business of the world." In his comprehensive study, "Public International Unions," Dr. Paul S. Reinsch declares that "The most important fact of which we have become conscious in our generation is that the unity of the world is real."

In this chapter only coöperative undertakings outside of the League of Nations are considered, but it must be remembered that through the League fifty-five nations are now in constant conference and coöperating in financial, educational, health, labor, economic and social welfare projects. The International Labor Organization is discussed in a preceding chapter.

During the nineteenth century, the development of rapid communication among all nations gave rise to problems which could not be solved and to activities which could not be administered by individual governments. The interests of individuals came to be less and less determined by national boundaries and had to be provided for by some form of international public or private organization.

Within the last half-century, about forty public and five hundred private international organizations have been established. In some cases, organizations originally formed by private individuals have developed into government agencies. In others, governments have associated themselves with private undertakings through representatives, but in many instances the initiative has been taken by the governments themselves.

Dr. C. Delisle Burns, in "A Short History of International Intercourse," calls attention also to a present tendency toward conference for exchange of experience between similar departments of different states, finance ministries, education departments, agricultural, and labor departments. "The tendency," he says, "points to an elaborate international contact of states, not unifying states, nor forming a world state, but federalising some of the functions of sovereign governments."

In the Interparliamentary Union, which was founded in 1904 and which held its twenty-fifth conference in Berlin in August, 1928, an opportunity is offered for consultation among another division of government officials. Its members are representatives in national parliaments, and the legislative chambers of the various governments are opened for its conferences. An effort is made to bring the members into agreement upon policies affecting international relations.

Joint regulation has been found necessary in connection with, among other things, systems of communication, the protection of certain forms of property including patents, health measures designed to control the spread of disease, and for the collection and distribution over wide areas of scientific information. In some cases the international organizations set up for the exercise of joint control consist of little more than information centers; in other instances, international commissions are empowered to propose measures for adoption by the national governments. In a few cases, the international body has administrative powers which amount to a considerable

INTERNATIONAL COÖPERATION

limitation of the sovereign powers of individual governments.

The Universal Postal Union is an example of the last type. In 1863, the cost of a letter from point to point varied from a few cents to more than a dollar, according to how it was routed. In sending a letter, it was thus necessary to indicate the route which it was to travel. If it happened to miss the vessel or train on which it was to begin its journey, it could not be sent by another route, but must wait sometimes many weeks. To improve this condition, upon the proposal of the United States, the representatives of fifteen nations met and agreed upon certain principles as a basis for future international postal agreements, but did not attempt to produce definite treaty regulations. The conference at which the Universal Postal Union was actually founded was called by the government of Switzerland in response to a suggestion from the German government, and met in 1874 with twenty-two countries participating. Many complicated questions had to be faced and the reluctance of a few nations to incur the immediate financial loss involved, and to submit to international regulation, was overcome only through the pressure of public opinion and of business interests.

The Universal Postal Union has continued in successful operation ever since, with modifications from time to time of the convention which established it. The Union is governed by a congress which meets every five years and in which each state has one vote, although it may have more than one delegate. The representatives of the United States are appointed by the Postmaster General. Decisions are made by a majority vote and are theoretically subject to ratification by the signatory state. In practice, they are final. In some instances, individual governments have strongly opposed certain changes in postal rates, but the proposed change adopted by majority vote has been put into effect, and no government can give up the incalculable advantage to its citizens of membership in the Union.

The Universal Postal Union proves that, in spite of conflicting interests, methods of procedure for international governmental control can be successfully worked out when individual governments recognize that, acting alone, they can no longer provide adequately for certain interests of their citizens. The degree to which national sovereignty has been surrendered in this field in order to secure national benefits is emphasized by Dr. Leonard S. Woolf in "International Government":

"In fact, so far has the surrender of independence to International Government gone in the Union, that the theoretical right of the State to refuse ratification to the Convention and Reglement as voted at a congress in practice hardly exists. The Administrations, adhering to the Union, never wait for formal ratification before putting the new regulations into operation, and the decisions of a Postal Congress are acted upon whether they are ratified or not.

"The result is that the nations of the whole world have for everything connected with the international exchange of letters and other postal matter submitted to International Government. Each national Administration can no longer determine the rates it will charge, the matter which it will or will not receive, or the methods on which it will conduct the foreign postal service. On all these subjects the national Administration is in practice bound to accept the decision of the majority of the Administrations adhering to the Union. In other words, the administration of postal communication between States has been internationalized. . . ."

The international bodies which have been granted the greatest power over national governments have been the International Sugar Commission and the International River Commissions. The International Sugar Commission was established for a limited period in order to put an end to the system of granting national bounties to sugar growers, a system which no nation acting separately could control. The Commission had the power to control by majority vote the tariff policies of member states so far as they affected the sugar industry. There was no appeal from its decisions to any higher body.

The International River Commissions afford another example of the ability of states to forego a certain degree of their sovereign power in order to achieve the benefits of coöperation. The Danube Commission, composed of representatives of ten states, has complete control over the conditions affecting the navigability of the lower Danube. The Commission imposes a tax on shipping to defray its own expenses; it acts under a guarantee of neutrality and has the right to use its own distinctive flag.

The International Institute of Agriculture, and the International Geodetic Union, are examples of a joint international effort to collect and distribute scientific information. The Union for the Protection of Industrial Property, the Sugar Commission and the Union for the Publication of Customs Tariffs illustrate the possibility of joint action in economic matters. The international organizations concerned with humanitarian reforms, which include the Opium Commissions, the Prison Congress, the Union for the Repression of the White Slave Traffic and the International Labor Organization, function with increasing effectiveness. International coöperation to protect health, particularly through the control of epidemics, which is carried on by the International Office of Public Hygiene in Paris, by the League of Nations, by the International Health Board in New York City, and by the Pan American Sanitary Bureau, is one of the most successful and interesting of these undertakings.

So long as European governments attempted to protect their people against epidemics of cholera by independent quarantines, they obstructed trade but not the spread of the disease. Reluctance to relinquish national rights, prevented common action until after the epidemic of 1892. The International Sanitary Convention and the Dresden Convention were then agreed upon, and there have been no more cholera epidemics.

In the Pan American Union a much more general form of international coöperation has been developed among the governments of the American continents. In 1889, the first of a series of Pan American Conferences was held in Washington. Preceding the calling of the conference, which was originally proposed by Secretary of State Blaine as a peace conference, Congress adopted a plan for coöperation among the American governments. As set forth in the call to the conference this plan provided for the consideration of "measures that shall tend to preserve the peace and promote the prosperity of the several American States."

This first conference created the International Bureau of American Republics in Washington under the direction of the Secretary of State of the United States, for the sole purpose of collecting and distributing commercial information. At the third Pan American Conference in 1906, the Bureau was reorganized and virtually made the executive organ of the Pan American Conferences. As finally reorganized in 1910, under the name of the Pan American Union, it now assists in securing the ratification of the resolutions and conventions adopted by the conferences, and promotes, in a variety of ways, the development of closer cultural, commercial and financial relations.

The governing board of the Pan American Union consisted until 1928 of all the Latin American diplomatic

INTERNATIONAL COÖPERATION 283

representatives accredited in Washington, with the American Secretary of State as president. At the Sixth Pan American Conference, in response to a criticism that the influence of the United States too greatly predominated, it was agreed that the states could appoint any representatives they desired, not necessarily the diplomats accredited to the United States who must be *persona grata* to it. The Union is supported by contributions, regulated according to their population, from the member states.

The United States has sought to limit action at the Pan American Conferences to economic matters. Among the conventions and treaties which the conferences have adopted are conventions protecting copyrights, patents and trade marks; a convention for the arbitration of pecuniary claims; a convention setting up a commission for the formulation of a code of international law; a convention on commercial aviation. At the Fifth Conference a treaty to prevent conflicts between the American states was adopted, and at the Sixth Conference an agreement was reached to hold in Washington within a year a special conference for the promotion of arbitration. Attempts to discuss such questions as tariff restrictions and the right of intervention have so far been fruitful only in calling attention to the need of arriving at agreements in these matters of mutual concern. In recent years an increasing number of Pan American Conferences representing special interests have been held with the coöperation of the Pan American Union, including those dealing with scientific, press, labor, commercial and health questions.

A proposal for a Pan European Union which was initiated as recently as 1923 by the publication of the book, "Pan Europe," by Count Richard N. Coudenhove-Kalergi, has grown with great rapidity and has received the endorsement of many European statesmen. The idea is to form an organization similar to the Pan American Union. The plan of the Union looks toward friendly coöperation with the League of Nations, as well as with other continents representing political units and rejects all intervention in questions of internal politics. It includes a system of commercial treaties, the formation of customs unions and of international cartels in certain industries. Speaking before the Chamber of Commerce of the United States, Thomas W. Lamont said of the plan for a Pan European Union:

"Such a development may take a long time in coming; on the other hand, it may move much more swiftly than we imagine. If it does, we shall be able within a short span of years to witness a Europe restored, industrious, stable, peaceful, far stronger in every way than it has ever been in the past, with armaments vastly reduced, with swords beaten into plowshares, and with a future bright with promise."

Two unofficial organizations for the development of better understanding and closer coöperation among the Pacific countries have been formed: the Pan Pacific Union, which has for a number of years arranged semi-official Pan Pacific Conferences of special groups, such as educators, scientists, business men and journalists; and the Institute of Pacific Relations, which held its first meeting at Honolulu in 1925. The Institute is unofficial; it takes no action, passes no resolutions, and reaches no conclusions. Its sole aim is to arrive at a better mutual understanding through a wider knowledge of facts. In order to achieve the greatest possible freedom of expression, its work is carried on chiefly through round-table discussions, which are not reported in the press.

The program of work of the Institute includes: the maintenance of central offices in Honolulu and committees of experts in each nation for the collection of data, and the dissemination of information. Biennially these national committees meet in a general conference to consider common problems and to develop an international understanding which will aid in their solution. The Institute considers one of its major functions to be the giving of wide and impartial publicity to facts bearing upon the problems of the Pacific peoples through periodicals, interchange of lecturers, study groups, and national and regional conferences. Its second biennial conference, lasting two weeks, was held in 1927, and was attended by 136 delegates, representing nine national groups. Among the difficult problems discussed were the rise of Chinese nationalism, the expansion of Japanese population, the American-Japanese Exclusion Act and naval power in the Pacific.

The number of group interests organized internationally increases daily. The League of Nations "Handbook" of international organizations for 1926 lists 398 organizations representing practically every human activity. Fifty-three international conferences to be held in 1928 are listed in a leaflet published early in the year by the Institute of International Education. Through these organizations, and conferences, there is a constant exchange of sentiments and ideas and a growing realization of common interests and of the possibility of coöperation. In "Public International Unions," Dr. Reinsch says:

"Millions are working together quietly, in the pursuit of their various living interests, toward the organization of world unity. It is not a thing imposed from above by force, or dictated only by a higher rationalism but it is the almost instinctive work of active men building wider and wider spheres of affiliation."

Civilization itself has been defined as a "capacity for coöperation."

CHAPTER XVI

INTERNATIONAL REDUCTION OF ARMAMENTS

Two experiments in basing security upon goodwill and common interest rather than force of arms have been successfully carried out in America.

William Penn's unarmed colony in Pennsylvania lived unattacked among savage tribes for seventy years, and only when Penn's principles of friendship and justice were no longer followed was a white man killed.

The second experiment was in a wholly different field. When the War of 1812 ended, the United States and Canada had each some forty-six forts on the shores of the Great Lakes and many shipyards employing hundreds of men. Word was received in this country of orders having been issued by the British Government to increase its naval force on the Great Lakes, and American officers urged Congress to increase appropriations for border defense. At this point Richard Rush, an official in the State Department, who shortly afterward became Attorney General, is credited with having suggested that, instead of a competitive building program, the Lakes be disarmed. The British Ambassador in this country, Charles Bagot, favored the proposal. On November 16, 1815, the Secretary of State, James Monroe, sent the following letter to our ambassador to England, John Quincy Adams:

"The information you give of orders having been issued by the British Government to increase its naval force on the Lakes is confirmed by intelligence from that quarter, of

REDUCTION OF ARMAMENTS

measures having been actually adopted for the purpose. It is evident, if each party augments its force there, with a view to obtain the ascendancy over the other, that vast expense will be incurred and the danger of collision augmented in like degree. The President is sincerely desirous to prevent an evil which it is presumed is equally to be deprecated by both Governments. He therefore authorizes you to propose to the British Government such an arrangement respecting the naval force to be kept on the Lakes by both Governments as will demonstrate their pacific policy and secure their peace. He is willing to confine it, on each side, to a certain moderate number of armed vessels, and the smaller the number the more agreeable to him; or to abstain altogether from an armed force beyond that used for revenue. You will bring this subject under the consideration of the British Government immediately after the receipt of this letter."

On January 31, 1816, Mr. Adams wrote Mr. Monroe in part, as follows:

"I can only now state in a summary manner that I think the proposal for mutually disarming on the Lakes of Canada, which I made conformably with your instructions will not be accepted. . . . Although Lord Castlereagh promised to submit the proposal to the Cabinet, his disinclination to accede to it was so strongly marked that I cannot flatter myself it will be accepted."

Two months later he wrote again:

"You may, however, consider as certain that the proposal to disarm upon the Lakes will not be accepted. In all the debates in Parliament upon what they call their military and naval peace establishment, the prospect of a new war with the United States has been distinctly held up by the ministers and admitted by the opposition as a solid reason for enormous and unparalleled expenditure and preparation in Canada and Nova Scotia."

In answer to this reluctance on the part of England, America did not turn its attention to a big navy program for the Lakes, but continued to press its plan. After a year and a half, in 1817, the Rush-Bagot Treaty was signed, stopping work on nearly one hundred fortifications and causing the immediate disarmament of more than a hundred warships. The persistence of American statesmen at this time contributed to the establishment of a period of peace which has lasted more than a century and which is now accepted so much as a matter of course that its significance is not appreciated.

Other efforts toward reduction in armaments have been effective chiefly in reducing the cost of war preparations, and in accustoming public opinion to the idea. Throughout the nineteenth century there was talk of restricting armaments. Proposals were made by various sovereigns and by such leaders as Garibaldi and Richard Cobden. The general discussion culminated in 1898 in the proposal of the Czar of Russia for an international conference to examine "the question of ending progressive development of existing armaments" in order to assure "to all nations the benefits of a real and lasting peace." The First Hague Conference in 1899, however, achieved nothing toward the actual reduction of armaments or military budgets. At the Second Conference in 1907 the subject was not included in the program, but the United States insisted upon its discussion and resolutions were adopted calling for a study of the problem.

Shortly after this, in 1910, the Congress of the United States passed a resolution requesting the President to appoint a commission of five members "to consider the expediency of utilizing the existing international agencies for the purpose of limiting the armaments of the nations of the world by international agreement, and of constituting the combined navies of the world an international force for the preservation of universal peace, and to consider and report upon any other means to diminish the expenditures of governments for military purposes and to lessen the probability of war."

In 1916, in connection with the naval building program, Congress adopted a "Declaration of Policy" which declared among other things that the United States looked "with apprehension and disfavor upon a general increase of armament throughout the world," but realized that "no single nation can disarm." In the light of these facts it requested the President to invite all the great governments to attend a conference which should formulate a plan for an international court and "consider the question of disarmament." It further provided that the navy building program might be suspended by order of the President, if an international tribunal competent to secure peaceful determinations of all disputes should "render unnecessary the maintenance of competitive armaments."

The reduction of national armaments "to the lowest point consistent with domestic safety" was next urged as one of the Fourteen Points set forth by President Wilson as a basis for the peace negotiations following the World War. The Covenant of the League of Nations provided for the reduction of armaments in Article 8, which reads in part:

"The members of the League recognize that the maintenance of peace requires the reduction of national armaments to the lowest point consistent with national safety and the enforcement by common action of international obligations.

"The Council, taking account of the geographical situation and circumstances of each State, shall formulate plans for such reduction for the consideration and action of the several Governments.

"Such plans shall be subject to reconsideration and revision at least every 10 years."

The Treaty of Versailles in the Preamble to Part Five,

which provided for the disarmament of Germany, declared that such disarmament was imposed

"In order to render possible the initiation of a general limitation of the armaments of all nations. . . ."

On July 16, 1919, M. Clemenceau wrote to the German Government in the name of the Allies:

"The Allied and Associated Powers wish to make it clear that their requirements in regard to German armaments were not solely with the object of rendering it impossible for Germany to resume her policy of military aggression. They are also the first steps toward that general reduction and limitation of armaments which they seek to bring about as one of the most fruitful preventives of war, and which it will be one of the first duties of the League of Nations to promote."

The terms of the disarmament of Germany included the reduction of its army to 100,000 men to be recruited by voluntary long-term enlistment, and the limitation of its navy to a few small boats for coast patrol, with no submarines and no fighting planes.

In 1921, at the invitation of the United States Government, nine countries met in Washington for discussion of limitation of armaments, and of Pacific and Far Eastern questions. The nations represented were, besides the United States, Belgium, Great Britain, China, France, Italy, Japan, the Netherlands and Portugal.

The Washington Naval Treaty, resulting from the conference, set a limit for the battleships and airplane carriers of the United States, Great Britain and Japan in the ratio of 5-5-3, with a lower figure of 1.67 for France and Italy. The original American proposal was intended to apply to cruisers, destroyers, submarines and other naval auxiliaries as well as to capital ships, but it proved impossible to carry out the proposal as regarding the auxiliary vessels. The treaty as negotiated and ratified involved the actual destruction of a large number of battleships built and building. Those destroyed totalled for the United States 842,380 tons, for Great Britain 447,750 tons, and for Japan 354,709 tons.

The treaty remains in force until December 1936, and can be terminated at that time or thereafter upon two years notice. According to its terms, the United States is to arrange, "in view of possible technical and scientific developments" for a conference of all the signatory powers eight years from the time of the treaty, that is in August, 1931. Preliminary plans for this conference have already been begun.

Meanwhile, in May, 1920, the Council of the League of Nations had formed a Permanent Advisory Commission on Military, Naval, and Air Questions, the members of which are representatives of their governments. In the same year the Assembly, believing that the Permanent Commission was limited too narrowly in its composition and its relation to the governments represented, asked the Council:

"To instruct a temporary commission, composed of persons possessing the requisite competence in matters of a political, social and economic nature, to prepare for submission to the Council in the near future, reports and proposals for the reduction of armaments as provided for by Article 8 of the Covenant."

This Temporary Mixed Commission on Armaments, in order that it might be more widely representative, was later reorganized as the Coördination Committee.

At every meeting of the Assembly of the League there was discussion of disarmament based upon the reports of these committees, but a prevailing feeling of insecurity prevented any agreement. It was seen from the discussions and reports of the Temporary Mixed Commission to be necessary to provide for security before progress could be made, and security, it was decided, must be based upon a system of compulsory arbitration. In 1924, in the Geneva Protocol, or the Protocol for Pacific Settlement, a plan was elaborated in which arbitration, security and disarmament were linked together in a general system for maintaining peace. Although the plan was not accepted it has influenced later negotiations, notably the Treaties of Locarno, regional security pacts which were negotiated shortly afterward. The Locarno treaties were in fact followed by a reduction in the French army. In this connection Denys P. Myers makes the following comment:

"The scale of armament indicates a state's conception of its lack of security. In the prewar period armament increased simultaneously with the increase of both the policy and practice of pacific settlement. The situation was logically contradictory. . . . The explanation, however, is obvious. The most important states, with the widest range of disputatious questions . . . were precisely those which reserved from the procedure of pacific settlement questions which might cause a war. As a consequence the development of pacific settlement did not have a direct effect on armament standards, which formed a nucleus for the breeding of suspicion. The proper relationship is beginning to exist, illustrated by French reduction of the army on the entrance into force of the Locarno treaties."

In 1925 the Sixth Assembly requested the Council to make a preparatory study with a view to a Conference for the Reduction and Limitation of Armaments.

A Preparatory Commission for the Disarmament Conference was formed to submit a preliminary draft for a disarmament agreement to the official Disarmament Conference. The Committee on which both the United

States and Russia are now represented, has considered seven questions:

"What is to be understood by armaments?

"Is it practicable to limit the ultimate war strength of a country, or must any measures of disarmament be confined to the peace strength?

"By what standards is it possible to measure the armaments of one country, against the armaments of another, e.g., numbers, equipment, expenditures, etc.?

"Can there be said to be offensive and defensive armaments?

"On what principles will it be possible to draw up a scale of armaments permissible to the various countries?

"Is there any device by which civil and military aircraft can be distinguished for purposes of disarmament? If this is not practicable, how can the value of civil aircraft be computed in estimating the air strength of any country?

"Admitting that disarmament depends on security, to what extent is regional disarmament possible in return for regional security? Or is any scheme of disarmament impracticable unless it is general? If regional disarmament is practicable, would it promote or lead up to general disarmament?"

At the meetings of the Preparatory Commission there developed radically divergent views on the part of the different states, which amounted to two distinct schools of thought, one invariably supported by France, with Poland and the Little Entente and varying additional adherents, and the other by the United States with the adherence of Great Britain and occasionally of other states.

France contended that in comparing armaments the resources and strategical position of the countries must be considered. The United States and Great Britain maintained that the military forces and material only should be taken into account. The French have held that land, sea and air forces are interdependent and a reduction must consider all three; the United States maintains the contrary. The French insisted,—and their views were adopted by a majority,—that in considering regional disarmament a region should be defined as a continent plus those states having liberty of action at sea, that is to say the whole world. The French also maintained that any system of regional agreements for limitation must depend upon a system of treaties of mutual alliance in case of aggression. The Americans, on the other hand, insisted that limitation would lead to security and that regional disarmament is a logical and practical forerunner of general disarmament. In general the French contended that security must be guaranteed by some form of military assistance against aggression as a necessary condition precedent to the reduction and limitation of armaments. The United States delegation held that the cause of security would be promoted through the reduction and limitation of armaments and the elimination of ill will and suspicion which may be expected to follow.

The discussions of the Preparatory Commission led to the creation, in 1927, of a Sub-Committee on Arbitration and Security, to consider measures capable of giving all states guarantees of arbitration and security necessary to enable them to fix the level of their armaments at the lowest possible figures. The United States, although invited, is not represented on this committee.

On February 10, 1927, the President of the United States announced that he had invited France, Great Britain, Italy, and Japan to empower their delegates to the next meeting of the Preparatory Commission on Disarmament to negotiate agreements for the further limitation of naval armaments, including classes of vessels not covered by the Washington Naval Treaty. This invitation was declined by France and Italy and accepted by England and Japan.

The Conference was held in the summer of 1927 but adjourned without agreement. Behind the difficulty of arriving at agreements on naval disarmaments lay the whole question of the freedom of the seas. Senator Borah has introduced a resolution in the United States Senate calling for a re-statement of international law on this point. An English naval expert, writing in *Headway* for December, 1927, declares:

"There is only one way out of this difficulty. Not to stick rigidly, as a private belligerent, to such claims as we were making in 1918. Not to go back to the old American Freedom of the Seas, immunity of private property from capture. But to go forward to the new Freedom of the Seas such as President Wilson indicated in the second of his Fourteen Points. The seas should only be closed, in peace or in war, by international agreement for the enforcement of international covenants."

The failure of the Conference led also to a general questioning of the practical wisdom of the appointment of naval officers to conferences designed to reduce the power and prestige of navies. It was recognized that such appointments in reality demanded of the same man the performance of two contradictory tasks.

The Eighth Assembly of the League of Nations, meeting on September 26, 1927, urged continued action in regard to disarmament and the convening of a conference on limitation and reduction of armaments as soon as possible, and recommended "the progressive extension of arbitration by means of special or collective agreements, including agreements between States Members and non-Members of the League of Nations, so as to extend to all countries the mutual confidence essential to the complete success of the Conference on the Limitation and Reduction of Armaments."

Although no actual reduction of armaments has been

obtained through the work of disarmament conferences, since the Washington Conference in 1921, they have served to hold the attention of statesmen upon the problem of maintaining peace and have educated public opinion to understand both the complexity of the problems involved and the necessity of finding a solution for them. To recognize the progress that is being made, it is only necessary to recall the fact that in 1907 it was impossible to place the subject of disarmament upon the agenda of the Second Hague Conference, while at the meeting of the Preparatory Commission in 1928 a thoroughgoing plan for complete world disarmament was presented by Russia and discussed. The Russian plan called for the disbanding of military personnel over a period of four years; the destruction of land, sea and air armaments; disarmed war vessels and military airplanes would be preserved for civil purposes. An international commission of control would be established with committees in each state. Each power would, within one year, enact legislation providing "that a breach of any of the stipulations of the convention shall be regarded as a grave offense against the state." A somewhat similar disarmament plan was presented to the League of Nations by Norway in 1922.

In the meantime certain closely related questions concerning the manufacture and sale of munitions are receiving attention. The United States in addition to its participation in the work of the Preparatory Commission has joined in three other movements under the auspices of the League of Nations which are closely connected with disarmament. These are the control of the traffic in arms, the control of the private manufacture of arms and the control of the use of poison gas in warfare.

With regard to the international traffic in arms, Article 23 of the Covenant of the League of Nations provides in part that "the members of the League will entrust the League with the general supervision of the traffic in arms and ammunition with the countries in which the control of this traffic is necessary in the common interest." As one result of the provisions of this article, the Convention of St. Germain to prevent the exportation of arms to certain defined areas inhabited by backward peoples was drawn up and signed by 23 states. The United States signed in September, 1919, but has not ratified. The United States participated in a further Conference for the Control of the International Trade in Arms, Munitions, and Implements of War which met at Geneva from May 4 to June 17, 1925. This Conference drew up a convention which was signed at the time by eighteen nations, and which is still before the Foreign Relations Committee of the United States Senate.

The Covenant of the League of Nations declares the "manufacture by private enterprise of munitions and implements of war is open to grave objections," and stipulates that:

"The Council shall advise how the evil effects attendant upon such manufacture can be prevented, due regard being had to the necessities of those Members of the League which are not able to manufacture the munitions and implements of war necessary for their safety."

A conference was held on this subject in the spring of 1927, but was without result. Upon the demand of the Assembly of the League for continued effort, conferences were resumed in August, 1928, at which the United States demanded full publicity for both government and private manufacture of arms. It was anticipated at the opening of the conference that a convention would be drafted and submitted to the 1928 Assembly.

In the United States various efforts have been made

to secure legislation "to take the profit out of war," but these bills have so far not been favorably received, in part because they have included conscription of labor without effectively providing for eliminating financial profits.

In December, 1927, Representative Theodore Burton introduced in the lower House of Congress a joint resolution to prohibit the exportation of arms, munitions, or implements of war to belligerent nations. No action was taken on this resolution.

Efforts to abolish certain forms of armaments have been made since the Washington Conference. Upon the initiative of the United States a treaty was negotiated with Great Britain, Japan, France and Italy for the prohibition of poison gas in warfare, but due to non-ratification by France it did not go into effect. At the International Conference on Traffic in Arms in 1925 the United States delegation attempted to extend the principles of this treaty to the whole world. In consequence, the Protocol for the Prohibition of the Use in War of Asphyxiating, Poisonous or Other Gases, commonly known as the Geneva Gas Protocol, was drawn up at Geneva in June, 1925. The United States Senate, although it ratified the Washington Treaty of 1922, has failed to ratify the Geneva Gas Protocol.

Recently, perhaps, the most hopeful sign has been the reaction of the people of the United States to the disappointing failure of the Coolidge Disarmament Conference in 1927, expressed in active opposition to the adoption, as a result of this failure, of any big navy program. A general demand also arose in all countries, following the negotiation of the Multilateral Treaty renouncing war, for a renewed attack upon the disarmament problem.

CHAPTER XVII
PACIFISM AND THE ABSOLUTE PACIFIST POSITION

PACIFISM in a general sense is used to refer to the peace movement as a whole and in that sense is the theme of this entire book. In its stricter sense it is applied to the doctrine of those who refuse to participate in war, primarily for reasons of individual conscience but also in the belief that such refusal is an effective method for bringing about the abolition of war. In this more limited meaning, pacifism calls for special discussion, since the principles behind it are often not clearly understood either by those outside of the peace movement or by those within the peace movement who advocate other methods of attacking war.

One of the clearest statements of the pacifist theory of life in contrast with the militarist theory of life has been given by Frederick J. Libby, Executive Secretary of the National Council for Prevention of War:

"Militarism in the past two decades has come to mean, not love of war, but reliance, solely or mainly, upon military force for the achievement of a nation's security, peace, and economic and political well being. Pacifism contrariwise means something much deeper than mere refusal to bear arms. It signifies reliance, solely or mainly, on spiritual forces such as goodwill, public opinion and the sense of justice on which all enduring governments rest, for the attainment of the same ends of security, peace, and economic and political well being; and it seeks these goods not for one nation at the expense of others, nor even singly, but for all together."

By Dr. Charles E. Jefferson pacifism is described as "one of the mightiest movements of our day."

"When you sneer at pacifism and pacifists," he says, "you are showing that you are belated—you do not know what is going on—you do not know in what direction the deepest currents of human life are flowing. Pacifism is a philosophy, a spirit, and a program. It is the philosophy of life which places the major emphasis on moral influence rather than on physical force. It is the spirit of goodwill, aiming to attain its objects not by violence, but by gentleness. It is a program in which the combatants in a dispute appeal to conscience and reason and not to guns."

The theory that love is the strongest of the forces available to man is very old. Prof. Clarence Marsh Case in his recent book "Non-Violent Coercion," a very valuable study of pacifism and to which this chapter is much indebted, quotes the teachings of philosophers before Christ. The founder of Taoism living in China in the sixth century before Christ asserted the power of meekness to conquer:

"He who excels as a warrior is not warlike.
He who excels as a fighter is not wrathful.
He who excels in conquering the enemy does not strive. This is called the virtue of not-striving. This is called utilizing men's ability. This is called complying with heaven,—since olden times the high test."

The founder of Buddhism said:

"The whole world dreads violence. By love alone can we conquer evil. Say no harsh words to thy neighbor; he will reply to them in the same tone."

Marcus Aurelius, representing the Stoic philosophy, urged men to "reflect that kindness is invincible provided only it be genuine; that meekness and gentleness are more human and manly, and it is he who possesses these that has strength, nerve, and bravery."

But these earlier teachers had in mind personal, rather than group relationships. They did not carry their theory through into state action, and their teachings never resulted in any formal sect organized around the doctrine of pacifism.

Christ emphasized, more than any other teacher, the irresistible power of love and the duty of loving one's enemies but neither is there in His teachings any clear statement of the implications of this theory in the relation of the individual to the state. Jesus devoted himself, according to Doctor Case, "to opening up in the personal experience of men streams of motive which it was assumed would reform social institutions by regenerating the individual life. . . . Jesus and the writers of the New Testament left not a doctrine to circumscribe but an ideal to leaven the moral and social life of mankind." Nevertheless, one by one the social institutions not compatible with the ideals of the Christian doctrine have been discarded by society—slavery, autocratic government, the bondage of women; and though he made no pronouncement on the subject of war, Christians in the very early days refused to participate in war, and endured martyrdom rather than bear arms against their fellow men. The chapter on the "Church and Peace" shows the early church for more than two centuries condemning war.

In the 14th century, there developed a conscious effort to extend the teachings of Christ from the dealings of man with man to all social relationships. Its beginnings can be traced in the activities of the Bohemian Brethren and later among the Anabaptists, Mennonites and Dunkers. Among these groups, however, the general rule was non-participation in all state affairs. The Mennonites did not permit their members to accept even civil offices which involved in their duties a violation of the principle of nonresistance. It remained for the Quakers to bring the effort to apply Christian teachings to state practices to full expression in William Penn's "Holy Experiment" in peaceful government in Pennsylvania. The Quaker demand was that Christians live, and that Christian states conduct their affairs in harmony with Christ's teachings. If this were done, the occasion for wars, they held, would be done away with. In "Quakerism and Politics," Isaac Sharpless asserts that the Quakers stopped at war because they believed that "the hatred, the killing, the stealing and all the immoralities which cluster around war were wrong in themselves, and could not be justified by the results gained, or the supposed inadequacy of right means to meet the situation."

But it was not until the World War that there were non-religious groups organized on the basis of refusal to participate in war. In this country there are now three groups outside the churches which refuse to take any part in war. They are the Women's Peace Union, the Women's Peace Society, and the Fellowship of Reconciliation. The first two are the only groups which require a membership pledge, never "to aid in or sanction war, offensive or defensive, international or civil, in any way."

The Women's Peace Union is attempting to secure the adoption of the following constitutional amendment:

"War for any purpose shall be illegal, and neither the United States nor any State, Territory, association, or person subject to its jurisdiction shall prepare for, declare, engage in, or carry on war or other armed conflict, expedition, invasion, or undertaking within or without the United States, nor shall any funds be raised, appropriated, or expended for such purpose."

The underlying principle of the Women's Peace Society is "A belief in the sacredness and inviolability of human life under all circumstances." It carries at the top of its letterhead a statement from William Lloyd Garrison:

"Non-resistance is not a state of passivity. On the contrary, it is a state of activity, ever fighting the good fight of faith, ever foremost to assail unjust power, ever struggling for liberty, equality, fraternity, in no national sense, but in a world-wide spirit. It is passive only in this sense,—that it will not return evil for evil, nor give blow for blow, nor resort to murderous weapons for protection or defense."

The Fellowship of Reconciliation, though not sectarian, is a religious organization. It requires no pledge of its members, but a statement of purpose, and its program is wider than opposition to war. It is

"A world-wide group of people of many races who feel called to seek with others such fundamental changes in the spirit of men and in the structure of the social order as shall make possible the full expression of love (as rendered in the teachings of Jesus) in personal, social, industrial, national and international life."

In England the number of men and women who have announced their refusal to take any part in war is much larger than in the United States. One hundred and twenty-eight thousand have signed what is known as the "Peace Letter" written and distributed by a member of Parliament, Arthur Ponsonby, and addressed to the Prime Minister. The letter reads:

"We, the undersigned, convinced that all disputes between nations are capable of settlement either by diplomatic negotiation or by some form of international arbitration, hereby solemnly declare that we shall refuse to support or render war service to any Government which resorts to arms."

The fact that opposition to war has received vigorous expression in England may be due in part to the traditional refusal of the Englishman to submit to government dictation, but it is more likely due, as Mr. Ponsonby maintains, to the clear evidence which all living Englishmen have had of the futility of war. Mr. Ponsonby, who is not himself a pacifist in the sense that he would refuse under any condition to take human life, bases his appeal for opposition to war upon its futility in the modern world, and quotes the phrase of the French peasant woman as she looked over her patch of field torn up in shell holes, "Comme c'est bête, la guerre!"

A peace letter campaign in the western part of Germany secured in three months one hundred and thirty-seven thousand signatures to a letter similar to the one circulated in England.

In France and Germany active branches of the "No More War" or "War Resisters" groups have been influential in bringing about friendlier relations between those two countries.

Certain of the absolute pacifist organizations have united in forming the War Resisters International, which now announces affiliated branches in 19 countries and meets in annual conferences. Behind all of these organizations is a sustaining moral conviction, which during the War enabled many of their members to endure persecution and extreme suffering, that war is wrong. By others war is attacked on economic and rational grounds, but by the absolute pacifist it is condemned on moral grounds as well.

Pacifist sects in the past and pacifist organizations today have made it clear that their refusal to participate in war is not incompatible with other service to the state. Such excellent citizens were the Mennonites that governments offered them inducements to come and settle in their territory. The attitude of the Quakers toward the state is shown in this statement in a report of a

Conference of All Friends quoted in "Non-Violent Coercion":

"We feel that the state in giving true service may well demand a loyal response, which the individual will gladly render. There may come, however, a point beyond which the claims of the state do not carry, where the enlightened conscience cannot bow to its commands, and where the individual gives the best service to the state by refusing to obey that which violates the august authority of conscience. This does not imply disregard of the state or free us from the obligation of service to it. This obligation we gladly and freely recognize, and it is of the greatest importance that we should make our policy positive, practical and helpful, not merely obstructive and negative."

This theory of a limitation to the authority of the state, and of what an individual's most valuable contribution to the state is, is upheld by Professor Harold J. Lasky in his book, "Authority in the Modern State":

"The only way the state can truly prosper is by sweeping into itself the active assistance of mind and conscience; and it will succeed in that effort only in so far as it respects them. Whatever, therefore, concerns the conscience of man, whatever brings its activity into operation, must, for the state, be sacred ground. . . .

"We dare not, in brief, surrender the individual conscience. Only upon its continuous exercise can our state be securely founded."

In asking for signatures of Englishmen to the letter referred to above, Mr. Ponsonby said:

"Men and women who sign the Peace Letter are simply declaring that for the good of their country and for the well-being of their fellowmen all the world over and for the protection of civilization they refuse to take any part in attempting to settle a dispute with another nation by means of massacre and devastation."

Lord Robert Cecil, as a member of the British Government, considering the relation of pacifism and patriotism, declared that it is

"Essential to create in the breasts of patriots a new purpose of patriotism, namely, to excel in the work of peace and in the prosperity of their own nation through the prosperity of humanity at large."

The right of the individual to follow the dictates of his religion, if not of his conscience, was recognized by the United States Government in the draft law, which exempted members of well-recognized religious sects whose creeds forbade their members to participate in war.

The National Defense Act, in so far as combatant service goes, makes exemptions on the ground of religious belief rather than membership in a religious sect, but exempts no one on either ground from such service as the President shall declare to be non-combatant.

The following letter from the Department of State, written since the war, October 22, 1926, to Roger N. Baldwin, director of the American Civil Liberties Union, seems to go somewhat further than either of these laws in the recognition of a citizen's right not to violate his conscience in the matter of bearing arms and the kind of service he performs for his country, without bringing his loyalty into question:

"The Department acknowledges the receipt of your letter of October 4, 1926, in which you state that you are wholly opposed to bearing arms for any purpose and that before making application for a passport you desire to be advised whether the words "support and defend the Constitution" means the bearing of arms or the supporting of war. . . .

"You are informed in reply that the Department does not construe an oath or affirmation of allegiance prescribed by the passport regulations as necessarily involving physical defense of the Constitution and consequently does not perceive any good reason why non-resistants should decline to accept it, especially as it is administered to women and to children old enough to understand its nature. However, if you have conscientious scruples against taking the oath as it stands, the Department will consider the matter of issuing a passport to you if you will file formal application for such a document supported by an oath or affirmation of allegiance to the Constitution in the following form:

> "Further, I do solemnly affirm that I will support the Constitution of the United States and will, so far as my conscience will allow, defend it against all enemies, foreign and domestic; that I will bear true faith and allegiance to the same; and that I take this obligation freely without any mental reservations or purpose of evasion. So help me God."

Non-participation in war is the phase of the absolute pacifist doctrine which has received chief emphasis in public discussion. Recently, however, there has been criticism in some instances by absolute pacifists themselves of exclusive emphasis on conscientious objection as the important part of the pacifist program. Harold C. Goddard declares that "to rely on the absence of armed force is just as materialistic as to rely on its presence. The things to rely on are national goodwill, national imagination, national self-control. The things to fear are national greed, national ignorance, and national passion."

In the May, 1928, issue of the *"Messenger of Peace,"* published by the Peace Association of Friends in America, Richard R. Wood urges the pacifist to do more than refuse to participate in war, and says that for the solution of the problems of peace the conscientious objector is likely to be inadequate because "absorbed in considering what his attitude is to be in case of another war. . . ."

"In the present generation the one supreme task is the prevention of war. The alternative is destruction. To waste time and energy in arguing about what to do in case war comes seems almost criminal in its futility. For this reason the policies and plans for action that cluster around the initials 'C.O.' are inadequate.

"The problem is two-fold. As Erasmus said, "Where God is not, Peace cannot come; where Peace is not, God cannot come.' The philosophy and program of conscientious objection is at most only one-half of the whole."

The great value of pacifism in the effort to abolish war may yet be found to lie in something other than its efficacy as a direct instrument. It is above all else an expression of the conviction—a conviction which is daily strengthened by a growing knowledge of the nature of the universe and of time, and by a closer insight into the teachings of philosophy and of religion—that the end can never justify the means. In the light of that conviction, war cannot persist.

CHAPTER XVIII

THE MILITARY POLICY OF THE UNITED STATES PAST AND PRESENT

The full significance of the present military policy of the United States can be properly understood only in connection with the history of our military establishment. The men who founded the United States of America definitely placed the military under the control of civilian authority. The Articles of the Constitution and the comments of early leaders leave no doubt of the importance to them of this arrangement.

In Article I of the Constitution, Congress alone was given power to declare war. The constitutional provision in Article II that the President should be Commander-in-Chief of the Army and Navy was designed as a fundamental check to the control of the government by any autocratic military party. The further constitutional provision that

"The Congress shall have power to raise and support armies, but no appropriation of money to that use shall be for a longer term than two years,"

was repeatedly cited in the early days to prove that even Congress did not have power to establish a permanent standing army. It gave the people frequent opportunity through their control of the membership of Congress to prevent the creation of a strong military machine by a group in temporary control of the government.

In giving Congress the power to call forth the militia

the Constitution specified the purposes for which it should be called forth, "to execute the laws of the Union, to suppress insurrection and to repel invasions." In another connection, Abraham Lincoln said of this constitutional caution in regard to the war-making power, in a letter to William H. Herndon, dated February 18, 1846:

"The provision of the Constitution giving the general war-making power to Congress was dictated, as I understand it, by the following reasons: Kings had always been involving and impoverishing their people in wars, pretending generally, if not always, that the good of the people was the object. This our convention understood to be the most oppressive of all kingly oppressions, and they resolved to so frame the Constitution that no man should hold the power of bringing this oppression to us. . . ."

The traditional close association of military power with autocratic forms of government led to steady opposition, in the early Congresses, to any suggestion for the establishment of a standing army and even to the appointment of a Secretary of War in times of peace.

When in 1783 a motion was made in the Continental Congress to create a land establishment of a few hundred men, it is stated by McMaster in his "History of the People of the United States," that

"The opponents of the measure, waiving all question of the need of troops, vehemently denied the right of Congress to levy them. No one, it was said, pretended to deny that the delegates of the States in Congress assembled had the right to raise troops in time of war. But it was far from clear that this authority could be construed into a right to make requisitions on the States for a land-force in times of peace. To say that the number was small, only eight hundred and ninety-six men, and the time limited to three years, was no defence. If the law could be interpreted to justify a requisition for a small number of men for a short time, what was there in it to forbid a requisition for a great number of men for an unlimited time? This was simply taking away the power of the States to deliberate on the matter and leaving them but the duty of obeying. ... The history of Greece, the history of Rome, and the history of England were then ransacked for examples of the ills of a standing army, and the conclusion reached that nothing but sophistry or Toryism could reconcile any army in time of peace with republican principles. ...

"Such was the persistency with which these objections were urged that Congress was soon as divided in opinion as the people. Motion after motion was brought forward to create a land force, and as often lost. ... A week later, the few troops in the service of Congress were disbanded. Eighty men, were, however, retained. ... The army having no longer any existence, the office of Secretary of War was left vacant."

Madison, in defence of the constitutional provisions "to raise and support armies," said in the *Federalist:*

"No less true is it, that the liberties of Rome proved the final victim to her military triumphs; and that the liberties of Europe, so far as they ever existed, have, with few exceptions, been the price of the military establishments. A standing force, therefore, is a dangerous, at the same time that it may be a necessary, provision. On the smallest scale it has its inconveniences. On an extensive scale its consequences may be fatal. On any scale it is an object of laudable circumspection and precaution. A wise nation will combine all these considerations; and whilst it does not rashly preclude itself from any resource which may become essential to its safety, will exert all its prudence in diminishing both the necessity and the danger of resorting to one which may be inauspicious to its liberties. ...

"Next to the effectual establishment of the Union the best possible precaution against danger from standing armies is a limitation of the terms for which revenue may be appropriated for their support. This precaution the Constitution has prudently added."

The "Journals" of William McClay which, according to Professor Charles A. Beard who has edited them, are one of the few documents reflecting the political events of the years 1789-91, contain illuminating comments on the early effort to subordinate the military power in the organization of this government. Their author was a Senator from Pennsylvania in the first Congress and is recognized as the forerunner in Congress of the Jefferson party. The closeness of the votes on the measures which McClay opposed during this formative period, indicates that the point of view expressed in these extracts from his "Journal" was not merely personal:

"March 30th, 1790. . . . The bill for the military establishment took up the rest of the day in desultory debate, and was finally committed to seven members. This bill seems laying the foundation of a standing army. The justifiable reasons for using force seem to be the enforcing of laws, quelling insurrections, and repelling invasions. The Constitution directs all these to be done by militia. Should the United States, unfortunately, be involved in war, an army for the annoyance of an enemy in their own country (as the most effective mode of keeping the calamity at a distance and enforcing an adversary to terms) will be necessary. This seems the meaning of the Constitution, and that no troops should be kept up in peace. This bill certainly aims at different objects. The first error seems to have been the appointing of a Secretary of War when we were at peace, and now we must find troops lest his office should run out of employment.

"April 15th, 1790. . . . I have opposed this bill hitherto as often as it has been before the House as the foundation, the corner-stone of a standing army. The troops are augmented one-half. The reasons hitherto given have been the distressed state of Georgia. Butler has blazed away on this subject at a great rate; declared over and over that Georgia would seek protection elsewhere if troops were not sent to support her, etc., etc., and said fifty Indians had penetrated into that State,

MILITARY POLICY

of which he had authentic information, etc. . . . This brought up Colonel Gunn. He declared he knew nothing of fifty Indians making any inroads into Georgia. He was just from there, and had the latest accounts. There existed no cause in Georgia for augmenting the troops; and since that was the reason assigned for it, he should vote against it.

"April 16th, 1790. . . . New phantoms for the day must be created. Now a dangerous and dreadful conspirator is discovered to be carrying on between the people of Kentucky and the Spaniards. . . .

"February 4th, 1791, Friday. . . . This day we had a large report from the Secretary of State transmitted to us from the House of Representatives respecting the fisheries of New England. The great object seems to be the making of them a nursery for seamen, that we, like all the nations of the earth, may have a navy. We hear every day distant hints of such things as these; in fact, it seems we must soon forego our republican innocence, and, like all other nations, set apart a portion of our citizens for the purpose of inflicting misery on our fellow-mortals. This practice is felony to posterity. The men so devoted are not only cut off, but a proportionate share of women remain unmatched. Had the sums expended in war been laid out in meliorating the kingdom of England, or any other modern Government, what delightful abodes might they have been made; whereas war only leaves traces of desolation."

Washington, Franklin, Jefferson, Hamilton, all alike bore testimony to this feeling of the people that large armies were antagonistic to the principles of democratic government. To Franklin they were "expensive machines to be maintained for the pomp of princes and the wealth of ancient states." Washington believed that "Overgrown military establishments are, under any form of government, inauspicious to liberty, and are to be regarded as particularly hostile to republican liberty." Jefferson said: "I am not for a standing army in time of peace, which may overawe the public sentiment, the good sense of the people will always be found to be the best army"; and again, "The spirit of this country is totally adverse to a large military force." Hamilton, arguing for the adoption of the Constitution, wrote in the *Federalist:* "The smallness of the army renders the national strength of the community an over-match for it; and the citizens, not habituated to look up to the military power for protection, or to submit to its oppressions, neither love nor fear the soldiery; they view them with a spirit of jealous acquiescence as a necessary evil, and stand ready to resist a power which they suppose may be exerted to the prejudice of their rights."

The traditional opposition to all things military was a controlling influence in the development of our government policy until the Civil War, and, in large part because of the attitude of Lincoln, held through that period and without serious impairment up to the World War. Before the Civil War the size of the army ranged from 5,000 to 17,000; between the Civil War and the Spanish-American War it averaged about 27,000; in the years following the Spanish-American War it grew to 70,000. In the "Military Policy of the United States," published as late as 1912 by the Government Printing Office, Major General Emory Upton refers to "the Anglo-Saxon prejudice" against "standing armies as a dangerous menace to liberty," and says:

"Whether we may be willing to admit it or not, in the conduct of war, we have rejected the practice of European nations and, with little variation, have thus far pursued the policy of China."

Francis Lieber, author of General Order No. 100, issued for the conduct of the armies in 1863, wrote:

"Standing armies are not only dangerous to civil liberty because directly depending upon the executive. They have

MILITARY POLICY

the additional evil effect that they infuse into the whole nation—especially when they are national armies, so that the old soldiers return continually to the people—a spirit directly opposed to that of a free people devoted to self-government. A nation of freemen stand in need of a pervading spirit of obedience to the laws; an army teaches and must teach a spirit of prompt obedience to orders. Habits of obedience and of contempt for the citizen are produced, and a view of government is induced which is contrary to liberty, self-reliance, self-government. Command ought to rule in an army; self-development of law and self-sustaining order ought to pervade a free people."

During and since the World War, owing in part to the military interpretation of the events of the war and to the influence of the European military systems with which many of our military men for the first time came in direct contact, there has been a fairly constant effort to secure legislation reversing this traditional policy, and to bring about instead the adoption of compulsory military service.

The adoption in 1916 and the amendment in 1920 of the National Defense Act, regarded by the military officials as the next best thing to universal compulsory military service, changed the military establishment of the United States in several fundamental respects. The amendments adopted in 1920 included the provision under which military training is being introduced into our educational institutions. The vote on this amendment to the act in the House of Representatives was 237 for, 107 against and 83 not voting. There was no record vote taken in the Senate.

A persistent campaign during this same period for a big navy met with strong opposition from Congressional leaders, and when the 1916 program was adopted, it was accompanied by this declaration:

"It is hereby declared to be the policy of the United States to adjust and settle its international disputes through mediation or arbitration, to the end that war may be honorably avoided. It looks with apprehension and disfavor upon a general increase of armament throughout the world, but it realizes that no single nation can disarm, and that without a common agreement upon the subject every considerable power must maintain a relative standing in military strength. . . .

"If at any time before the construction authorized by this Act shall have been contracted for there shall have been established, with the coöperation of the United States of America, an international tribunal or tribunals competent to secure peaceful determinations of all international disputes, and which shall render unnecessary the maintenance of competitive armaments, then and in that case such naval expenditures as may be inconsistent with the engagements made in the establishment of such tribunal or tribunals may be suspended, when so ordered by the President of the United States. . . ."

The vigorous support of the limitation of arms conference in 1921 and the public veto put upon the "big navy" program proposed to Congress in the spring of 1928, demonstrated the opposition on the part of the people of the United States to the initiation of a naval race with any other nation. An increased naval program does not, however, carry with it the same power to influence the psychology of the nation as does a program for general military training. The danger of a big navy is rather in its effect on other nations and in the temptation it offers a government to adopt a policy of aggression. These dangers are also more readily recognized than are those of a steadily growing military-training program and consequently more easily met.

The early determination to keep the United States a non-military nation in the interest of establishing a republican form of government should be borne in mind in considering the following facts of the country's present military establishment as it is developing under the National Defense Act.

The National Defense Act authorizes a regular army of 19,100 officers and 280,000 enlisted men. The actual strength of the army is, however, under the Constitution, controlled by Congress through appropriations for two years. On October 31, 1927, the regular army was composed of 118,597 enlisted men and 11,784 commissioned officers.

Speaking before the House of Representatives on February 3, 1928, on the Army Appropriation Bill, Representative Ross Collins of Mississippi called the attention of the House to the fact that the actual strength of the army was far in excess of these figures. Including the highly efficient National Guard, with the Organized Reserves and R. O. T. C. and the large numbers trained in the Citizens' Military Training Camps, Mr. Collins asserted "we are face to face with the fact that we have a military establishment of over 600,000 men and its gain over 1927 will be in excess of 22,000 officers and men." He continued, commenting on these numbers:

"I hope members of Congress will carefully consider these statements. I think it is necessary that they do so; otherwise a military sentiment will soon grow up in our Republic, whose power and influence will be too large to cope with, a sentiment not in keeping with American traditions and ideals."

The state militia is brought by the National Defense Act more closely than ever before under federal control. Under its terms the "militia" is divided into the "organized militia," now known as the National Guard, and the "unorganized militia," consisting of all the male population between the ages of 18 and 45. The country is divided on a basis of military population into corps areas, each containing at least one division of the National

Guard. The members of the National Guard who were previously paid from state funds, as members of the state militia, are now paid by the War Department, which also supplies them with armament, equipment and uniforms. The instruction of the National Guard is prescribed by the Secretary of War and its discipline is made to conform with that of the regular army. The Adjutant General in each state and territory is appointed by the governor subject to the approval of the Secretary of War and he reports to the Secretary of War.

By providing that the President may "draft into the military service of the United States" any or all members of the National Guard whenever Congress authorizes the use of armed forces in excess of the regular army, the National Defense Act, in contrast to earlier limitation of the purposes for which the militia could be employed, places the members of the militia on the same footing as the regular national forces.

The Act authorizes a National Guard strength of 435,000. The appropriation bill passed in 1928 allowed for 188,000 men. Army officers have already announced that in 1929 the program will be for 190,000 and that immediately after that they will seek to increase the number to 210,521. Forty-eight drills a year are provided for these troops and fifteen days of intensive training in camp. The *per capita* cost of members of the guard to the Federal government is given at $175.53 but actually, according to calculations of members of the Military Affairs Committee of the House, if the pay of army officers detailed to National Guard work and the supplies issued are included, it is nearer $500 for each man.

In order that there may be trained officers ready to take command of the militia, the National Defense Act establishes an Officers' Reserve Corps, and that there may be a source of supply for the Officers' Reserve Corps, provides for a Reserve Officers' Training Corps, commonly known as the R. O. T. C. and for Citizens' Military Training Camps, or C. M. T. C. In order to secure the necessary supplies as well as man power for the army, the National Defense Act provides also for the mobilization of industry under an Assistant Secretary of War. The development of the R. O. T. C. and the mobilization of industry campaign are not under such direct control by Congress, as are the size of the Regular Army and the National Guard, for appropriations made for these activities can be supplemented by the Department from its other funds and no stipulation is made as to the number of officers assigned to this branch of the service or as to the supplies and equipment distributed.

Before the introduction of R. O. T. C. units, the only courses in military training, except those in military schools, were the courses offered in the so-called Land Grant Colleges. Under the law covering the Land Grant Colleges, known as the Morrill Land Grant Act, which was passed in 1862, military training courses must be provided by such colleges, though they need not be compulsory. The States received for the establishment and maintenance of these institutions an allotment of land from the Federal government. The original Morrill Land Grant bill granting this educational aid to the States, which passed both houses of Congress in 1859, contained no provision for military training. This first bill was, however, vetoed by President Buchanan, for reasons of economy and on the question of the constitutional right of Congress to dispose of public lands for educational purposes. The veto had nothing to do with the question of military training in the colleges. In 1862, a war year, the bill was reintroduced and the clause, "including military tactics," was inserted parenthetically by the Senate. The act provides in brief for the

"Maintenance of at least one college where the object shall be, without excluding scientific and classical studies, and including military tactics, to teach such branches of learning as are related to agriculture and the mechanic arts, in such manner as the legislatures of the states may respectively prescribe, in order to promote the liberal and practical education of the industrial classes in the several pursuits and professions in life."

In 1923 the act was officially interpreted to mean that the courses need not be compulsory. This decision was rendered when the War Department protested against the action of the University of Wisconsin, a Land Grant institution, in changing its military training from a compulsory to an elective course. The Secretary of the Interior, whose responsibility it is to see that the Land Grant Colleges live up to the obligations of the Morrill Act, replied to the protest:

". . . . According to the Act approved July 2nd, 1862 (the Morrill Land Grant Act), it is clear that the branches of instruction, which include military tactics, are to be taught 'in such manner as the legislatures of the States may respectively prescribe. . . .'

"Instruction in military tactics is obviously a requirement on the States as are the other branches which are mentioned. It does not appear, however, from the Federal legislation that instruction in military tactics is any more obligatory on the individual student than is instruction in agriculture or mechanic arts."

In a letter to Mr. Walter C. Longstreth, May 14, 1927, the Secretary of the Interior further said:

"A Land-Grant College, by changing its course in military training from a compulsory to an elective course, would not suffer any diminution in the appropriations that it now receives from the United States Government under any of the Acts of Congress providing aid for such institutions. . . ."

MILITARY POLICY   321

The creation of the R. O. T. C. greatly extended military training in universities and colleges and introduced it for the first time into the public high schools of the United States. The junior branch of the R. O. T. C. is organized in high schools and similar educational institutions and gives to boys of fourteen or over who are "physically fit" a three-year course in military drill and tactics.

The importance from the military man's point of view of the Junior R. O. T. C. is indicated in this statement by Major William Faller Edwards in the *Infantry Journal* for October, 1924: "The high school boy in his sophomore year is in his most plastic and enthusiastic stage. He is at the age of hero worship and idealism, unblighted by the cynicism of later youth. Once fairly launched upon enthusiasm for the R. O. T. C., he will most certainly continue it, either at college or elsewhere."

The senior branch of the R. O. T. C. is organized in colleges and includes two courses, the basic course covering the first two years and an advanced course covering the last two years. The classes may be in infantry, artillery, cavalry, medical or other army corps work. Naval R. O. T. C. units were authorized by Congress in 1925 and have been established in some of the large universities. Air units also are now organized at a few of the larger institutions.

No institution other than the Land Grant Colleges is compelled to introduce any military course, and any institution which does introduce such a course may make it elective or compulsory as it sees fit. To secure the introduction of R. O. T. C. courses and to secure attendance at the C. M. T. C's., the War Department is therefore confronted with the necessity of popularizing military training.

In November, 1922, the Secretary of War summoned a

group of college and school officials and leaders of boys' activities to meet in Washington for a conference with army officers. The reason for calling such a conference was indicated by the Secretary of War in his opening and closing addresses, in which he said:

"The War Department finds itself in a peculiar dilemma. While the Federal government is responsible for national defense, for the raising and maintenance of armies and a navy, the physical, moral and mental education of our youth is reserved to the States and to the people. The Federal government finds itself with a large responsibility, but with no jurisdiction over the fundamental factors upon which success ultimately depends. . . ."

. . . .

"If the War Department had the appropriations available for the purpose (promoting a military training program) and were to undertake to do this by itself, criticism would at once be raised that we were doing it entirely for military purposes. Hence, it is necessary for you and others who may be drawn into this matter to work and even to take the lead in making examinations and reports on which future action must be based. We must be practical in this world."

As an inducement to introduce military training courses, the War Department is able to offer a school or college a notable increase in its equipment and its faculty, at the expense of the Federal government. The equipment occasionally reaches a value of as much as half a million dollars. All students receive uniforms, and those in the advanced course of the senior branch covering the last two college years are granted a cash allotment as commutation of subsistence amounting on an average to $200 for the two years. In addition, students receive mileage and advanced students approximately 75 cents a day for attendance at summer camps, or for participation in naval cruises. These opportunities to earn and to save money as well as other attractive features, such as the free use of polo ponies, state rifle matches, and camping expeditions, are advertised by the colleges in their catalogues.

The colleges on their part agree that their students shall devote to these courses a minimum of three academic hours a week for the first two years and five academic hours a week for the last two years; that the courses shall be two-year courses and such as are prescribed by the Secretary of War; that for students entering either of these courses their completion will be necessary for graduation. The advanced course counts toward credit for graduation, the amount of credits to be determined by the college authorities. Students having had military training in a high school R. O. T. C. are not excused from the basic course in college. Boys taking military training in high school and college therefore have a seven-year course in it. The president of a college binds himself in the contract "to promote and further the object for which the training corps is organized," an agreement easily interpreted by officers of the R. O. T. C. to justify protests against any member of the faculty whose teachings are not in complete harmony with the R. O. T. C. program.

The character of the courses given in the various R. O. T. C. units is determined by the Secretary of War, who is authorized by the National Defense Act "to prescribe standard courses in theoretical and practical military training." The claim is frequently made for the courses that they train students for citizenship, but from the above provision in the act it is apparent that such training can be given only in so far as courses in theoretical and practical military training supply it. The Secretary of War in 1921 explained that "the Reserve Officers' Training Corps has a more definite mission than was anticipated at the time of its inception. It was proposed then to prepare young men for an undefined service in the event of an emergency. It is proposed now, under the new law, to prepare young men to be officers in a definitely organized Citizen Army." The object of the course is variously stated. The students themselves in R. O. T. C. manuals are told that "success in battle, whether attack or defense, is the aim of all military training. Everything that you have studied in this course, and everything that you will study in your further course of military training, has that great end in view—success in battle, or victory." In a manual addressed to fathers and mothers the purpose is stated to be "Not to make soldiers out of your boys, but to develop them physically, morally and mentally into the best type of citizens, capable of defending our flag should an emergency arise."

Graduates of R. O. T. C. courses are available for commissions in the Reserve Officers' Corps and practically all graduates receive commissions. The total enrollment in military training courses in schools and colleges for the school year 1926-27 was 108,957. Of this number 70,809 students were in colleges and 38,148 in high schools and military schools. The number of educational institutions offering courses was 223, the schools of a given city being counted as one.

Attendance at a Citizens' Military Training Camp for four seasons also makes a man eligible for a commission in the Reserve Officers' Corps. A link is created between military training camps and educational institutions by scholarships and credits. The Military Training Camp Association in 1925 sent a letter to the presidents of colleges and universities urging them to offer scholarships to the foremost young men at the nearest camps. The same letter called attention to the fact that "many State Boards of Education have already authorized high school credit for attendance at a Citizens' Military Training Camp."

In 1927, 38,597 men and boys were trained at these camps. According to the testimony of officers in charge of this branch of the service, it is hoped ultimately to provide for training 100,000, and to reach 60,000 by 1930 or 1931.

Citizens are also given a training useful to the army and brought into sympathetic touch with military affairs, through the civilian clubs of the National Rifle Association and the national rifle matches held each two years. In the speech of Representative Collins in the Lower House referred to above, the cost of these rifle matches is put at a million dollars. In the 1927 report of the Secretary of War the following statement appears in regard to this particular activity of the army:

"Assistance to the National Rifle Association, civilian rifle clubs, and schools was continued during the year. Every effort is being made to encourage organizations interested in rifle shooting and to withdraw assistance from those not making proper use of the facilities furnished by the War Department."

The War Department is finding an opportunity for popularizing the Reserve Officers' Corps among the members of boys' organizations. Army officers are encouraged to act as scout masters in the Boy Scout troops as a means of interesting the civilian population in the military establishment. Scout troops are entertained at army camps and are reviewed by high ranking officers. The practice has also been started of having American Legion posts adopt Boy Scout troops.

Arguments against military training in schools and colleges are compiled at length in the publications of the Committee on Militarism in Education and other groups.

In 1926 Winthrop D. Lane published a study of the present extent and effect of military training in schools and colleges of the United States, which was presented to the public by a notable group of men and women, among them Dr. John Dewey, Senator William E. Borah, Rabbi Stephen S. Wise, Mrs. Carrie Chapman Catt, Dr. Francis E. Clark, Zona Gale, Dr. Henry M. McCracken, Dr. Mary E. Woolley, Dr. Charles Clayton Morrison, George Foster Peabody, and Francis B. Sayre. These sponsors of the pamphlet urged not only thoughtful consideration of its statements but "action to secure to American youth such educational influences as will make unequivocally for peace."

Military training from the point of view of its effect upon the individual student is condemned by many educators and by students themselves. In March, 1926, 1,783 students at Cornell, out of the student body of 2,074, signed a petition that military training be made optional. A vote among the students of Ohio University showed 1,330 against military training and 465 for it. In compliance with the desires of the students the University of Wisconsin, Pomona College, Boston University, and The College of the City of New York have been added to the forty some universities in which courses in military training are optional. Columbia University and the University of North Carolina have abolished military training.

Aside from the fact that only students "physically fit" are admitted to military training courses and therefore these courses cannot benefit those most in need, the claim that military training is physically beneficial to students is denied by experts in physical education and by army men themselves. Lieut. Colonel Herman J. Koehler, who was in charge of the physical training of officers' training camps during the war, says:

"The use of the musket as a means of physical development for any one, be he man or boy, is more than worthless. It is, in my opinion, positively injurious. I deny absolutely that military drill contains one worthy feature which cannot be duplicated in every well-regulated gymnasium in the country today. A thorough physical training develops all the necessary soldierly qualities to the greatest degree and does it without injury. If we have athletes, we shall never be without soldiers."

Military training as far as the development of character goes is also condemned by educators as tending to contradict the whole modern theory of education for self-discipline and self-government.

Winfred Ernest Garrison, Professor in the University of Chicago, enlarged upon this point in an article in the *Christian Century:*

"Military discipline for boys, just in the proportion in which it succeeds in accomplishing the only thing that it can be reasonably expected to accomplish, conceals its deeper failure. Highly specialized 'obedience, promptness, and orderliness' under highly artificial conditions make a beautiful impression—while those conditions last. The boy learns the proper reaction to the military stimuli which cover his day from reveille to taps. How can anyone tell what he is thinking about inside? How can one judge of his possession or lack of the qualities which will make him an acceptable member of normal society? The teacher-officer is in the position of a physician trying to make a diagnosis of a patient encased in armor. . . .

"The development of the character of a boy is no such simple matter. Military training has no part or place in it. Military training has just one use—preparation for military service."

Sterling G. Brinkley of Emory University has said:

"Blind, unquestioning obedience to orders and authority which the individual has had no voice in deciding and setting up is a quality we do not want. Neither do we want the attitude on the part of our leaders of expecting such obedience."

Speaking before the House Military Affairs Committee, Professor William Bradley Otis from The College of the City of New York, who was sent to France by the Government in 1919 to lecture to the members of the expeditionary force on the terms of the treaty of peace, characterized military training as "utterly foreign to American ideas, utterly counter to American traditions," and said:

"Never before, gentlemen, in American history has the freedom of our higher educational institutions been thus threatened by an Army bureaucracy. It is an insidious influence and has gained headway largely because the American people have not been aware of what is going on."

Supplementing its methods for enlisting the man power of the nation, the War Department is organizing a far-reaching plan for securing supplies for the army. The War Department Business Council, composed of fifteen men representing large business concerns, and an Industrial Preparedness Committee of the National Association of Manufacturers have been formed. The United States has been divided into procurement areas on the basis of the kind of supplies each district can provide, and district headquarters are maintained, the heads of which are usually civilians. Army officers act as executive assistants, and each has a staff of key men, most of whom are executives in manufacturing organizations. Contracts to go into effect upon a declaration of war have been tentatively given, it is stated, to 14,000 plants. In carrying out this program, the army claims it is seriously handicapped by the provision of the National Defense Act which restricts the manufacture of reserve supplies to Government-owned arsenals and factories "unless they can be produced on a more economical basis elsewhere," and it is now seeking authorization to distribute what are called "educational orders" to private firms.

In order to have officers trained in procuring supplies for the army, a plan has recently been worked out, although funds have not yet been provided, for the organization in educational institutions of "munitions battalions" in accordance with which college seniors will be enlisted in the army for 18 months. For three months before and 6 months after their senior year they will be given an intensive course in soldiering and in procurement problems. During their final college year they will be free from military duties, will not be in uniform and will receive their tuition free and the regular allowance of enlisted men when away from troops. It is believed that when men who have had such training enter industry they "will always think of industry in relation to the army's problems."

Obviously to keep up such activities as these it is necessary to have not only widespread interest and support, but steadily increasing appropriations. Therefore the army makes every effort to have its point of view presented to the public as frequently as possible in the press and before social and business organizations and at the same time seeks to prevent the expression of any criticism likely to discourage appropriations. What army officials cannot do themselves along these lines members of the Reserve Officers' Corps frequently do through their membership and influence in a great variety of civilian organizations. How great this influence of the Reserve Officers' Corps may be and to what extent it is being utilized to promote the military program is indicated by the two statements that follow.

The Chairman of the Sub-Committee on Military Appropriations of the House Committee on Military Affairs, said to the president of the Reserve Officers' Association when he appeared before the committee in 1927 to ask for larger appropriations:

"I very strenuously object to the system which is apparently in vogue of, year after year, bringing outside pressure to bear on this committee for the purpose of increasing the appropriations for those items. We are glad to have you appear in your official capacity to give us any information or to make any statement that you care to make to us but as a member of the committee, I do object to the systematic pressure that is brought upon this committee and upon Members of Congress year after year for this purpose. I think it sets a very bad precedent, and one that is liable to grow into a very vicious system if it is permitted to continue."

The Sub-Committee on Appropriations for the Navy, in its report to the House of Representatives in the spring of 1927, said:

"The committee believes that the attention of the House should be called to the reserve situation generally. That the reserves have a necessary and important place in our scheme of national defense there is no question. That there should be a limit, however, there should be no question. To keep it within the proper limits under existing laws seems to fall to the lot of this committee, which should not be. Unless it is watched and closely watched it will expand to the point where we will have accomplished by indirection what we have always striven to avoid directly, and that is the establishment of a large force in this country possessing military views and tendencies which will outnumber and outweigh in voice our regular establishments. This is not believed to be an overstatement of what may be reasonably expected if we should fail to watch the situation closely."

The *Army and Navy Register* of November 10, 1923, carried several suggestions from an army officer to army officers, indicating how the army enlists the support of reserve officers and civilians:

"Become personally acquainted with every reserve officer assigned to the regiment,—know them, their business relations and their personal interests.

"Promote your acquaintance with the leading professional and business men of the community—make as many personal friends as possible. One of the means open for this is through the Chamber of Commerce and the leading business clubs.

"Become a member of business clubs which have weekly luncheons—Rotary and Kiwanis. After a while you may be able to have a regular military committee included in their organization. In any event whenever things of a military nature come up for discussion you are pretty sure to be consulted.

"Enter into the social life of the community and become an active member of the Country Club. A reasonable amount of time spent on the golf links is not wasted. Many opportunities will here be found to talk national defense to influential men at a time when they will listen.

"Take an active part in the community Boy Scout movement. If there are no Boy Scouts, do what you can to get the movement under way.

"Cultivate the press. Furnish news items of a personal and local nature built around the name and address of members of the regiment. This is always news and will generally get by. Occasionally you will have an opportunity to prepare an editorial and here is where you can explain the principles of national defense."

In its system of Civilian Aides who are appointed for each State, but who report directly to the Secretary of War, the War Department has established a further close connection with civilian life. There have also recently been indications that the army is coöperating directly with the moving picture industry, by supplying "supers" from the troops, and tanks and other armaments, and in return having military activities widely advertised. Mr. Will Hays, president of the largest moving picture organization in the country, has been made a colonel in the Reserve Officers' Corps, under the Adjutant General's office.

The War Department has also very successfully enlisted the assistance of other departments of the Government in promoting its campaigns, as for instance the Post Office Department which has authorized a cancellation stamp carrying the slogan, "Let's go! Military Training Camps," which has attracted attention in foreign countries and led to protests from many American citizens who desire to see this country build up international goodwill, and feel that such a slogan misrepresents to other nations its true spirit.

A consideration of the above statements and extracts, which give a partial picture of the wholesale preparation which modern warfare calls for, should make it clear that, first, if states propose to continue to carry on wars they must be prepared to be completely absorbed in that undertaking; second, in the present contest between the old idea of organization for war and the new idea of organization for peace, the forces working for peace need on their side a government department officially and persistently presenting, with the prestige and power of the government behind it, the fact that under present conditions peace is a national and world necessity.

The dangers apprehended from the present policy and program of the military establishment of the country have to do first with their effect on the development of the individual young men undergoing military training, and second with their effect upon the traditional governmental policies of this country. A warning against the danger to the fundamental principles of democratic government in a program which leads to military influence in civilian fields of activity, was voiced by President Coolidge in an address to the American Legion in 1925:

"Whenever military powers start to dictate to civil authorities, by whatsoever means adopted, the liberties of the country are beginning to end."

An impressive protest against the influence of military men appeared in an editorial in the *Advocate of Peace* for December, 1927, which concluded, "The welfare of States is best promoted under civilian control. It is not the business of our military experts to fix, to criticize, or to direct through the public press or other agency of propaganda the course of our public policy." The argument that increased military preparedness is the way to protect the country against foreign foes was succinctly answered by President Coolidge in a speech at the graduation exercises of the United States Naval Academy in June, 1925, when he said:

"I am not unfamiliar with the claim that if only we had a sufficient military establishment no one would ever molest us. I know of no nation in history that has ever been able to attain that position. I see no reason to expect that we could be the exception."

The facts and statements cited in this chapter lead inevitably to the question, Is it possible to be "prepared" for war and at the same time maintain the democratic institutions of this nation? The fundamental issue is not whether certain army officers are attempting to militarize the nation; the fundamental issue is the incompatibility of the demands of the war system with the needs and traditions of democratic government.

CHAPTER XIX

THE MONROE DOCTRINE

The conviction of both Latin Americans and many citizens of this country that the policies of recent administrations have extended and distorted the original purpose of the Monroe Doctrine, coupled with the insistence of the United States, as expressed in the Covenant of the League of Nations and in the World Court reservations, that no question concerning the doctrine shall be submitted for decision to any international body or to any other nation, is creating a persistent demand for a clear definition by the Government of the United States of its meaning and application. Uncertainty as to the implications of the Monroe Doctrine leads undoubtedly to the acceptance of policies toward Latin American states which would otherwise be more carefully considered by the citizens of this country.

The original declaration of the doctrine came as the direct result of a threat of European intervention to restore to Spain her revolted colonies in the Western Hemisphere. An effort to restore them was in line with the accepted policy of Europe at that time, which was to put down revolution, wherever it occurred, in the interests of all established monarchical governments. A change of government within a state was considered not a domestic but an international affair. The United States had recognized the independence of the revolted Spanish colonies immediately after the ratification of the treaty with Spain for the transfer of the Floridas. Great Britain, because of trade relations which she had developed with the newly independent states, was opposed to their restoration to Spain, although she had not recognized their independence, and approached the United States with the idea of arriving at an understanding with regard to the Spanish-American colonies and then making a clear statement to the rest of the world of the principles agreed upon.

At about this time Russian traders coming south from Alaska had established a fort in what is now California. John Quincy Adams, as Secretary of State, on July 17, 1823, informed the Russian Minister that "we would contest the right of Russia to any territorial establishment on this continent and that we should assume distinctly the principle that the American continents are no longer subjects for any European colonial establishments." On December 2, 1823, President Monroe, in his annual message to Congress, described the Russian situation, stating that the matter was being handled successfully in the ordinary diplomatic way, and adding:

"The occasion has been judged proper for asserting, as a principle in which the rights and interests of the United States are involved, that the American continents, by the free and independent condition which they have assumed and maintain, are henceforth not to be considered as subjects for future colonization by any European powers."

Joined with this statement of the non-colonization principle was a definition of the attitude the United States would assume in case of an attempt to restore the revolting American colonies to the Spanish Crown:

"We should consider any attempt on their part to extend their system to any portion of this hemisphere as dangerous to our peace and safety. With the existing colonies or dependencies of any European power we have not interfered and shall not interfere. But with the governments who have declared their independence and have maintained it, and whose independence we have on great consideration and on just principles acknowledged, we could not view any interposition for the purpose of oppressing them or controlling in any other manner their destiny, by any European power, in any other light than as the manifestation of an unfriendly disposition toward the United States."

At the time, the power of this declaration, although it was made by the United States alone and included the non-colonization principle which had not been suggested by Great Britain and which was contrary to its views, rested in large part upon the known attitude of Great Britain toward a restoration of the Spanish colonies.

In 1870 the doctrine was further defined when President Grant in urging the annexation of Santo Domingo gave expression to a corollary which had for some time been recognized:

"The doctrine promulgated by President Monroe has been adhered to by all political parties, and I now deem it proper to assert the equally important principle that hereafter no territory on this continent shall be regarded as subject to transfer to a European power."

During the 19th century all applications of the Monroe Doctrine had to do with the protection of the American continents against European invasion, or contact.

As late as 1901 Theodore Roosevelt, as President, said of the Monroe Doctrine in a message to Congress:

"This doctrine has nothing to do with the commercial relations of any American power, save that it in truth allows each of them to form such as it desires. In other words, it is really a guarantee of the commercial independence of the Americas. We do not ask under this doctrine for any exclusive commercial dealings with any other American state. We do not guarantee any state against punishment if it misconducts

THE MONROE DOCTRINE

itself, provided that punishment does not take the form of the acquisition of territory by any non-American power."

In 1902, in connection with the situation which developed out of the foreign indebtedness of Venezuela and involved the threatened intervention of the powers, Dr. Luis Drago, Minister of Foreign Affairs of Argentina, announced what has since been known as the Drago Doctrine:

"The public debt of an American state cannot occasion armed intervention or even the actual occupation of the territory of American nations by a European Power."

Secretary of State John Hay replied to this pronouncement by quoting Roosevelt's statement that the United States did not guarantee any state against punishment for misconduct provided that punishment did not take the form of the acquisition of territory by a non-American Power. In 1904, however, President Roosevelt stated in discussing the problem arising out of the foreign debts of Santo Domingo:

"Chronic wrongdoing or an impotence which results in the general loosening of the ties of civilized society may in America, as elsewhere, ultimately require intervention by some civilized nation, and in the Western Hemisphere the adherence of the United States to the Monroe Doctrine may force the United States, however reluctantly, in flagrant cases of wrongdoing or impotence, to the exercise of an international police power."

From this time to the present—a period during which the investments of American citizens in Latin America have grown to enormous proportions—Latin American states claim that the United States government has distorted the Monroe Doctrine to suit its own purposes. Felipe Barreda, Professor of Pan American History in San Marcos University, Lima, Peru, analyzes recent applications of the doctrine in *Current History* for March, 1927:

"A study of the various cases of the modern interpretation and application of the doctrine in the last twenty years makes it clear that it has been employed in the following ways, typical of the new conception which has superseded Monroe's own formulation of his ideas:

(1) In cases of internal political strife or revolution in Latin American countries the Government of the United States assumes the right to declare which is the constitutional party to be supported by the military and naval power of the United States. (First intervention in Nicaragua, 1912.)

(2) When the conclusion is reached that a Latin American country is not able to maintain an independent and competent government to keep order and discharge its international obligations, the United States assumes the right to take political and economic control of such country. (Intervention in Haiti, 1915.)

(3) The United States assumes the right to intervene in the political government and economic administration of a debtor nation in Latin America to enforce and secure the cancellation of public debts. (Santo Domingo, 1916.)

(4) The United States Government assumes the right to intervene in the internal affairs of the Latin American countries, when, in its opinion, political or economic ideas may endanger the private interests of American citizens. (The controversy with Nicaragua and Mexico.)

Dr. Samuel Guy Inman in the same issue of *Current History* suggests a further reason for Latin American suspicion of the policies of this country in the extension of the "practice of non-recognition of Latin American Governments, announced by President Wilson as applying to governments obtaining power through revolution, to non-recognition when a government enforces laws regarded as unfavorable to the citizens of the United States." The strong feeling of Latin Americans against the fixed attitude of the United States that the definition, interpretation and application of the Monroe Doctrine are its exclusive concern, is also expressed by Professor Barreda. This attitude was first definitely proclaimed by the demand of the United States for the insertion in the Covenant of the League of Nations of Article 21:

"Nothing in this Covenant shall be deemed to affect the validity of international agreements, such as treaties of arbitration or regional understandings like the Monroe Doctrine, for securing the maintenance of peace."

In 1923, the centennial year of the Monroe Doctrine, in an address before the American Bar Association on August 30, and later in an address in Philadelphia under the auspices of the American Academy of Political and Social Science, on November 30, Secretary of State Hughes recognized the suspicion with which the Monroe Doctrine is at present regarded in many Central and South American states and attempted to correct misunderstandings as to the scope and purpose of the doctrine.

"The policy of the Monroe Doctrine," he said, "does not infringe upon the independence and sovereignty of other American states. Misconception upon this point is the only disturbing influence in our relations with Latin American states. . . ."

The definition of the Monroe Doctrine, as given by Mr. Hughes in identical language in both addresses, was the following:

"Properly understood, it is opposed (1) to any non-American action encroaching upon the political independence of American states under any guise, and (2) to the acquisition in any manner of the control of additional territory in this hemisphere by any non-American power."

In both addresses he insisted with emphasis that "the Monroe Doctrine is not a policy of aggression; it is a policy of self-defense," that it does not infringe upon the sovereignty of other American states, and "does not attempt to establish a protectorate" over them; and that, as it is "distinctively the policy of the United States, the Government of the United States reserves to itself its definition, interpretation and application." In regard to the Caribbean region he said further:

"So far as the region of the Caribbean Sea is concerned, it may be said that if we had no Monroe Doctrine we should have to create one. . . . What has taken place of late years in the region of the Carribbean has given rise to much confusion of thought and misapprehension of purpose. As I have said, the Monroe Doctrine as a particular declaration in no way exhausts American right or policy; the United States has rights and obligations which that doctrine does not define. And in the unsettled condition of certain countries in the region of the Caribbean it has been necessary to assert these rights and obligations as well as the limited principles of the Monroe Doctrine. . . .

"We have established a waterway between the Atlantic and Pacific Oceans—the Panama Canal. Apart from obvious commercial considerations the adequate protection of this canal— its complete immunity from any adverse control—is essential to our peace and security. We could not afford to take any different position with respect to any other waterway that may be built between the Atlantic and Pacific Oceans. Disturbances in the Caribbean region are therefore of special interest to us not for the purpose of seeking control over others, but of being assured that our own safety is free from menace. . . ."

The most definite effort on the part of Latin American states to combat recent developments in the Latin-

American policies of the United States, was made at the Sixth Pan American Conference in Havana, when certain Latin American delegates attempted to secure the adoption of the principle of non-intervention. The United States delegation succeeded in postponing any far-reaching discussion of this subject until the next Pan American Congress which will not meet until 1933. But, as the *Sun* of Baltimore, from which the following editorial is quoted, points out, consideration of the right of intervention is bound to take place at the Pan American Conference on Conciliation and Arbitration agreed upon at Havana and scheduled to meet in Washington in December, 1928:

"For the purpose of the scheduled conference (of conciliation and arbitration) is to reduce to systematic form, preliminary to embodiment in treaties, such matters as the American republics are willing to arbitrate with each other. In the case of the weaker Latin American nations this will probably mean virtually every cause of international dispute, for they have everything to lose by resisting the impartial judgment of a neutral tribunal. In the case of the United States, however, every issue submitted to arbitration vis-à-vis a country like Haiti will be a concession from our previous position, which in the case of our smaller neighbors has come to be one of virtual dictation. Whether these concessions can be of real practical value without severely limiting our intervention policy as recently practiced remains to be seen.

"Viewed in this light . . . it will be realized that we have practically declared for a new Latin American policy and a more liberal definition of the Monroe Doctrine. We avoid any pledge never to intervene, which might open the road for other nations to land their troops in Central America. But we also tacitly abandon the irritating thesis that we are of divine right the policeman of the New World."

CHAPTER XX

IMPERIALISM

The ill-defined term imperialism is used to describe a group of policies by which "backward" countries are brought under the control of the technically more advanced nations.

The reasons for the establishment of such control have been the desire, chiefly on the part of industrialized nations, for access to raw materials necessary to industry and to national defense, such as oil, coal and iron; for markets for manufactured products; for opportunities for the profitable investment of surplus capital; for outlets for possible surplus population; for coaling stations for merchant ships and warships; and for political prestige.

To achieve these objects, ten nations of the world have brought under their domination more than one-half of the total land surface of the earth and more than one billion alien people. The nations exercising this control over the destinies of the human race are, in the order of the geographical extent of the countries they dominate, Great Britain, Russia, France, Portugal, Belgium, the United States, Holland, Italy, Spain, and Japan. If this list were arranged according to the population of the territories controlled, the United States would stand seventh in the list; if according to the amount of commerce carried on, the United States would stand fifth.

The figures given above are from "Imperialism and World Politics," by Professor Parker T. Moon of Columbia University, the most comprehensive recent study of the problem of imperialism.

In the 70's and 80's of the 19th century, because of the general adoption of factory production which resulted in many nations' having a surplus of manufactured articles to be disposed of abroad, and the erection of tariff barriers against competitors, colonial markets which could be controlled by export and import duties for the benefit of the home country became necessary. At the same time the development of rapid communication made economic penetration and military control of remote backward countries possible. The accumulation in the more developed and industrialized nations of surplus capital led to a demand for opportunities for investment in countries where capital was scarcer and development more profitable, and this in turn to the demand that stable governments be maintained in these regions. The further fact that tropical products have become necessary in the manufacture of many modern necessities and that the native population of tropical countries does not ordinarily supply either a stable government or efficient workers, have served as further reasons for the assumption by a few nations of control throughout large territories.

There is obviously no easy solution to the problem to which imperialism has so far been the answer. The resources of the undeveloped countries are needed and to fail to bring them into use is to delay economic and social progress. If, however, in the present economically interdependent world, peace is the first requisite for prosperity, some other method must be found for their development. Imperialism carries a double threat of war. Exploiting, or at best imposing alien control and alien modes of living upon increasing areas of the earth rouses the resentment and ill will of millions of people; among other things defeating the purpose of imperialism by preventing full development of international trade. The more immediate war danger lies in the rivalry of imperialistic powers. By many in every country the rivalry of the great powers for control of the economic resources of the earth is held to make war inevitable. The financial interests of England and the United States are declared to be engaged in a struggle for world mastery, and the determined efforts of both to obtain control of the earth's supply of oil, it is frequently stated, can have but one outcome,—war. If allowed to pursue its customary course to its conclusion, such rivalry certainly would end in war. But new considerations have entered into the situation. An economic advantage cannot today be won by means of war. Prosperity is primarily dependent upon peace. Recognition of war as an assault upon the stability of civilization makes it incumbent upon governments to seek some modification of policies that imply war and some method of rational adjustment of the economic interests of their citizens.

In the United States imperialistic policies have met with an opposition which they have not encountered in other countries, because they have been generally felt to be contrary to the principles upon which this government was founded. It is true that all through the history of the United States there have been certain groups ambitious to extend its territory, and it is also true that in the methods by which this has been accomplished, particularly in the case of the Mexican War, there is much that is morally indefensible. Nevertheless, the United States has recognized in theory and repeatedly insisted upon the right of every nation to self-determination, so that it has never entered wholeheartedly or unchecked by the dissent of its own citizens upon imperialistic adventures. Washington and Franklin alike protested against such policies as Europe had pursued in acquiring territory and increasing trade. Washington urged "timely

IMPERIALISM

provisions, to guard against those acts of our own citizens which might tend to disturb peace with other nations, and to put ourselves in a condition to give that satisfaction to foreign nations which we may sometimes have occasion to require of them." He "particularly recommended" prevention of "those aggressions by our citizens on the territory of other nations, which, furnishing just subject of complaint, might endanger our peace with them. . . . Peace with all the world is my sincere wish. I am sure it is our true policy."

To Franklin it seemed "that neither the obtaining nor retaining of any trade, how valuable soever, is an object for which men may justly spill each other's blood; that the true and sure means of extending and securing commerce is the goodness and cheapness of commodities; and that the profit of no trade can ever be equal to the expense of compelling it, and of holding it by fleets and armies. . . . If statesmen had a little more arithmetic or were more accustomed to calculation, wars would be much less frequent."

Recently, however, the charge of imperialism is persistently made against the United States. It is based chiefly on the relations of this government with the countries of the Caribbean area, on its delay in granting promised independence to the Philippine Islands, on the method pursued in the annexation of Hawaii, and on the government's policies, generally covered by the Monroe Doctrine, in regard to the countries of South America.

Criticism of the Latin American policies of the United States is voiced not only by laymen but sometimes by our own government officials. In general, Democrats criticize "imperialistic" activities carried out by Republican administrations and the Republicans similar policies of the Democrats. Former Secretary of State Hughes, in an address at Amherst in 1924, declared the criticism of this government's occupation of Santo Domingo "just," and added that it was the belief of many that the occupation would never have occurred "had President Wilson had the opportunity or time . . . to become fully cognizant of the situation existing in the Dominican Republic." In a campaign speech before his election President Harding, speaking of Haiti, said,

"I will not empower an Assistant Secretary of the Navy to draft a constitution for helpless neighbors in the West Indies and jam it down their throats at the points of bayonets borne by United States Marines, nor will I misuse the power of the Executive to cover with a veil of secrecy repeated acts of unwarranted interference in the domestic affairs of the little republics of the Western Hemisphere, such as in the last few years have not only made enemies of those who should be our friends, but have rightfully discredited our country as their trusted neighbor."

President Cleveland publicly condemned the preliminary steps leading to this country's annexation of Hawaii, and the House of Representatives passed a resolution condemning the diplomatic representative of this country for "illegally aiding in overthrowing the constitutional government of the Hawaiian islands."

Neither the extent of United States control over other countries nor the methods by which it exercises that control are generally known to the citizens of this country. The whole situation came in for fuller and more open discussion in the press in connection with the Sixth Pan American Conference, at Havana, in 1928, than it ever had before. The following extracts from a syndicated dispatch from Paris to American papers at the opening of the Havana Conference indicated the general line of criticism:

"The attention of European statesmen is now centered on Havana. The issue is believed here to be whether or not the

IMPERIALISM

Latin American states will be able to resist encroachments of 'United States imperialism.' The matter is conceived to be one of world equilibrium. Asia also is concerned for Latin America is thought to sympathize with Asia on the race issue."

Professor Moon gives the following table indicating the regions over which today the control of the United States extends:

	Area (Square Miles)	Population	Commerce
Outlying Territories			
Alaska	590,884	60,000	$ 88,905,000
Hawaii	6,449	307,000	188,541,000
Dependencies			
Philippine Islands	115,026	11,076,000	243,356,000
Porto Rico	3,435	1,347,000	172,478,000
Virgin Islands	132	26,000	2,559,000
Samoa	58	8,000	294,000
Guam	210	13,000	967,000
Wake and Midway Is.	29		
Leased Territory			
Panama Canal Zone Guantanamo, Fonseca Bay, Corn Island	527	27,000	
Total Possessions	716,750	12,864,000	$ 697,100,000
Nominally Independent Dependencies			
Cuba	44,164	3,369,000	$ 724,595,000
Haiti	11,072	2,045,000	28,872,000
Dominican Republic	19,325	897,000	51,843,000
Panama	33,667	443,000	16,250,000
Nicaragua	49,200	638,000	21,797,000
Liberia	36,834	1,500,000	2,528,000
Total nominally independent dependencies.	194,262	8,892,000	$ 845,885,000
Grand total	911,012	21,756,000	$1,542,985,000

The belief on the part of many Americans that the policies of recent administrations toward Latin America are contrary to the democratic principles and traditions of this country; the resentment on the part of Latin

American countries toward these policies, affecting not only political but commercial relations; and the distrust to which they are giving rise in Europe, make it imperative for citizens of the United States to give diligent consideration to the whole situation. A fair understanding of what this government has done and is trying to do, of the good and the evil results of its domination of other countries, can be gotten only from a study in each instance of a detailed statement of facts. Books which afford a basis for such study are listed in the bibliography.

Conflicting claims are made as to the purposes for which United States control of neighboring countries has been established. On the one hand, the purpose of the United States is declared to have been to maintain stable governments and make development possible, largely for the sake of their own people, and to provide protection for the lives and property of foreigners which European governments would otherwise take steps to provide. By others, the purpose of the control is believed to be the economic advantage of small groups of citizens of the United States, while by an increasing number of well-informed students of the Caribbean situation political and military purposes are held to play a greater part than "dollar diplomacy." Protection of the Panama Canal probably mainly accounts for the insistence of this government upon a general control of conditions in the Caribbean area.

The methods by which the United States has established its control vary in the different countries.

When Cuba, over which a protectorate was secured as a result of the Spanish American War, was granted political independence, a considerable degree of control was kept under the provisions of the Platt Amendment. This "amendment," so called because it was originally adopted in 1901 as a rider on the Army Appropriation Bill, is incorporated in the Cuban constitution and in a permanent treaty with the United States. Under it

"The government of Cuba consents that the United States may exercise the right to intervene for the preservation of Cuban independence, the maintenance of a government adequate for the protection of life, property, and individual liberty...."

In addition, Cuba is prohibited from incurring any debts which her current revenues cannot meet, and grants the United States land necessary for coaling and naval stations.

In the case of Haiti, Santo Domingo and Nicaragua, United States control has been secured through actual military occupation by marines, whose officers have gone so far as to bring about the dissolution of a national assembly which refused to grant certain investment privileges desired by foreign citizens.

In other cases threats of force, such as the mere presence of warships in nearby waters, have been enough to secure the carrying out of policies favored by the United States. In still others, notably in the case of Mexico, refusal of recognition to governments whose policies were not in accord with those of the United States has served the same purpose.

Several countries are subject to the indirect control of the United States under the terms of loans made in this country. If a country in which the government is subject to frequent change and in which the financial policies are somewhat erratic, desires to negotiate a loan, it is necessary for it to grant the interests making the loan direct control of some part of its financial assets. For one of the less well-established Latin American countries, therefore, to negotiate a loan in a European country would lead to a situation which under the Monroe Doctrine the United States will not tolerate. This government consequently encourages loans by American banks, and political and financial interests are led into close cooperation in maintaining security and encouraging policies in conformity with those of the United States.

Financial control is exercised in various ways. In some instances "commissions of three," two of the commissioners being citizens of the United States chosen by the banking interests, are appointed for the general control of the borrowing country's economic policy. Several Latin American governments employ citizens of the United States as financial advisers. In other cases representatives of the interests making the loan are put in charge of the collection of customs. Only in cases of actual occupation by the military forces of the United States are these officials appointed directly by the government of the United States.

In the case of Salvador, under the terms of a loan made by a banking firm of the United States, any dispute regarding the payment of the loan, for which 70% of the country's custom revenues were pledged to the United States creditors, was to be referred to the Chief Justice of the Supreme Court of the United States. The interpretation put upon this provision by banking interests is indicated in the following statement from an advertising circular which was issued by a firm of investment bankers:

"It is simply not thinkable that, after a Federal Judge has decided any question or dispute between the bond holders and the Salvador Government, the United States Government should not take the necessary steps to sustain such decision. There is a precedent in a dispute between Costa Rica and Panama, in which a warship was sent to carry out the verdict of the arbitrators."

The State Department vigorously objected to the issuance of the above statement.

In March, 1922, the State Department issued a circular to American bankers expressing the hope that in view of the possible international interests involved, "American bankers will inform the Department of State of contemplated loan transactions, so that an opportunity may be afforded to express an objection." The circular stresses the fact that the Department of State "will not pass upon the merits of foreign loans as business propositions, nor assume any responsibility whatever in connection with loan transactions." Yet the failure of the State Department to object to a loan has been looked upon in many instances as in a measure committing this government to protect investors, and the question has been raised as to whether this policy may not increase seriously the dangers from foreign investments. The policy has also been severely criticized as an illegal assumption of power on the part of the State Department, and as an attempt to use the financial power of this country for carrying out political purposes. Former Secretary of the Treasury Carter Glass of Virginia, in a statement quoted in the *New York Times* of October 14, 1927, said: "Private business has no right to ask or to receive the imprimatur of the Government on its credit transactions, nor should foreign governments be required to get the permission of our State Department to engage in the ordinary commerce of credits or commodities with American business concerns. Such concerns should be left to conduct their business on their own responsibility and at their own risk."

The constant danger of war involved in a close relation between financial and political interests is obvious. In an attempt to do away with this threat to peace and for the protection of weaker nations, the Brazilian jurist, Calvo, formulated a theory in which he maintained that investors in foreign countries had no right to expect their governments to intervene with either military force or diplomatic action which must sooner or later lead to military force, but that foreigners should have the same status as citizens and have the same legal protection for life and property. In 1890, at the first Pan American Conference, the Latin American countries voted for a resolution endorsing this doctrine. The delegates from the United States opposed it. Their objection was that foreigners do not have the political power to protect their interests which citizens have, and that if they could not look to their own government for protection they would inevitably seek by illegal means to interfere in local politics. In several Latin American countries contracts now include a clause by which a foreign investor "renounces all right to prefer a diplomatic claim in regard to obligations derived from the contract." The United States has insisted, however, upon the doctrine laid down by Secretary of State Bayard in 1888:

"This Government cannot admit that its citizens can, merely by making contracts with foreign powers, or by other methods, not amounting to an act of expatriation, or a deliberate abandonment of American citizenship, destroy their dependence upon it or its obligations to protect them in case of a denial of justice."

There is no doubt that the time has come for a reconsideration of this entire question. Former Secretary of Commerce Hoover is quoted by Norman Hapgood in his *News Letter* as having said, "The time for making war to protect foreign investments has passed." The reaction of the press and the public to the threat of war with Mexico in the winter of 1926 and 1927 over that country's oil-land laws, indicated the strength of public feeling on this subject.

The present United States Ambassador to Mexico, Mr.

IMPERIALISM

Dwight W. Morrow, in the *New York Evening Post* of September 27, 1927, is quoted as saying:

"Differences of opinion between states are the incidents of international life. The acknowledgment of the possibility of such differences is the effective way of preventing serious consequences arising therefrom. . . .

"Entirely apart from the immorality of putting human lives to the hazard of modern war where the sole issue is a pecuniary claim, there is a conclusive practical reason against such a course, in that war, in the great majority of cases, does not and cannot accomplish the desired result."

Even among investors themselves there is apparently an increased number who do not feel they are entitled to ask soldiers, enlisted for the defense of the nation, to risk their lives in order to protect the economic interests of individual citizens. William Kent of California gave expression to this point of view in a letter to President Taft when war threatened with Mexico in 1912:

"As one interested in Mexican investments, I wish to commend in the highest terms your policy of non-interference. Every American dollar and every American life in Mexico is there subject to the risk of the possessor. If I would not myself go to Mexico to risk my life in defense of my property interests, I would be no less than a murderer to ask that the men in our army assume such a risk."

In 1925 the Women's International League for Peace and Freedom secured the introduction in Congress of a resolution, since reintroduced at each session, calling upon the President to direct the various departments of the Government to refrain, without authorization from Congress, from engaging the responsibility of the Government to supervise the fulfillment of financial arrangements between citizens of the United States and foreign governments or committing the Government to any form of military intervention to compel the observance of alleged obligations on the part of foreign governments. Various other proposals have recently been made to prevent governments from becoming involved in military action through the activities of foreign investors. William Culbertson, former member of the Tariff Commission, in his book, "International Economic Policies," has suggested that international judicial machinery be established through which investors may as individuals, not as representatives of any special country, secure adjustment of any discriminatory treatment.

Another proposal suggests an international commerce commission somewhat like the Interstate Commerce Commission, with international boards of reference, which shall have the power to pass on concessions when originally proposed in order to protect the interests of backward peoples and to insure fair competition and coöperation between the different national groups concerned.

Several tendencies can be pointed to as indicating effort on the part of governments to solve the problems which have given rise to the dangers of imperialism. Sir Arthur Salter, Director of the Economic and Financial Section of the League of Nations, in an article in the *Yale Review* for July, 1925, calls attention in this connection to the fact that under the Covenant of the League of Nations countries entrusted with the administration of mandated areas are to "secure equal opportunities for the trade and commerce of other members of the League . . . a very significant limitation of the power of sovereignty in the sphere of economic competition."

With special regard to American problems, Mr. Hughes, when Secretary of State, in a speech before the Canadian Bar Association in 1923, urged the possibility of arranging for commissions of inquiry to advise legislative bodies as to the interests of other states affected by their legislation. He said:

"In relation to domestic questions which have an international bearing, it would be quite possible to make more frequent use of this method, not to decide but to inform, not to arbitrate but to investigate, to find the facts and to report to the governments of the states represented the effect of measures and where injury would lie."

He went on to recommend a permanent commission to which would automatically be referred

"for examination and report as to the facts, questions arising as to the bearing of action by either government upon the interests of the other, to the end that each reasonably protecting its own interests would be so advised that it would avoid action inflicting unnecessary injury upon its neighbor."

Prof. Charles Cheney Hyde of Columbia University, referring to this proposal of Mr. Hughes in an article in *The Annals of the American Academy of Political and Social Science,* for July, 1927, suggests the development of this proposed plan to meet the needs of Mexico and the United States.

"It is believed that there exists what may roughly be termed an American-Mexican interest—a certain solidarity of economic interest derived from geographical propinquity, interchange of population and financial investment. Both nations may well give fresh thought to the extent and reality of the community of interest by which they are bound, and to the harm which each must sustain from any conduct detrimental to that interest. . . . Above all, both need to consider whether the present situation does not justify and possibly demand the employment of a joint high commission consecrated to the task of safeguarding their community of interest, and alert to warn both governments whenever the conduct of either threatens to weaken it."

Other suggestions for the solution of the problems arising out of the relationships between the states of the American continents are made by Professor Moon. Among them, the substitution of a mutual guarantee for the Monroe Doctrine; the substitution of Pan American intervention for United States intervention; and of international receiverships for United States financial protectorates.

Many students of American life agree that the United States has drifted into imperialism scarcely realizing the implications of its policies. On the whole its policy has been, it is said, "an unconscious, an absentminded sort of imperialism."

Professor John W. Dewey, in an article in *Mexican Life,* for September, 1927, points out the danger of this very unconsciousness on the part of the public of the growth of imperialistic policies in the government:

"Given, on one hand, a nation that has capital and technical skill, engineering and financial, to export, plus manufacturers in need of raw material, especially iron and oil, and, on the other hand, an industrially backward country with large natural resources . . . and it does not require intention or desire to involve the first nation in imperialistic policies. . . .

"Imperialism is a result, not a purpose or plan. It can be prevented only by regulating the conditions out of which it proceeds. And one of the things which most stands in the way of taking regulatory measures is precisely the consciousness on the part of the public that it is innocent of imperialistic desires. . . ."

Recent discussions in the press indicate a growing awareness on the part of the public of the discrepancy between theory and fact in the government's foreign policy. It is also encouraging to realize that whatever the practice of this country, its avowed opposition to the principles of imperialism and the energetic repudiation by its responsible statesmen of any imperialistic purposes have strengthened the forces which will ultimately compel the abandonment of policies that involve exploitation, unfair domination, and international rivalry threatening the peace of the world. General recognition of the futility of war as a means of assuring economic progress will hasten the abandonment of economic policies based upon it. The public must at the same time be ready to accept a modification of shortsighted national aspirations in the interest of true national welfare, and also the development of international agencies of adjustment.

CHAPTER XXI

WORLD POPULATION AND THE IMMIGRATION POLICY OF THE UNITED STATES

THE direct bearing of population problems upon international relations is leading to an organized attempt to find out what the facts of world population are.

The International Labor Organization, in accordance with a provision in the preamble of the Treaty of Versailles which gives it supervision over the interests of immigrants, is steadily collecting at its Geneva office information on this subject which may facilitate understanding and general discussion.

The first World Population Conference ever held took place in Geneva from August 30 to September 3, 1927. The Conference, which was purely scientific in its nature, revealed the extreme complexity of the population question and the need for further study. A permanent International Union of Population was therefore organized. The committee of scientists chosen to draw up a plan of work included from the United States Dr. William Welch, Dr. E. M. East and Dr. Raymond Pearl. The subjects discussed at the conference indicate the nature of the general problem. They were biology of population growth, optimum population, population and food supply, effects on race of differential birth rate, fertility and sterility in relation to population, migration and its control. In connection with the last subject two important questions arose: Have peoples a natural right to reproduce beyond their economic resources and then demand the soil of others? Have peoples a natural right to conserve soil of which they are not making use and from which they cannot produce the maximum?

Recent figures and estimates on world population are to be found in an article by Dr. Imre Ferenczi in the *Review of Nations* for October, 1927, which are taken, in part, from the *Annuaire de l'Institut Internationale de Statistique,* and in "Christianity and the Race Problem," by Dr. J. H. Oldham.

The population of the world is estimated to be 1,894,874,000. If the earth's surface were utilized in the most efficient manner as regards production and transport, 7,869 million people instead of the present 1,900 million, it is believed, could be supported without any further technical improvement.

The number and density of the population per kilometre of the various continents in 1910 and 1924 were as follows:

		Population	Density
Europe	1910	447,480,000	45.7
	1924	462,227,000	48.2
America	1910	180,397,000	4.1
	1924	227,133,000	5.2
Africa	1910	126,854,000	4.4
	1924	137,361,000	4.8
Asia	1910	858,497,000	20.7
	1924	1,060,238,000	24.3
Oceania	1910	6,866,000	0.8
	1924	7,915,000	0.9

The figures indicate an increase in the world's population during the last 200 years of 900 millions. It is pointed out by Dr. Ferenczi that this increase coincides with the rapid expansion of the white race in non-European countries, population both native and foreign having increased wherever Europeans have established their institutions and influence. During the eighteenth and nineteenth centuries emigration from Europe grew from

3 million to from 35 to 40 million. Only where European civilization has not yet penetrated, as in China and central Africa, has the population remained stationary or declined.

The fact that as yet sufficient effort has not been made to collect reliable figures in this field on which to base government policies, is indicated by the wide discrepancy in the figures, quoted by Dr. Oldham, from "The Rising Tide of Color," by Lothrop Stoddard, and from "Mankind at the Crossroads," by Edward W. East. Dr. Oldham maintains in comparing the figures that it needs to be borne in mind that Dr. Stoddard sets out to prove a theory, and that Dr. East has no theory to prove. Professor East's figures are for 1916 and Dr. Stoddard's are for 1914.

		Whites	*Yellows*	*Browns*	*Blacks*
East	(1916)	710,000,000	510,000,000	420,000,000	110,000,000
Stoddard	(1914)	550,000,000	500,000,000	450,000,000	150,000,000

As to the rate of increase Dr. Stoddard asserts that whites tend to double in number in 80 years, yellows and browns in 60 and blacks in 40. Professor East arrives at the conclusion that at present rates of increase whites may be expected to double in 58 years, browns in 278, yellows in 232 and blacks in 139. If Professor East's calculations are correct the white race will within a quarter of a century actually outnumber all other races combined.

As to the relation of war to population Dr. Oldham says:

"The temptation, which now exists, to encourage the growth of population for reasons of national defence would be removed (if war were abolished). The energies and resources at present required for defence against war would be available for dealing with the problems of population and food supply by scientific research and popular education. Experience seems to show that those whose livelihood is precarious and whose sense of responsibility is thus weakened tend to multiply more rapidly than other classes in the community; and that the motives which lead to restriction of numbers in a family operate most strongly when a certain standard of comfort has been reached. A general improvement in the standard of living might therefore prove to be the most effective of all means of limiting the growth of population."

The three possibilities open to governments with a surplus population are (1) to secure the economic advantage of their citizens at the risk of denationalization in oversea countries, (2) to employ their surplus population as far as possible within the country or to settle it by home colonization; (3) to endeavor to obtain the assignment of colonial territory for group settlements of their nationals, with self-government and such rights of sovereignty as will secure certain economic and financial interests of the mother-country. The Japanese Government is attempting home colonization and has prepared a plan by which six million persons will in the course of twenty years be settled with government assistance on the Island of Hokkaido.

Dr. Ferenczi sees in the need of industrialized nations for markets, that is for buying power among large portions of the earth's population, hope for beneficial adjustment and believes it may lead nations which rule over excessively large territories to open a portion of those territories for settlement by over-populated nations.

Seen against this world background, the immigration policy of the United States takes on increased importance and interest.

From the Revolutionary War to the Civil War, the dominant idea behind our immigration policy was to offer an asylum to the oppressed peoples of Europe and to build up the population of a wide and undeveloped country. During the period from 1820 to 1860, 2,000,000 immigrants were admitted.

The Civil War was followed by a period of industrial expansion, when great numbers of both skilled and unskilled laborers were needed to build the transcontinental railroads and man the rapidly developing factories. Between 1866 and 1914, the total number of immigrants was 27,312,726.

From 1820 to 1883, 90% of the total arrivals were from Great Britain, Germany, Scandinavia, Belgium, the Netherlands, France, and Switzerland. The movement from these countries is generally referred to as the "old" immigration. After 1883, Italy and Austria, and in general, the countries of southern and eastern Europe, became the principal sources of immigration.

The first attempt to regulate immigration was made with respect to immigration from China. Chinese immigration on the Pacific Coast began about 1840 as a result of severe economic depression in China and of exaggerated advertising in that country by American shipping companies of the California gold fields. In 1868, the Burlingame Treaty was concluded regulating conditions affecting immigration. Its terms were conciliatory and did little or nothing to restrict the number of immigrants. In 1880, a treaty was negotiated which gave the United States the right to limit, regulate, or suspend Chinese immigration, but not to prohibit it. In 1882, at the instigation of California, a law was passed excluding Chinese laborers for ten years. The passage of this law is credited by political students to the fact that in 1882 California was a doubtful State and both parties were eager to win the approval of the California Workmen's Party which advocated Chinese labor exclusion. The law was extended in 1892 and 1902, and exclusion made

WORLD POPULATION AND IMMIGRATION 363

permanent by a law passed in 1904, in contravention of the 1880 treaty. A test case was brought under this law in 1898 in the belief that the Supreme Court would declare laws that contravene treaties unconstitutional. The judgment of the court was as follows:

"It must be conceded that the Act of 1882 is in contravention of the treaty of 1868 and of the supplemental treaty of 1880, but it is not on that account invalid. . . . It (a treaty) can be deemed . . . only the equivalent of a legislative act, to be repealed or modified at the pleasure of Congress. . . . It is the last expression of sovereign will and must control. "The question whether our government was justified in disregarding its engagements with another nation is not one for the determination of the courts. . . . This court is not a censor of the morals of the other departments of the government."

Justice Field said of this decision:

"This made it clear that a treaty is not the 'supreme law of the land' except as Congress makes it so. Congress can, without violation of the Constitution, repeal or amend any part of a treaty even without securing the consent of the other party to the treaty, and even without conference."

A law affecting immigration in general was passed in 1882, which barred criminals, lunatics, and those likely to become public charges. The immigration of contract labor was prohibited by law in 1885.

In 1907, immigration from Japan was restricted by means of what is known as the "gentleman's agreement" between that country and this, by which Japan agreed to refuse passports to America to its nationals of the laboring classes and also agreed, in order to prevent circuitous entry, to include in the prohibition, territories contiguous to the United States.

To reduce immigration in general, measures imposing a literacy test were passed by Congress during the administrations of Cleveland, Taft and Wilson, but were vetoed on the ground that it was contrary to the traditional custom of America to bar an immigrant because he failed to meet educational qualifications.

During the war, immigration was, of course, greatly reduced, but it was anticipated there would be an overwhelming increase following the war. In 1917, because of the belief that there would be a flood of immigration from India, the Asiatic barred zone was created, including India, China, part of Afghanistan, a section of the country between the Caspian Sea and China, and islands adjacent to the continent of Asia.

During the post-war years, investigations were conducted resulting in the conclusion that immigration could not be considered exclusively as an economic problem, and that the number of immigrants arriving was too large to be properly assimilated. It was also made clear by these investigations that a change in the character of immigration was taking place.

In 1921, a law was passed by Congress as a temporary measure, which for the first time attempted to apply a principle of selection according to the degree of supposed assimilability of the various nationalities. The desire was to force the immigration current back to its earlier sources. The numbers of aliens admissible under this law in any year was limited to 3% of the number of foreign-born persons of that nationality in the United States as determined by the census of 1910. The total number admissible from all countries under the act was fixed at 367,000 a year.

The immigration law of 1921 caused great hardships to immigrants who came to this country only to be turned back because the quotas were already full. Ellis Island was so crowded during the early months of the year that it was practically impossible to maintain proper

WORLD POPULATION AND IMMIGRATION

conditions of health and comfort. Foreign governments protested to the government of the United States and the ill feeling engendered among the immigrants and carried back to their own countries might well have developed serious international ill will.

In 1924 the second selective immigration law was enacted, which included three important changes:

(1) The number of aliens admissible was changed from 3% of the number included in the 1910 census to 2% of the number of each nationality according to the 1890 census. Countries of the Western Hemisphere were exempted from the quota reservations. The total number admissible in any one year was set at 165,000. The change from the census of 1910 to that of 1890 was made in the belief that it would increase the proportion of immigration from northern European countries. This basis of determining the quota was to be followed until July 1, 1927, when what is known as the "national origin" system of determining the quotas was to be put into effect. By this system, the total number to be admitted each year, 150,000, would be allocated to the different nationalities upon the basis of proportionate numerical strength in the total population of the United States, as recorded in the census of 1920.

The date for inaugurating the "national origin" system was later postponed until July 1, 1929. One reason for the delay was the fact that it was found that the national origin system would reduce immigration from the Scandinavian countries and from Ireland and Germany.

(2) The 1924 act, by providing for the inspection of immigrants at the port of embarkation and for the control of the quota by American consuls in foreign ports rather than after arrival, greatly improved the conditions of immigration and thereby removed causes of international friction.

(3) The 1924 act excluded as immigrants all aliens not eligible to citizenship. Certain classes, including scholars, professional people and tourists coming into the country for temporary travel or residence, were excepted.

To understand why this last provision affected only Japanese, a little history is necessary. The first naturalization law of 1790 provided for the naturalization of "any alien being a free white person." In 1870, this law was amended and citizenship declared open to aliens who were "free white persons and to those of African nativity or to persons of African descent." In 1882 by act of Congress Chinese were excluded from the privileges of naturalization. According to careful students of this question, the original naturalization law of 1790 had as its aim the maintenance of liberty and democracy and sought only to deny citizenship to slaves. It is claimed, further, that until 1906, the naturalization laws of 1870 were understood to admit to naturalization all the races from the extreme white to the extreme black, except the Chinese, who had been specifically excluded. In 1906, the naturalization bureau on its own initiative adopted a more rigid interpretation of the law and excluded Japanese, but Hindus, Mexicans and others were still regarded as eligible for naturalization. In 1922, the Supreme Court declared that the term "free white person" did not include the Japanese, but only the races commonly called white or Caucasian. Hindus continued, as Caucasians, to be naturalized under this decision until 1923 when a ruling by the Supreme Court deprived them of eligibility. Justice Sutherland who rendered the opinion, stated:

"What we *now* hold is that the words 'free white persons' are words of common speech, to be interpreted in accordance with the understanding of the common man. . . ."

By this interpretation, Hindus were excluded from citizenship. The law disastrously affected from 3,000 to 5,000 Hindus, most of them farmers on the Pacific Coast who had already established themselves in this country, depriving them of the right to hold land, and also depriving many who had already become citizens, of their citizenship.

Since all other nationalities which might have been affected were thus excluded by the law of 1917, the exclusion provision of the 1924 immigration act was obviously aimed at the Japanese, and was the culmination of a series of anti-Japanese laws that had been passed by Pacific coast States, beginning in 1893. In this act, Congress abruptly abrogated the "gentleman's agreement" which the United States Government admitted had been scrupulously observed by Japan. Japan's proposal for a conference was refused.

When the 1924 act was pending in Congress, Secretary of State Hughes wrote the Chairman of the Immigration Committee, who was Congressman Johnson of Washington, protesting against the Japanese exclusion provision as inconsistent with the existing treaty between the United States and Japan. His letter contained the following paragraphs:

"The practical effect of Section 12 (b) is to single out Japanese immigrants for exclusion. The Japanese are a sensitive people, and unquestionably would regard such a legislative enactment as fixing a stigma upon them. . . .

"The question is thus presented whether it is worthwhile thus to affront a friendly nation with whom we have established most cordial relations and what gain there would be from such action. Permit me to suggest that the legislation would seem to be quite unnecessary even for the purpose for which it is devised. It is to be noted that if the provision of subdivision (b) of Section 12 were eliminated and the quota provided in Section 10 of the proposed measure were to be applied to Japan, there would be a total of only 246 Japanese immigrants entitled to enter under the quota as thus determined. . . . We now have an understanding with the Japanese Government whereby Japan undertakes to prevent the immigration of laborers from Japan to the United States except the parents, wives and children of those already resident here. Furthermore, the Japanese Government, incidentally to this undertaking, now regulates immigration to territory contiguous to the United States with the object of preventing the departure from Japan of persons who are likely to obtain surreptitious entry into this country.

"If the provision of Section 12 (b) were to be deleted and the provision in regard to certificates for immigrants to this country were to become applicable to Japan, we should with the present understanding with the Japanese Government be in a position to obtain active coöperation by the Japanese authorities in the granting of passports and immigration certificates. We could in addition be assured that the Japanese Government would give its assistance in scrutinizing and regulating immigration from Japan to American territory contiguous to the United States. It is believed that such an arrangement involving a double control over the Japanese quota of less than 250 a year would accomplish a much more effective regulation of unassimilable and undesirable classes of Japanese immigrants than it would be practicable for us, with our long land frontier lines on both North and South to accomplish by attempting to establish a general bar against Japanese subjects, to the loss of coöperation with the Japanese Government in controlling the movement of their people to the United States and adjacent territories."

The passage of the Japanese exclusion provision of the 1924 act, contrary to the recommendations of the Secretary of State, led to very wide-spread protests in Japan, and among such groups in this country as the Federal Council of Churches, the National Committee for Constructive Immigration, and the Friends General Conference. July 1, the day the act went into effect, was observed throughout Japan as "Humiliation Day."

In presenting the matter to the Japanese Diet the Minister of Foreign Affairs made the following declaration:

"Until our just contentions have been given satisfaction we shall maintain our protests and shall continue our best possible endeavors to seek an amicable adjustment of the question and to ensure forever the traditional friendship between the two nations."

Hon. Cyrus E. Woods, American Ambassador to Japan, when the act was passed said:

"The Japanese Exclusion Act was, in my judgment, an international disaster of the first magnitude,—a disaster to American diplomacy in the Far East, a disaster to American business, a disaster to religion and to the effective work of our American churches in Japan."

The following statement was made at the Institute of Pacific Relations, by Yusuke Tsurumi, prominent Japanese publicist, who since then has been elected to the Japanese Parliament:

"I have sounded America throughout, and I know that, in spite of the immigration laws, her heart is right. I have gone home and told this to the Japanese people, as they came in thousands to my lectures to hear eagerly about America. And I want to tell America in return that the heart of Japan, too, is right. We understand America's difficulties, we recognize her right to legislate for herself, and while we deplore the manner of the legislation, I want America to know that the Japanese people will wait with patience and with dignity and confidence until again the American tradition of fair play comes into its own."

The passage of the act was supported by the American Federation of Labor, and at its 1926 convention the Federation adopted this resolution:

"Whereas, the American Federation of Labor has for years demanded from Congress, and with coöperation of other organizations and interests finally secured passage of a law excluding aliens ineligible to citizenship as a measure of protection to American citizens, and as a logical condition of the national policy of restricted immigration. . . .

"Resolved, that we again direct the Executive Council to forcibly present to Congress and the proper committees of both houses organized labor's vigorous and emphatic protest against any modification of the Federal law excluding aliens ineligible to citizenship. . . ."

In a message to the American people on Japan from the American Friends Service Committee arguments in opposition to the admission of Japanese are answered factually:

"They are said to drive out American labor by accepting low wages and bad living conditions. As a matter of fact, they have largely replaced Chinese labor, and the labor they compete with is largely Mexican or South European; while in their special agricultural work no white man wishes to take their place. The low wages which they accepted were a menace to American standards before the Gentlemen's Agreement took effect, but since 1907 Japanese immigrants have gone through the same history as most other immigrant groups; their living conditions have improved and their wages are now generally equal to those paid to white workers. They now own and operate some of the most prosperous small farms in the West. Many of them have gone into the professions. Those born in this country are more American than Japanese; they are so completely assimilated that they have lost all touch with Japan, and often even with their Japanese parents who could not learn English.

"Until recently there was a law in Japan which created a form of dual citizenship; but recently that law has been abolished; and Japan no longer claims such rights over those who have left her country and have become citizens of another nation. To the latter only they owe allegiance."

So far immigration from Canada and Latin America has been unrestricted. The immigration act of 1924 exempts native-born citizens of countries of the Western Hemisphere from the quota provisions. The Commissioner General of Immigration advocated in his report for the fiscal year of 1926 the extension of the quota system to these countries.

The opponents of the proposal to restrict Canadian and Latin American immigration claim that freedom of movement across the Canadian border is traditional, and that the Canadians make good citizens; that immigration from Spanish American countries, other than Mexico, is inconsiderable and that the movement from Mexico is necessary to supply labor for the development of the Southwest.

In 1926, the number of immigrants from the West Indies and Central and South America was less than 8,000, but during the last few years, Canada and Mexico have contributed almost as many annually as has Europe. Immigration from Mexico was very small before the World War, but during the war years, the American demand for labor, aided by disturbed conditions in their home country, led to a considerable movement of Mexicans into the United States. It is estimated that whereas in 1900 Mexicans formed only 1% of our foreign-born population, they now form nearly 10%. The Mexican government does not favor the loss of its nationals and the Mexican Federation of Labor is attempting a restriction of emigration.

It will be evident from this brief survey of past and present immigration policies that the problem is closely bound up with questions of international goodwill. From this point of view, there are three elementary considerations which could, it would seem, be taken into account in any immigration policy adopted, however drastic:

First: avoidance of arbitrary discrimination against individual nations.

Second: avoidance of methods of enforcing our immigration policies which are unnecessarily irritating to other nations.

Third: fair and honorable treatment of the citizens of other countries who become residents of this one, in order that the impressions they carry back to their home countries may be such as to increase the number of our friends.

The ordinarily accepted theory that "immigration is a matter of purely domestic concern" was reiterated at the Sixth Pan American Congress by the United States delegates in the form of a reservation to the immigration resolution.

Whether, however, the claim that each government has the right to absolute control over the extent and character of immigration continues to be upheld, or whether these questions, as the tendency seems to be at present, are recognized as a phase of international politics, they must finally be determined in the light of world facts. The question presses for consideration because the movement of population, which before the World War was largely individualistic, has since the war through the restriction of immigration and emigration been subjected to the interference and control of governments.

At the invitation of the Italian government, an International Conference on Emigration and Immigration met in Rome, May 1924, at which 57 countries, the League of Nations and International Labor Office were officially represented. The discussions dealt with questions of protection and welfare of immigrants and with "general principles which should be adopted in treaties of immigration and emigration." A second International Conference met in March 1928 at Havana. Whether or not these conferences result in definite modification of the legislative policies of any nation, they at least indicate an attempt to regard the problem of emigration and immigration as a common problem and to study it from the world point of view.

CHAPTER XXII

THE WAR-MAKING POWER IN THE UNITED STATES GOVERNMENT

IN an article on "The Executive Assumption of the War-Making Power," published in the *National University Law Review* for May, 1927, Albert H. Putney, Professor of Constitutional Law in the National University, calls attention to "the gradual passing of the war-making power, at least in so far as war can be made with the military and naval forces already authorized, from the hands of the Legislative Department of the Government into those of the Executive."

The granting of the war-making power to Congress by the Constitution, Prof. Putney declares, was one of the greatest innovations in the direction of greater human liberty and justice made by the Constitution, and presented a striking contrast to the rule previously followed in European monarchies. He asserts that one of the most important questions confronting the citizens of the United States today is whether an assumption of this war-making power by the Executive is to be acquiesced in. The following brief discussion is summarized from Professor Putney's article referred to above.

The Constitution of the United States provides in Article I that "The Congress shall have power . . . to declare war." This power of Congress has been declared by the Supreme Court of the United States to be an exclusive one:

"By the Constitution, Congress alone has the power to declare a national or foreign war. . . . The Constitution confers on the President the whole executive power. . . . He is Commander-in-Chief of the Army and Navy of the United States. . . . He has no power to initiate or declare a war either against a foreign nation or a domestic state."—The Prize Cases, 2 Black, 635, 668, 17 L. Ed., 459, 477.

The Supreme Court has also interpreted the term "war" to embrace all attempts by a country to maintain its rights by the employment of force:

"Every contention by force between two nations, in external matters, under the authority of their respective governments, is not only war, but public war."—Bas. v. Tingy, 4 Dallas, 37, 40, 1 L. Ed., 731, 732-3.

The historical background of the war-making provision of the Constitution is described in this paragraph from a speech made by Senator Sumner of Massachusetts:

"By the Constitution it is solemnly announced that to Congress is given the power 'to declare war.' This allotment of power was made only after much consideration and in obedience to those popular rights consecrated by the American Revolution. In England and in all other monarchies at the time, this power was the exclusive prerogative of the Crown, so that war was justly called the last reason of kings. The framers of our Constitution naturally refused to vest this kingly prerogative in the President. Kings were rejected in substance as in name. The One-Man Power was set aside and this kingly prerogative placed under the safeguard of the people, as represented in that highest form of national life, an Act of Congress. No other provision in the Constitution is more distinctive or more worthy of veneration. I do not go too far when I call it an essential element of Republican institutions, happily discovered by our fathers."

Professor Putney traces through the various administrations the acts of the Executive Branch of the Government and the statements of Presidents and Secretaries of State which bear upon this question, showing that until the end of the nineteenth century the war-making power was jealously guarded by Congress and acknowledged by every President. Among the striking statements which he quotes are these:

President Jackson in connection with the question of the recognition of Texas referred the question to Congress as one "probably leading to war" and therefore a proper subject for "a previous understanding with that body by whom war can alone be declared and by whom all the provisions for sustaining its perils must be furnished."

Again, when difficulties threatened war with Spain, President Jackson hurried instructions to our minister to discuss the matter with the Spanish Government, in order that before its adjournment the matter might be laid before Congress, "the constitutional judges of what is proper to be done when negotiations for redress of injury fail."

In connection with the rendering of military assistance to Texas before its annexation, the Secretary of State of the United States had occasion to write the American Minister to Texas: "The employment of the Army or Navy against a foreign power with which the United States are at peace is not within the competency of the President."

President Buchanan, in his Annual Message in 1858, said:

"The executive government of this country in its intercourse with foreign nations is limited to the employment of diplomacy alone. When this fails it can proceed no further. It cannot legitimately resort to force without the direct authority of Congress, except in resisting and repelling hostile attacks."

Again in his Annual Message of 1859 this President stated:

"Congress possesses the sole and exclusive power under the Constitution 'to declare war.' They alone can 'raise and support armies' and 'provide and maintain a navy.' But after Congress shall have declared war and provided the force necessary to carry it on, the President as Commander-in-Chief of the Army and Navy, can alone employ this force in making war against the enemy. This is the plain language and history proves that it was the well-known intention of the framers of the Constitution. It will not be denied that the general 'power to declare war' is without limitation and embraces within itself not only what writers on the law of nations term a public or perfect war, but also an imperfect war, and, in short, every species of hostility, however confined or limited. Without the authority of Congress the President cannot fire a hostile gun in any case except to repel the attack of an enemy."

President Harrison in connection with an attack upon sailors of the United States when on shore leave in Valparaiso, and President Cleveland in connection with a boundary dispute between Great Britain and Venezuela, both made it clear that they claimed no authority to use force without the express authorization of Congress.

Professor Putney cites the action of President Roosevelt in connection with the revolution in Panama in 1903 as the first exercise of the war-making power by a President without the consent of Congress but calls attention to the fact that President Roosevelt

"Adopted for his own administration, and urged upon others, a principle which, if followed by his successors, would have almost entirely eliminated the practical evils which have resulted from later interventions based upon the precedent which he created.

"The principle referred to was that against the use of force for the recovery of contract claims against a foreign country.

In his Fifth Annual Message, dated December 5, 1905, in discussing the troubles in Santo Domingo and the foreign claims against that country, he said: 'Our own Government has always refused to enforce such contractual relations on behalf of its citizens by an appeal to arms. It is much to be wished that all foreign governments would take the same view.'"

"The latest chapter in the history of the gradual usurpation of the war-making powers by the Executive," according to Professor Putney, "is a short one. It comprises merely the sending of marines into Nicaragua to support the tottering rule of the revolutionary president, Adolfo Diaz, and the President's argument in support of this action in his Message of January 10, 1927, which concluded:

" 'It has always been and remains the policy of the United States in such circumstances to take steps that may be necessary for the preservation and protection of the lives, the property, and the interests of its citizens and of this Government itself. In this respect I propose to follow the path of my predecessors.

" 'Consequently, I have deemed it my duty to use the powers committed to me to insure the adequate protection of all American interests in Nicaragua, whether they be endangered by internal strife or by outside interference in the affairs of that Republic.' "

This statement as to what the policy of the United States has always been is contradicted by citations from the messages of Jefferson and Madison and Daniel Webster when Secretary of State. In his first Annual Message Jefferson recounted the sending of an American squadron to Gibraltar when Tripolitan cruisers were blockading United States commerce in the Mediterranean. One of the cruisers engaged a small American schooner and was captured, but since the American naval forces were "unauthorized by the Constitution without the sanction of Congress to go beyond the line of defense, the vessel being disabled from committing further hostilities was liberated with its crew." "The Legislature," Jefferson continues, "will doubtless consider whether by authorizing measures of offense also they will place our force on equal footing with that of its adversaries."

Commenting on this message Professor Putney says:

"President Jefferson clearly recognized and stated the distinction between those cases where the use of force abroad for the protection of American lives and property is really defensive and where, therefore, it may be authorized by the President without the consent of Congress, and those cases where it is offensive in its character and, therefore, only permissible when authorized by Congress. In the case of actual physical attacks upon American citizens or their property, or the immediate danger of such attacks, the forces of the United States may be used for strictly protective purposes without the consent of Congress, which it is manifestly impossible to obtain in such cases. When, however, any attempt is made to take over the control of territory, to use force for the collection of claims due to American citizens, to interfere with the military operation of foreign troops, or above all to interfere between two governments each claiming to be the legal government of the country, war (perhaps only partial war, but still war) is waged, and this can only be constitutionally done under the authorization of Congress. There is here no question of any surrender of American rights, or any failure to protect American interests, it is merely a question as to which department of the government has been granted the power of deciding upon the question of the necessity of war. The framers of the Constitution felt that this was too great a power to be safely placed in the hands of any one man, and expressly granted it to Congress. For more than a century the Presidents of the United States acquiesced in this decision."

The message of President Coolidge quoted above, Professor Putney declares, "in effect asserts that the President of the United States has the power to wage an offensive war, upon his own authority, against any country, and for any reason which in his opinion appears to affect 'the lives, the property and the interests of its citizens and of this Government itself.' If this claim is correct it would only be necessary to appeal to Congress if an increase in the numbers of the land and naval forces were required."

The Power of Congress to Outlaw War

Another interesting point in regard to the war-making power in the United States Government, which has recently come up in connection with outlawry of war treaties, is the claim that it would be unconstitutional for the treaty-making power of the United States, the President and the Senate, to negotiate outlawry of war treaties, because by the Constitution the war-making power belongs to Congress. This claim is, however, contradicted by Professor J. P. Chamberlain of Columbia University, in the following statement:

"Important treaties have been made by the United States to limit the exercise of other powers vested in Congress and vital to the national defense.

"Article I, Section 8, also grants to Congress power 'to provide and maintain a navy.' This power is also unlimited; but the treaty-making power, with the approval of the nation, signed and ratified the convention of Washington, February 6, 1922, of which Section 1 reads: 'The contracting powers agree to limit their respective naval armament as provided in the present treaty.'

"The treaties of arbitration of 1908 and 1909 known as the Root treaties, and the treaties of investigation and conciliation of Mr. Bryan in 1913 and 1914 also constitute international obligations morally limiting the right to declare war."

CHAPTER XXIII

WAR DEBTS AND REPARATIONS

THE war debts owed to the United States by European nations present a problem which has not yet been satisfactorily settled and which will call for further expression of opinion on the part of American citizens. Although the whole subject, as in the case of many others connected with world peace, is of so technical a nature that it can be understood only through detailed study, the public should be familiar with its broad outlines in order that popular prejudice may not influence future decisions in regard to it. In answer to criticism of the present settlements as not sufficiently generous on the part of this country it has been stated by Secretary Mellon that "neither the people nor the press nor Congress" expressed any such opinion as would have warranted cancelling any amount of the indebtedness which it was feasible to collect.

The facts in regard to the present agreements for the settlement of the debts are these: the obligations given by the Allies during the war were demand obligations. Because it was necessary that these be funded into long-term obligations, Congress in 1922 created the World War Foreign Debt Commission. It provided that the Commission should have no power to extend the time of maturity of any obligations beyond 1987, or to fix the rate of interest at less than the rate borne by outstanding liberty bonds. The act which contemplated payment in full further required that each agreement be approved

WAR DEBTS AND REPARATIONS 381

by Congress before going into effect. It was found by the Debt Commission that it was impossible to enforce the provisions of this act, and Congress agreed to the arrangements entered into by the Commission.

The basis of the negotiations carried on by the Debt Commission was the foreign nation's "capacity to pay," and it was explicitly and repeatedly stated by the American negotiators that the debt payments must be considered independently of reparation payments to be received by the debtors from Germany. The amounts of indebtedness and the total payments required under the existing agreements, and the rates of interest applying, are shown in the following table. The time of payment allowed is, in all instances, sixty-two years:

Country	Amt. Advanced	Payments To be made	Int. Rates
Armenia	$11,959,918	$16,655,179	Not funded
Austria	24,055,709	33,437,435	" "
Belgium	379,087,200	727,830,500	1.790%
Cuba	10,000,000	Paid	
Czechoslovakia	91,879,671	312,811,433	3.327%
Esthonia	13,999,146	33,331,140	3.306%
Finland	8,281,926	21,695,055	3.306%
France	3,404,818,945*	6,847,674,104	1.640%
Great Britain	4,277,000,000	11,105,965,000	3.306%
Greece	15,000,000	19,125,000	Not funded
Hungary	1,685,836	4,693,240	3.306%
Italy	1,648,034,051	2,407,677,500	.405%
Latvia	5,132,287	13,958,635	3.306%
Liberia	26,000	Paid	
Lithuania	4,981,628	14,531,940	3.306%
Nicaragua	166,604	298,818	Not funded
Poland	159,666,972	435,687,550	3.306%
Rumania	37,922,675	122,506,260	3.321%
Russia	192,601,297	275,504,668	Not funded
Yugoslavia	51,758,487	95,177,635	1.030%
Totals	$10,338,058,352	$22,488,561,093	

*French agreement not yet ratified by French Parliament or Congress of the United States.

According to Treasury estimates, these settlements—on the basis of their "present worth"—represent a cancellation by the United States of over $5,489,000,000 of indebtedness.

The two schools of thought in the United States, on the subject of debt payments, are most clearly set forth in a statement issued early in 1927 by members of the faculty of political science of Columbia University, and later endorsed by members of the faculty of Princeton University, and in the reply of Secretary of the Treasury Mellon to this statement. These documents may be obtained in full in *International Conciliation* for May, 1927, published by the Carnegie Endowment for International Peace. Summarized briefly, the Columbia University statement urges the complete reconsideration of the debt settlements in the light of present knowledge. It does not recommend cancellation. It maintains:

That war debt settlements have produced distrust and misunderstanding, and that when in Europe century-old political enmities are yielding to common sense, an international financial problem of recent origin, whatever its magnitude, should not be allowed to threaten the foremost gain in international relations since European nations began.

That our money advances to the Allies during the war were regarded by Congress as "a joint contribution to a common cause." Many statements made in Congress and by public men at the time the loans were made are quoted in support of this contention. March 25, 1926, on the floor of the Senate, Senator Smoot said, as a member of the World War Foreign Debt Commission:

"Those of us who were here in 1917-18 know how we felt then. There was no thought of commercial loans or of investment of our resources in the bonds of the Allies. We were bound together in a common cause; money was all we had to give and we gave it freely. It was, of course, expected that if we won the war some day in some way

WAR DEBTS AND REPARATIONS

all obligations of foreign governments which we received for the sums advanced would be honored and adjusted."

That the loans were for different purposes, and that the debt settlements did not take this fact sufficiently into account. (Of the total sum advanced, $7,000,000,000 was advanced before the Armistice. A large part of this money was, by agreement, spent in the United States for war and other supplies; a part was used for the purchase of supplies later sold to the citizens of the debtor nations. England borrowed in part in order to loan to her allies and has agreed to cancel her debt to them in so far as her indebtedness to the United States is cancelled.)

That to the minds of our debtors, the core of the controversy is the question of what equivalent, moral or material, was rendered by them for the sums advanced. In other words, that while we loaned money toward winning the war, the Allies sacrificed lives.

That a nation's capacity to pay cannot be determined.

That the wide discrepancy in liberality of the settlements is unjust.

That our debt settlements are part and parcel of a whole network of settlements between other powers, and should be considered in an international conference in which our negotiators should be given the power to come to an agreement calculated to promote the future peace and prosperity of the world.

The Secretary of the Treasury, Mr. Mellon, in answer to this statement, asserts:

That Congress, from the wording of the Liberty Loan acts, clearly intended the sums advanced to the Allies to be loans, and not subsidies.

That the advances made after the Armistice cannot be considered as a contribution pending effective entry into battle or as saving American lives, and that large amounts of the sums agreed upon in the debt settlements are taken up in the payment of these post-war advances.

That the reparation payments due European nations from

Germany under the Dawes plan are in the case of all our principal debtors, except Great Britain, larger than the amounts due us.

That neither the people nor the press nor Congress expressed any such opinion as would have warranted the government's officials who were acting as trustees for the American people in cancelling any amount of the debt which it was feasible to collect.

That a recognition of their external obligations by the European nations and an undertaking bravely to meet them within their capacity, such as each country has accepted, is a moral force of great service to permanent prosperity in the world.

Aside from the feasibility of obtaining payment, and aside from any theory of generosity, the question is raised by many economists whether it would be to the financial advantage of the United States to accept payment of the war debts in full or in large part. Secretary Mellon is quoted in the annual reports of the World War Foreign Debt Commission as having said before the funding negotiations that:

"The entire foreign debt is not worth as much to the American people in dollars and cents as a prosperous Europe as a customer. A business man would prefer making $100 in his business than being repaid $5 of a debt. The farmer or the laboring man would rather have a market for our surplus in Europe than save a dollar of Federal taxes."

In this connection it should be noted that the payments which the United States receives under the agreements amount to less than one-third of 1% of our annual national income at present, and will never exceed one-half of 1% of the probable national income. If they were applied in full to a reduction in the personal income tax rate, they would make a difference of only $2 a year to a taxpayer with a net income of more than

$5,000. To the 90% of the people who pay taxes on an income of less than $5,000 the reduction would be even less.

The argument was made in Congress, however, that whatever the value to the United States of the payment of the debt, full payment should be exacted because the debtor nations are spending larger sums for armaments than they are called upon to pay the United States, and that any relaxation in the debt settlements would merely increase the amounts expended for military purposes. The answer made to this is that the reduction in armaments depends upon the creation of international goodwill, and that the present settlements tend to add to the ill will and distrust in the world.

The extent of the ill will engendered may be seen in the statement quoted below from a representative of the nation which has raised less objection than any other to the debt-collection policy of the United States. A. G. Gardiner, English author, in an article, "Prospects of Anglo-American Friendship," in *Foreign Affairs* for October, 1926, says:

"The chief cause of estrangement is the debt settlement. . . . The British taxpayer, burdened as he is with a weight of taxation unprecedented in history, would be more than human if he did not feel some mortification at the fact that for every pound sterling he earns, he has to pay 9d. to a creditor whose economic position he has come to regard as being in almost every respect vastly more comfortable and happy than his own.

"But there is more in it than that. The resentment which really counts is based on less ignoble feelings. In the main your Englishman, though like other men he hates parting with his money, is too much of a business man to harbor malice at having to meet an obligation which he has contracted in the course of straight business. He will dislike losing the money, but he will consider himself under a moral obligation to pay, and though he may envy his creditor, he will not like him any the less for it. But the whole point is that, in this case of the war debt, he does not feel that at bottom there does exist the same moral obligation. He cannot persuade himself that it was contracted in the normal course of business. He cannot agree that war debt and debts contracted in ordinary business are on the same footing. He regards the expenditure on the war as being expenditure incurred for a common object, and he cannot bring himself to believe that the mere bookkeeping entries of such expenditure have the same binding force as they have in the more material relations of commerce.

"On an impartial view of the matter, he has some justification for this attitude. If we did wage a common war—and I have yet to hear the man who denies it—is it really possible to allocate the burden on purely commercial principles? No one has attempted to apply such principles to the sacrifice in men. Is there any more justification for applying them to materials? If America sent a detachment of machine-gunners plus equipment for the reinforcement of our defenses, no indebtedness of this strictly computable nature was incurred. The sacrifices she made were agreed to be invaluable. But if she sent equipment only, apparently the sacrifice was to be assessed on quite a different basis. . . .

"It is notorious that if America had not insisted upon a 'business settlement,' England would have been quite ready, in the common interest, to cancel all debts due to her."

The *New Republic* of May 23, 1928, takes vigorous exception to the tendency in England to demand reduction on moral grounds, and puts the need for revision entirely on economic grounds. Just as the Allies have learned that the cost of war cannot be recovered from the vanquished, the United States has need to learn that it is impossible to collect large sums loaned for war purposes: "Tribute exacted for defeat in war tends to throw out of balance the economic integration of the world; and no less a disturbance is likely to arise from insistence on full repayment of loans advanced for destructive purposes."

The Dawes Plan

Although the United States has insisted that the war debts and German reparations should be considered separately, the two things have necessarily been closely interwoven in European thought. The inability of Germany to continue to meet reparation payments would undoubtedly lead to a demand for a reconsideration of the debt-funding agreements with the United States.

During the war and during the Peace Conference the peoples of the Allied nations of Europe were for political reasons led to believe that a defeated Germany could be made to pay fabulous sums to the victors. Having put this idea into the minds of the people it became exceedingly dangerous for any government to attempt to disillusion them. The fact that Germany could not pay the amounts expected was recognized by economists and statesmen long before any effort was made to educate the public to the fact. The Reparation Commission which was established by the Treaty of Versailles, and on which the United States, since it asked for no reparations, was not represented, made little or no effort to remove the question of reparations from the political to the economic field.

In October, 1922, the Secretary of State of the United States proposed the appointment of a committee of experts to attempt a solution of the reparation problems. France refused to agree to this proposal. On December 29, 1922, Secretary of State Hughes repeated the suggestion in a public address before the American Historical Association. Mr. Hughes in this speech declared the question of reparations was an economic problem which should be taken out of politics. He expressed the belief that the committee of experts should be free "from any responsibility to foreign offices and from any duty to obey political instruction" and hoped that the way might be found "for a frank discussion and determination of what is essentially an economic problem."

European governments still paid no attention to this plan of the Secretary of State of the United States and continued to stand by their political promises of huge reparations. Early in 1923 the French government sent an army into Germany and occupied the Ruhr. By this attempt to enforce a demand which could not be met the whole situation was brought to a crisis, and when some ten months later the President of the United States declared the State Department proposal was still open for acceptance, the government of England began correspondence with the United States as to ways and means of putting the plan into effect.

It was finally agreed, with the concurrence of France, that the Reparation Commission should appoint a committee of experts to study means of balancing the German budget and stabilizing German currency. The United States, invited to participate in these committees, declined, but stated that it viewed with favor the acceptance by American experts of invitations to participate. How hard it was to clear the air of the political aspects of the reparation problem was indicated by the vigorous objections which the French government made in a press campaign to an alternative proposal for an international conference on reparations, at the same time it was quietly accepting the proposal for a committee of experts.

The report of the Committee of Experts, of which Charles G. Dawes served as Chairman, was made to the Reparation Commission on April 9, 1924, and with the agreement of Germany the plan recommended was put into operation on September 1, 1924. The Dawes Plan has been clearly explained for the average reader by J. Henry Scattergood of Philadelphia. Mr. Scattergood uses a tank by way of illustration: the filling of the tank is the payment by Germany, the emptying of the tank is the receipt of the payments by the Allies. The tank is to be filled from three sources, from taxation, from earnings of the railways of Germany and from a mortgage secured by all German businesses except agriculture. It is in the method of emptying the tank that a difficult problem, known as the transfer problem, arises. Mr. Scattergood points out that the payment put into the tank by Germany cannot be taken out in the form of gold since Germany has no gold, nor in the form of paper money since this would have to be sold for francs or sterling or dollars and unless Germany were to have a balance of exports over imports, the transaction would soon drive down the value of the mark. It would then soon be worthless and the fund in the tank would accordingly melt away in the hands of the Agent General for reparation payments. The only way to make payments (aside from the temporary expedient of foreign loans) is, therefore, in goods or services, that is, Germany must export more than she imports and thus establish a trade balance in an amount sufficient to meet the payments. But no nation wants to receive abnormally large quantities of Germany's goods. America's answer is a high tariff; France on her part has never been willing to accept free German material or to permit German labor to come into the devastated regions and work freely, because of the effect on her own industrial and labor market.

The first four annual payments under the Dawes Plan have been promptly met by Germany, but the amount to be paid increases by more than one-third beginning with 1928-1929. Also the payments so far have been made possible by the negotiation of a loan from American and other investors which in turn has first claim on German resources. The test of the plan is recognized as still in the future and the necessity of some modification, as, for instance, agreement upon the total amount to be paid, which the Reparation Commission had no authority to fix, has been indicated by the American Agent General for Reparations, Mr. Seymour Parker Gilbert.

Another unsettled issue to which Dr. Moulton calls attention is the inter-relation between the reparation and the inter-Allied debt problems.

"If," he says, "the Allies—particularly those countries having the largest share in the reparation claim—are to be expected to accept greatly reduced reparation sums, the inter-Allied debt problem must also be conceived in different terms. No one has ever succeeded in doing anything but delude himself by assuming that the reparation settlement and the inter-Allied debts constitute two separate and distinct problems. The fact that they originated differently is of mere technical interest. There will never be any final solution of the reparation problem until a comprehensive adjustment of both the international debt and reparation problems is worked out."

Whatever truth lies behind the statement that when the original war debt funding negotiations were being conducted, "the public" would not tolerate any considerable reduction in the claims of the United States, when the situation is reconsidered, as it apparently must be within the next few years, there should be a sufficiently widespread realization of the inter-relation of financial problems involved, and of the interdependence of the economic prosperity of all nations, to prevent any obstruction of later efforts at reasonable adjustment.

CHAPTER XXIV

WHAT WAR IS

THERE are only a few hundred men in the world who know in detail what plans are being made for another war, and only a handful of them are giving out so much as an occasional hint. With very few exceptions, the members of legislatures and government officials who are daily deciding issues in a way which leads toward or away from war, are not among those who know the present meaning of the word war.

Thousands of men know intimately what the last war was like, but they are eager to forget, and do not pass their knowledge on. There are pictures from which some of the truth about the last war could be learned, but they are not shown. Only once have the men, who carry in their persons evidence of what war is, gathered together and marched before a public accustomed to seeing soldiers on dress parade. In Paris, on Armistice Day, 1924, after a brilliant ceremony over the tomb of the Unknown Soldier, at which the picked troops of the French army had been reviewed, another army, this time of the *Mutilés,* gathered at the Arc de Triomphe and marched through the streets. The Universal News Service sent this dispatch to its papers:

"First came the seriously wounded in wheel chairs and on stretchers, a few carried by relatives. Then came hundreds of blind men, led by children born when Verdun's guns were booming. Following that division came the men with one leg, men with one arm, and then "smashed mugs." There were men with noses off, men with no chins, and men with only half heads. Never has there been such a tremendous spectacle since wars began . . . and over all was an overwhelming silence—the silence of the wrecks who marched, and the silence of the horrified multitude who watched."

Yet the last war is admitted to have been only a preliminary experiment in the use of modern weapons. In considering a next war mankind is confronted by an entirely new situation, which calls for new judgments based on present facts.

To illustrate the difference between the last war and the next it needs only to be remembered that at the beginning of the last war there was no airplane carrying a gun, that for some time air men fought with rifles, that the greatest weight of bombs dropped in any one month was 12 tons, while today it is possible with the airplanes of France alone to drop 120 tons in one raid. Chemists had hardly begun to experiment with poison gases. Today gas warfare is worked out to so fine a point that it is planned to fill the air with a deadly gas and then to let loose an irritating gas which will compel men to tear off their gas masks. The *Chicago Daily News* of September 8, 1924, cites a report made to the League of Nations by a special committee on chemical warfare as authority for the statement that there is no conceivable limit to the power, efficacy and variety of chemical warfare. The principal chemicals which are already used are "tear gas, which blinds temporarily; sneeze gas, which causes uncontrollable sneezing, intolerable headaches and fits of suffocation; mustard gas, which blisters the skin, eats away the mucous membranes, and penetrates the clothing and the earth and is dangerous for days; asphyxiating gas, which kills by hemorrhage of the lungs, and syncopetoxic gas, which kills by instant paralysis. Furthermore the possibility is seriously considered of dropping disease germs in glass globes on cities, and of ravaging harvests by similarly scattering parasites."

It is sometimes asserted that the evils of chemical and aircraft warfare are greatly exaggerated, that it is pleasanter to be gassed than shot, and that cities can be protected against aircraft. The statements of the men in a position to be best informed contradict these claims. General Pershing has said:

"Chemical warfare should be abolished among nations as abhorrent to civilization. It is a cruel, unfair and improper use of science. It is fraught with the gravest danger to noncombatants and demoralizes the better instincts of humanity. . . . Scientific research may discover a gas so deadly that it will produce instant death. To sanction the use of gas in any form would be to open the way for the use of the most deadly gases and the possible poisoning of whole populations of noncombatant men, women, and children. The contemplation of such a result is shocking to the senses. It is unthinkable that civilization should deliberately decide upon such a course."

Major-General Mason M. Patrick, U. S. A., retired chief of the United States air corps during the War, in an address before the Michigan Branch of the League of Nations Non-Partisan Association at Detroit, January 31, 1928, said:

"We are just at the beginning of the era of air transportation. Every one knows that aircraft will play a most important part in any future war, and that the aircraft of the future will be vastly more powerful machines, more effective weapons, than those of today. Flying at great heights, travelling at great speed, carrying huge bombs filled with explosives, or with noxious gases, (for gas will be used in war, international agreements to the contrary notwithstanding), they can rain down death and destruction, and it can be readily imagined what would be the effect of such an air attack upon this or any other of our large cities. It is repeated, we should surely avail ourselves of any means which will render less likely the necessity of our engaging in so sanguinary a conflict."

As for the protection of cities against aircraft, Brigadier-General Groves, Director of Air Operations of the British Air Forces in 1918, made the following statement, in an address given before the Royal Institute of International Affairs in London on March 29, 1927:

"The consensus of opinion in aviation circles is that local defence is of negligible value; that no adequate means of protection against aircraft attack are yet in view; that the best defence against such an attack is the aerial counter-offensive; and that the only effective deterrent to aerial aggression is the threat of reprisals in kind."

Referring to the experience of the last war, he said further:

"It may be argued that it will be possible to protect the big cities by means of anti-aircraft defences. The following considerations will show that that view is fallacious. In 1918 the London anti-aircraft defences consisted of 11 specially trained night-flying squadrons of aeroplanes, 180 guns on the ground, in addition to a number of guns mounted upon motor vehicles, 10 balloon aprons, and a large number of searchlights. The number of aircraft was nearly 300, and the total number of men employed some 30,000—i.e., the equivalent of two divisions of infantry. In addition, there were a number of specially prepared night landing grounds, extensive telephone installations, and a large headquarters staff to co-ordinate and direct the whole defensive organization. Great as was the scale of these defences, London was bombarded, although the largest number of aeroplanes in any single raid was only 36. Obviously, it would be impossible to maintain defences on the above scale for every city and other nerve centres in a state; but even if it were possible, such defence would be useless against aerial attack delivered by thousands or even by hundreds of aircraft."

The English officer, Commander J. M. Kenworthy, in his recent book, "Peace or War," one of the most startling revelations of what war today means, points out that, although guns and projectiles have been improved and there are gas shells capable of producing a gas barrage in the air,

"It is exceedingly difficult to gauge the height, speed and course of attacking aircraft at night, and it is difficult to make these barrages effective. The improvement in artillery has not kept pace with the improvement in aeroplane engines and aeroplane design; aircraft can now fly much higher, at greater speed, and therefore with greater immunity from attack from the ground. Three hundred miles an hour is a practical speed for aeroplanes."

He calls attention also to the great areas that must be protected and to the difficulty that the defending airplanes have in finding the enemy planes at night, and in distinguishing friend from foe, and to the many casualties resulting from the falling shrapnel and shells of defense guns. He refers to Brigadier-General Lord Thomson as saying that the most effective form of defense against air attack is confined to bombing squadrons—that is, to reprisals.

Marshal Foch has stated:

"The carrying power of the airplane is increasing. Improvements are almost daily enabling greater and greater weights to be carried. These developments introduce an entirely new method for the large-scale use of poison gas. By the use of bombs, which are becoming increasingly efficient and of greater capacity, not only have armies become more vulnerable, but the centers of population situated in the rear and whole regions inhabited by civilians will be threatened.

Chemical warfare thus acquires the power to produce more terrible effects over much larger areas."

On another occasion Marshal Foch declared that in another war not only men but women and children would be combatants, that the fighting would not be localized in any sense, and that the whole world would be involved.

Brigadier-General Groves, following maneuvers of the Royal Air Force in 1927, admitted that:

"During the next war large areas of the country will probably be submerged in a sea of gas spread by enemy airplanes.

"How to protect civilians from the perils of gas attack, and how to move them in time of need from the town to safe quarters, above and below the ground, are problems which are now occupying some of the best technical brains in the country."

The discussion at a recent meeting of the Red Cross in Brussels, reported in the *New York Times* May 27, 1928, gives a sense of immediate reality to these warnings:

"Assuming that in future wars large populations will be sprayed with poisonous gases . . . the Red Cross recently assembled experts on the subject in an international conference. . . . The meeting adopted various suggestions, which will be submitted to the international committee of the Red Cross.

"As conceived by these experts, the next war will be one in which the gas-besieged civilian will be in much the same predicament as a passenger in one of the lower cabins of a sinking ship. He may have some chance to survive, but not much. For the clouds of chemicals that will envelop his city will settle upon reservoirs, poisoning the water supply; will penetrate warehouses and shops, making food inedible; will hunt him out in his house or cellar, as well as in subterranean shelters, penetrating every crevice and cutting off all sources of fresh air except that which may be artificially produced within hermetically sealed enclosures. And if such enclosures existed, only a very small proportion of the population could utilize them.

"If the civilian is provided with an effective gas mask . . . and can get it on and make a dash for an entirely air-and-gas-proof cellar, and if he has an artificial supply of oxygen readily at hand, and if the gas cloud lifts before long and is not renewed, he may escape and live. . . . The careful citizen may have to purchase many masks, getting a new one each time an improved brand appears. The present ones cost about $4 each.

"If the recommendations of the experts were fully carried out, cities would have to be almost entirely rebuilt. The expense of even a moderate number of gas-proof caverns, gas-proof buildings and masks would, of course, be enormous. Some of the experts at the conference expressed the view that no reliable means of immunization existed, even assuming that a nation was prepared to pay the price of the elaborate construction conceived by the technicians."

H. G. Wells, in his introduction to Commander Kenworthy's book, recounts the fact that when the question of teaching the use of gas masks to children in the infant schools was raised in a debate on the Air Estimates Bill in the House of Commons in 1927, it was greeted with laughter by the members present. He goes on to say that "nothing could better illustrate the happy carelessness with which we move towards the next catastrophe. . . . Today the huge majority of people in the world think no more about the prevention of war than a warren of rabbits thinks about the suppression of shotguns and ferrets. They just don't want to be bothered about it. It is amazing how they accept the things that will presently slaughter them. . . ."

As a matter of fact even those who know most about present war plans know only with what weapons and devices another war would be begun. "The late war brought surprises, the next would add to them." Two things, only, seem reasonably certain: It will be fought from the air with gas and flame, and carried on against whole populations.

The dispatch from the *Chicago Daily News* mentioned above refers to the report of the special committee on chemical warfare of the League of Nations as saying that the next war will treat civilians the same as soldiers, that it will strike at great cities by long-range guns and aircraft and that protection of combatants against gases will be difficult, and protection of civilians almost impossible.

Attacks will be directed against centers of industry, against sources of food supply and lines of communication. Breaking down the morale of the enemy people will be one of the chief objectives.

The Right Honorable Winston S. Churchill, formerly First Lord of the Admiralty, Minister of Munitions, Secretary of State for War and Secretary of State for Air, in an article which was published in *Nash's Pall Mall Magazine,* September 24, 1924, under the title "Shall We Commit Suicide?" pointed out the lines along which the plans for another war are being made:

"It is established that henceforth whole populations will take part in war, all doing their utmost, all subjected to the fury of the enemy. . . . Mankind has never been in this position before. Without having improved appreciably in virtue or enjoying wiser guidance, it has got into its hands for the first time the tools by which it can unfailingly accomplish its own extermination. . . .

"As for Poison Gas and Chemical Warfare in all its forms, only the first chapter has been written of a terrible book. . . . A study of disease—of pestilences methodically prepared and deliberately launched upon man and beast—is certainly being

WHAT WAR IS 399

pursued in the laboratories of more than one great country. Blight to destroy crops, anthrax to slay horses and cattle, plague to poison not armies only but whole districts—such are the lines along which military science is remorselessly advancing."

In an article, "War—Man's Greatest Industry," published in the *New York Times* for March 13, 1922, Charles M. Lincoln after long research and investigation makes this statement:

"The British Army Council foresees the use of chemicals on the offense in these ways: From cylinders along the ground, in clouds, by shell or projectile bombardment, by bursting grenades, and by projectiles and containers dropped from airships.

"Instruction of troops in the discharge of liquid fire is beginning, each soldier to carry on his back two tanks of volatile oil which high pressure will enable him to shoot 150 feet through a hose.

"Great progress is being made by all the nations in the wireless control of pilotless planes. The possibilities of radio are being developed by all the nations. . . . In a few countries consideration of the use of bacteria as a war weapon has accompanied the research in chemicals. But no nation has thus far had the hardihood to openly include bacteria in its category of weapons, as gases and chemicals have been included. But, at that, another great war might bring the use of disease germs. . . . They are cheap, can be produced in abundance, and might prove quite effective."

The tremendous property losses of war conducted according to modern methods are indicated by Will Irwin in "The Next War":

"Perhaps a better way of breaking up the 'resistance of the rear' would be to exterminate not the human Paris but the physical Paris. That could be done in one gigantic conflagration started by inextinguishable chemicals dropped from a few aircraft. The method is practicable even now, in the infancy of chemical warfare; and the military chemists of Europe are experimenting further alone these lines. Such a campaign would of course not be confined to Paris, it would be aimed also at the great ports, at a hundred little cities which do their part in making munitions. . . . Such a campaign could in a few weeks nearly equal the property losses of the Great War."

General Lincoln C. Andrews, as Chief of the New York Bureau of Military Training, declares that to him it is incredible when he hears men talk about the next war in a matter-of-fact way. "It cannot be," he says, "that they have any conception of what the next war will be like. It will be so hideous in its devastation that it will matter little which side wins, for both will be ruined."

One of the things which Dr. William P. Merrill, President of the World Alliance, says the individual man or woman can do to help mobilize for peace is to know and keep making known the facts about what war today is:

"Nothing," he says, "should stop us in this work. One grave danger threatening mankind is that a new generation will come up trained and accustomed to look back on war from a distance, as a glorious and wonderful affair. We must not let the sense of the hideous gruesomeness of the horrible business of fighting fade out. The best of our fighting men came back with their lips sealed. They would not talk about war. Can we wonder? Yet they ought to talk. They ought never to let anyone forget what war is, as waged today. We ought to read and pass on and keep in circulation such books as Will Irwin and Philip Gibbs and others have been writing. Strong influences are at work to suppress or set aside such discussions of the nature of war. . . . Every lover of peace should put thought and energy into the task of keeping unveiled the grim horror of this business of war."

CHAPTER XXV
WHAT WAR COSTS

It is possible after a fashion to estimate the number of dollars that the World War cost; it is even possible to estimate in round numbers the loss of life which it entailed. But it is not possible to compute the whole cost of the war for it would have to be added up in the unknown terms of the future. This fact, and the fact also that the cost will be borne by victor and vanquished alike are revealed in a very striking statement made by Dr. Ales Hrdlicka of the Smithsonian Institution, which is quoted by Dr. David Starr Jordan in his book, "War and the Breed":

"Armies in the past have had little heavy artillery, with none of the powerful modern high explosives, and other conditions of warfare were such that deep mental and nervous shocks must have been far less frequent.

"But it is not only the direct injuries to the brain or nervous system which come into consideration. Perhaps even greater harm, both in the way of resulting defective personalities and following defective progeny, will result from the extreme and prolonged tension that must be sustained in many cases by the soldier in the trenches, for days and often weeks at a time, from the infectious diseases, and from the disease of the various important organs contracted through overstrain, exposure or direct injuries. All such conditions will leave lasting marks on the organism. They will produce a large class of invalids, and these invalids, at best, will not be able to give the proper care to their progeny; but in many cases they will, doubtless, not be able any more to transmit to their progeny a 'healthy mind and a healthy body.'

"Viewed in this light, modern warfare becomes a great enemy of the human race. It not only kills many of the most healthy and competent but it will create and perpetuate on a larger scale many serious organic defects, which, like the proverbial sins, will plague humanity for generations. The victor and the vanquished will suffer alike."

On the monetary cost of war comprehensive studies have been made by Professor Ernest L. Bogart, which have been published by the Carnegie Endowment for International Peace, under the title, "Direct and Indirect Costs of the Great World War":

SUMMARY OF THE DIRECT COSTS OF THE WAR

	Gross	Advance to Allies	Net Cost
United States	$ 32,080,266,968	$ 9,455,014,125	$ 22,625,252,843
Great Britain	44,029,011,868	8,695,000,000	35,334,011,868
Rest of British Empire	4,493,813,072	....	4,493,813,072
France	25,812,782,800	1,547,200,000	24,265,582,800
Russia	22,593,950,000	....	22,593,950,000
Italy	12,313,998,000	....	12,313,998,000
Other Entente Allies	3,963,867,914	....	3,963,867,914
TOTAL	$145,287,690,622	$19,697,214,125	$125,590,476,497
Germany	$ 40,150,000,000	$ 2,375,000,000	$ 37,775,000,000
Austria-Hungary	20,622,690,600	....	20,622,960,600
Turkey and Bulgaria	2,245,200,000	....	2,245,200,000
TOTAL	$ 63,018,160,600	$ 2,375,000,000	$ 60,643,160,600
GRAND TOTAL	$208,305,851,222	$22,072,214,125	$186,233,637,097

SUMMARY OF INDIRECT COST OF THE WAR

Capitalized value of lives lost:
    Soldiers ....$ 33,551,276,280
    Civilians 33,551,276,280
Property losses:
    On land 29,960,000,000
    Shipping and cargo 6,800,000,000
Loss of production 45,000,000,000
War relief 1,000,000,000
Loss to neutrals 1,750,000,000

Total indirect costs $151,612,552,560
Total direct costs, net 186,233,637,097

Grand total costs of the war $337,846,189,657

WHAT WAR COSTS

The average daily cost of the war was more than $215,000,000 or $9,000,000 per hour. Dr. Frank Crane visualizes this amount of money in these comparisons:

"If the money which the war cost were brought together in silver dollars and these dollars were placed edge to edge they would lap around the world 236 times; they would belt the earth at the equator with a silver girdle 29 feet wide; piled on one another would reach 1⅔ times the distance to the moon; rolled into rails they would make a railroad twice around the equator; divided equally among the entire population of the globe they would allow each human being about $170."

There are no records from which the cost of the war in lives can be more than roughly estimated. The war records of the various countries show the number of known dead to have been as follows:

Country	Soldiers Killed
United States	107,284
Great Britain	807,451
France	1,427,800
Russia	2,762,064
Italy	507,160
Belgium	267,000
Serbia	707,343
Rumania	339,117
Greece	15,000
Portugal	4,000
Japan	300
Total	6,938,519

Country	Soldiers Killed
Germany	1,611,104
Austria-Hungary	911,000
Turkey	436,924
Bulgaria	101,224
Total	3,060,252
Grand total	9,998,771

The loss of life from the decline in the birth rate and the increase in the death rate is estimated by the Danish

Research Society in a study on the "Social Results of the War" to have been:

	Decline in Birth Rate	Increase of Death Rate
Germany	3,600,000	2,700,000
Austria-Hungary	3,800,000	2,000,000
Great Britain, Ireland	850,000	1,000,000
France	1,500,000	1,840,000
Belgium	175,000	400,000
Italy	1,400,000	880,000
Bulgaria	155,000	130,000
Rumania	150,000	360,000
Serbia	320,000	1,330,000

To all this should be added the public loss in constructive power and the private cost in suffering and misery which these figures indicate:

20,297,551 wounded
5,983,600 prisoners
10,000,000 refugees
9,000,000 war orphans
5,000,000 war widows.

When it comes to the cost of war to the race, it is, as Dr. Hrdlicka's statement suggests, impossible to do more than indicate that the cost is heavy. In "War and the Breed," Dr. David Starr Jordan assembles the opinions of many biologists and students of questions of race inheritance to the effect that far from insuring the "survival of the fittest," war kills off or disables the best, leaving the physically unfit as fathers of the race.

Dr. Caleb Williams Saleeby, discussing "The Long Cost of War," says:

"We all find reasons for the fall of the Roman Empire according to our creeds, instincts and prejudices. But some of the reasons advanced actually have reason in them. The incessant drain of the right kind of military stuff from the population of Rome, led in the long run to the production of that degenerate people who wished only for bread and circuses. The recruiting officer rejected the halt and blind, feeble-kneed, the easily fatigued, saying, though he did not know it: 'You are not good enough to be a Roman soldier; stay at home and be a Roman father.' The future was ruthlessly sacrificed by militarism to the present."

Professor Vernon Kellogg states:

"War to the biologist seems, above all else, stupid. It is racially dangerous. It flies in the face of all that makes for human evolutionary advance, and is utterly without shadow of serious scientific reason for its maintenance. It is not natural selection in Man, nor in any way the counterpart of it.

"France has kept for over a century an interesting set of official records (of conscripted youths) which offers most valuable data for the scrutiny of the biological student of war . . .

"From the recruiting statistics as officially recorded, it may be stated with confidence that the average height of the men of France began notably to decrease with the coming of age, in 1813 and on, of the young men born in the years of the Revolutionary Wars (1792-1802), and that it continued to decrease in the following years with the coming of age of youths born during the Wars of the Empire.

"Running nearly parallel with the fluctuation in number of exemptions for undersize is the fluctuation in number of exemptions for infirmities. These exemptions increased by one-third in twenty years. Exemptions for undersize and infirmities together nearly doubled in number. But the lessening again of the figure of exemptions for infirmities was not so easily accomplished as was that of the figure for undersize. The influence of the Napoleonic Wars was felt by the nation, and revealed by its recruiting statistics, for a far longer time in its aspect of producing a racial deterioration as to vigor than in its aspect of producing a lessening stature."

So far from considering war a cause of progress, as is often claimed, Darwin wrote in the "Origin of Species":

"In every country in which a large standing army is kept up, the finest young men are taken by conscription or enlisted. They are thus exposed to early death during war, are often tempted into vice, and are prevented from marrying during the prime of life. On the other hand, the shorter and feebler men, with poor constitutions, are left at home, and consequently have a much better chance of marrying."

Following any future wars the cost to the race would be much heavier, for as Will Irwin says in "The Next War":

"So far, wars in general have struck at the strength of the male strain alone. However much the women have been massacred, there has been no scientific selection in the choice of victims. The strength of woman has been left to war-depleted nations to renew their blood. Already, the general staffs of Europe are saying that the recruiting of women in the late war was irregular, hit-and-miss, wasteful. . . . It would be far more efficient and economical to mobilize them all and select the war-workers by scientific methods. . . . We shall take the young unmarried women, and choose from them by scientific test the strongest and most brilliant, rejecting the weakest and most stupid. That process was begun in the late war. The best managed munitions works gave no woman a job until medical and psychological tests proved that she had the body and brains for the work. Just as with the men, we shall send the culls back to civilian life, free to pour their inferior blood into the veins of the new generation. . . . In the next war, munitions works and services of the rear will be special objects of attack. There, as at the front, we shall kill by wholesale not by retail, and we shall kill our selected female breeding stock. So to the anti-social effects of the next war we must add one never accomplished before in human history: the sapping of the feminine strength in the human race."

But besides the drag upon the future the indirect

WHAT WAR COSTS

costs of war in terms of human welfare are very heavy. Immediately following the war, Homer Folks traveled through Europe to make a survey in the interest of the work of the Red Cross of the "Net Results of the War upon Human Welfare." He has published the results of his survey in "The Human Costs of War." The increase in loss of life by sickness due to the war, he points out, is one of the things that cannot be estimated for the bills "come later." But the facts he cites in regard to tuberculosis are indicative of what the cost was:

"The anti-tuberculosis movement was local, state, national and international, voluntary and governmental, medical and lay; the best organized effort to stamp out a widespread disease yet known. Progress was slow. In a period of twenty or thirty years the disease might be reduced by 50 per cent. But everywhere it was being reduced. Now comes the war. This decrease in tuberculosis is immediately arrested and in two or three years the hard-won gains of twenty are lost.

"In Italy there was an increase of 16 per cent in two years; in the cities of Italy, an increase ranging from 30 to 50 per cent. In England there was an actual increase in 1917 of 16 per cent over 1913 and of 30 per cent over what probably would have been the rate in 1917 had there been no war. Even in America, far removed as we were from the seat of war and late as we entered it, the rate of decrease in the tuberculosis death-rate, which had been fairly continuous for many years, was abruptly reduced."

Beyond these things there is still the cost in character which must be included in the total against war. The old idea that war develops heroism and desirable traits of character is repeatedly contradicted by those who have had an opportunity to see its effect on men. Major General O'Ryan has declared on more than one occasion:

"We soldiers are not ashamed of the way we fought, but those of us who know anything know that fighting is not glorious. No matter how righteous the cause, the experience of a soldier at the front tends to lower his finer sensibilities. If any soldier came out of this war a better man than when he entered, it is in spite of and not because of his battle experience. War is the denial of Christianity, and of all the most sacred things in life. It exalts force. It thrives on lies. It is the product of hate and fear and cannot by any stretch of the imagination be waged humanely."

Ellen Key, as a citizen of a neutral country, watched the effect of war on European families from the woman's point of view. She says in her book, "War, Peace and the Future":

"Even in those cases where women regain their loved ones without any great physical or mental hurt, they often find them so changed in character that the mother or wife has the feeling that she is confronted with a different man to the one who left her; a sad man instead of a merry, a hard man instead of a sensitive, a brutal man instead of a refined man."

And even yet the total is not all summed up. There is the constructive work that war delays or makes impossible.

The following paragraph from Francis Delaisi suggests the human power for production which war usurps:

"Imagine a gigantic workyard where fifteen million hands, provided with formidable machinery, are busily employed day and night. Behind them, fifty-five million men are exclusively occupied in manufacturing and transporting all that is necessary for their upkeep, their equipment, their supplies and the renewing of their plant. And behind them the inhabitants of twenty-nine nations reducing their consumption to a minimum (sometimes, even below) and devoting their privations and their savings to feeding this gigantic gang of workers. All the resources of the universe were transported to this workyard where fifteen million men were employed not in production, but exclusively in the destruction of everything they could lay their hands on, and of themselves."

It has been estimated that the labor and raw material consumed every month during the last year of the war by the ordnance department of the United States Army alone, was equal to the cost of the Panama Canal. So much for what the war cost,—what we got out of it, according to Mr. Bruce Barton who quotes Eugene Debs as "the man who was most right about the last war" was " 'influenza and the income tax.' "

In "The Next War" Will Irwin considers a few of the productive undertakings which release from war would make possible:

"In our government are a number of bureaus concerned with increasing production, fighting disease, supervising the agencies which conserve life and increase production. . . . Go into any of these Washington bureaus and some specialist, some practical dreamer, struggling along at a salary running from fifteen hundred dollars to three thousand dollars a year, will tell you what 'his people' could do to multiply production and improve human conditions, to lengthen and fortify life, to increase the beauty and usefulness of the world 'if we only had the money.' But they haven't the money. For these activities, the Government grants less than one per cent of the National revenue. In 1920, the existing army and navy absorbed thirty-eight per cent; and the whole war bill, was ninety-three per cent."

It is an analysis of the taxes that tells this story most vividly. The Report of the Secretary of the Treasury for the fiscal year ending June 30, 1927, shows 82 cents of every tax dollar going to pay the bills of past wars and of preparation for future wars. The report contains these statements:

". . . in modern times the Federal tax burden of one generation is largely determined by the military activities of the preceding one. In the fiscal year 1927 expenditures for interest on the public debt exceeded by over $140,000,000 the aggregate amount of ordinary civil expenditures, while military expenditures were almost twice civil expenditures.

"When the average citizen grumbles over the size of his income tax payment he often visualizes his hard-earned money being spent by the Government to compile reports on business or agricultural conditions, or to erect public buildings, send diplomats abroad, carry on scientific investigations, or make and enforce laws. As a matter of fact, a small part of the taxpayer's dollar goes into work of this sort, only about one-sixth being used for all the multitudinous types of ordinary civil functions added together. One-half of each tax dollar is used for the service of the public debt (due except for a fraction of one per cent to wars). The remaining one-third of the taxpayer's dollar is spent on military expenditures for national defense or payments to military veterans."

The total appropriation for present national defense and past wars is estimated at 82 per cent of the budget for 1927, or $2,511,141,563, as follows:

Pension Office, Interior Department	$199,015,000
Veterans' Bureau, including bonus, Army and Navy insurance, etc.	405,500,000
War Department, for military parks, Soldiers' Home, etc., included in so-called non-military activities	10,606,805
Interest on public debt	830,000,000
Public debt retirements	484,766,130
Army and Navy, military activities	581,253,628
Total	$2,511,141,563

WHAT WAR COSTS

The following tables from this report show the expenditures for national defense in pre-war and in post-war years:

Year	Army	Navy	Total National Defense	Total Expenditures	Per Cent of Total Expenditures
1907....	$ 92,142,000	$ 97,866,000	$190,008,000	$579,129,000	32.87
1908....	103,436,000	118,780,000	222,216,000	659,196,000	33.71
1909....	121,871,000	116,316,000	238,187,000	693,744,000	34.19
1910....	122,572,000	123,974,000	246,546,000	693,617,000	35.54
1911....	122,294,000	120,729,000	243,023,000	691,202,000	35.16
1912....	108,676,000	136,390,000	245,066,000	689,881,000	35.52
1913....	113,816,000	134,093,000	247,909,000	724,512,000	34.21
Totals..	$784,807,000	$848,148,000	$1,632,955,000	$4,731,281,000	34.51

Year	Army	Navy	Total National Defense	Total Expenditures	Per Cent of Total Expenditures
1921..	$472,161,000	$650,717,000	$1,122,878,000	$4,468,713,000	25.12
1922..	318,440,000	476,348,000	794,788,000	3,195,685,000	24.86
1923..	273,629,000	323,218,000	596,847,000	3,244,717,000	18.39
1924..	242,490,000	331,095,000	573,585,000	2,946,401,000	19.47
1925..	244,688,000	344,603,000	589,291,000	2,464,169,000	24.29
1926..	267,260,000	312,743,000	580,003,000	3,030,387,000	19.13
1927..	270,809,000	318,909,000	589,718,000	3,000,000,000	19.66
Totals	$2,089,477,000	$2,757,633,000	$4,847,110,000	$22,350,072,000	21.68

The Sun of Baltimore published these tables with this comment:

"Probably the best way to compare expenditures of one group of years with the other, in the opinion of statisticians here, would be to reduce the dollars to a common basis by using the 1913 index of the retail cost of living . . .

"Employing this figure and averaging it for each group of years, it is found that the $1,632,955,000 which national defense cost from 1907 to 1913, is equivalent to $1,694,975,000 of the 1913 value and that the $4,847,110,000 cost of national defense from 1921 to 1927 is equivalent to $3,231,406,000 of the 1913 value.

"In other words, in actual dollars the cost of defense trebled, while in dollars converted to a common basis of value, the cost just about doubled."

And after all the material costs of actual warfare have been met, there is yet another—the cost of the toleration of war. Upon every effort toward freedom and human welfare, upon the labor movement, the woman's movement, the child welfare movement, upon democracy, the toleration of war is a heavy drag. It contradicts in principle each one of these, by denying the value of human life and the worth and dignity of the individual. As Dr. Charles C. Morrison has said in "The Outlawry of War," because the establishment of peace "has been supposed to depend upon the realization of the brotherhood of man," men "have failed to see that so long as war remains, all dreams of a higher social order are in vain."

PART IV
MATERIALS FOR A WORKING PROGRAM

CHAPTER XXVI

WHAT YOU CAN DO FOR PEACE [1]

A ROUGH survey, such as the preceding chapters contain, of the forces making for world peace and of opposing influences, leads to two convictions: the first is that the peace movement today is strong enough to have a chance of success not in the remote future, but now; the second is that to achieve success it must find expression in every community big and little. No single effort of any group or any individual can be spared, nor is it possible to foresee what effort may open the way for the universal demand for peace which lies just beneath the political surface, to break through and compel action. The fate of the "big navy" program, which the militarists attempted to put through Congress in the spring of 1928, left no doubt of the extent of peace sentiment nor of the power of peace forces when their strength is focused. It was at first taken for granted in Congressional circles that the "big navy" program of seventy-one ships would be adopted. Leaders in Congress who were opposed to it believed that it would pass because there had been so little expression of opinion against it. At that point a few of the national peace organizations sent out detailed statements of what was happening. Almost overnight the churches, the women's groups, hastily created emer-

[1] The addresses of peace organizations mentioned in this chapter will be found at the end of the chapter, those of other organizations are included in the text.

gency committees, and scattered individuals everywhere sent in such a protest as Congress had not received on any issue in years. The navy program was reduced in committee from seventy-one ships to sixteen. More than this, peace sentiment was recognized as a political force to be carefully considered.

Forming a Committee

It is not necessary to wait for a committee or organization to be formed in a community in order to work for world peace. There is much that an individual or group of individuals consulting together informally, can do. But the most effective work can be accomplished if a large committee of active, well-informed citizens is gathered together and divided into sub-committees each of which can devote its energy to some one phase of the work.

A committee may sometimes be more easily formed in the first place for some specific activity, such as a mass meeting for a prominent speaker, or an open forum for the discussion of some current problem or important measure before Congress. Armistice Day and Goodwill Day offer opportunities to organize for community action.

The work of a permanent committee can be divided in various ways. One effective way is to have a sub-committee for each different group to be reached so that the peace problem can be studied and presented from the special point of view of that group. The member chosen to interest the local labor groups, for instance, should not only understand the effect of war upon labor but should know what labor organizations have done to promote peace, so that local unions can be made to realize that in taking up peace work they are joining in an activity of their own group.

Meeting Opposition

The organizers of a peace committee must be prepared for a certain amount of opposition. It is inevitable that a movement seeking to bring about so profound a change as the elimination of war, affecting as it does long-established institutions, should be attacked. One method which has been employed to obstruct efforts toward peace has been, not to charge local groups with deliberately evil intent, but to assert that they are the dupes, either indirectly, through national peace organizations, or directly of "red" and "foreign" and "socialistic" influences. Local committees should know that the attacks upon national peace organizations and their officers have been fully answered and demonstrated to be without foundation, and that these answers are available. They should know also that there has been vigorous remonstrance and division within the ranks of such organizations as the American Legion and the D. A. R., officers of which have been instrumental in preventing speeches and public meetings designed to promote peace. Unquestionably in so difficult a problem as the organization of world peace, there is room for honest difference of opinion as to the methods that should be pursued, and the peace movement, knowing the facts and the future are on its side, should be willing in all instances to meet honest opposition with reason and without resentment. Even in the case of attacks rising consciously or unconsciously out of interested motives, the peace movement has no energy to spare for counterattacks. But peace workers need to be informed as to the source and motives of any charges made in order that they may be properly discounted and impotent to check the progress of the movement.

Among the publications from which information on these points can be obtained are: "Professional Patriots," by Norman Hapgood, published by Albert and Charles Boni; "The Blue Menace," by Elizabeth McCausland, published by *The Springfield Republican,* Springfield, Massachusetts, 10 cents a copy; the articles by Mrs. Carrie Chapman Catt which appeared in the *Woman Citizen* for June and July, 1927; an article in the *American Legion Monthly* for July, 1927, "There's Only One Kind of Americanism," by Rupert Hughes; and "Our Threatened Heritage," a letter of protest to the Daughters of the American Revolution by members objecting to the methods employed by the officers of the organization in combating the work of peace organizations, copies of which can be ordered from the D. A. R. Committee of Protest, 371 Broadway, Cambridge, Massachusetts.

There is an old saying, "When you wish to start a fire, put your match to the dry end of the stick." The organization of a community for peace work should be begun, therefore, where success promises to be quickest, for each step gained helps in taking the next, and energy is not tied up in a long struggle.

Through Libraries

The library as a center of information offers a logical point at which to begin. Many libraries will be found willing to arrange a special table or shelf of books and magazines dealing with international affairs. If necessary a committee can undertake to raise money to purchase them.

The Carnegie Endowment for International Peace has established "International Mind Alcoves" in over 150 libraries, the majority in small communities. These alcoves are designed "to stimulate the international mind —to assist readers to gain a wider knowledge of the peoples of the world and thereby a larger interest in them." The books number about 100, and are chosen from the most recent publications. They are presented to the library a few at a time. Any library may apply to the Endowment for such a collection. There is, however, a waiting list, so that requests cannot be immediately filled. A report on "International Mind Alcoves," very helpful in any work with libraries, can be obtained by writing the New York offices of the Endowment, at 405 West 117th St. If a selection of books on Latin America is to be started, the Pan American Union, Washington, D. C., can give valuable suggestions and material.

Through consultation with the State Library Commissions, it will often be found possible to arrange for the inclusion of books on international affairs in their traveling libraries and extension work. State library organizations in ten States are already receiving the books included in the International Mind Alcoves.

If a special collection of books on international affairs is arranged in the library, publicity should be given it by a notice and, if possible, editorials in the local papers. When a foreign country, or a special problem affecting world peace is prominent in the news, a bibliography on the subject can be prepared, preferably by the local librarian, to be posted on the library bulletin board and for publication in the papers.

In a number of instances the city libraries have coöperated with local clubs in preparing and printing bibliographies on international affairs, among others the Public Library of Newark, New Jersey, and the St. Louis Public Library. The Public Library of Newark in collaboration with the Newark Museum also arranges exhibits on foreign countries in connection with which it issues bibliographies for children and adults on various phases of the life of the people and their relations with the United States. Helpful suggestions in arranging similar projects can be obtained by writing the Director of the Library, John Cotton Dana.

The children's room in the library should be supplied with books and pictures about the children of other nations, and such others as will give children a sense of the unity of mankind and the interdependence of nations. International Mind Alcoves for children to interest them in "their friends of other lands" have recently been started by the Carnegie Endowment, and are proving popular. An attractive feature can be made of children's books of other nations by arranging them to suggest a trip around the world, for instance, by putting them around a small globe of the earth standing at the center of a table, or around the edge of a world map; or a map can be hung on the wall behind the table of books, with the names of the books about each country printed in the margin.

Through Public Discussion

Public meetings are particularly important in emergencies when legislation is pending which needs to be supported or opposed. For large meetings and for meetings on technical problems, out-of-town speakers and authorities on the subject are desirable from every point of view, including that of publicity, through which a message can be carried to many more people than will attend the meeting. A mass meeting which has aroused general interest may be followed by smaller meetings in the city and vicinity addressed by local speakers who can report on the larger meeting and lead a discussion.

As a part of a year-round program, speeches should be arranged before regular meetings of all organizations. At any such meeting the peace speaker should secure the adoption of a resolution on the need for persistent government effort toward peace, which can be sent to state and national legislative representatives and political leaders, and should arrange for the formation of a peace committee. From the Pennsylvania Branch of the Women's International League for Peace and Freedom, 1525 Locust St., Philadelphia, a sample form can be obtained which will be found useful in building up a list of speakers for local meetings.

In addition to routine meetings a series of open forums, if possible periodic open forum luncheons, can be held. Forum luncheons at which both sides of a problem are presented with time allowed for discussion, were inaugurated immediately after the war by the Foreign Policy Association in New York and have continued in that city and been extended to many others. Suggestions as to how to proceed can be obtained from the Foreign Policy Association. Where out-of-town speakers are not available for such luncheons, local representatives of various groups can be asked to discuss peace as the necessity of the modern world, from their particular points of view. At one, a local editor may tell what the press is doing to promote peace, at another a clergyman may describe the work of the churches, and at others representatives of teachers, of women's clubs, of business men, of labor and farm organizations and of young people may be the speakers. Such a series has been tried out with success by a committee of Friends in England.

Suggestions for conferences on the general topic, "The Cause and Cure of War," carrying out the idea of the successful conferences held by women's organizations in Washington for the last three years, can be obtained from the National Committee on the Cause and Cure of War. Regional, state, county, city, town, village and rural conferences are planned by this committee, during the fall and winter of 1928, in support of the Kellogg treaty renouncing war, and special programs on this subject are available. General suggestions for organized joint conferences based on material originally prepared by the Y. W. C. A. may be obtained from the National Council for Prevention of War. Two programs for state conferences are described below.

The Indiana Council on International Relations arranged an all-day state-wide conference on "A Constructive Program for World Peace—Indiana's Responsibility." In addition to special speakers local men and women were asked to assist in the discussion period and their names were included on the program. Churches of all denominations coöperated in a mass meeting and a public luncheon gave the people who could not attend the sessions an opportunity to hear part of the discussion. At a similar conference arranged by the Connecticut Council on International Relations, separate luncheons were given for the men's and women's groups with speakers on subjects of special interest to each; the afternoon was devoted to round table discussions so arranged that delegates might attend more than one, and an evening dinner was held in a hall with a gallery so that the general speeches could be heard by a large audience.

Public discussion on foreign affairs has been greatly stimulated during recent years by the summer institutes arranged under the auspices of a rapidly increasing number of universities. The first of these institutes, organized at Williams College in 1921, known as the Williamstown Institute of Politics, has been addressed by leading statesmen and thinkers from all sections of the world. Similar institutes on public and international affairs are held at the University of Virginia, the University of Georgia, the University of Chicago, the University of Porto Rico, the University of New Hampshire, the University of Washington and the University of California. A conference of a little different character is held annually at Eliot, Maine, under the auspices of *World Unity*. It is known as Green Acre Institute and its purpose is to make available to the general public "those findings of modern science and philosophy which tend to supply a new basis for faith in the possibility of human brotherhood and world coöperation."

A number of brief summer schools for the discussion of peace problems have been held during the last few years. Among the organizations which regularly hold such schools and from which information can be secured as to how to arrange others, are the Fellowship of Reconciliation and the Women's International League for Peace and Freedom.

Peace committees might find it profitable to follow the example of universities which send students abroad for study, and send a representative to attend a conference or summer school or one of the many institutes on international relations, who would be able to bring a report and something of the inspiration of the meeting back to the community.

During political campaigns public meetings at which congressional candidates can be asked to state their own opinion and their party's position on peace questions are particularly important.

The value of public meetings, large or small, can be greatly increased by the distribution of inexpensive fliers setting forth salient facts in connection with the subject under discussion, or giving a list of books for further study, or a list of suggestions as to what an individual can do. Suggestions for fliers and samples of those already printed can be obtained from the National Council for Prevention of War.

Through the Churches

Armistice Sunday has come to be almost universally observed in the churches by special services and sermons. A community peace service is usual. It may be preceded by a series of evening sermons in preparation for the day. Special programs are issued annually by the Federal Council of Churches. A Goodwill Service for Armistice Sunday is published by Dr. Lincoln Wirt, Western Secretary of the National Council for Prevention of War; an "International Church Service" by the League of Nations Non-Partisan Association and an International Vesper Service, the price of which is ten for 30c, published by the Y. W. C. A. The Y. M. C. A. and Y. W. C. A. issue special programs for services of international friendship in connection with the Week of Prayer and World Fellowship, celebrated throughout the world by these organizations each autumn. The Board of Religious Education of the United Church of Canada, at Toronto, is publishing a service of "Peace and Goodwill" for Rally Day, 1928.

The Sundays nearest Christmas and Goodwill Day also offer an opportunity for special church programs. Material helpful in building up a church peace service will be found in the peace sermons and articles by religious leaders which are issued by the American Institute of Sacred Literature, Hyde Park, Chicago, by the World Alliance for International Friendship through the Churches. Reprints of sermons and a leaflet of "Songs of Fellowship," published by the Fellowship of Reconciliation, can be obtained from the National Council for Prevention of War. A comprehensive collection of peace hymns has been made by Dr. George H. Donaldson of Cliffside, New Jersey, but has not yet been published.

Sunday Schools and Vacation Bible Schools

In the Sunday Schools and Vacation Bible Schools a steadily increasing effort is being made to teach the ideals of peace. The International Council of Religious Education at its 1928 meeting recommended world peace as one of the three subjects to be emphasized in the Sunday Schools. Sunday School courses are being revised not only with the idea of including special peace lessons but with that of considering the whole course from the point of view of its effect on the fundamental peace teaching of the Christian religion and Sunday Schools should make use of these new editions. A study of "The God of the Old Testament in Relation to War," by Marion J. Benedict, recently published by Teachers College, Columbia University, will be found very useful in the preparation of a Sunday School course, as is likewise a scholarly pamphlet, "The Words of Christ Quoted for or Against War," which has been prepared by the New York Presbytery and may be obtained from Mr. Harold A. Hatch, 70 Leonard St., New York City.

The General Sunday School Association of the Universalist Church, 176 Newbury St., Boston, Mass., issues a peace program particularly appropriate for Goodwill Day or for any patriotic holiday. In addition this association sends out special goodwill programs including hymns, scripture readings, prayers and general suggestions, six weeks in advance of Goodwill Day, Armistice Sunday and other appropriate occasions, as a part of a loose-leaf notebook service with which it supplies all superintendents of its Sunday Schools.

For adult classes the courses on Christianity and Peace listed in a later section of this chapter are appropriate, notably "Christian Fellowship Among the Nations," by Dr. Jerome Davis and Dr. Roy B. Chamberlin.

For the younger classes, "Peace Lessons for Sunday

Schools," by Anna FitzGerald Van Loan, graded for pupils from six to sixteen years of age, is among the recent non-denominational publications of special value. It is published by Fleming H. Revell, New York, in three volumes at $1.00 a volume. "Projects in World Friendship," by John Leslie Lobingier, arranged for primary, junior and high school departments, is published by the University of Chicago Press for $1.85. "Programs of World Service for Primary Children," also by Mr. Lobingier, is being issued by the Committee on Missionary Education of the Congregational Churches, 14 Beacon St., Boston. In "Peace Crusaders—Adventures in Goodwill," by Anna Bassett Griscom, published by Lippincott and available from the American Friends Service Committee for $1.50, there is much material that will be found of interest and value in Sunday School work.

Helpful suggestions can be obtained from the Missionary Education Movement, 150 Fifth Ave., New York City, the Federal Council of Churches and the World Alliance. Lists of additional Sunday School material, including Christmas plays and Armistice Day programs, can be obtained from the National Council for Prevention of War.

Missionary Societies

The relation of the work of missionary societies to world peace is receiving wide attention. In several instances Missionary Boards have taken the position that no call must be made for protection by armed forces, and, equally fundamental, a new attitude is being adopted, expressed in this statement by the executive secretary of the Institute of Social and Religious Research:

"That some radical changes in policy and emphasis in the missionary movement in order to make it more completely

WHAT YOU CAN DO FOR PEACE

conducive to world-mindedness are demanded must be obvious to everyone who has thought deeply on the situation.

"Should not missions be rebased on the principle of mutuality, of reciprocity, that is, of the interchange among all countries, whether so-called Christian or so-called non-Christian, of the best ideas and personalities? The sending nations must recognize that they, too, are non-Christian when seen under the white light of Christ himself."

Material of special interest to missionary groups will be found in the reports of the 1926 convention of the Religious Education Association published in its *Journal*. Abstracts of the speeches delivered on this occasion as well as church resolutions on this subject and a statement on "Missionaries and Armed Forces," issued by the Society of Friends in England, are obtainable from the National Council for Prevention of War. The publications of the Missionary Education Movement, notably its books by Basil Mathews, are of particular value in this field.

For work with young people's societies excellent suggestions can be secured from the World Christian Endeavor Society which has recently entered upon a "Crusade for Peace" in which other Christian young people's organizations are joining. The Epworth League and the Girls' Friendly Society have also undertaken to promote international goodwill. The Committee on World Friendship among Young People of the Federal Council of Churches has issued valuable material, including "International Friendship Projects" in which are many practical suggestions. The interest of young people of high-school age in the churches of Ohio has been aroused through Peace Declamation Contests. Full information and a book of selections suitable for declamations can be obtained from the Ohio Council of Churches in Columbus.

Dr. Sidney L. Gulick, Secretary of the Commission on International Justice and Goodwill of the Federal Council, makes these suggestions as to how the individual can begin work within his own church:

"Talk to your pastor. Urge him to start study classes in the Sunday School. The various adult groups of men and women can give time to the study of these questions. Suggest the formation of a Church Committee on International Goodwill. The Committee may be asked to be responsible for finding the best books on the problem and placing them in the Sunday School library. It may arrange for pageants and concerts and lectures dealing with these questions. When several churches have such committees they may join in holding big public rallies on world questions once or twice a year. This committee will be the connecting link between the local church and the national agencies of the churches.

"One wide-awake, consecrated, intelligent, resourceful individual in each church can accomplish wonders if he has faith and will really do what he can."

If they are not already receiving them, the bulletins and publications of the Federal Council of Churches and the World Alliance for International Friendship through the Churches should be sent not only to ministers but to Sunday School officers and church leaders in the community.

Through Women's Clubs

By resolutions, at least, practically all national women's organizations are exerting an influence on the side of world peace, but many local branches are not actively carrying out the line of work suggested by the resolutions or the programs of the national bodies. Where they are not, a member may be asked to bring the matter up at a meeting and if possible have a special committee on international relations appointed to arrange a study course, coöperate with other clubs in a general program, or carry on an independent project in connection with the library, schools or churches. A program for a special club meeting may be suggested, based on the outlines at the end of this chapter. Reports of peace work in the club bulletins are important in creating and sustaining interest.

A plan for interesting women's groups which could well be imitated in other communities has been worked out by the Adams County Y. W. C. A. at Hastings, Nebraska. The Association has organized a Women's Council on International Relations including the presidents of all the local women's organizations in the community. Monthly meetings are held from which each member takes books, information and peace material back to her organization. Round-table discussions are arranged to which other women are invited and speakers sent out to the meetings of other organizations.

Where it is a question of coördinating various active women's groups consultation with the Women's Council for the Promotion of Peace, Hippodrome Annex, Cleveland, Ohio, through which 115 organizations have very successfully carried out an active program, will prove helpful.

A list of the national women's organizations taking part in the effort to establish peace will be found in the chapter on Women and Peace. The latest resolutions of these organizations can be obtained from their national offices or from the National Council for Prevention of War.

Through Young People's Groups

The national bodies of young people's organizations have nearly all adopted some plan for increasing international goodwill and understanding of international problems. Whether or not a local group carries out this part of the program depends largely on the local leader, who may be glad to put additional emphasis on the peace work if interest is expressed in it.

The Y. M. C. A., which is organized in 56 different countries, offers various opportunities for boys of different nations to become acquainted with each other. Besides the "World-Y" tours and borderline camps which it arranges, it publishes two magazines, *World Youth and Foreign Flashes,* which tell stories and show pictures of what boys of other nations are doing. It sends out exhibits of foreign photographs and objects to be used as a basis for talks and for study. It awards a World Brotherhood Charter to boys' groups which take part in its international program. At its international camps a dramatic ceremony is held around the last campfire. A line of boys, each draped in the flag of his country, marches out of the darkness into the light of the fire. Stepping forward one by one each says in his own language, "The boys of my country desire to join hands with young people everywhere," at the same time lighting a peace torch at the fire, to signify that he carries the flame of peace into all parts of the world. This ceremony can be used also at local camps, the American boys all joining hands and repeating the pledge of the Campfire together. Complete information as to how local branches can take part in the organization's international work can be obtained from the national headquarters. A special program for Y. M. C. A. camps is issued by the National Council for Prevention of War.

The Y. W. C. A. publishes many suggestions for pageants, plays and special programs, as well as for study groups on international questions, which can be ordered from the national headquarters. The Week of Prayer arranged by the World Committee of the Y. W. C. A.

each November is in some cities called World Fellowship Week and provides an excellent opportunity for peace programs. The September issue of the *Womans Press* is devoted to material useful in promoting international goodwill.

The Boy Scout and Girl Scout organizations and the Campfire Girls all provide channels, including international correspondence departments in their magazines, through which the young people of different nations can be brought into touch with each other. Their national resolutions and programs not only authorize but call for work in promotion of world peace and goodwill. The fact that those interested in popularizing military training in this country are seeking to encourage it through such organizations as the Scouts, makes it all the more important to be sure that local groups understand and are carrying out the fundamental "aims and ideals" of their organizations. The Boy Scout International Conference recently declared its aims to be "directed toward the development of a spirit of harmony and goodwill between individuals and between nations." In the 1927 Handbook of the Boy Scouts, war is vigorously condemned:

"War is one of the tragedies of the life of the world. In its wake stalk sorrow, poverty, disease, moral let down, debt, hatreds, fears. . . .

"The insane thing about war is that, after killing and destroying, *then* folks must gather around the table—find what the points at issue are and adjust them finally. In a sane world this would be done *first*. It is not *conflict* but *conference* that settles—therefore have it first. . . .

"The Boy Scout Movement around the world is creating world friendships, making community of interest among nations, and should help prevent future wars.

"What individuals and cities and states have learned fairly

well, namely, to settle their differences before impartial judges, may yet be realized between nations.

"Why not? And the Scout who *lives* goodwill and fairness and peace is helping the world recover from the disease of *war*."

The Girl Scouts, in order that there might be no misunderstanding of their purposes, in 1928 authorized a change in the Scout uniform from khaki cloth, cut in a somewhat military style, to green, made in a more typical sports fashion.

The ideals of international goodwill are likewise encouraged by the following organizations of which local branches can be formed if none already exists: the Knighthood of Youth, which is being promoted by the National Child Welfare Association, 70 Fifth Ave., New York City, with Dr. Frank Astor as managing director, and is designed for children from seven to twelve years of age; the Hi-Y Clubs, which are organized in high schools in connection with Y. M. C. A. work; the Sportsmanship Brotherhood, which was organized by a group of men interested in promoting international goodwill through sports, and about which full information can be secured from the Executive Secretary, Daniel Chase, 342 Madison Ave., New York City; and the Woodcraft League of America, 70 East 45th St., New York City, organized by Ernest Thompson Seton.

Besides the opportunity which many of these organizations offered their members for correspondence with young people of other countries, a direct exchange of letters with selected young people abroad can be arranged for American boys and girls through the National Bureau of International Correspondence, which has its headquarters at Peabody College, Nashville, Tennessee, and is a branch of the Musée Pédagogique, which is under the direction of the French Minister of Public

Instruction; or through Miss Mary N. Chase, Proctor Academy, Andover, New Hampshire. For boys, Dr. Sven V. Knudsen has developed a very interesting plan for direct correspondence, under the title "My Friend Abroad," which is carried out through the *Open Road* magazine, 248 Boylston St., Boston. Dr. Knudsen is publishing a directory of a thousand names of boys in different countries who want to exchange letters. At the end of the first year the American boys had written an average of twenty-six letters and already received an average of fourteen replies. One boy had written seventy-nine letters to twenty-three countries and had thirty-six replies from fifteen countries. Prizes are offered for the largest number of letters and for the best.

A Youth Peace Contest, a declamation contest for boys and girls from nine to fifteen years of age, has been arranged by the American Friends Service Committee. Any community may take part. Silver, gold and diamond medals are awarded. Complete directions may be obtained from the Committee.

Summer Camps

Young people can also be reached at their summer camps. A practical and varied collection of camp programs is published by the League of Nations Non-Partisan Association. Through routine life out of doors it is possible to make clear the part which coöperation played in man's development and to bring about a realization of how men wherever they live are occupied with the same tasks of finding food, clothing, shelter, and rest. The saying, "We are citizens of the earth together," can be given a new meaning. A camp program developing this idea is issued by the National Council for Prevention of War.

Goodwill Teams and Peace Caravans

Any young people's group might organize an International Goodwill Team following the plan originated by the Y. M. C. A., or a Caravan for Peace such as those sent out by the American Friends Service Committee. Members of a Goodwill Team inform themselves on international topics, subscribing to appropriate magazines and always making it a point to read at least one book on international affairs a week. A team meets once a week to discuss current events, rehearse programs and plan methods of carrying its ideas afield. Two members spend their time making engagements, two others take charge of collecting pamphlets and posters suitable for distribution, and songs, magazines, maps and charts that can be used with different groups or clubs. Members of the club then speak or give other programs in churches, schools, clubs—"anywhere that people meet to hear programs in the city or surrounding country." Bibliographies on topics discussed are distributed at meetings.

In the Caravans for Peace, men or women college students travel in automobiles supplied with banners and literature for distribution and speak outdoors or indoors to any audience, and wherever possible arrange for local committees to be formed to continue the peace work. The Caravaners are given a week's training before starting out. Letters from the Caravaners of 1928 telling their remarkable adventures and showing how much they have need to be in earnest and well fortified with facts, have been issued in mimeographed form by the American Friends Service Committee.

Service Civile

In Europe young men and women have organized what is known in Switzerland as the *service civile* in which they give their services for the summer months in constructive work for their country. In Switzerland these volunteers have repaired the damages done in a little Alpine town by an avalanche, rebuilt the parts of another town damaged by a landslide, and graded and levelled Alpine pasturages which the people of the neighborhoods could not handle by themselves. The government has reduced the railway fare to these young workers, army supply depots issue army blankets and other equipment, and the villagers supply their simple food. International teams are also being formed to go wherever they are needed.

This plan seems to carry out the suggestions of William James in his "Moral Equivalent of War":

"If now—and this is my idea—there were, instead of military conscription, a conscription of the whole youthful population to form for a certain number of years a part of the army enlisted against *Nature* . . . the military ideals of hardihood and discipline would be wrought into the growing fiber of the people; no one would remain blind, as the luxurious classes now are blind, to man's real relations to the globe he lives on, and to the permanently sour and hard foundations of his higher life.

"Such a conscription, with the state of public opinion that would have required it, and the many moral fruits it would bear, would preserve in the midst of a pacific civilization the manly virtues which the military party is so afraid of seeing disappear in peace. We should get toughness without callousness, authority with as little criminal cruelty as possible, and painful work done cheerily because the duty is temporary, and threatens not, as now, to degrade the whole remainder of one's life. . . . The only thing needed henceforth is to inflame the civic temper as past history has inflamed the military temper. . . ."

It is entirely possible that were enough requests received Congress might arrange for the Department of the Interior and the Department of Agriculture during the summer months to give groups of young people some insight into and some training in the constructive and often heroic work carried on for the benefit of the country by many of their branches.

Through Rural Groups

To reach people in outlying districts is a special problem. Talks over the radio, if they can be arranged, offer one opportunity, and articles in the country papers offer another. Special speakers can be sent to meetings and picnics of farm organizations, and to county and state conventions of ministers and teachers, where a large proportion of those who attend are usually leaders in country districts. In addition to the speeches that are made, literature should be distributed, resolutions proposed and permanent committees formed.

A calendar of county fairs should be kept by a local committee, and speakers, literature, and, if possible, a peace exhibit sent from one fair to another. A booth decorated with posters and stocked with books and magazines, where people may sit and rest, makes an ideal center for the distribution of literature and for an occasional talk. An adjoining sand pile where children may be left to play under supervision would be a valuable addition to the booth. A register should be kept of visitors, with notes, when possible, of what questions they were particularly interested in and of ways in which they would be willing to help with peace work in their communities. Individuals may be found willing to start a circulating library of books in their homes—the books to be provided by a group of people, by the State Library Commission or a nearby city library. Others may be willing to urge action for peace at local or national meeting of farm organizations. An excellent plan of work with county fairs has been carried out by the Yearly

Meeting of Friends in Philadelphia for several years. An automobile delivery wagon in which a machine for showing moving pictures by daylight and a phonograph are installed, travels from fair to fair. From it speeches are delivered and literature distributed in paper shopping bags on which are printed the words, "War ruins both winner and loser. What we need is security against war." The younger members of farm organizations can often be interested in arranging international pageants and programs for local meetings and fairs.

Through the Press

When a peace committee is being organized in a community, the editors of the papers should be among the first persons consulted and informed. It is important that they should understand exactly what the purpose of the committee is and the program of work it proposes to carry out. The first story announcing the formation of the committee is likely to be the best news story that the committee will have to offer for some time and the success of the work may depend upon the impression it makes. An account of the organization meeting, including a statement, preferably by the chairman of the committee, as to its purposes and plans, should be taken by some member of the committee to the editors in order that there may be an opportunity for conference with them and any questions they have may be answered. A page of "facts" should be prepared for the convenience and guidance of reporters, including the list of officers, the date of organization, statement of purpose, program of work, dates of meetings, and, if there is to be affiliation with a national group, a statement of the officers and purpose of the national group. A paragraph on the international character, extent and strength of the peace movement may well be appended.

Editors should be consulted about the kind of material they can use, and copies of the information bulletins issued by peace societies shown them so that they may choose those they wish to receive regularly.

A prize may be offered through a paper for the best article suggesting how an individual working in his own community can further international goodwill. The publication of a special feature or page on Armistice Day or Goodwill Day may be suggested and an offer made to help in collecting material. One way not only to reach the public through the press but to attract the attention of the press itself is to run half or full page advertisements on appropriate days setting forth startling facts and arguments for peace. The advertisements should be signed by those who pay for them. This idea has been tried in several cities with notable success. Merchants may be persuaded on Goodwill Day and Armistice Day or at Christmas to carry a line of goodwill across their large advertisements. At Christmas, the line might read simply, "Peace on Earth, Goodwill to Men." On Armistice Day it might be "We can end war in our time if we get on the job"—Major-General John F. O'Ryan; on Goodwill Day, "Science has made us Neighbors; Let Goodwill make us Friends."

The country papers are fully as important as the city papers. By consultation with the editors, the publication of feature articles with a local angle, news notes of local activities, book reviews or letters from men and women of influence in rural life may often be arranged.

It is important that those who interview editors have in mind a correct idea of the relation of the press to the development of better international understanding. The press as a whole is confronted today with the tremendous task of collecting news from every corner of the earth and of distributing it to the front door of the world

twice in every twenty-four hours. To meet the technical
difficulties and responsibilities of that task, it is steadily
increasing its international organization and contacts.
In 1924 the Press Congress of the World was organized
at the suggestion of American editors. In 1926 it held
its third conference in Geneva. Twenty-four countries
were represented, with eighty-four delegates from the
United States. The Congress declared its prime purpose
to be "to bring about the utmost coöperation through
the press in preventing wars, and to forward the attainment of permanent world peace through the better
understanding of all peoples by means of a free, courageous, and responsible press." The Council of the
League of Nations in 1926 called a Conference of Press
Experts, attended by 120 delegates, including an
influential group from the United States, which met in
Geneva, August 24 to 28, 1927. The preamble of the
resolutions adopted speaks of "the work of the press in
its great and responsible mission of accurately and con-
scientiously informing world public opinion and hence
contributing directly to peace and the advancement of
civilization." A Pan American Congress of Journalists
met in Washington in April, 1926, for the purpose of
creating bonds of sympathy and closer understanding
through the newspapers of North and South America, by
securing a fuller interchange of news and by guarding
against the misrepresentation of the peoples concerned.
The Congress declared that its constituent members
should neglect "no endeavor to give their readers the
important, constructive, educational news of all countries, limiting as far as possible that which is merely
sensational, trivial or likely to create antagonisms or
jealousies."

Two facts are pointed out by editors as militating
against constructive international news in the daily

papers. The importance of speed in the gathering and writing of news leads to selecting salient news which is oftener than not destructive. In the second place, lack of knowledge of foreign conditions and foreign politics on the part of the reading public stands in the way of constructive foreign news dispatches, for a complete explanatory story cannot be printed with each new development from day to day. Sensational, personal foreign news is easily understood. In several cities newspapers, with the coöperation of a member of a local college faculty or other authority, are printing courses on current topics including international relations—an idea that should be imitated in as many cities as possible. Information in regard to carrying out such a plan can be gotten by writing to the editor of the *News-Leader* of Richmond, Virginia.

The relationship between governments and the press in some instances also tends away from full accurate news reports. In the United States the World War brought about far-reaching changes in the relationship of the government and the press. The cessation of criticism of the government and the coöperation between the press and the government at that period has led, according to one journalist, to the news reporter's thinking of himself as "an ambassador abroad and a statesman at home," whose business it is to carry out government policies. Public insistence on freedom of the press can help this situation.

The creation of travel fellowships for journalists, in some instances by governments themselves, as in Czechoslovakia, Latvia and Jugoslavia, and in others by federations of journalists, as in Denmark, Esthonia and Norway, and in others through private funds, as in the case of the English-speaking Union, which each year sends an American to England and two British journalists to the United States, indicates a realization of the importance of journalists' being well informed on foreign affairs. The Carnegie Endowment for International Peace arranged a European tour for a large number of American editors in 1927. Local peace organizations might well offer, when possible, travel fellowships for local members of the press.

To stimulate a discussion by the press itself of what it can do to aid the present world-wide effort to develop better international relations, would probably do more than any other one thing to increase its conscious activity in this direction. The charge of a member of the press itself, Mr. Bruce Bliven, editor of the *New Republic,* that editors in general show an "inveterate bellicosity" might serve as the needed stimulus to such discussion. Mr. Bliven gave eight reasons for his condemnation of the attitude of editors, in a speech which he made before the first Conference on the Cause and Cure of War. He holds the press bellicose,

"For permitting hostilities to develop between governments without giving the public warning (e.g., the chief chancelleries of the world knew that the late war was impending, but the press gave no advance information concerning the situation); because it encourages a belligerent attitude on the part of its own government, editors in general exhibiting an inveterate bellicosity; because it tells lies at the behest of secret interests or of the government (Reuter's Agency, for example, admits having been turned over to the British Government during the war); because it continues to foster hate after war is over, producing 'a frame of mind incompatible with justice and reason'; . . . because it fails to tell the truth about foreign countries and foreign peoples; fails to encourage government officials in the effort to lay a foundation for better international relations; fails to tell the truth about modern warfare—does so inadequately in peace time and not at all in war; and fails to support movements for peace; specifically, the press has never given the League of Nations a fair deal."

A form of advertising useful in supplementing newspaper publicity, that of billboards, is rapidly gaining popularity. At Flushing, Long Island, sixty organizations are coöperating in erecting an anti-war signboard fifty feet long and four feet high at a crossroads where it will be passed by thousands of motorists daily. A special meeting was planned for its dedication. Details of the plan can be obtained by writing Mr. Morris L. Beard, Flushing, Long Island, New York.

Through Motion Pictures

The organization of the motion picture business makes it difficult for the public to exert an immediate influence upon the character of pictures being shown. Protests against pictures which tend to glorify war or to create ill will, may, however, influence the choice of later subjects. Protests should be sent to the local manager, to the office of the producing company, and to the President and Secretary of the Motion Picture Producers and Distributors of America, 469 Fifth Avenue, New York City.

The number of war pictures has recently increased, and since, even when such pictures do not glorify war they cannot accurately represent it, and lead to war's being accepted as a normal part of life, protests against them are being made both in England and the United States. In England the War and Navy Departments are officially coöperating with the motion picture producers by permitting the use of soldiers, ships and armament. In the United States similar coöperation is extensive. In an article recently published, a "distinguished film critic of England" insists that no film can give an honest picture of the suffering and horror and filth and stench of war, and declares that the real menace of the war film is:

". . . not its bitterness, its social distortion, nor its incitement to hatred, but its half-deference to the honour of the battlefield, its half-suggestion of the comradeship of slaughter. . . .

"I feel, as each of these showy, sentimental war films comes marching along, a fierce desire to stand up and cry out that the whole thing is an abomination, a dishonour to our country, and to the men who now plaster their faces with studio mud and blood and mimic their own agony."

Commander J. M. Kenworthy of England in his book, "Peace or War" warns the public that:

"Films that glorify war and enhance its romance will have a cumulative effect on the mind of humanity. And if ever we tackle this question (of war) at the root, we shall ban such films from the screen for all time."

Besides their possible use in glorifying war, motion pictures are a powerful influence for the development of international goodwill or ill will. This phase of their influence should be closely watched by the citizens of the United States since, according to reports, the film producers in this country are faced with the necessity of expanding through greater sales in foreign countries or with becoming stagnant. It has been suggested that if the State Department finds it necessary to supervise foreign investments in the interest of international goodwill, it should also oversee the production of films for foreign distribution in order that the character and sentiment of the people of this country may not be misrepresented to the people of other nations.

An International Cinema Congress, held in 1926 at the suggestion of the International Committee on Intellectual Coöperation of the League of Nations, and attended by 450 representatives of different nations, voted for an international bureau to maintain a catalogue of educational films and adopted these resolutions:

"The International Motion Picture Congress recommends authors, scenario-writers, publishers, and, in general, all persons interested in the artistic and industrial aspects of film production:

"(a) To avoid carefully scenarios liable to arouse a spirit of animosity between nations and tending to perpetuate the idea of war;

"(b) To avoid presenting foreign nations or races in a degrading or ridiculous light on the screen;

"(c) To show the characteristics and qualities of a foreign people in such a way as to arouse sentiments of interest and sympathy in their favour, and to utilise the resources of the cinema to the fullest possible extent to bring about international peace and universal progress."

Mr. Will Hays, President of the Motion Picture Producers and Distributors of America, writing in the August, 1927, number of *Pan Pacific Progress,* declared the motion picture industry to be intent upon bringing about better international understanding:

"The motion picture knows no barrier of distance. We are apt to look upon the distant group or nation as something different from ourselves and therefore inimical. The motion picture knows no barrier of language. We are apt to regard those who do not speak our own tongue as different and inimical. But a few thousand feet of celluloid film in a metal container can be sent to the ends of the earth. . . . Our own government is coöperating closely, and we are ourselves determined that at every opportunity a true portrayal of American life and ideals shall be given to the world and that to the nationals of all countries shall go a true message of the lives of the nationals of all others."

In speeches before the World Federation of Education Associations in 1927, Mr. W. W. Black, Assistant Director of the Education Department of the Pathé Exchange, 35 West 45th St., New York City, and Mr. Carl E. Milliken, Secretary of the Motion Picture Producers and Distributors of America, indicated a growing sense of responsibility among motion picture producers in regard to the international influence of motion pictures.

Mr. Black urged the formation of a centrally controlled clearing house through which authentic pictorial records of the different nations could be obtained.

Mr. Milliken said:

"It is the purpose of the motion picture industry, moreover, to develop relations of peace and amity with all nations of the world in every way possible."

Expressing the hope that pictures may be made revealing the backgrounds, ideals, customs and hopes of different people, he said further:

"Such pictures, exhibited in times of strained relations when misunderstanding has drawn taut the line that holds nations at peace, might be the cause of averting an international disaster. It might be the means of preserving peace when war seems inevitable."

These statements may be of help in persuading directors of local motion picture theaters to use their influence for international goodwill.

The Paramount Company, according to the announcement of Jesse L. Lasky, first vice-president, has recently appointed a counsellor of foreign affairs whose duty it is to see that pictures of foreign countries are technically correct and that there is nothing in them to offend other countries.

In the United States several groups have been formed for the promotion of educational motion pictures. The National Board of Review of Motion Pictures, 70 Fifth Ave., New York City, furnishes information about films available on different subjects; the Federal Council of Churches has created a committee on motion pictures; the Religious Motion Picture Foundation, 105 East 22nd St., New York City, has recently been established, and although so far it has not produced films dealing with the peace teachings of Christianity, it may do so if the demand for them becomes evident.

Films showing life in foreign countries can be secured, not only from several commercial houses, but from the following organizations: The Junior Red Cross, the Pan American Union and the Bureau of Commercial Economics, all in Washington, D. C. In many instances lectures are supplied with the films.

On special occasions, such as Armistice Day and Goodwill Day, it may be possible to arrange with the managers of moving picture theaters to have special films or slides shown, or to have a speaker between shows. Further suggestions are included in the programs for these days given below.

Through the Radio

In connection with Armistice Day or Goodwill Day it is often possible to arrange special radio programs. An effort should be made to have the speeches at any large peace meeting broadcast.

In 1925 the principal radio organizations of Europe formed an International Union of Broadcasting Organizations. It is expected that the radio companies of other nations will later become members of this group. According to a statement of the Secretary General of the Union, the members "have mutually pledged one another not to employ their stations for the radiation of material likely to give offense to neighboring countries; they have passed a resolution advising their members to assist in forwarding the League of Nations ideal and to broadcast whenever possible the speeches of great statesmen in favor of better international relations; they are arranging a series of national nights upon which each station broadcasts a program of some one nation's music and literature." The League of Nations Association of Japan inaugurated last year what may be termed a radio "chair" on international affairs in coöperation with the Atago Broadcasting Station. Besides talks on the League of Nations and discussions of current international affairs, the lectures included the subjects, "War and Peace," "Armistice Anniversary," and "World Peace from an Economic Point of View." These facts may be of interest to the officials of local broadcasting stations in connection with any request for goodwill programs.

The practicality of arranging radio programs was proved by the publicity department of the Women's International League for Peace and Freedom, under the direction of Mrs. Carrie S. Weyl of Philadelphia. During the World Court campaign arrangements were successfull made for broadcasting three forums, and from the spring of 1926 to the spring of 1927 a series of forums was broadcast on such subjects as the French debt, immigration laws, our Latin American relations, the problems of disarmament, Mexico and China.

The League of Women Voters has arranged a radio "Voters' Service" which is broadcast from Washington. The discussions by well-known men and women in public life include many international topics. When it is possible to arrange for afternoon radio talks on world affairs, their value can be increased by holding "radio teas" during the time of the talk, as is done in Los Angeles by the Council of International Relations.

Through Art Galleries and Museums

Because the creative art impulse of men is essentially one with their longing for unity and demands peace, and because art is a universal language through which all men may understand each other, artists must come to play an increasing part in building up a world at peace. Professor Frank Jewett Mather, Jr., of Princeton University, enlarged upon this theme in the February, 1912, issue of *International Conciliation:*

"Whenever the predilection for peace is established it will consist of a complex of motives. . . . And among the most valuable motives available should be and may be the love of beauty, the respect for the creator of it,—the artist, and the artist's own passionate preference for a social adjustment that excludes disorder, violence, ugliness. Among art-loving nations in the past the artist enjoyed amid wars an ambassadorial immunity. This fact E. H. Blashfield, the well-known mural painter, has recalled eloquently in a recent address before the American Academy of Arts and Letters. 'The artist,' he said, 'so far as his personal security was concerned, carried the truce of God with him. Through the fourteenth century Italy was a battle-field, but Giotto and his painters, Giovanni Pisano and his sculptors, Arnolfo and his architects, went up and down the battle-field unharmed, and entered through the breached walls of cities to paint allegorical pictures of the blessings of peace in the town halls.' . . . Devoid of the bitterness of industrial competition, perforce an exemplar of orderliness and disciplined enthusiasms, the artist is in the nature of things the friend of peace, and whoever enlarges the demand for art in the world and thereby increases the influence of the artist is measurably furthering the peace of the world."

The larger art galleries may be interested in arranging exhibits showing the influence of the art of one nation on another, or of prints of famous paintings showing artists' conceptions of the horror of war, and others celebrating peace; great portraits of famous men who have worked for peace might be included.

Museums are frequently able to arrange temporary exhibits of material showing the life of the people of other nations, the exchange of products, and the contribution of different nations and ages to the development of objects in common use today, illustrating the unity of the world and of civilization. From Mrs. Theodora Rhoades, 333 East 41st St., New York City, who has had much experience in arranging international exhibits, valuable suggestions for making such an exhibit a success can be obtained.

Through the Schools

In any work with the schools it must be made clear in the beginning that the question is not one of "propaganda." The interest of peace workers in education is to see to it that certain new facts are not omitted from those which children are taught, among them the facts that today all nations are interdependent; that nations are already acting together in many fields and organizing internationally; that arbitration is being more and more widely accepted; that modern war in the modern world presents a new problem; that there is a worldwide effort to abolish war; and that there is no misrepresentation of fact or perpetuation of outgrown conceptions in regard to the world situation and international relations.

Where military training has been introduced in the high schools of a community and there is a desire to do away with it, consultation with the Committee on Militarism in Education and with school authorities in cities, such as Cleveland, Ohio, where military training has been abolished, will prove helpful in deciding upon the best methods to be pursued.

What is being done by international and national educational organizations and by individual schools and teachers to promote international goodwill, a partial account of which is given in the chapter on "Education and Peace," should be known to all teachers and school officials so that no school may find itself left out of this movement. In many schools peace projects are now carried on throughout the school year, and individual teachers of various school subjects have worked out ways of increasing international understanding and friendliness. Suggestions along these lines which may be discussed with teachers are given below.

In addition to such plans as these, which may be carried out by peace committees to stimulate interest in schools and colleges, the programs of national organizations working with the schools can be promoted locally.

The American School Citizenship League, of which Mrs. Fannie Fern Andrews has been the Executive Secretary since its organization in 1908, prepares and distributes material and information to aid teachers in training children in the ideals of world friendship. It has published a comprehensive graded course edited by educational authorities for use from the first to the eighth grade under the title "An American Citizenship Course in United States History."

The American Junior Red Cross with headquarters in Washington, D. C., arranges for the exchange of letters and illustrated portfolios between the schools of different nations. The portfolios are prepared by the children as a part of their classroom work. In 43 countries nine million school boys and girls are now taking part in this exchange and so coming into friendly contact with boys and girls of their own age in other countries. An illustrated booklet called "International School Correspondence," describing the fascinating portfolios exchanged and

WHAT YOU CAN DO FOR PEACE

the pleasure the children take in preparing as well as in receiving them, and instruction as to how to proceed in introducing the plan in a school, may be obtained from the headquarters of the organization.

The Federal Council of Churches through its Committee on World Friendship Among Children, publishes material for teachers, and has for two years carried out interesting projects in connection with the schools. In 1927, 13,000 doll messengers of friendship were sent to the children of Japan to take part in their doll festival. To show their delight and appreciation the Japanese children sent a return gift of 200 beautiful dolls which were taken on a tour to visit the school children in this country. In 1928, school friendship bags are being sent to the children in Mexico. They contain articles to use in school and to play with, and carry the message, "Friendship and goodwill have been packed into this bag and we hope you will be happy to receive it. A true friendship must continue to grow between the children of our two countries."

The League of Nations Non-Partisan Association, the National Child Welfare Association, the Missionary Education Movement and the National Council for Prevention of War are constantly publishing material for teachers.

A list of books, pamphlets, programs, pageants, songs, bibliographies, maps and posters available for school work will be sent upon request by the National Council for Prevention of War.

A particularly interesting plan for a school exhibit which might be called to the attention of teachers is that originated by Miss Estelle Downing, Chairman of the International Relations Committee of the National Council of Teachers of English, and member of the faculty of the Michigan State Normal College, at Ypsilanti.

Miss Downing has prepared an "international hope chest" containing posters, scrap-books, flags, songs, outline programs, bibliographies, and other goodwill material. This chest is shipped to teachers, who may keep it for three days and make it the center of interest for a school program on international goodwill and peace.

If there is a normal school in the vicinity, the plan followed each year by the Committee on Peace and Service of the Philadelphia Yearly Meeting of Friends, of sending literature on world peace to the graduates of normal schools, can be imitated.

The Cincinnati Peace League, 2215 Upland Place, offers a fellowship to enable a student in a local university to attend the Geneva School of International Studies for a summer course, awarding the fellowship by preference to a member of the junior class so that the inspiration of the experience may be brought back to the other students. The Riverside Council in California offers $100 each year for the best school essay on "How the United States Can Aid in Preventing War in the World."

Prize Contests

National prize contests arranged annually or occasionally by national organizations also offer an opportunity to stimulate interest in internationl questions among teachers and students.

Complete information in regard to participation in annual peace essay contests in normal, high, and secondary schools, for which Miss Mary and Miss Helen Seabury offer prizes, will be sent by the American School Citizen League. The Intercollegiate Peace Association, which has its offices at Antioch College, Yellowsprings, Ohio, is in charge of annual oratorical contests in which college students compete for the Seabury prizes. In 1927,

WHAT YOU CAN DO FOR PEACE

542 orations and essays were written in 100 colleges in 17 states.

The Brooks-Bright Endowment, formerly called the Brooks-Bryce, offers an annual prize in the secondary schools for pupils between 12 and 20 years of age, throughout the English-speaking world, for essays on the maintenance of friendly relations between Great Britain and the United States. The first prize in America is a return trip ticket to Great Britain and a letter of credit for $500. The endowment was established in 1923, with an office at 19 West 31st Street, New York City.

The League of Nations Non-Partisan Association has for two years awarded a prize of a trip to Europe to the high school student winning first place in a national essay contest on the League. In 1928, 1604 students in 802 high schools participated.

Prize contests that have been carried out under the auspices of the National Council for Prevention of War indicate the great value which such projects may have in promoting interest in the development of international goodwill and world unity. In 1928, $1200 was offered in prizes for the twelve best essays on world heroes. The contest was an international one open to students in high schools and schools of comparable grade throughout the world. Each school participating in the contest sent to the Committee of Award a list of twelve names of the men and women whom its pupils considered most worthy to be remembered for heroic service to humanity of a permanent character. The school was allowed also to submit one essay on each of the heroes chosen. Nearly 1,000 schools and half a million students participated in some way, either in the selection of heroes or in the writing of the essays. Essays from 563 schools, 195 in the United States and 368 in other countries, were admitted as eligible.

In 1927 a competition was arranged by a group of prominent educators, authors and editors for the best translation of the speech made by M. Aristide Briand upon the occasion of the entry of Germany into the League of Nations. The Briand speech competition, it has been estimated by Mr. Arthur Charles Watkins, who acted as Secretary of the Committee in Charge, with Dr. Henry Grattan Doyle of George Washington University as Chairman, brought to the attention of more than 100,000 students the eloquent plea of the French Premier for amicable methods of settling the disputes of nations. More than 2,500 translations were submitted and from these a very interesting composite translation was made which has been published, along with the plan and results of the competition by the Committee in Charge, which can be addressed at 532-17th St., N. W., Washington, D. C.

The following suggestions for promoting a knowledge of world unity and of international interdependence through the different subjects in the curriculum have been gathered from many sources.

History

In the introduction to a scheme for "A First Course in General History," prepared by teachers in the schools of Wales, there occurs this statement:

"The Peace, by ending an historical period (1815-1918), caused us to take a general survey of the century, and it became obvious that its most outstanding feature was the improvement of communications—railway, steamship, airplane, telegraph, telephone, wireless—whereby every part of the globe had become economically dependent on every other. Henceforth it is clear that history will be world history. All the tributary histories have joined a single stream. But, since the value of history is to explain the present as a result of the past, this implies that past history as well as future history has become one. The pasts of all countries now form one history, because their effects are today all coöperating."

The theme of history teaching, it is reiterated by teachers, should be the "unity of civilization." "The aim of history teaching must be to show mankind its common heritage in the past and its common hopes for the future. . . . Consciousness of a common history is one of the most unifying agents." The story of man's life on earth should be told as one story. Professor G. P. Gooch of England, who has perhaps written more on this subject than any other teacher, explains the phrase, "unity of civilization," as meaning that "civilization is a collective achievement, a common heritage, and a joint responsibility."

Among the specific suggestions which have been made for teaching history from this point of view are these:

Tell the story of world development and the story of national development as a part of it.

Create a clear realization of development from age to age and of the contributions made by successive generations, discussing the future as well as the past and what this generation may contribute to it. The use of time charts to show change from century to century, is recommended in this connection. A booklet on time charts is published by the Historical Association, 22 Russell Square, London.

Show in the past and in the present the coöperation of men of different nations in creating civilization, in the sciences, the arts, and industry. "History in general is too much inclined to show people meeting only on the battlefield, as if their only contact were in war."

Trace the development of organized living together in tribes, cities, provinces, states, empires and federations of states, to the present League of Nations and world organization.

Trace the developments which have led to closer intercourse among men; the conquests of the Roman Empire; the organization of the Church; the development of trade and travel routes during the Middle Ages; the contact between the East and West following the Crusades; the establishment of trade routes across the seas; and finally the era of constant communication between all parts of the earth.

Teach history around great personalities, marking its periods not by the names of rulers but by the changes that ideas have wrought in the life and the thought of the world, as, in the case of Galileo, Copernicus, Newton, Socrates, Plato, Kant.

In the schools of countries belonging to the League of Nations, the question of the history of international coöperation centers naturally around the League and very interesting programs have been worked out to give children a conception of its aims, activities and significance. In the schools of the United States the same emphasis does not naturally fall upon the work of the League, but its growing importance means that it must be discussed fully as a fact of international life and must be included in any course dealing with history, civics or international relations. Complete and varied material can be obtained from the League of Nations Non-Partisan Association, 6 East 39th St., New York City.

In teaching the history of war periods, the following points are recommended for emphasis:

To the scattering of the nations over the earth, war made a contribution at however great expense, but interdependence, and the invention of weapons of wholesale destruction, have made the problem of war a new problem.

War has not "always been." Coöperation is older than combat. The natural "struggle for existence" among animals and men is with their environment, or, in the case of animals, with creatures other than their own kind. Coöperation is a factor of survival and of intellectual development. "Man did not make society—society made man."

In dealing with specific wars, consideration should be given to these points:

There are historical, economic, scientific, and geographic causes for the point of view of both parties in past wars. If this is understood, animosity will be directed toward conditions rather than people.

The cost of a war should be estimated in terms of the daily lives of the people, and should include the constructive work which expenditures for war make impossible.

How could the war have been avoided? Have similar disputes been settled by other means?

The history of the effort toward peace, which can be followed through the centuries, deserves adequate attention in all history courses. At present there is scarcely a line in history texts to indicate that the statesmen of the world have ever made an effort to abolish war, or that the people of the world have ever organized to secure peace. In connection with United States history the omission is particularly glaring.

The relations of the United States with Latin American republics is another neglected phase of its history. To enable teachers to include courses in Latin American history without further crowding their program, the *History Teacher's Magazine* in June, 1918, published an "Outline for Incidental Study of Latin American History," by Mary Wilhelmine Williams.

Geography

Respect, sympathy, understanding—these, according to Professor J. Russell Smith of Columbia University, are the three great spiritual possibilities of the geography class.

If children are to have respect for other nations, Professor Smith points out, they must be taught that there is a reason for the difference between nations; that it grows out of different environmental conditions, and does not mean inferiority or superiority. They must appreciate the skill of foreign peoples in terms of their adaptation to their environment; the skill of the Eskimo who makes a boat that nothing we have can rival; the skill displayed in the boomerang made by the Bushman of Australia. Professor George Cons has said on this point:

"Our presentation of the personal habits of primitive people should be related to the demands of their environment; the contrast to civilized habits should not be stressed; habits of primitive people, often objectionable to our civilized sensitivity, generally are the personal response to secure economy of effort made necessary by their type of life."

In order that children may have sympathy they need to be taught to look upon the people of other countries as engaged in the same jobs that they are. "All the world is a great group of fellow craftsmen, who are engaged upon the endless task of feeding themselves. . . . The farmer with his reaper is engaged in the same task as is the Hindu or the Chinese or the Japanese or the Filipino who wades about his rice paddy."

To give a child understanding, he must be made to see that foreigners who do not behave exactly as we do are not doing "foolish things but natural things; that they are doing very much what we should do under the same circumstances." He should be led to see also the value of differences and how all nations contribute to a common civilization. The National Foreign Trade Council in a publication entitled "Our Imports and Who Use Them," tells these interesting facts of how other nations contribute to make our daily lives what they are.

"As soon as you get up in the morning, the genii of foreign trade begin to minister to your needs and conveniences. The East Indies have contributed their vegetable oils to your bath

WHAT YOU CAN DO FOR PEACE

soap and shaving cream; your sponge is either a plant growth from the tropical waters of the Caribbean, or the modern imitation made of rubber from Sumatra and Brazil. You brush your teeth with fine bristles from the Far East, and smooth your hair with long vigorous bristles from China and England. Imported materials are essential to the making of the porcelain equipment of your bathroom. Imported tin is in the tubes that hold your shaving cream or tooth paste. Your comb may be made of imported rubber. Before you even get your clothes on, many widely separated parts of the world have been of service to you.

"Proceeding to dress, you call upon all parts of the world for your personal adornment. Silk worms in Japan and China may have contributed to your hosiery, shirt and tie; imported wool enters into much of your outer clothing; your shoes are built up of material from all parts of the globe; your garters and suspenders owe their elasticity to the rubber plantation of Sumatra; while your white linen collar and your linen handkerchief are made of flax from Ireland, Canada, Belgium and the Netherlands.

"Hurrying down to breakfast, you find either coffee from Brazil, tea from the Far East, or cocoa from tropical countries. To sweeten these beverages you use sugar from Cuba and the tropics. Your breakfast china contains English clay, the glasses are wrought from foreign substances, and the knives, forks and spoons may contain imported aluminum and tin. You may start the meal with a banana from Honduras or a grape fruit from Cuba.

"Leaving your house, you walk over asphalt from Trinidad and take a train, the safety of which depends on air-brake hosing made of imported rubber. You may be lightening your travels by walking on rubber heels, and if the day is wet, wearing rubber overshoes and a rain coat.

"You reach your office and sit down at a desk of mahogany. On the desk are to be found pencils, the lead of which is made of graphite from Mexico, Ceylon, Chosen, Canada and Madagascar. On the end of the pencil is an eraser of imported rubber set in a cap of imported tin. The finger grip of your pen is of cork from Spain or of rubber. The telephone and the dictaphone use imported asphalt, carbon, flax, mica, platinum, nickel, rubber, shellac, silk and tin in their construction. The typewriter in the office, and other pieces of office machinery, contain many kinds of alloy steels, often coated with nickel.

"At the end of the day you pick up your hat, which is made either of straw braid from the Far East, or of fur from all parts of the world."

In some class rooms parallel columns are kept on the blackboard in which from time to time, at the suggestion of the children, items which they use are listed with the country from which they come in whole or in part. Pictures from newspapers and magazines showing the gathering of raw materials or the manufacture of goods in other nations can be combined with such a list to lead the children to think of foreign people as contemporaries. The exports of the pupil's country, too, should be traced to the people who use them, and the contribution of their own nation to the wealth of the world made clear.

In teaching the geography of the Pacific region the close relationships and future possibilities for international coöperation among the countries bordering on that ocean should be discussed. Theodore Roosevelt once pointed out that "the Mediterranean era died with the discovery of America. The Atlantic era has reached the height of its development. The Pacific era, destined to be the greatest, is just at the dawn." A Japanese educator, Baron Matsui, has said of the close relations among Pacific peoples:

"There is no East and there is no West today. Commerce and communication have broken down the barriers. The world is coming together. It is not growing apart. The world is one. The Occident and the Orient must stand or fall together. The white man and the yellow man must join

WHAT YOU CAN DO FOR PEACE

hands and march together into a greater and more glorious future, or else go down to doom together. There is no other choice."

Pan American relations deserve far greater attention than they usually receive. Interesting materials, including illustrated booklets and lantern slides, are sent out by the Pan American Union for use in geography classes.

Art

In the study of art the attempt to create beauty is seen to be a common human impulse shared by men of all times and all places, while the influence of races and peoples upon one another can be traced in the art of all modern nations.

In Japan the Government has organized an International Fine Arts Society for the furtherance of international understanding and the development of the fine arts. Commenting on it, the *Japan Advertiser* points out:

"Fine art objects cannot be created independently of the trend of the times and the force of environment, but their influence upon us rises above time and environment. . . . This is because the fine arts not only delineate the individual elements of a nation, but also give expression to sentiments common to all human beings and true through all ages and places. The comprehension of these sentiments broadens our minds and deepens our sympathy."

Athletics

The need for carrying the spirit of sportsmanship into all of the relationships of life, including the international relationships, is increasingly recognized. John Galsworthy has declared that the spirit of sport is the great hope of the world:

"Sport, which still keeps the flag of idealism flying, is perhaps the most saving grace in the world at the moment, with its spirit of rules kept, and regard for the adversary, whether the fight is going for or against. When, if ever, the fair-play spirit of sport reigns over international affairs, the cat force which rules there now will slink away and human life emerge for the first time from the jungle."

Athletics offers an opportunity for learning the games and sports of other nations. A group of five or six may study a game and teach the rest of the class how to play it, telling as much as possible about its origin, and the people who play it. In *The American Schoolmaster*, for December, 1927, it is emphasized that goodwill and ill will are to a large extent habitual attitudes of mind; that these habitual attitudes are largely formed by experience in dealing with others with whom we have conflicting interests; that one of the most effective ways to develop the spirit of goodwill is in competitive sports and games in which the organization is carefully controlled and fair play carefully and uniformly assured. The publications of the Sportsmanship Brotherhood, 342 Madison Ave., New York City, contain excellent material on the possible contribution to the movement for world peace, notably a booklet, "Sportsmanship, a Bridge of Understanding between the Nations of the World," to which Dr. John H. Finley contributes an introduction.

Biography

Through the study of biographies in connection with English or history work, pupils can be given an understanding of other peoples; an appreciation of the fact that races and nations have made different contributions to the intellectual and spiritual progress of humanity as well as to material civilization; and a knowledge that scientists, artists and men of learning have world power and influence. The study of famous men and women leads also to a discussion of what heroism is. Its three principles have been defined as nobility of character, fearless and self-sacrificing devotion to a great cause, and constructive work for humanity of a permanent character. In an International World Hero Contest, conducted by the National Council for Prevention of War, in which these qualities were used as a basis of judgment, the following were selected by the school children: Louis Pasteur, Abraham Lincoln, Christopher Columbus, George Washington, Benjamin Franklin, Woodrow Wilson, Florence Nightingale, Joan of Arc, Socrates, Johann Gutenberg, David Livingstone, and George Stephenson. A portfolio with portraits and the prize-winning essays has been published.

As the culmination of a study of the men and women who have led humanity in its struggle for freedom and for the recognition of the worth of the individual, there should be a discussion of those who have tried to win it freedom from war. Through the centuries the great statesmen and philosophers have labored for world peace, among them Dante, Erasmus, Grotius, Kant, Fox, Penn, Franklin, Tolstoi. As a short project in this connection a brief account of the winners of the Nobel Peace Award might be compiled.

The study of biography leads naturally also to the study of heroism today. Instances of men and women who are making great contributions to the progress of humanity and of those who display heroism in the daily routine of life, can be gathered from the newspapers and magazines by the students. William James's "Moral Equivalent of War" should be read in this connection.

Botany
Many of our garden flowers come to us from foreign

countries, particularly from the Orient, and suggest the beauty of the East. The tea and rambler roses, the parents of the modern rose, were brought to England from China. Chrysanthemums, camelias, peonies, primroses and azaleas also came from China.

"All the old-fashioned garden favorites," according to "The Aristocrat of the Garden" came from the Far Eastern countries. "Rosa alba, the musk rose, cinnamon, moss, sweet briar and damask roses came from wild species of Persia, Asia Minor and Europe, or from their garden forms."

The study of plants and flowers—their dependence upon insects for pollenization and the dependence of animal life upon them—brings out clearly the fact of the inter-relation of all forms of life and shows the principle of coöperation to be a universal law.

Civics

New textbooks on civics clearly reflect a new conception of this study. In "Community Civics," the author, Arthur W. Dunn, former director of the American Junior Red Cross, emphasizes government as a means of coöperation. In "International Civics," the authors, Pitman B. Potter and Roscoe L. West, discuss existing means of coöperation among national governments and how they must be developed to meet the conditions of modern life. Statements by American educators in the chapter on "Education and Peace" stress the importance of the international aspects of this study.

Current Events

Aside from the interest in international affairs which their subject matter develops, current event courses offer an opportunity to train students to read the newspapers and current periodicals with discrimination. They should be made to realize the difficulty which newspapers face in securing unprejudiced reporters to collect daily full and accurate facts about important events in all parts of the world. Reports of an important event in one paper should, whenever possible, be checked up by comparison with accounts of the same occurrence in other papers. The habit should be formed of noting the source of all news reports and of reading them carefully to determine whether definite statements are made and authorities cited or whether they purport to be no more than general impressions. In the case of signed articles as much as possible should be learned about the writer.

The general reliability of a publication can be gauged by keeping notes of its statements on important questions and checking them by later developments.

Domestic Science

In the domestic science courses there is opportunity to teach the inter-relation of all countries through a study of the sources of foods, of the raw materials used in the making of fabrics, and the foreign origin of many kinds of fabrics brought to the West originally by early traders. Some schools have also utilized these courses as an opportunity for children to take part themselves in developing world friendship by making garments for foreign children who are in need.

English

Study of the English language shows it to have been created and influenced by many civilizations. Its words come from the Greek and Roman civilizations and many new words to meet new ideas come from Germany, France, Spain, and Italy. Advanced study brings out the common source and close relationship of all European languages. The history of the alphabet leads back through the Phœnicians and Egyptians to the pictorial writings of early man everywhere. "The child who has learned that the language it is using every day has come to it by all of these wonderful routes will have a different conception of its own and its country's relation to other countries." Dr. Otto F. Ege of the Cleveland School of Art has put the fascinating story of the alphabet into two books which are listed in the bibliography.

Accurate use of words and their definition, so important for arriving at mutual understanding, can be made the basis of discussions which will help individuals to escape from the limitations of prejudices and develop independence of thought. One teacher, at the beginning of the school year, without discussion, asks her high-school class to define words like the following: Internationalism, trade unionism, socialism, religious. The papers are graded so that the answers will not be haphazard or careless. There is no direct discussion based on the answers but, from time to time, as the words occur in class work there is some consideration of the ideas they represent. The middle of the year, the same test is given the class and a measurement thus made of the students' progress in accurate thinking and careful use of terms.

In the study of English literature children may be led to enter sympathetically into the life of other peoples. In *The American Schoolmaster* for December, 1927, the following suggestions are made for building international goodwill by the careful choice of the things that children **read:**

"If reading is to function in the lives of boys and girls, the gaining of factual information must become merely a secondary aim. Social attitudes and values that express themselves in living experiences are the ends to be sought. These ends can be most successfully achieved through emotionalized experiences. Because of its dual appeal, to the intellect and to the emotions, literature is one of the most effective means of encouraging desirable attitudes and developing a sense of worth while values. In proportion as it is vivid and stirring, it will succeed in overcoming our provincialisms and giving to the world beyond our horizons the greatest possible reality. Thus the parish mind will be made capable of living in ever larger units. Thus through literature we shall be transformed into world citizens."

Because great thinkers throughout the history of the world have urged peace it is possible in connection with many of the authors studied to select readings on this theme. In Emerson, Longfellow, Tennyson, Whittier, Lowell and Whitman there are excellent selections. In Hawthorne's "Tanglewood Tales," "The Golden Fleece" points the folly of war. In Burke's "Speech on Conciliation" an opportunity is given for discussion of the use of force in international relations. An interesting project in English classes is for the students to find what the authors they are studying have said on peace and war, or to collect the peace poems of American writers.

Debates

There have recently been two interesting developments in debate work: the increasing number of international debates held in the larger universities which emphasize the fact that there are common problems to be solved by the joint effort of leaders in different nations; and the growing realization that we must modify methods of debating so that the result will be an effort to arrive at truth rather than an effort to make one opinion prevail over another. In an article in *Progressive Education* for the second quarter of 1925, Dr. Harry A. Overstreet points out that if we are to cultivate openmindedness—the "will to see farther"—which is the first essential of the international mind, there must be substituted for the technique of debate the technique of social exploration and discussion. In the course of a debate the student does not try to learn something nor to incorporate something of which he has been previously ignorant, and which, when incorporated, will modify his conclusions. His one object is to win. To the truly broad-minded person, however, the only victory worth while is that of truth over error. "Group coöperation in the pursuit of . . . truth" should be the object of discussions. Each side should aim to bring out the best possible arguments on that side in order to arrive at correct conclusions. The spirit in which the debate is conducted should never lead to antagonism for it is important to acquire the habit of not confusing differences and antagonisms. In "The New State" Mary P. Follett voices a warning against permitting diversity to arouse hostility:

"Suppose a friend says something with which I do not agree. It may be that instantly I feel antagonistic, feel as if we were on opposite sides, and my emotions are at once tinged with some of the enmity which being on opposite sides usually brings. Our relations become slightly strained, we change the subject as soon as possible, etc. But suppose we were really civilized beings, then we should think, 'How interesting this is; this idea has evidently a larger content than I realized; if my friend and I can unify this material we shall separate with a larger idea than either of us had before!'"

There is also an opportunity in debating to cultivate in students the habit recommended by John Dewey, of "discriminating tested beliefs from mere assertions, guesses and opinions; and to develop a lively, sincere and open-minded preference for conclusions that are properly grounded."

Following a debate, the members of the two teams might continue friendly conversations on the basis of all the material gathered on both sides and stage a second contest in which the award should go to the student giving the best reasons for the final opinion of the discussion group as a whole or of a majority of its members. At one point in the debates of the Constitutional Convention of 1787 when the delegates had reached such a deadlock that certain groups were threatening to withdraw, Benjamin Franklin secured an adjournment for three days and gave the delegates this advice:

"Spend the time of this recess not in associating with your own party and devising new arguments to fortify yourselves in your old opinions, but mix with members of opposite sentiments, lend a patient ear to their reasonings, and candidly allow them all the weight to which they may be entitled."

Foreign Languages

The reading of current periodicals and newspapers from the countries the languages of which are being studied, as well as masterpieces of literature, can do much to promote better international understanding.

The study of a common auxiliary language, such as Esperanto or Ido, is being given renewed consideration because of the development of the international radio. It has been suggested that if an auxiliary language were called the "Radio" language it would promote its popularity.

The International Auxiliary Language Association of America has recently been organized and endowed for research study of all questions involved in the establishment of one synthetic language secondary to all national languages which may be taught in educational systems throughout the world.

Classes in Esperanto have already been introduced in the public schools of Lithopolis, Ohio. They are not compulsory but are reported to be very popular. The courses have been endowed by Mr. and Mrs. R. J. Jones, of Northport, L. I., N. Y., who hope later to establish an Esperanto College for adults in Lithopolis.

Hygiene

The fight to control disease has produced great heroes and thrilling tales of adventure. The stories of Pasteur, of Lister, of Walter Reed, of Grenfell, of Trudeau, may well be told in any class where the problems of health are discussed. The Metropolitan Life Insurance Company has published for teachers a series of small books on "Health Heroes."

A discussion of the problems of health gives an interesting opportunity to point out the necessity for international coöperation. As early as 1851 there was an international congress to consider ways of dealing with cholera, the plague and yellow fever. In 1903 an international commission was set up at Suez to act as a barrier to protect Europe and America against the epidemics coming from the East, and at this time it was agreed that governments should assist one another by issuing information as to epidemic diseases in their territories. Under the League of Nations a health organization has been created which has not only the direct support of the nations in the League, but of the International Health Board in the United States.

Mathematics

The history of the development of mathematical science and of the sciences that have grown out of it is another chapter in the story of interdependence among the ages and the nations. Our system of notation leads back to the Arabs and to the natives of India. Several mimeographed pages of examples selected from "Problems About War for Classes in Arithmetic; Suggestions for Makers of Textbooks and for Use in Schools," by D. E. Smith, published by the Carnegie Endowment for International Peace, but now out of print, can be obtained from the National Council for Prevention of War.

Music

Wherever or however they live, people sing their children to sleep, sing to express their joy and sorrow, and in teaching music it is possible to make children realize that it is a language all the world shares. Much of our music, of course, comes from other nations. Many of our common songs had their origin abroad. The air of "The Star Spangled Banner" is taken from an old English drinking song. The music to which "America" is sung is also the music to the national songs of Great Britain, Germany and Switzerland.

In an article on "World Brotherhood Through Music" in the *Journal of the National Education Association,* for May, 1926, Frances Elliott Clark says:

"Everywhere we now sing 'Santa Lucia,' 'All Through the Night,' 'Praise Ye the Father,' 'Silent Night,' and 'Auld Lang Syne,' and cease to remember that we owe them to Italy, Wales, Netherlands, Tyrol, and Scotland. . . . We sing the beautiful hymn, 'My Saviour As Thou Wilt,' and care not at all that it was written into the overture of an opera by the German, von Weber. 'Won't Go Home Until Morning' or 'He's a Jolly Good Fellow' is the old French 'Malbrook,' and it in turn was brought from the Crusades. We sing to our babies 'Rock-a-Bye Baby,' (English), 'There is a Happy Land' (Hindustan), Brahms' 'Lullaby' (German), 'Slumber, Baby, My Little Brother' (French), 'Sweet and Low' (English), and 'Hey Baloo' (Scotch)."

In singing the songs of other lands, many of them made familiar here by people who have left their own countries to live and work with us, an appreciation of the foreign groups in America can be cultivated.

Science

Science knows no national boundaries, and in it all ages are united. To the perfection of every great invention men of many nations and many centuries have contributed. The great scientists are thought of as belonging to the whole world, not to any nation, for they have served the world. The achievement, for instance, of Charles Lindbergh in flying across the Atlantic was made possible by the combined work of the scientists of the world, many wholly unknown. It was suggested, indeed, by Alfred Korzybski, author of the "Manhood of Humanity" that it would have been appropriate had there been a monument to the "unknown scientist" as well as to the unknown soldier upon which Lindbergh might have laid a wreath.

It is science which by its discoveries and inventions has brought the nations of the world into their present close relationship. James Bryce in "International Relations" makes the interesting comment that "electricity is the most potent of the unifying forces for the purposes of knowledge and interchange of thought, as steam has been for commerce." Today men make use of these inventions of science without understanding the fundamental laws, the discovery of which have made them possible. A more profound study and more general knowledge of science may give an insight into universal laws, which will mean intellectual "control" over the machine age which at present tends to dominate mankind.

The cultivation of the scientific attitude of mind— insuring patience, willingness to investigate and to test and to be corrected, unwillingness to dogmatize, and acceptance of facts regardless of their effect upon earlier beliefs—and its application to the study of social and international relations is probably the most important contribution that can be made to the solution of these questions.

In *The American Schoolmaster* for December, 1927, methods of teaching science so that it will contribute to broader international sympathies are pointed out:

"In the first place, the emphasis in science should be placed on the service it can render mankind. Science can be so taught as to make service the dominating passion of those who are to recruit the ranks of scientific men of the future.

"The important study of the biographies of great scientists breeds international respect. . . . An impartial survey of the facts will reveal that other nations have made quite as notable contributions as our own in the field of applied science."

The adventurous work of scientists in connection with irrigation and other constructive projects carried on by the Department of the Interior, and with the work of the Forestry Service needs to be better known. Excellent illustrative material can be gotten from both departments. In these undertakings there is

"Not yesterday's obsolete war, that of Man against Man, but rather a new life, dispensing War for Man's mastery over the earth and its forces, an ever-youthful war, of which we have probably not fought out yet a millionth part."

On Pasteur's seventieth birthday, when delegates from learned societies of all nations met in Paris to do him honor, he said to them:

"And you, delegates from other nations, bring me the deepest joy that can be felt by a man whose invincible belief is that Science and Peace will triumph over Ignorance and War —that nations will unite, not to destroy, but to build, and that the future will belong to those who have done the most for suffering humanity."

Programs for Special Days

Although Armistice Day and Goodwill Day are the two occasions during the school year when special programs can be entirely devoted to world peace, other holidays also offer an opportunity for emphasizing the facts and attitudes of mind which make for peace. Detailed graded programs for Goodwill Day, and Armistice Day, can be obtained from the National Council for Prevention of War. Excellent programs and program material can be obtained from Miss E. Estelle Downing, Chairman of International Relations Committee of the National Council of Teachers of English, Michigan State Normal College, Ypsilanti, Michigan; from the Auxiliary Committee on World Friendship of the Los Angeles Public Schools, which has published a book entitled, "World Friendship," by Miss Evaline Dowling, the price of which is 50 cents; from the League of Nations Non-Partisan Association, 6 East 39 Street, New York City, which publishes an *International Guide to Material Descriptive of Many Lands and Peoples,* price 10 cents; and the American School Citizenship League, Boston. *The American Junior Red Cross News* devoted its issue for May, 1928, to suggestions for Goodwill Day.

Whenever possible Armistice Day and Goodwill Day should be made the occasion for undertaking some class project which will give the children a definite part in the worldwide peace movement—as, for instance, sending letters or broadcasting a message of goodwill to children in other lands.

School Projects in World Friendship

A Trip Around the World.—A conductor of the tour is elected by the senior class. One or two members from each class, who act as guides for each country, are chosen to make the tour. Groups are selected to represent the people of the various nations visited. These, in appropriate costume, act out a scene or give a series of tableaux illustrating the life of the country which they represent—incidents in its history, the work, the recreation, and the art of the people.

Trips Abroad.—A very much simpler travel program can be carried out by forming various groups of from three to five students. Excused from the auditorium periods or from certain of their classes for a few days in order that they may visit, by means of the library, some chosen country, they "return" and tell about their journey. At the end of the reports, a vote can be taken as to which the students have given the most vivid picture of the country they visited.

Make a Chart showing the decrease in the earth's size measured in time of travel from point to point during the last one hundred years.

World Peace, Month by Month.—On the last day of each month, a member of the senior class reports on the most notable event affecting peace during that month. Members of the other classes make reports, based on material gathered by their class as a whole, of news items and editorials which have appeared during the month injurious to the cause of world peace or tending to promote it.

A Bulletin Board for Foreign News.—A bulletin board, on which newspaper articles about foreign countries or international relations can be posted, will lead not only to interest in foreign affairs, but to a more careful reading of the daily papers. The articles should be discussed in class from the point of view of their accuracy and checked up with later items in the same or other papers. Such a bulletin board for little children can be carried out in pictures.

The World as Shopkeeper.—Representatives are chosen

for each country, who study the products of that country, what it has to sell to the rest of the world and what it must secure from other countries. When the groups have completed their studies, an afternoon can be devoted to an international shopping tour. On tables labeled with the names of the various nations, there are objects or printed cards indicating what that nation produces for export. In turn, the nations go from one stand to another, securing what they need and do not produce themselves.

The World Market.—The fact that the world is an economic unit and that war is no longer compatible with modern industrial life can be made clear by having pupils collect from newspapers and magazines advertisements that show that manufacturers think in terms of the world and find their markets in the four corners of the earth.

World Unity.—By coöperation among the teachers of special subjects, an interesting survey of the extent of world unity as revealed in science, history, economics, and art, can be made. Reports by different groups on these subjects could form the program for a special day, such as Armistice Day or Goodwill Day.

Monuments to Peace.—An interesting essay or talk illustrated with lantern slides could be based on the peace monuments which have been erected on international border lines or in commemoration of peace agreements and acts of goodwill. Among these peace monuments are The Christ of the Andes between Chile and the Argentine Republic; the Peace Portal in Blaine, Washington; the International Bridge across the Niagara River at Buffalo, which was dedicated with ceremonies of friendship in August, 1927; the Granite Arch at Che Foo, China, on which there is this inscription, "Erected in honor of the citizens of America, our friends across the sea. May there be eternal peace between the two peoples"; and the

"Alabama" Room in the City Hall of Geneva, Switzerland. It was in the "Alabama" Room that the "Alabama" claims case between England and the United States was settled in 1871-72. The conclusion of this case marked the beginning in Europe of a popular movement in favor of the pacific settlement of disputes. In the room is a plowshare made from the swords of officers in the Civil War who at a peace meeting in Philadelphia in 1876 gave them for this symbolic purpose. The story of the "Alabama" Room has been written by Mr. George Huntington Donaldson and is distributed by the National Council for Prevention of War.

Model Assemblies of the League of Nations.—As a means of teaching the present extent of international coöperation and organization, the staging of "Model Assemblies" has become popular not only in colleges but in high schools. Full information will be supplied by the League of Nations Non-Partisan Association.

A Book of Peace.—The preparation of a book of peace, such as the low eighth grade of the Durant School of Oakland, California, compiled and bound under the title "The Dawn of Peace" and which contained poems, quotations, original essays and comments, cartoons and reproductions of paintings depicting scenes of war or peace, affords an interesting project for classes of any age.

A Scrap Book of Peace-Time Heroes.—Accounts of people performing self-sacrificing services for others, or carrying on constructive work for the benefit of humanity, which appear in the daily press or in current periodicals, may be brought in and voted upon for inclusion in a peace hero scrap book.

An International Museum.—A school "museum" can be started of articles from foreign countries to which brief accounts of the country can be attached.

A World Peace Edition of the school paper can be

arranged to appear on Armistice or Goodwill Day. Such an edition was printed by the High School of Bell, California.

Teaching Little Children

From certain points of view, what little children are not taught is even more important than what they are. Parents today have been fairly well trained to avoid saying or doing anything which will make their children afraid of the dark or of animals or of strangers. It is recognized that such fears limit a child's powers. It should be realized as clearly that all prejudices shut some door of knowledge or of opportunity for wider experience, and every effort should be made to guard children against acquiring them.

The teaching of world-mindedness and the development of independence of thought can be begun very early. Nearly all children are interested in knowing how things came to be as they are. Through this interest in beginnings, a child can be given very early a conception of progress from generation to generation, of the fact that people in every age have contributed to give us what we have today. In this connection, it is not hard to make a child understand that the different races and nations, living in all parts of the earth—some where it is hot, some in the mountains, some by the sea—have learned different ways of doing things, so that today each one has something to teach the others.

A sense of progress from century to century makes it seem natural that ways of life should change. Children should feel the wonder of the fact that they are living today at a turning point in history, that new adventures lie ahead, and that no one can be sure that anything is impossible—to prove it, tell them how often people used to say to each other, "You can no more do that than fly!"

Since, as someone has said, the whole earth is every child's treasure chest and workshop and playroom, children should think of the earth as a whole and be familiar with its various parts. A globe and a little later a map should be part of the furnishings of every child's room. The countries to which things made in his own country are sent and the ones from which come the things he uses every day can be pointed out to him, or bright-colored threads used to follow the lines of ·the voyages. An around-the-world frieze of pictures of the children of different nations can be arranged on the walls of a young child's room, and later, photographs of places of special interest or of the products of different countries put in their place. Newspaper pictures make it a simple matter for a child to begin an "Around the World" scrap book, to which he can add for many years.

Through music and through art children can learn that all nations are alike in their love of beauty, that they influence one another, and that each makes its contribution. Reproductions of great paintings can be obtained now in excellent and inexpensive prints, which will help to give a child a love of beauty and a sense of the unity inherent in beauty, as well as a knowledge of the art of different nations. A list of prints for children can be ordered from the *Woman's Home Companion.*

There are several paintings by great masters from which a love of peace can be more directly inspired. Among them is "A Knight of Rhodes," by Pinturicchio, which shows a member of this order of knights who were not warriors but were healers of men. "An Angel before the Walled City," by Lippi, offers an imaginative suggestion of the conflict between material and spiritual forces. Among the portraits of men who have labored in the cause of peace are "Dante and His Book," by di Michelino; "Erasmus," by Holbein,—Erasmus was the first man to be known as a citizen of the world; and "St. Francis Preaching to the Birds," by Giotto.

An ambitious and well-informed teacher or mother may arrange "other nation" days, perhaps one a month, when a child pretends he is a child of another nation, dresses as the other child does or wears at least some part of his dress, eating as nearly as possible the same kind of food, playing the games, and learning as much as possible about the other's country, and possibly some phrase of his language. If such a plan is too elaborate, at least the games of other children can be played. The fact that all children play such games as hide and seek, blind man's buff, and London Bridge, and the little differences that there are in the way other children play them, can be pointed out. Books of such games are listed in the bibliography. The National Council for Prevention of War issues descriptions of games in mimeographed form.

To develop independence of thought in little children, it is well to permit them to discriminate between the facts older people tell them that can be demonstrated, and the opinions they express. Another method is to teach them to test their own opinions by continued observation, and not to be troubled at finding an earlier opinion wrong but to see that it is a matter of growth.

Psychologists point out the necessity of bringing children up without fear if they are to be without hate, since the two are closely associated, and of giving them some constructive skill through which their will-to-power can be satisfied.

It is also important, of course, to "disarm" nurseries, but toy soldiers and B. B. guns are bound to be encountered. The best protection against bad effects from them is to give children as true a picture as possible of what war is, so that it may not be confused in their minds with marching down a sunny street to gay music.

WHAT YOU CAN DO FOR PEACE

Through the Celebration of Special Days

Armistice Day and Goodwill Day are the outstanding peace days, but other holidays afford appropriate opportunities to call attention to the world effort to secure peace. Material helpful in arranging international and goodwill programs is published by an increasing number of organizations. The National Young Women's Christian Association and the National Missionary Education Movement publish large collections of pageants, plays, folk-songs and dances. Descriptive lists of material with information as to where it can be obtained are supplied by the League of Nations Non-Partisan Association and by the National Council for Prevention of War, both of which organizations also publish plays, pageants, and dramatic readings. Sources from which school programs can be gotten are mentioned in the section, "Through Schools." Information in regard to motion picture films is given in the section on that subject. Lantern slides showing life in other nations can be obtained from the Pan American Union, the Young Men's Christian Association, and among the commercial firms from the Keystone View Company of Meadville, Pennsylvania, and Williams, Brown and Earle, 918 Chestnut St., Philadelphia. Lantern slides showing actual war scenes can be obtained from the Keystone View Company or from Radiguet and Massiot, 15 Boulevard des Filles-du-Calvaire, Paris. A collection of such slides can also be rented from the National Council for Prevention of War. Flags of all nations, needed in many programs, can be ordered from the Westminster Press, Philadelphia, in a set of 42, size 11 x 16 inches, for $4.25, or in practically any size from Annin and Company, Fifth Ave. and 16th St., New York City. Colored plates from which flags can be made were published in the *National Geographic Magazine* for October. 1917.

Armistice Day, November 11

Much program material is suitable for either Armistice Day or Goodwill Day, but the important thing on Armistice Day is to remember—to remember the two things that were uppermost in men's minds on the first Armistice Day, when the world that knew war went mad with joy because war was ended. The first thing is, the full horror, and cost, and waste, and suffering, and interruption of war. The second is that hundreds of thousands of men died in the belief that they were fighting to end war and that the only true honor therefore that we can do them is to carry their work to completion. In a letter to the Commander of the American Legion, President Coolidge said of the purposes of the day:

"Armistice Day ought to be celebrated not simply by thinking of the war and the men who died in the war but by dedicating all to the cause of perennial peace and the outlawry of war."

The Sunday nearest Armistice Day should be observed in all churches and is very generally. Suggestions for church programs will be found in the section, "Through the Churches." There should also be a community celebration on Armistice Day itself. A public luncheon, dinner or evening meeting to discuss what the community is doing to carry out the purpose for which the war was fought, is one appropriate form of celebration. A community international children's party is also an inspiring way to celebrate.

In Carson City, Michigan, a celebration of Armistice Day in which the people of the town and surrounding country took part, was arranged by the First Congregational Church. An all-day program held on Armistice Day itself included morning and afternoon services at which well-known ministers of the nearby towns gave addresses. All business houses closed at 10:30. The superintendent of schools, accompanied by members of his faculty and a large group of students, marched to the morning services, preceded by a flag bearer and bugler. A quarter-page advertisement was carried in the local papers with the names of the local men who had been killed in the war, and below them these sentences:

"We invite every patriotic citizen, and every Christian man, woman and child in our community to make this Armistice Service a memorial for our honored dead. Let us keep in mind the ideals for which they gave themselves. In the World War they died to make that the last war. Let us dedicate ourselves to finish their task."

Extra copies of the advertisement were run off and distributed widely through the nearby towns. Information as to the details of such a program can be obtained from the minister of the Carson City Congregational Church, Dr. W. S. Shelly.

The Committee for World Friendship of Plainfield, New Jersey, has made it a practice to conduct poster campaigns during Armistice week, and in 1928 arranged with the managers of moving picture houses to show a trailer at every performance during the week. Among the sentences carried on the slides were these:

"Fighting for peace is the truest way to honor those that died in a 'War to end War.'"

What You Can Do To Prevent War

"Try to understand other nations.
"Teach your children to practice tolerance.
"Ask your minister to preach against war.
"Elect Congressmen who advocate:
  Open Diplomacy;
  Universal Reduction of Armaments;
  Compulsory Arbitration.

"The American people can end war in our time if they get on the job.—Let us wage peace!—I should be a traitor to my country if I did not do everything in my power to abolish war."—Major General John F. O'Ryan, Commander of the 27th Division.

Figures on the cost of war in lives and in dollars can be dramatically shown on such movie slides or on posters.

In Ottawa the League of Nations Union secured a shop window for Armistice week and arranged a miniature scene showing the desolation and destruction wrought by modern war. On either side were placards bearing the words, "War Wastes," "Unless we end war, war will end us," "Peace Pays," "What do you know about the League of Nations?" This idea can be enlarged upon by a general display of cost of war posters or of the "pie chart" showing the percentage of the taxes paid by the people which go to pay the cost of wars past and future. In the smaller cities a parade can be held in which the salient facts of the cost and nature of modern war are carried on banners, and in which all the organizations which are in any way furthering peace work can be represented. It should be followed by an indoor or outdoor meeting where the facts displayed on the banners may be explained and an account given of what is being done for peace.

One of the simplest ways of celebrating the day is for the peace groups of a city at the beginning of the school year to offer a prize for the best essay on some such topic as, "The Difference Between War Yesterday and Today," and to award these prizes and have the essays read on Armistice Day; or a prize to be announced on Armistice Day can be offered through the local newspaper for the best article on, "How This Community Can Help Free the World From War."

WHAT YOU CAN DO FOR PEACE 485

Lincoln's Birthday, February 12.

In no man has the spirit of human brotherhood been more clearly portrayed than in Lincoln. His policy of conciliation following the Civil War is one of the great contributions to the realization of peace. The spirit of Lincoln inspires a poem by Vachel Lindsay, "Abraham Lincoln Walks at Midnight," of which this is one of the stanzas:

> He cannot rest until a spirit-dawn
>   Shall come: the shining hope of Europe free;
> The league of sober folk, the Worker's Earth
>   Bringing long peace to Cornland, Alp and Sea.

Washington's Birthday, February 22.

The whole story of Washington's life is not told if his work for world peace receives no mention. When he was President, the first commission of Americans was sent to Europe to negotiate treaties of commerce with other nations and he wrote to its secretary:

"My first wish is to see this plague to mankind (war) banished from the earth and the sons and daughters of this world employed in more pleasing and innocent amusements than in preparing implements and exercising them for the destruction of mankind."

The revival in modern history of arbitration as a method of settling international disputes was due to Washington. When many men in this country were demanding another war with England, President Washington sent as a special ambassador his Chief Justice, John Jay, to London, and the treaty which was arranged began the long list of arbitration treaties which the nations of the world have signed during the last century. When a memorandum suggesting this arbitration treaty with England was given to him, he wrote across it "and with all other nations." His birthday is a fitting time for Americans to stop and consider just what they have done to carry out Washington's "first wish" and how near they are to banishing the plague of war from the earth.

Goodwill Day, May 18.

Goodwill Day is the anniversary of the opening of the First Hague Peace Conference in 1899. Its observance was proposed in 1900 by European members of the International Council of Women and promoted by that organization, by the American Peace Society, and by the American School Citizenship League. Since the war the World Federation of Education Associations has urged that this day be made "a significant landmark in the movement for international friendship."

Although celebrated chiefly in the schools, the day lends itself also to community programs and offers an opportunity to do two things, to cultivate a spirit of goodwill and to undertake projects that will give evidence of goodwill. The origin of the day makes it appropriate to observe it with meetings on the subject of arbitration and the steadily increasing acceptance of peaceful methods of settling international disputes. Material on this subject can be secured from the World Peace Foundation, the American Peace Society, the National Council for Prevention of War, the Foreign Policy Association, and the American Foundation.

The special object of the day should be to increase knowledge and sympathetic understanding of other nations. In cities with a cosmopolitan population it can be made the occasion for an international program which will lead to permanent coöperation among the different local groups. An international luncheon or dinner can be arranged by a committee representing the different national groups in a community, or can be given by older citizens each one of whom invites a foreigner as a guest. An interesting decoration for such a dinner is a large map of the world in outline with the countries represented in the community filled in in color. Any international gathering of this sort can be appropriately concluded with the impressive candle-lighting ceremony in which representatives of the different nations stand in a circle, each holding a candle. One candle is lighted by the presiding officer and from it the next and so on around the circle, each one repeating as he lights his candle the name of his country and in his own language the words, "As light begets light so goodwill kindled in these meetings shall never die out."

In Rock Springs, Wyoming, the Lions Club arranges an annual international night which is attended by the Governor and prominent citizens. National groups give songs and dances and conclude with the candle-lighting ceremony described above. In St. Paul a Cosmopolitan Club has been formed in which thirty-eight groups are represented, each having one member on the Board. An account of the activities of the club can be obtained from the President, Mr. Henry W. Libby. In Baltimore an International Folk Festival included a handicraft exhibit which was kept open for a week. In Cleveland one of the daily papers, *The Press*, arranged a dance of nations which enlisted the enthusiastic coöperation of the whole community. For cities where it is possible to stage an elaborate spectacle, a "Festival of the Nations," an epic of world relationships, in four colorful scenes in which several hundred people participate, has been arranged by Mr. Chalmers Brooks Fithian, Dean of the National Pageant Association. Information about the successful staging of this festival in Southern California can be secured from the Council of International Relations of

Southern California, Chamber of Commerce Building, Los Angeles.

"Reconciliation trips," inaugurated in New York City by Clarence V. Howell and Ida Oatley Howell, are being imitated in other large cities. The program for one month in New York included trips to the Japanese, Latin American, Chinese, Negro and Russian communities where special facilities had been arranged for meeting the people and understanding their point of view. In the summer of 1928, the first world "reconciliation tour" is being conducted on which a group of Americans will visit several European nations and have special opportunities for meeting the people.

In cities where the population is less cosmopolitan, the idea of world unity can be emphasized in several ways. A public dinner or evening meeting can be held for the discussion of world unity from their special points of view by a scientist, an artist, a minister of the gospel and a business man, all of whom should have interesting things to say on this theme.

The economic interdependence of all nations can be called to the attention of the public in a series of posters, or in window displays built up around articles manufactured by local firms, showing the countries in which the materials used in the articles are produced, and the countries to which the articles are sent. A simultaneous display of this kind by manufacturers and merchants for a week would attract wide attention and could be utilized by the schools. Suggestions for such a display will be found in the chapter on "Commerce and Peace" and in the preceding section, "Through the Schools."

An international evening can be provided by showing moving pictures or lantern slides of other countries. The sources from which they can be obtained are listed above.

An entire community where there is a broadcasting

WHAT YOU CAN DO FOR PEACE 489

station may be interested in having its children join those of other nations in broadcasting a message of goodwill, such as the following one which the children of Wales have sent out for several years and which on Goodwill Day in 1927 was repeated from powerful stations not only in Europe but in Canada:

"We boys and girls of the principality of Wales and of Monmouthshire, greet with a cheer the boys and girls of every other country under the sun. Will you, millions of you, join in our prayer that God will bless the efforts of the good men and women of every race and people who are doing their best to settle the old quarrels without fighting? Then there will be no need for any of us, as we grow older, to show our pride for the country in which we were born by going out to hate and to kill one another. Long live the League of Nations— the friend of every Mother, the protector of every Home, and the guardian angel of the Youth of the world."

Memorial Day, May 30

Several cities are now honoring on Memorial Day not only the soldiers who have given their lives in battle, but men and women who have been "heroes of social construction." Programs for carrying out such a celebration on Memorial Day can be gotten by writing the Peace Heroes Memorial Society, 3431 Larona Avenue, Cincinnati, Ohio. Something of the spirit of the celebration can be gathered from the following paragraphs of the invitation issued to citizens to take part in it:

"Miners, railroaders, builders, electricians, mechanics, firemen, policemen, explorers, physicians, nurses, mothers and others upon whose risks and sufferings life depends, form an army larger than any fighting force of which history has record. It is an army serving without intermission and knowing no armistice, an army that endures both pain and privation. It numbers its losses of life by the tens of thousands every year and its other casualties by the hundreds of thousands. It goes to its hard perilous battles without decorations and without honors. . . . Yet it is the army of our real national defense against hunger, cold, sickness, exposure, disorder, exhaustion, extinction; ultimately perhaps our true defense against foreign foes. . . .

"Shall not we who honor the army that slays . . . honor the army that heals and preserves? We acclaim the heroism of the fighter. Shall we not acclaim the heroism of the worker, the investigator, the mother?"

Independence Day, July 4

July fourth is the natural occasion for the expression of pride in America and for a renewal of the spirit and ideals which inspired the men who founded it. This day has been made the occasion in several cities for ceremonies welcoming people of foreign birth to citizenship. In pageants, processions, international dinners, there can be shown the contributions which many nations have made to the development of the United States in the days of exploration and settlement and through the years of its industrial growth to the present period.

Two editorials on July 4, 1927, one in the New York *Herald Tribune* and one in the New York *Times*, suggest new interpretations of the spirit of this day. The New York *Herald Tribune* said:

"Of all our wars and victories deserving of commemoration on Independence Day few are more stirring to the imagination than the victory, won by a devoted handful of American officers and men, which freed the world from the terrible menace of yellow fever. . . . Their heroism had the rare reward of a complete success. The war against yellow fever, waged with the knowledge gained by the experiments to which they submitted themselves, has gone on, until the disease which year after year through centuries had been taking its hundreds of thousands of lives has been driven from the homes of men. Few armies have won a victory of that magnitude."

The New York *Times* editorial read:

" 'Are and of right ought to be free and independent' was written one hundred and fifty-one years ago. It was the preamble and the peroration of an announcement that the United Colonies were absolved from allegiance to the British Crown and that all political connection between them and Great Britain ought to be dissolved. . . . To infer from this a lack of responsibility to the rest of the world, a refusal to adhere to a society of nations to promote the peace of mankind, or the assumption of political, social or economic self-sufficiency, would be to misinterpret this historic utterance. . . .

"With the raising of the standards of living the wants of man cannot be satisfied locally. As he ascends to a higher range of existence, whether in mere creature comforts or in intellectual commerce, the wider does the horizon of his needs become and the more insistently do they call for the removal of artificial barriers. Freedom the world around urges not only respect for the independence of the individual nation but also—and more and more strongly—the recognition of the interdependence of all nations."

A poster, "America First," based on a sermon by Bishop G. Ashton Oldham in which he covets for America the leadership toward a time when "war shall be no more," printed in black and red in various sizes, is issued by the National Council for Prevention of War and will be found very appropriate for Independence Day programs. The poster reads:

America First
Not merely in matters material, but in things of the spirit. Not merely in science, inventions, motors, and skyscrapers, but also in ideals, principles, character.

Not merely in the calm assertion of rights, but in the glad
assumption of duties.
Not flaunting her strength as a giant, but bending in helpfulness over a sick and wounded world like a Good Samaritan.
Not in splendid isolation, but in courageous coöperation.
Not in pride, arrogance, and disdain of other races and peoples, but in sympathy, love, and understanding.
Not in treading again the old, worn, bloody pathway which ends inevitably in chaos and disaster, but in blazing a new trail, along which, please God, other nations will follow, into the new Jerusalem where wars shall be no more.
Some day some nation must take that path—unless we are to lapse once again into utter barbarism—and that honor I covet for my beloved America.
And so, in that spirit and with these hopes, I say with all my heart and soul, "AMERICA FIRST."

International Flag Day, July 2

A first International Flag Day, calling attention to the unarmed boundary between the United States and Canada and to their hundred years of peace, was organized in 1927 with impressive ceremonies attended by Canadian and American officials, held at the Peace Portal in the State of Washington. The celebration falls between America's Independence Day and Canada's Dominion Day and it is hoped will extend all along the border line. The Peace Portal standing near the western end of the line was built to commemorate the one hundred years of peace that have existed between America and Great Britain. It is near the city of Blaine, and rests half on British soil and half on American. On one side is the flag of Great Britain and on the other that of the United States. On the American side are the words, "Children of a Common Mother"; on the Canadian,

"Brethren Dwelling Together in Unity." Below one of the doors is inscribed, "Open for One Hundred Years"; and below the other, "May These Doors Never Be Closed."

Near the eastern end of the boundary is the Bridge of Goodwill and Peace between Buffalo and Fort Erie. The piers of this bridge mark the places where once stood American and British forts, and where, over a hundred years ago, during the War of 1812, there had been desperate fighting. Cities wishing to take part in the celebration of International Flag Day may secure further information from Mr. G. A. Miller, of Bellingham, Washington.

Columbus Day, October 12th

Through the *Journal* of the National Education Association, Dr. Leo S. Rowe, Director of the Pan American Union, has made the suggestion that Columbus Day be celebrated as a Pan American Friendship Day. Dr. Rowe points out that it is the "one date that has equal significance for all the republics of the Western Hemisphere." He goes on to say:

"To the vision, courage, and leadership of the great admiral we all alike owe the beginnings of European civilization on this continent.

"It is well that we of the United States should stop to realize to what extent we are indebted to Spanish explorers and missionaries for the taming of our great wilderness.

"While during colonial days North and South America had few contacts, with the beginning of the struggles for independence there began an era of sympathetic interest which has continued to the present time. South American patriots drew their inspiration from the American and French revolutions and their efforts toward liberty awakened the intense sympathy of such Americans as Henry Clay, some of whose most passionately eloquent utterances were devoted to the cause of South American independence."

Interesting material for Latin-American programs, including lantern slides, can be obtained from the Pan American Union.

Christmas Day

Christmas offers a natural occasion for an expression of goodwill and of the desire for peace. A community Christmas tree celebration emphasizing world unity and goodwill, and including songs such as Whittier's "Christmas Carmen" set to music by Daniel Batchellor, is published by the National Council for Prevention of War. Plays and programs for Sunday Schools may be obtained from the Federal Council of Churches, the Missionary Education Movement, the League of Nations Non-Partisan Association and the National Council for Prevention of War.

THROUGH DISCUSSION PROGRAMS

It leads to greater interest in the peace movement if members of an organization have an opportunity to carry on discussions themselves, as well as to hear special speakers. Many of the discussions suggested below may be impromptu.

An Afternoon of Prejudices.—The course on Prejudice by Professor Edwin L. Clarke, described in Chapter II, lends itself to group discussion. A memeographed copy of one of Dr. Clarke's lectures can be ordered from the National Council for Prevention of War. Professor Clarke says in the outline of his course:

"A person who desires to have intellectual power should carefully consider each important subject with which he has to deal, to see if he is prejudiced. If such is the case, he must try to determine the source of his bias. Once recognized, it can be fought. . . . This means that he must read literature presenting both sides. . . . He must get acquainted with intelligent and educated persons who hold the point of view which he dislikes, and must try to comprehend the reasons for the stand they take. . . . The acquisition of open-mindedness in regard to any single subject tends to make easier open-mindedness in others."

A Group Intelligence Test.—The object is not to find out what individuals know, but what the group as a whole knows of current world affairs. Questions can be based on the current news. Committees should be appointed to secure information and report back on the questions which cannot be answered.

Taking an Inventory.—Both in starting peace work and at regular periods while a program is being carried out, take stock of exactly what influences for peace are at work in the community. The discussion can be based upon the chart shown in Chapter I. Interest is increased by noting on a blackboard or similar surface what is being done. A similar inventory can be taken of influences in the community making for unfriendly relations, followed by suggestions as to how they can be met.

"Ask Me Another," questions and answers on international affairs issued by the Department of International Coöperation to Prevent War of the National League of Women Voters, and arranged in eight sets. Full instructions for conducting meetings based upon them accompany the sets; price 10c.

"Is the United States Coöperating to Build Permanent Peace?" A questionnaire prepared by The Inquiry, the Y. M. C. A. and a member of the faculty of New York University.

"Thinking Peace, A Quiz." Published by the Women's Missionary Society of the Reformed Church in the U. S., 1505 Race Street, Philadelphia; price 10c.

"Is America Blocking the Way to World Peace—How Can the Average Citizen Work for the Cause of Permanent Peace?" A detailed outline for discussion with helpful suggestions for leaders, published by the New York League of Women Voters, 420 Lexington Avenue, New York City; price 25c.

"Arbitration the Only Substitute for War," 150 questions and answers on this subject, published by the Committee on the Cause and Cure of War; price 15c.

"What Do You Mean by 100% American?" A stimulating discussion published by the Young Women's Christian Association as a part of a pamphlet, "Program Help on International Relationships"; price 30c.

"Our Foreign Policy," a discussion in the form of questions and answers, published by the New York Federation of Progressive Women, 15 E. 40th Street, New York City; free.

"A World Outlook," a discussion course for young people including the following topics: The World Neighborhood, Tolerance, The Fight Against War and the Development of Organized Government. It is issued by Glenn D. Adams, Young Men's Christian Association of Chicago, 19 South La Salle St., 15 cents each in quantities of ten or more.

"What To Do With Goodwill," the first of a series of one-day discussion programs for women's clubs, with reference material free, which is being issued by the League of Nations Non-Partisan Association.

Through Study Courses

Three types of study courses designed to bring about a better understanding of world problems are available:

Courses calculated to develop what may best be described as a scientific attitude of mind.

WHAT YOU CAN DO FOR PEACE

Courses on the general background problems of war and peace.

Courses on special problems involved in the establishment of peace.

Attitude Courses

The most carefully worked-out courses along these lines are those prepared by The Inquiry, under the following titles:

"What Makes Up My Mind On International Questions?" Price $1.00 in cloth, 75c in paper.

"Coöperative Technique for Conflict"; price 20c.

"Creative Discussion," Contrasted with debate; price 35c.

"And Who Is My Neighbor?" On race relations in America; price 75c.

General Background Courses

Under the title, "Information for Study Groups," the International Relations office of the American Association of University Women issues helpful suggestions for organizing and conducting courses; free. It also has in preparation a handbook for Leaders. Among the suggestions offered, are these:

"Where a controversial subject is under consideration, the various aspects of the points of conflict may be presented by different members. When this is followed care should be taken to prevent the discussion from becoming a formal debate.

"In the face of the bewildering mass of articles and books that confront the student of international affairs, the most efficient way of studying a particular problem is to read first a general account and to take notes in outline form on that account. With the striking phases of the situation in mind, further material may be chosen to elucidate obscure points and to explain points of view. It is also essential to be aware of the identity of the authors whose materials are studied—to know something of their standing and the factors which may give them a bias in their writing."

"Syllabus on International Relations."—By far the most comprehensive and authoritative course on international relations, by Parker Thomas Moon, Ph. D., of Columbia University, issued by the Institute of International Education and published by the Macmillan Company. Its main divisions are as follows: Introductory Discussion of International Relations; Nationalism, Territorial Conflicts and War; Imperialism and World Politics; Militarism and Armaments; History of International Relations to 1914; History of International Relations Since 1914; Summary Review of Policies of Great Powers; Economic Problems of International Relations; Problems of Diplomacy; International Ororganization, the League and the World Court. The price is $3.50.

"Syllabus of a Course of Twelve Lectures on the History of International Relations and the League of Nations," by C. Delisle Burns, published by the League of Nations Union 15 Grosvenor Crescent, London, S. W. 1; price 15c. This is an excellent outline of the study of the general peace problem.

"Adventuring in World Coöperation," by Jerome Davis and Daniel A. Poling, published by the United Society of Christian Endeavor; price 25c. The course which includes many interesting quotations and helpful outlines for discussion, is divided into four parts: Our World Contacts; Our Misunderstandings; Our Conflicts; and Friendship as an Instrument.

"The Science of Social Relations," by Hornell Hart, published by Henry Holt & Co., is particularly valuable because it is both comprehensive and direct in its method of approach. It includes written assignments based on each chapter. The price is $4.50.

"Patriotism," three discussion outlines for young people, for social workers, and for church people, published in one of the *Occasional Papers* issued by The Inquiry, under date of May, 1928.

"Conflict or Coöperation," a study outline with bibliographies, is prepared by the American Committee of the World Youth Peace Congress, 104 East 9th Street, New York City; price 25c.

"On Earth Peace," by Rhoda E. McCulloch and Margaret E. Burton, is published by the Federation of Women's Foreign Mission Boards of North America and the Council of Women for Home Missions. The chapter headings are: Christian Missions and World Peace; Inter-Racial Coöperation and World Peace; Causes of War; the Cure for War; The Christian Way of Life; and Programs and Suggestions; price 30c.

"World Peace Primer," a series of 21 simple lessons by Mrs. E. K. Bowman, Helena, Montana, price 25c.

"A Study Course on World Peace," in connection with which the material in the various chapters of this book would be found useful, is issued in outline form with lists of books and pamphlet material by the National Council for Prevention of War under the following heads: War in Relation to the Modern World; What Is Being Done to Protect the World Against War; Policies, Practices and Beliefs Which Endanger World Peace; Foreign Relations of the United States; and The Unique Position of the United States in Relation to World Peace.

Courses on Special Topics

The courses in this section are listed according to subjects in the following order: General, Arbitration, Christianity and Peace, Foreign Policy, Latin America, the League of Nations and World Court, the National Defense Act, the Problems of the Pacific, Racial Questions, the United States Government.

"Guidance Material for Study Groups" is issued by the American Association of University Women on these topics: European Diplomacy; The Evolution of International Organization; Fuel and Raw Materials in International Politics; Establishing the New World Order; Pan American Policies and Problems; The Foreign Policy of the United States; Problems of the Pacific; International Economics; and Mexico. The price of each is 20c.

"Arbitration." Material for study of this topic can be secured from the World Peace Foundation, the Federal Council of Churches; the American Foundation; the Foreign Policy Association; the National Committee on the Cause and Cure of War; the National League of Women Voters; and the National Council for Prevention of War.

"Christian Fellowship Among the Nations," by Jerome Davis and Roy B. Chamberlin, published by the Pilgrim Press, Boston, price 25c.

"The Churches and World Peace," a syllabus published by the Federal Council of Churches at 25c a copy, or ten for $1.00.

"International Problems and the Christian Way of Life," by Rhoda E. McCulloch, published by the Association Press, 347 Madison Avenue, New York City, 30c a copy.

"Testing Modern Life by Jesus' Way of Living," by Gerald Birney Smith, published by the American Institute of Sacred Literature, Hyde Park, Chicago, as one of its series of Outline Bible Study Courses.

"Working for World Peace Through Organized Justice and Goodwill," a six weeks' discussion course, published by the Commission on International Relations of the National Council of the Congregational Churches, 287 Fourth Ave., New York City, price 10c.

"The Search for Peace," "What Contribution Has Christianity to Make in the Promotion of Peace?", by Laura F. Boyer, published by the National Council of the Protestant Episcopal Church, 281 Fourth Avenue, New York City, price 25c.

"The Message of Jesus to Our Modern Life," by Shailer Mathews, published by the American Institute of Sacred Literature, Hyde Park, Chicago, price 75c.

"Christ and the Nations," issued by the American Baptist Publishing Society, Philadelphia, price 25c.

"The Words of Christ Commonly Quoted for or Against War," a compendium prepared for study groups by a committee of the New York Presbytery, distributed by Harold A. Hatch, 70 Leonard St., New York City.

"Thinking It Through," a discussion on world peace, by Evelyn Riley Nicholson, approved by the Board of Education of the Methodist Episcopal Church, published by the Methodist Book Concern, New York City; price 40c.

"Missions and World Problems," a comprehensive syllabus with bibliography, published by The Inquiry; price 75c.

"Know Your Own Foreign Policy," questions and answers prepared by the National League of Women Voters on the following subjects: the League of Nations; the World Court; the State Department; the Powers and Responsibility of the President for International Affairs; the Monroe Doctrine; Current Questions on the

Disarmament Conference; the price is 20c each. Orders should be sent to New York office.

"What Should Be the Foreign Policy of the United States Regarding Neutrality and Neutral Rights—What Policy Will Contribute Most Toward World Peace?" An outline of a 7-weeks' course for group study, with references; issued by the Peace Committee of the Philadelphia Yearly Meeting of Friends.

"International Relations of the United States," a series of brief summaries for busy men and women issued by the Federal Council of Churches; price $1 a hundred.

Information on questions related to the foreign policy of the United States, prepared in such form as to serve readily as the basis for a study course, can be obtained from the Foreign Policy Association. The pamphlets available are listed in the Association's index of publications, which will be supplied upon request.

"Hispanic American History," a syllabus of 169 pages by Professor William Whatley Pierson, published by the University of North Carolina Press, Chapel Hill, North Carolina. A comprehensive outline with bibliographies; price $1.50.

"Ventures in Inter-American Friendship," the trend of thought on social, political and religious problems in Latin America. Written by Samuel Guy Inman and published by the Missionary Education Movement of the United States and Canada, New York City. Price 50c.

The Pan American Union supplies outlines and interesting material for study groups, on Pan American problems.

"A Study Course on the League of Nations, the World Court, and the International Labor Organization," a very interesting, complete and well-organized course issued by the League of Nations Non-Partisan Association; price

WHAT YOU CAN DO FOR PEACE

10c. It includes bibliographies and references to documents with suggestions for discussions under each topic.

"The National Defense Act," a summary and series of questions and answers issued by the National League of Women Voters; price 15c. Order from the New York office.

"Primer on Outlawry of War," questions and answers, published by the National League of Women Voters, price 2c. Order from the New York office.

"Problems of the Pacific," an analyzed and annotated bibliography by Raymond Leslie Buell, published by the World Peace Foundation, which could readily be followed as a study course on Pacific problems. The price is 5c.

The reports and publications of the Institute of Pacific Relations, Honolulu, will be found useful in studying Pacific questions.

"All Colors," a study outline on woman's part in racial relations prepared by The Inquiry and distributed by the Woman's Press. 153 pages with bibliographies and suggestions for discussion leaders; price $1.00.

"Toward Friendship with China," issued by the Federation of Women's Boards of Foreign Missions of North America.

"Of One Blood," a short study of the Race Problem by Robert E. Speer, published by the Council of Women for Home Missions and the Missionary Education Movement of the United States and Canada, New York City; price 75c.

"The Outline of Government in the United States," for reference or study, published by the National League of Women Voters; price 50c.

Through Reading Courses

Study Courses Under the Auspices of the National Committee on the Cause and Cure of War.—These courses are based on a carefully selected list of readings which may be followed by an individual or by a group. The main topics recommended for 1927-28 were: the Causes of War and the Agencies That Deal with Them; the Cures of War and the Agencies That Deal with Them; Foreign Policy; Arbitration; Asiatic Problems Emphasizing China, Japan, and the Philippines; Problems of the Americas: United States and Mexico; European Problems, Emphasizing International Debts.

"World Unity Reading List of Current Books," published by the World Unity League, 22 East 34th Street, New York City; price 10c.

The Foreign Relations of the United States, by Paul Scott Mowrer, published by the American Library Association, 86 East Randolph Street, Chicago; price 15c. In many cities it can be obtained from the local library.

What an Individual Can Do

The fact that the movement for world peace can be furthered by individuals as well as organizations has many striking illustrations, from those who have given millions of dollars to the promotion of the cause, to the men and women who supply their local libraries with the publication of some peace organization or a magazine on international affairs. Among the notable gifts to the peace movement have been the Carnegie Endowment for International Peace, organized by Andrew Carnegie with a fund of $10,000,000, and his creation of the Church Peace Union with an endowment of $2,000,000; the endowment of $1,000,000 given by Edwin Ginn to the World Peace Foundation; Mr. James H. Causey's gift of $1,500,000 to the University of Denver for the establishment of a chair to promote international goodwill; and Alfred Nobel's endowment of the annual peace award. Small endowments have been made to colleges for the purchase of books or for special lectures on international topics, and for essays on peace subjects.

Other individuals have given large sums of money in prizes for peace plans or ideas tending to promote international understanding. Mr. Edward Bok's gift of $50,000 for the best plan to promote world peace, which was won by Charles H. Levermore in 1924, was followed by the offer of similar prizes by Mr. Edward A. Filene to the citizens of European countries. A prize of $25,000 was offered by Raphael Herman for the best plan for peace education, and awarded to David Starr Jordan in 1924. The Misses Seabury of New Bedford, Massachusetts, have for many years offered annual prizes in both high schools and normal schools for the best essays on questions affecting world peace.

A contribution of a different kind, but comparable in value and influence, is the work of men and women who have devoted their lives to writing and speaking for peace. The influence of the writings of a man like David Starr Jordan, who has published more than 450 books and articles on questions of peace, and of Dr. and Mrs. Edwin D. Mead of Boston, has reached around the world.

What one person can do without large means is nowhere better illustrated than by Mrs. E. K. Bowman of Helena, Montana, who because of her unique peace work was entered by the Director of the North Pacific Section of the American University Women as a candidate for the *Pictorial Review* Achievement Award in 1927. Mrs. Bowman, who has done her own housework and raised a family of five children, has found time without financial help and without office equipment to write and distribute several editions of a "World Peace Primer"; she has arranged essay contests in the schools of her State, sending 300 package libraries of material to teachers; she has developed a system of letters which are sent to a large mailing list as often as funds for postage can be gotten; she has prepared a lecture with lantern slides, which is circulated, and has given over a hundred lectures herself; she has persuaded the Bar Association, the Federation of Labor, and the American Legion of her State, to allow her to send speakers to their annual conventions; and she has organized a speakers' bureau with key men in various towns who keep themselves informed on international affairs and on opportunities for speeches.

If this seems too ambitious a program for imitation, there are other simpler things that can be done to help hold the attention of the public on the problem of peace. Letters to newspapers and magazines here, there, everywhere, answering articles, commenting on editorials, praising those which stand for peace, have a cumulative influence. One person working in this way who should have helpful suggestions to offer as to how to proceed, is Miss Lydia G. Wentworth of Brookline, Massachusetts. Another excellent plan carried out by many men and women is to buy a good book on international affairs as often as possible, even one a year is well worth while, and keep it in circulation among friends.

The methods of Mr. C. W. Johnson of Springfield, Massachusetts, could be imitated by many others. Among other devices for promoting peace, he has printed on the front of envelopes the words, "Build Friendships, not Warships, for National Defense," and on the back this quotation,

"The world has tried war with force and has utterly failed. The only hope of success lies in peace with justice." President Calvin Coolidge, Cambridge, Mass., July 3, 1925.

Packages of such envelopes can be obtained from Mr. Johnson at 128 Orleans Street.

Goodwill Day, May 18th, offers one of the best opportunities for an individual to interest a community in peace work. In San Jose, California, Mr. J. W. Wells, an "anti-war Civil War veteran" has encouraged the observance of the day in the schools in many ways, among others by making pennants with the names of different nations on them and a large placard with the words, "Greetings of Goodwill to all Nations." The students assemble, display the pennants and placard, and photographs taken of them are widely published and sent to schools abroad. Pennants displayed around the placard in an auditorium or entrance hall would lead to interesting discussion.

The Detroit News of April 4, 1928, in an editorial, "Put Punch Into All Your Peace Promotion," suggests a further way in which any individual anywhere can help to undermine the institutionalized habit of war;

"There is nothing that the world needs more than a general campaign to induce positive thinking in behalf of peace. When world public opinion favors peace there will be no more war. We approach that state. Nowhere any longer is there willingness to say a good word for war, but there remain the fearful. . . .

"It is the duty of individuals to talk peace positively; to stop repeating rumors of war; to refuse to credit malice to people of other races and nationalities, and to insist to the limit of their influence on banishing those acts and words that may be mistaken for threats."

Fliers carrying sixteen useful suggestions for the individual volunteer peace worker, compiled by Mrs. J. Malcolm Forbes, may be obtained from the National Council for Prevention of War.

Because publications dealing with current questions go very rapidly out of date, organizations do not make it a policy to keep such material in print for any great length of time, and the date of the publication of this book should be noted before ordering material listed in the preceding chapter. It is frequently better to ask for material on a given subject rather than for a special pamphlet. Where a publication found to be out of print is particularly desired, if it is referred to in this book, the National Council for Prevention of War will make an effort to supply a copy at least for temporary use.

ORGANIZATIONS WORKING FOR PEACE

The following organizations offer an opportunity for coöperation in their programs and serve as sources of information and material. The list is not complete, but includes the larger organizations formed primarily for peace work, and others whose addresses are needed in connection with programs of work outlined in Chapter XXVI. Under the title, "Organizations in the United States That Promote Better International Understanding and World Peace," the National Council for Prevention of War publishes a list of more than one hundred and fifty organizations with the names of officers and statements of purpose and activities. The same organization is also able to supply copies of the Peace Year Book published in England, and mimeographed lists of organizations in many of the countries of Europe, Asia, and Latin America. A Peace Year Book containing a great deal of interesting general material is published in Germany by the Friedensgesellschaft, but is not translated. Information in regard to foreign peace societies can also be obtained through the International Peace Bureau, rue Charles Bonnet, 8, Geneva, Switzerland.

American Association of University Women,
    1634 Eye St., N. W., Washington, D. C.
American Committee for the Outlawry of War,
    134 South La Salle St., Chicago, Ill.
American Federation of Labor,
    Massachusetts Ave., and Ninth St., Washington, D. C.

American Foundation,
 565 Fifth Ave., New York City.
American Friends Service Committee,
 20 South 12th St., Philadelphia, Pa.
American Peace Society,
 Colorado Bldg., Washington, D. C.
American School Citizenship League,
 405 Marlborough St., Boston, Mass.
Association for Peace Education,
 5733 Blackstone Ave., Chicago, Ill.
Carnegie Endowment for International Peace,
 2 Jackson Pl., Washington, D. C.
Church Peace Union (See World Alliance)

Committee on Militarism in Education,
 387 Bible House, Astor Pl., New York City.
Committee on Peace and Service, Philadelphia Yearly Meeting
 of Friends,
 15th and Race Sts., Philadelphia.
The Epworth League,
 740 Rush St., Chicago, Ill.
Federal Council of Churches of Christ in America,
 105 East 22nd St., New York City.
Fellowship of Reconciliation,
 383 Bible House, Astor Pl., New York City.
Foreign Policy Association,
 18 East 41st St., New York City.
The Inquiry,
 129 East 52d St., New York City.
League of Nations Non-Partisan Association,
 6 East 39th St., New York City.
Mennonite Church, Peace Problems Committee, Akron, Pa.
National Board of the Young Women's Christian Associations,
 600 Lexington Ave., New York City.
National Committee on the Cause and Cure of War,
 1010 Grand Central Terminal Bldg., New York City.
National Council for Prevention of War,
 532 17th St., N. W., Washington, D. C.
 and 205 Sheldon Bldg., San Francisco, Calif.

ORGANIZATIONS WORKING FOR PEACE 511

National Council of the Young Men's Christian Associations,
 347 Madison Ave., New York City.
National Grange,
 630 Louisiana Ave., N. W. Washington, D. C.
National League of Women Voters,
 532 17th St., Washington, D. C.
 Department of International Coöperation to Prevent War,
 1010 Grand Central Terminal Bldg., New York City.
National Woman's Christian Temperance Union,
 1730 Chicago Ave., Evanston, Illinois.
  Director, National Department of Peace,
  Mrs. May Bell Harper, Unionville, Connecticut.
Peace Association of Friends in America,
 Richmond, Indiana.
Peace Committee of Philadelphia Yearly Meeting of Friends,
 304 Arch St., Philadelphia.
Rotary International,
 221 East Cullerton St., Chicago, Ill.
United Society of Christian Endeavor,
 41 Mt. Vernon St., Boston, Mass.
Women's International League for Peace and Freedom,
 522 17th St., N. W., Washington, D. C.
Women's Peace Society,
 20 Vesey St., New York City.
Women's Peace Union,
 39 Pearl St., New York City.
World Alliance for International Friendship Through the Churches,
 70 Fifth Ave., New York City.
World Peace Foundation,
 40 Mt. Vernon St., Boston, Mass.
World's Student Christian Federation,
 347 Madison Ave., New York City.

BIBLIOGRAPHY

A UNIQUE Library on international affairs and the peace movement is maintained by the Carnegie Endowment for International Peace at its headquarters in Washington, under the direction of Miss M. Alice Matthews. The Library contains over 37,000 catalogued volumes and pamphlets including valuable special collections of documents relating to foreign affairs and receives over 200 periodicals and newspapers. Comprehensive reading lists on various phases of the peace problem are issued at frequent intervals and may be obtained free of charge by addressing the Library at 2 Jackson Place, Washington, D. C.

The reading lists issued by the Division of Bibliography of the Library of Congress, Washington, D. C. under the direction of Mr. William A. Slade, Chief Bibliographer, include many titles of interest to students of international relations and world peace; they will be sent on request to any library.

The World Peace Foundation issues at intervals a publication "International Book News" which it distributes free of charge upon request.

In the following list of bibliographies, the abbreviation "LCar," is used for the Library of the Carnegie Endowment for International Peace, and "LC" for the Library of Congress.

COMPREHENSIVE BIBLIOGRAPHIES ON SPECIAL SUBJECTS*

GENERAL

Aids to International Understanding, a booklet with notes; compiled by the Newark Public Library. Published by the New Jersey Federation of Women's Clubs, Miss Margaret Buttenheim, Chairman, Committee on International Relations, 44 Crescent Road, Madison, New Jersey, 10c.

War and Peace. St. Louis Public Library.

Recommended Books. League of Nations Non-Partisan Association, New York.

ARBITRATION

International Arbitration. LCar.

Taft, Root and Bryan Treaties. Women's International League for Peace and Freedom, Washington, D. C.

ARMAMENTS

Limitation of Armaments. LC.

Disarmament, special reference to naval limitation. LC.

Traffic in Arms and Munitions of War. LCar.

Disarmament and Substitutes for War. Public Library of the City of Boston.

CONSCIENTIOUS OBJECTORS. LCar.

EDUCATION

Education and Internationalism. Friends' Book Centre, Euston Road, London, N. W. 1, 2s.

Education and International Peace. LCar.

History in School Text Books. LCar.

* Where there is only one bibliography title forms topical subject.

A Bibliography for School Teachers of History, Eileen Power. Methuen, London, 1s. 6d.

Europe

European Diplomacy. American Association of University Women, Washington, D. C., 20c.

The Europe of Our Day, Herbert Adams Gibbons. American Library Association Reading Course. (Obtainable at most libraries.)

Immigration

American Immigration. LC.

Japanese in America. LC.

Foreign Language Groups Handbook—Bibliography. Missionary Education Movement, N. Y., $1.25.

Racial and Nationality Backgrounds. Woman's Press, 600 Lexington Ave., N. Y., 50c.

Americans from Abroad, John Palmer Gavit. American Library Association Reading Course. (Obtainable from most libraries.)

International Law

International Law, Codification of, LC.

Recognition in International Law, with Special Reference to Russia. LCar.

International Organization

International Communication. LC.

International Status of Panama Canal and Similar Waterways, LC.

International Relations

General

Recent Publications on International Relations. LCar.

Democratic Control of Foreign Affairs. LC.

Ways of Learning, brief reading list of authoritative sources of material on international affairs, American Foundation, N. Y., or LC.

Economic

> *American Investments in Foreign Countries.* LC.
> *Intervention with Special Reference to Protection of Foreign Loans and Investments.* LCar.
> *Fuel and Raw Materials in International Politics.* American Association of University Women, Washington, D. C.
> *Training for Foreign Service.* United States Commissioner of Education, Washington, D. C. (With bibliography for advanced study on questions of foreign trade.) 10c.

Foreign Relations of the United States

> *Foreign Relations of the United States* (List of government publications). Superintendent of Documents, Washington, D. C. Ten cents.
> *The Foreign Relations of the United States*, Paul Scott Mowrer, American Library Association Reading Course. (Obtainable at most libraries).
> *The Foreign Policy of the United States.* American Association of University Women, Washington, D. C., 20c.

LABOR AND PEACE

> *Labor and World Peace.* LCar.
> *International Labor Organization—1919-1926.* International Labor Office, Geneva. Pamphlet, 50c. May be obtained from the Washington Branch of the International Labor Office, Lenox Bldg.

LATIN AMERICAN TOPICS

> Comprehensive reading lists on Latin American nations and on a wide range of subjects bearing upon Latin American relations and affairs may be obtained from the Pan American Union, Washington, D. C.
>
> *The United States and Latin America.* LC.
> *Economic and cultural relations between the United States and Latin America.* LCar.

League of Nations
  Current Reading Lists. League of Nations Non-Partisan Association, N. Y.
  League of Nations. LC.
  League of Nations Covenant. LCar.
  Locarno Treaties. LCar.

Mexico, Present Situation. LC.

Military Training. LC.

Nicaragua
  Nicaragua, with Special Reference to her Relations with the United States. LC.

Outlawry of War
  Outlawry of War. LC.
  Outlawry of War. LCar.

Pacific Problems, Raymond Leslie Buell. World Peace Foundation, Boston, 5c.

Peace and the Peace Movement. LCar.

Philippine Independence. LC.

Population. Its decrease and increase with economic results. LC.

Reparations Problem. LC.

Tariff Question Pro and Con. LC.

United States Government
  Constitution of the United States. LC.
  The Founders of the Republic, Claude G. Bowers. American Library Association Reading Course. (Obtainable at most libraries.)
  The United States in Recent Times, Frederick L. Paxon. American Library Association Reading Course. (Obtainat most libraries.)

Conflicts in American Public Opinion, William Allen White and Walter E. Myers. American Library Association Reading Course. (Obtainable at most libraries.)

WAR

Causes of War. LCar.
Conscription of men, material resources and money in time of war. LCar.
Cost of War. LCar.
Cost of European War. LC.
War and the Race. Bibliography of Eugenics. University of California Press, Berkeley, Cal.
War and Religion. LCar.
Referendum on War. LCar.

WAR DEBTS

Cancellation of Allied Debt. LC.
War Debt Problems. LCar.

WORLD COURT

Permanent Court of International Justice. LC.
Permanent Court of International Justice. LCar.

WORLD UNITY

Reading List of Current Books. World Unity Publishing Co., 4 East 12th St., N. Y. 10c.

YOUTH MOVEMENT. LCar.

BOOKS FOR THE GENERAL READER CLASSIFIED ACCORDING TO VARIOUS PHASES OF THE PEACE MOVEMENT

Descriptive leaflets or tables of contents of the books listed below may be obtained from the publishers. A few books that are out of print have been included, most of which can be found in city libraries. Pamphlets and magazine articles are listed when books covering the same points are not available. In the case of related subjects, such as imperialism and nationalism, books dealing with either should be looked for under both heads. Under each heading books suited to serve as a general introduction to that subject are starred.

I. BACKGROUND MATERIAL

A. *The Unity of the Universe.*

Allee, W. C., and others, *The Nature of the World and Man.* University of Chicago Press, Chicago, 1927, $5.00.

Shapley, Harlow, *Starlight.* Doran, N. Y., 1926, $1.00.

*Shapley, Harlow (editor), *The Universe of the Stars.* Radio talks. Harvard Observatory, Cambridge, Mass., 1926, $2.00.

B. *The Unity of Civilization*

Bury, J. B., *History of the Freedom of Thought.* Holt, N. Y., 1913, $1.00.

Follett, M. P., *The New State.* Longmans, Green, N. Y., 1918, $3.00.

*Parsons, Geoffrey, *The Stream of History.* Scribner, N. Y., 1928, $5.00.

Perry, W. F., *The Growth of Civilization.* Dutton, N. Y., 1923, $2.50.

Randall, J. H., *The Making of the Modern Mind.* Houghton Mifflin, Boston, 1926, $3.50.

Wells, H. G., *Outline of History.* Macmillan, N. Y., 1926, $5.00.

C. *The State.*

Burns, Cecil Delisle, *The World of States.* Stokes, N. Y., 1918, $1.00.

*Brown, Philip M., *International Society—Its Nature and Interest.* Macmillan, N. Y., 1923, $1.50.

Hocking, William Ernest, *Man and the State.* Yale University Press, New Haven, Conn., 1926, $4.00.

D. *Economic Interdependence.*

Angell, Norman, *The Great Illusion.* Putnam, N. Y., 1913, $1.50.

Bosanquet, Helen, *Free Trade and Peace in the Nineteenth Century.* Putnam, N. Y., 1924, $4.20.

Culbertson, W. S., *International Economic Policies.* Appleton, N. Y., 1925, $3.50.

Delaisi, Francis, *Political Myths and Economic Realities.* The Viking Press, N. Y., 1927, $4.00.

Fraser, H. F., *Foreign Trade and World Politics.* Knopf, N. Y., 1926, $3.25.

Notz, William F., *The International Cartel Movement.* Editorial Research Reports, Washington, D. C., 1928, $1.00.

*Redfield, William C., *Dependent America.* Houghton Mifflin, Boston, 1926, $2.50.

Taussig, Frank W., *Selected Readings in International Trade and Tariff Problems.* Ginn, Boston, 1921, $3.00.

Warbasse, James Peter, *Coöperative Democracy.* (An account of Coöperative Associations and their international development.) Macmillan, N. Y., 1927, $3.00

E. *Public Opinion.*

Angell, Norman, *The Public Mind.* Dutton, N. Y., 1927, $3.00.

Dewey, John, *The Public and Its Problems.* Holt, N. Y., 1927, $2.50.

Lasswell, Harold D., *Propaganda Technique in the World War.* Knopf, N. Y., 1927, $5.00.

Lippmann, Walter, *Public Opinion.* Harcourt, Brace, N. Y., 1922, $3.00.

Ponsonby, Arthur, *Falsehood in War-Time.* Allen & Unwin, London, 1928, 2s. 6d.

*Scott, Jonathan French, *Five Weeks: The Surge of Public Opinion on the Eve of the Great War.* John Day Co., N. Y., 1927, $2.50.

Sisson, Edward O., *Educating for Freedom*. Macmillan, N. Y., 1925, $1.40.

II. INTERNATIONAL RELATIONS

Bryce, James, *International Relations*. Macmillan, N. Y., 1922, $2.50.

Buell, Raymond Leslie, *International Relations*. Holt, N. Y., 1925, $5.00.

*Burns, C. Delisle, *A Short History of International Intercourse*. Oxford University Press, N. Y., 1924, $1.75.

III. INTERNATIONAL ORGANIZATION

A. *General*

Brailsford, Henry N., *Olives of Endless Age*. Harper, N. Y., 1928, $3.50.

Coudenhove-Kalergi, R. N., *Pan-Europe*. Knopf, N. Y., 1926, $2.00.

*Hughan, Jessie W., *A Study of International Government*. Crowell, N. Y., 1923, $2.75.

Lawrence, Thomas J., *The Society of Nations: Its Past, Present and Possible Future*. Oxford University Press, N. Y., 1919, $1.50.

Morrow, Dwight Whitney, *The Society of Free States*. Harper, N. Y., 1919, $1.25.

Potter, Pitman B., *Introduction to the Study of International Organization*. Century, N. Y., 1928, $4.00.

B. *The League of Nations*

All official publications of the League of Nations are distributed in the United States by the World Peace Foundation, 40 Mt. Vernon Street, Boston, Mass.

Bassett, John Spencer, *The League of Nations—A Chapter in World Politics*. Longmans, Green, N. Y., 1928, $3.50.

Duggan, Stephen P. and others, *The League of Nations: The Principle and the Practice*. Atlantic Press, N. Y., 1919, $2.50.

Hudson, Manley O., *American Coöperation with Other Nations through the League of Nations.* World Peace Foundation, Boston, 1926, 5c.

*Price, Burr, *The World Talks It Over.* Henkle, N. Y., 1927, $1.75.

Rappard, William E., *International Relations as Viewed from Geneva.* Yale University Press, New Haven, Conn., 1925, $2.50.

Rappard, William E., and Patterson, Caleb Perry, *The League of Nations.* "International Conciliation," (pamphlet, June, 1927) Carnegie Endowment for International Peace, 1927, 5c.

Williams, Bruce, *State Security and the League of Nations.* Johns Hopkins Press, Baltimore, Md., 1927, $2.75.

Wilson, Florence, *Origins of the League Covenant.* Hogarth Press, London, 1928.

C. *Permanent Court of International Justice*

All official publications are distributed in the United States by the World Peace Foundation, Boston, Mass.

Bustamente, A. S., de, *The World Court.* Macmillan, N. Y., 1925, $3.00.

Hudson, Manley O., *The Permanent Court of International Justice.* Harvard University Press, Cambridge, Mass., 1925, $4.00.

*Hudson, Manley O., *The World Court 1922-1928.* (Pamphlet.) World Peace Foundation, Boston, 1928, 30c.

*Johnsen, Julia E., *The Permanent Court of International Justice.* H. W. Wilson, N. Y., 1923, 90c.

Wickersham, G. W., *World Court.* (Pamphlet.) Workers Education Bureau Press, N. Y., 1927, 25c.

D. *International Labor Organization*

All official publications are to be had from the World Peace Foundation, 40 Mt. Vernon St., Boston, Mass.

*Barnes, George N., *History of the International Labor*

Office. Williams and Norgate, London, 1926, $1.00. (International Labor Office, Washington, D. C.)

Perigord, Paul, *International Labor Organization.* Appleton, N. Y., 1926, $3.50.

E. **International Law, Its Development and Codification**

Hudson, Manley O., *Progressive Codification of International Law.* In the *American Journal of International Law,* October, 1926.

Hughes, Charles Evans, *The Development of International Law.* Reprinted from the *Advocate of Peace,* June, 1925, by the American Peace Society, Washington, D. C., 10c.

*Nippold, Otfried, *Development of International Law after the World War.* Oxford University Press, N. Y., 1925, $2.50.

Oppenheim, Lassa F. L., *The Future of International Law.* Oxford University Press, N. Y., 1921, out of print.

*Read, Elizabeth, *International Law and International Relations.* American Foundation, N. Y., 1927, $1.00.

Scott, James Brown, *The Gradual and Progressive Codification of International Law.* In the *American Journal of International Law,* July, 1927.

The Codification of American International Law. Pan American Union, Washington, free.

F. **International Administrative Coöperation**

*Hudson, Manley O., *Current International Coöperation.* Calcutta University Press, Calcutta, 1927. (May be purchased from Harvard Coöperative Society, Inc., Cambridge, Mass., $1.50.)

Reinsch, Paul S., *Public International Unions.* World Peace Foundation, Boston, 1916, $1.65.

Sayre, Francis Bowes, *Experiments in International Administration.* Harper, N. Y., 1918, $1.50.

*Woolf, Leonard S., *International Government.* Brentano's, N. Y., 1916, $2.00.

IV. The Government and Policies of the United States

A. General

*Baker, Crothers H., and Hudnut, R. A., *Problems of Citizenship*. (College textbook.) Holt, N. Y., 1924. (Immigration, International Relations, War and Peace, Means of Preventing War, The Hague, The League.) $2.75.

Beck, James M., *The Constitution of the United States*. Doran, N. Y., 1924, $2.50.

Becker, Carl L., *Our Great Experiment in Democracy*. Harper, N. Y., 1927, $3.00.

Call, Arthur Deerin, *Our Country and World Peace*. American Peace Society, Washington, D. C., 1926, $1.25.

Hamlin, C. H., *The War Myth in United States History*. Vanguard Press, N. Y., 1927, 50c.

Jordan, David Starr, *Democracy and World Relations*. World Book Co., Yonkers, N. Y., 1918, $1.60.

Mead, Edwin D., *Washington, Jefferson and Franklin on War*, Old South Association, Boston, 10c.

Moley, Raymond and Rocca, Helen M., *The Outline of Government in the United States*. (Includes the Constitution.) National League of Women Voters, Washington, D. C., 50c.

*Tufts, James H., *Our Democracy*. Holt, N. Y., 1917, $1.50.

The Federal Convention. American Peace Society, Washington, D. C., 1924, 25c.

B. Foreign Relations of the United States

1. General

Blakeslee, G. H., Recent Foreign Policy of the United States. Abingdon Press, N. Y., 1925, $2.00.

Corwin, Edward S., *The President's Control of Foreign Relations*. Princeton University Press, Princeton, N. J., 1917, $1.50.

*Dealey, J. Q., *Foreign Policies of the United States*. Ginn, Boston, 1926, $2.80.

Foreign Policy Association, *Open Diplomacy and American Foreign Relations.* (Pamphlet.) N. Y., 1926, 35c.

Jessup, Philip C., *American Neutrality and International Police.* World Peace Foundation, Boston, 1928, $1.25.

Latané, J. H., *History of American Foreign Policy.* Doubleday, Page, N. Y., 1927, $4.00.

Potter, Pitman B., *The Myth of American Isolation.* (Pamphlet.) World Peace Foundation, Boston, 1921, 5c.

Putney, Albert H., *Executive Assumption of the War Making Power.* In *National University Law Review*, May, 1927, Washington, D. C., 75c.

Wright, Quincy, *The Future of Neutrality.* Carnegie Endowment, N. Y., 1928, 5c.

2. Latin American Relations and the Monroe Doctrine

A Brief History of the Relations between the United States and Nicaragua, 1909-1928. Documents assembled by the State Department, U. S. Government Printing Office, Washington, 1928, 15c.

Alvarez, Alejandro, *The Monroe Doctrine.* Oxford University Press, N. Y., 1924, $3.00.

*Balch, Emily Greene (editor), *Occupied Haiti.* The Writers Publishing Co., N. Y., 1927, $2.00.

*Beman, L. T., *United States Intervention in Latin America.* H. W. Wilson, N. Y., 1924, $2.40.

Chapman, C. E., *A History of the Cuban Republic: A Study in Hispanic American Politics.* Macmillan, N. Y., 1927, $5.00.

Cox, Isaac Joslin, *Nicaragua and the United States 1909-1927.* World Peace Foundation Boston, 1927, 30c.

Haring, Clarence H., *South America Looks at the United States.* Macmillan, N. Y., 1928, $2.50.

Hughes, Charles Evans, *Pathway of Peace.* Harper, N. Y., 1925, $4.00.

Inman, Samuel Guy, *Problems of Pan Americanism.* Doran, N. Y., 1925, $2.00.

Knight, Melvin M., *The American in Santo Domingo*. Vanguard Press, N. Y., 1928, $1.00.

*Page, Kirby, *The Monroe Doctrine and World Peace*. Doubleday, Doran, N. Y., 1928. (Pamphlet.) 10c.

*Rippy, J. Fred, *Latin America in World Politics*. Knopf, N. Y., 1928, $3.50.

*Rodo, José Enrique, *Ariel*. Houghton Mifflin, Boston, 1922, $1.25.

Stimson, Henry L., *American Policy in Nicaragua*, Scribner, N. Y., 1927, $1.25.

Thomas, David Y., *One Hundred Years of the Monroe Doctrine, 1823-1923*. Macmillan, N. Y., 1923, $4.00.

Walling, William English, *The Mexican Question*. Robins Press, N. Y., 1927, $2.00.

3. *Pacific Problems*

A. *General*

Condliffe, J. B. (editor), *Problems of the Pacific*. Proceedings of Second Conference of the Institute of Pacific Relations, 1927. University of Chicago Press, Chicago, 1928, $3.00.

*Morley, Felix, *Our Far Eastern Assignment*. Doubleday, Page, N. Y., 1926, $2.00.

B. *Special*

Ball, E., *Independence for the Philippines*. (Compilation.) H. W. Wilson, N. Y., 1927, 90c.

Carnegie Endowment for International Peace, *Diplomatic Relations Between the United States and Japan, 1908-1924*. N. Y., 1925, 25c. ("International Conciliation" pamphlet.

Gulick, Sidney L., *Reëstablishing Right Relations with Japan*. Federal Council of Churches of Christ in America, N. Y., 1925, 25c.

Johnsen, Julia E., *Selected Articles on China Yesterday and Today*. H. W. Wilson, N. Y., 1928, $2.40.

Lew, T. T., and others, *China Through Chinese Eyes.* 2 vols. Committee on Reference and Counsel, 419 4th Ave., N. Y., $1.50.

*McKenzie, R. D., *Oriental Exclusion.* University of Chicago Press, Chicago, 1928, $2.00.

Monroe, Paul, *China—A Nation in Evolution.* Macmillan, N. Y., 1928, $3.50.

Soyejima, Michimasa, *Oriental Interpretations of the Far Eastern Problems.* Chicago University Press, Chicago, 1925, $2.00.

Storey, Moorfield, *The Philippines and the United States.* Doran, N. Y., pamphlet, 10c.

C. *Immigration*

Buell, Raymond L., *Japanese Immigration.* (Pamphlet.) World Peace Foundation, Boston, 10c.

Fairchild, H. P., *Immigrant Backgrounds.* John Wiley & Sons, N. Y., 1927, $2.75.

Jenks, J. W. and Lauck, W. J., *The Immigration Problem.* Funk & Wagnalls, N. Y., 1913, $1.75.

Johnsen, Julia E., *Japanese Exclusion.* (Compilation.) H. W. Wilson, N. Y., 90c.

Panunzio, Constantine, *Immigration Crossroads.* Macmillan, N. Y., 1927, $2.50.

*Stephenson, G. M., *A History of American Immigration.* Ginn, Boston, 1926, $2.40.

D. *War Debts and Reparations*

Bass, J. F., and Moulton, H. G., *America and the Balance Sheet of Europe.* Ronald Press Co., N. Y., 1921, $3.00.

Bergmann, Carl, *The History of Reparations.* Ernest Benn, Ltd., London, 1927, 21s.

*Carnegie Endowment for International Peace, *The Inter-Allied Debts: Statements as to the Desirability of an Early Revision of Existing Arrangements.* N. Y., 1927, 5c. ("International Conciliation" pamphlet.)

BIBLIOGRAPHY

*Gerould, J. T. and Turnbull, L. T., *Inter-Allied Debts and Revision of the Debt Settlements*. H. W. Wilson, N. Y., 1928, $2.40.

Moulton, Harold G., and McGuire, C. E., *Germany's Capacity to Pay*. McGraw-Hill Book Co., N. Y., 1923, $2.50.

Moulton, Harold G., and Pasvolsky, Leo, *World War Debt Settlements*. Macmillan, N. Y., 1926, $2.00.

E. Foreign Trade and Investments

Dunn, Robert W., *American Foreign Investments*. Viking Press, N. Y., 1926, $5.00.

*Winkler, Max, *America, the World's Banker*. Foreign Policy Association, N. Y., 1927, 50c.

F. National Defense

Beman, L. T., *Military Training:* (Compilation.) H. W. Wilson, N. Y., 1926, 90c.

Bywater, Hector C., *Navies and Nations*. Houghton Mifflin, Boston, 1927, $4.00.

*Johnsen, J. E., *National Defense*. (Debaters Handbook Series.) H. W. Wilson, N. Y., 1928, $2.40.

*Palmer, John McAuley, *Statesmanship or War*. Doubleday, Page, N. Y., 1927, $2.50.

V. PROBLEMS OF WAR AND PEACE

A. General

Bakeless, John, *The Origin of the Next War*. Viking Press, N. Y., 1926, $2.50.

Bakeless, John, *Economic Causes of Modern War*. Moffat, 1921, $4.00.

Barnes, Harry Elmer, *History and Social Intelligence*. Knopf, N. Y., 1926, $5.00.

Dickinson, G. L., *War: Its Nature, Cause and Cure*. Macmillan, N. Y., 1923, $1.50.

Fisher, Herbert Wescott, *Alias Uncle Shylock*. Albert & Charles Boni, N. Y., 1927, $2.50.

Glasgow, George, *From Dawes to Locarno*. Harper, N. Y., 1926, $2.50.

James, William, *The Moral Equivalent of War*. ("International Conciliation" pamphlet.) Carnegie Endowment for International Peace, N. Y., 1910, 5c.

*Johnsen, Julia E., *War—Cause and Cure*. (Collection of articles.) H. W. Wilson, N. Y., 1926, $2.40.

*Kenworthy, J. M., *Peace or War*. Boni & Liveright, N. Y., 1927, $2.50. (Vivid chapters on the "next war.")

Kenworthy, J. M., and Young George, *The Freedom of the Seas*. Hutchinson, London, 1928, 18s.

McDougall, William, *Janus: The Conquest of War*. Dutton, N. Y., 1927, $1.00.

*Page, Kirby, *War: Its Causes, Consequences and Cure*. Doran, N. Y., 1923, $1.50. (Pamphlet 15c.)

Pollard, Francis E., *War and Human Values*. Peace Committee of the Society of Friends, Euston Road, London, 1927, 2s.

Ponsonby, Arthur, *Now Is the Time*. Independent Labor Party, London, 1925, 2s.

Russell, Bertrand, *Why Men Fight*. Century, N. Y., 1917, $1.50.

The Peace of the World, Union of Democratic Control, London. Distributed by American Friends Service Committee, 20 South 12th St., Philadelphia, 15c.

The Problems of Peace. Lectures delivered at the Geneva Institute of International Relations, August, 1926. Vol. I, 1927, Vol. II, 1928, Oxford University Press, N. Y., 1927 and 1928, $4.25, each.

Reports of the Conference on the Cause and Cure of War. National Committee on the Cause and Cure of War, 1010 Grand Central Terminal Bldg., N. Y., 3 vols., 50c each.

B. Arbitration

Adams, Mildred, *A Review of Arbitration*. National League of Women Voters, N. Y., 1927, 10c.

Field, Noel H., *Banishing War through Arbitration*. National Council for Prevention of War, 1926, 10c.

Jessup, P. C., *The United States and Treaties for the Avoidance of War*. Carnegie Endowment, N. Y., 1928, 5c.

Myers, Denys P., *Arbitration and the United States*. World Peace Foundation, 1926, 10c.

*Scott, James Brown, *The Judicial Settlement of International Disputes*. Oxford University Press, N. Y., 1927, $1.50.

Scott, James Brown, *Instructions to the American Delegates to the Hague Peace Conferences and their Official Reports*. Oxford University Press, N. Y., 1916, $1.50.

Trueblood, Benjamin F. *International Arbitration at the Opening of the Twentieth Century*. American Peace Society, Washington, D. C., 5c.

Development of Methods for the Pacific Settlement of International Disputes, Pan American Union. (Mimeographed pamphlet.) Supply exhausted. Copy may be borrowed from the National Council for Prevention of War.

The Multilateral Treaty Notes Exchanged Between the United States and Other Powers on the subject of a Multilateral Treaty for the Renunciation of War. U. S. Government Printing Office, Washington, 1928, 10c.

Page, Kirby, *The Renunciation of War*. Doubleday, Doran, N. Y., 1928, 10c.

The Multilateral Treaty. Department of International Coöperation to Prevent War of the National League of Women Voters, N. Y., 1928, 5c.

C. The Outlawry of War

*Morrison, C. C., *The Outlawry of War; A Constructive Policy for World Peace*. Willett, Clark & Colby, Chicago, 1927, $3.00.

D. Problems of Imperialism

Denny, Ludwell, *We Fight for Oil.* Knopf, N. Y., 1928, $3.50.

Gilchrist, Huntington, *Imperialism and the Mandates System.* (Pamphlet.) League of Nations Non-Partisan Association, N. Y.

Hopkins, J. A. H., and Alexander, M., *Machine-Gun Diplomacy.* Copeland, N. Y., 1928, $2.50.

*Moon, Parker T., *Imperialism and World Politics.* Macmillan, N. Y., 1926, $3.50.

Page, Kirby, *Dollars and World Peace.* Doran, N. Y., 1927, $1.50; pamphlet, 15c.

Page, Kirby, *Imperialism and Nationalism.* (Pamphlet.) Doran, N. Y., 1926, 15c.

Peffer, Nathaniel, *The White Man's Dilemma.* John Day Co., N. Y., 1927, $2.50.

Smith, George Otis, and others, *Raw Materials and Their Effect upon International Relations.* ("International Conciliation" pamphlet.) Carnegie Endowment for International Peace, N. Y., 5c.

Tramerye, Pierre de la, *The World Struggle for Oil.* Knopf, N. Y., 1923, $2.75.

Viallate, Achille, *Economic Imperialism and International Relations During the Last Fifty Years.* Macmillan, N. Y., 1923, $2.00.

Woolf, Leonard S., *Imperialism and Civilization.* Harcourt, Brace, N. Y., 1928, $2.00.

E. Problems of Nationalism

Barker, Ernest, *National Character.* Harper, N. Y., 1927, $3.50.

*Hayes, C. J. H., *Essays on Nationalism.* Macmillan, N. Y., 1926, $3.00.

F. Racial Problems

Hankins, F. H., *The Racial Basis of Civilization.* Knopf, N. Y., 1926, $2.75.

Mathews, Basil, *The Clash of Color*. Doran, N. Y., 1924, $1.25, pamphlet, 75c.

*Miller, H. A., *Races, Nations and Classes*. Lippincott, Philadelphia, 1924, $2.00.

Oldham, J. H., *Christianity and the Race Problem*. Doran, N. Y., $1.00.

*Speer, Robert E., *Of One Blood*. Missionary Education Movement, N. Y., 1924, 50c.

G. *The Problem of Armaments*

Baker, Philip, J. N., *Disarmament*. Harcourt, Brace, N. Y., 1926, $4.00.

Bullard, Arthur, *A B C's of Disarmament and the Pacific Problems*. Macmillan, N. Y., 1921, $1.25.

*Enock, A. G., *The Problem of Armaments*. Macmillan, N. Y., 1923, $1.50.

Levermore, Charles H., *Disarmament on the Great Lakes*. World Peace Foundation, Boston, 1914, 5c.

*Myers, Denys P., *The Staggering Burden of Armament*. (Pamphlet.) World Peace Foundation, Boston, 1921, 10c.

Reely, M. K., *Disarmament*. (Debaters Handbook Series.) H. W. Wilson, N. Y., 1921, $2.25.

*Smith, Rennie, *General Disarmament or War?* National Council for Prevention of War, London, 1927. Can be obtained from the National Council for Prevention of War, Washington, D. C., 25c.

H. *World War Guilt*

*Barnes, Harry Elmer, *Genesis of the World War*. Knopf, N. Y., 1927, $5.00.

*Gooch, A. P., *Recent Revelations of European Diplomacy*. Longmans, Green, N. Y., 1927, $3.00.

Morel, E. D., *Truth and the War*. National Labour Press, London, 1918, 2s.

VI. WAR

A. War and Human Nature

Carter, John, *Man Is War*. Bobbs Merrill, Indianapolis, 1926, $3.50.

Ellis, Havelock, *Essays in Wartime*. Constable, London, 1916, 5s.

Ellwood, Charles Abram, *Cultural Evolution: A Study of Social Origins and Development*. Century, N. Y., 1927, $2.50.

*Kropotkin, P., *Mutual Aid*. Knopf, N. Y., 1919, $1.75.

Nasmyth, George, *Social Progress and the Darwinian Theory*. Putnam, N. Y., 1916. (Out of print.)

Nicolai, G. F., *The Biology of War*. Century, N. Y., 1918, $3.50.

Trotter, W., *Instincts of the Herd in Peace and War*. Macmillan, N. Y., 1919, $2.50.

B. What War Is Today

Friedrich, Ernst, *The War in Pictures*. International Federation of Trade Unions, Amsterdam, Holland or Committee on Militarism, N. Y., $1.50.

Gibbs, P. H., *Now It Can Be Told*. Harper, N. Y., 1920, $3.00.

Gibbs, P. H., *More That Must Be Told*. Harper, N. Y., 1921, $2.50.

Hart, B. H. Liddell, *Paris or the Future of War*. Dutton, N. Y., 1925, $1.00.

*Irwin, Will, *The Next War*. Dutton, N. Y., 1921, $1.50.

Peat, Harold R., *The Inexcusable Lie*. Barse & Hopkins, N. Y., 1923, $1.50.

A Manual of the Medical Aspects of Chemical Warfare. War Office, London, England.

C. The Cost of War

Bodart, G., *Losses of Life in Modern War, Military Selec-*

tion and Race Deterioration. Oxford University Press, N. Y., 1923, $2.00.

*Bogart, Ernest L., *Direct and Indirect Costs of the Great World War.* Oxford University Press, N. Y., 1919, $1.00.

Folks, Homer, *Human Costs of the War.* Harper, N. Y., 1920. (Out of print.)

Jordan, David Starr, *War and the Breed.* Beacon Press, Boston, Mass., 1915, $1.50.

VII. THE PEACE MOVEMENT

A. *General*

Call, Arthur Deerin, *The Will to End War.* (Pamphlet.) American Peace Society, Washington, D. C., 1920, 15c.

*Ernst, Richard, *God's Path to Peace: The Evolution of Forces Converging toward Peace.* Abingdon Press, N. Y., 1914, 75c.

Lape, Esther Everett, *Ways to Peace.* Scribner, N. Y., 1924, $3.00. (Plans submitted for Bok Peace Award.)

Marvin, F. S., *The Evolution of World Peace.* Oxford Unisity Press, N. Y., 1921, $4.75.

Mead, Lucia Ames, *Swords and Ploughshares.* Putnam, N. Y., 1912, $1.50.

Moritzen, Julius, *The Peace Movement of America.* Putnam, N. Y., 1912, $3.00.

Perris, G. H., *Short History of War and Peace.* Holt, N. Y., 1911, 90c.

Shotwell, James T., *Plans and Protocols to End War: Historical Outline and Guide.* Carnegie Endowment for International Peace, N. Y., 1925, 5c.

Whitney, Edson L., *The American Peace Society, A Centennial History.* American Peace Society, Washington, D. C., 1928, $3.00.

**Building International Goodwill,* by various authors. Macmillan, N. Y., 1927, $1.50.

B. *The Church and Peace*

*Cadoux, C. J., *The Early Christian Attitude to War*. Swarthmore Press, London, 1919, $2.00.

*Fosdick, Harry Emerson, *Christianity's Supreme Rival*. Park Avenue Baptist Church, N. Y., 10c.

Gulick, Sidney L., *Christian Crusade for a Warless World*. Macmillan, N. Y., 1922, $1.00.

Holmes, John Haynes, *Patriotism Is Not Enough*. Greenberg, 112 East 19th St., N. Y., 1926, $2.00.

Jefferson, Charles E., *Christianity and International Peace*. Crowell, N. Y., 1915, $1.25.

Lynch, Frederick Henry, *Mobilising for Peace*. Revell, N. Y., 1924, $2.00.

*McCutcheon, M. F., and others, *The Christian and War: An Appeal*. McClelland & Stewart, Toronto, 1926, $2.00.

Mygatt, Tracy D. and Witherspoon, Frances, *The Glorious Company*. Harcourt, Brace, N. Y., 1928, $3.00.

Oxnam, G. Brownley, *Youth and the New America*.

Page, Kirby, *The Sword or the Cross*. Doran, N. Y., 1922, 15c.

C. *Education and Peace*

(Note: A large part of the literature on this subject is in the form of magazine articles, a reading list of which can be secured from the Library of the Carnegie Endowment for International Peace, Washington, D. C. The following magazines have devoted special issues to the teaching of international goodwill: *The Journal of the Progressive Education Association*, April-May-June, 1925, Washington, 50c; *The American Schoolmaster*, December, 1927, Ypsilanti, Mich., 20c; *The Advocate of Peace*, September, 1928, Washington, is devoted to the report of the Commission on the International Implications of Education which met as a part of the World Conference on International

Justice held in celebration of the centennial of the American Peace Society, 30c.

Dewey, John, *Democracy and Education.* Macmillan, N. Y., 1922, $2.50.

Kilpatrick, William Heard, *Education for a Changing Civilization.* Macmillan, N. Y., 1927, $1.00.

Knapp, Forrest L., *An Experimental Measurement of the Value of Certain Instructional Materials for Peace Education.* To be published by the Religious Education Association, Chicago.

Neumann, George B., *A Study of International Attitudes of High School Students.* Teachers College, Columbia University, N. Y., 1926, $1.50.

Pierce, Bessie L., *Public Opinion and the Teaching of History in the United States.* Knopf, N. Y., 1926, $3.25.

Power, Eileen, *The Teaching of History and World Peace.* Chap. XI. in *The Evolution of World Peace* by F. S. Marvin. Oxford University Press, N. Y., 1921, $4.75.

*Scott, Jonathan F., *The Menace of Nationalism in Education.* Macmillan, N. Y., 1926, $1.10.

Taft, Donald R., *Historical Textbooks and International Differences.* Association for Peace Education, Chicago, 1925, 5c.

Tigert, John J., *A Practical Program of Education for the Promotion of International Goodwill.* U. S. Department of the Interior, Bureau of Education, Circular No. 9, free.

Tuell, Harriet E., *The Study of Nations.* Houghton Mifflin, Boston, 1920, $1.00.

Walsh, Walter, *Moral Damage of War to the School Child.* American Peace Society, Washington, D. C., 1911, 5c.

Watson, Goodwin B., *The Measurement of Fair-Mindedness.* Teachers College, Columbia University, N. Y., 1925, $1.50.

Woellner, Frederic P., *Education for Citizenship in a Democracy.* Scribner, N. Y., 1923, $1.60.

*Zimmern, Alfred, *Learning and Leadership.* League of Nations, 1927. World Peace Foundation, Boston, 50c.

Proceedings of the Conferences of the World Federation of Education Associations. 2 vols. To be ordered from the Federation.

Proceedings of the First Pan Pacific Conference on Education. U. S. Department of the Interior, Washington, D. C., 1927, $1.00.

Report of Conference on the Teaching of History. Association for Peace Education, Chicago, 1925, 25c.

Training the Emotions Controlling Fear. Report issued by the Boston Public Schools, 1928, 25c.

D. Labor and Peace

American Federation of Labor, *Disarmament.* Official record of support of disarmament and peace. Pamphlet. American Federation of Labor, Washington.

Angell, Norman, *War and the Workers.* National Labour Press, London, 1916. 2s.

Johnson, A. S., "War and the Interests of Labor," *Atlantic Monthly,* March, 1914; reprinted as "International Conciliation" pamphlet, Carnegie Endowment for International Peace, N. Y., 5c.

Muste, A. J., "American Labor and Peace." *World Tomorrow,* N. Y., Feb., 1924.

Neill, C. P., "The Interest of the Wage-Earner, in the Present Status of the Peace Movement." "International Conciliation" pamphlet, Carnegie Endowment for International Peace, N. Y., 5c.

Sharp, Evelyn, "British Labor's Recent Work for Peace." *World Tomorrow,* N. Y., Jan. 1922.

E. The Press and Peace

*Bliven, Bruce, *Address at the Conference on the Cause and Cure of War, 1925.* Report published by Committee on the Cause and Cure of War, 1010 Grand Central Terminal Bldg., N. Y., 50c.

Deming, William C., *Opportunity and Duty of the Press in Relation to World Peace*. ("International Conciliation" pamphlet.) Carnegie Endowment for International Peace, N. Y., 1913, 5c.

Lippmann, Walter, *Liberty and the News*. Harcourt, Brace, N. Y., 1920, $1.00.

Yost, Casper S., *The Principles of Journalism*. Appleton, N. Y., 1924, $1.50.

F. Women and Peace

Addams, Jane, *Peace and Bread in Time of War*. Macmillan, N. Y., 1922, $1.75.

Addams, Jane and others, *Women at The Hague*. Macmillan, N. Y., 1915, 75c.

Boyle, Ruth, *Let Us Have No More War*. Good Housekeeping, N. Y., April, 1928, 25c.

*Key, Ellen, *War, Peace and the Future*. Putnam, N. Y., 1916, $1.50.

Langdon-Davies, John, *A Short History of Women*. Viking Press, N. Y., 1917, $3.00.

*Norris, Kathleen, *What Price Peace*. Doubleday, Doran, N. Y., 1928, 75c.

Royden, Maude, *Women at the World's Crossroads*. Woman's Press, N. Y., 1922, $1.25.

Schreiner, Olive, *Woman and War*. Stokes, N. Y., 1914 (from *Woman and Labor*), out of print.

G. Young People and World Peace

Eddy, Sherwood, *Youth and World Problems*. Doran, N. Y., 1923, 10c.

*High, Stanley, *The Revolt of Youth*. Missionary Education Movement, N. Y., 1922, 75c.

Stewart, *Continental Youth Movements*. Association Press, N. Y., 1926, 35c.

*Wise, James Waterman, *Youth and the Old World.* Century Magazine, January, 1928, 50c.

H. Pacifism

*Case, C. M., *Non-Violent Coercion.* Century, N. Y., 1923, $3.00.

Graham, John William, *Conscription and Conscience.* Allen & Unwin, London, 1922, $3.25.

Thomas, Norman, *Is Conscience a Crime?* Vanguard Press, N. Y., 1927, 50c.

VIII. FAMOUS PEACE DOCUMENTS

The Universal Empire, 1315, Dante. Passages from the first book of *De Monarchia.* Old South Association, Boston, 10c.

The Complaint of Peace (Querela Pacis), Erasmus (1467-1536). Open Court Publishing Co., Chicago, 50c.

Le Nouveau Cynée, 1623, Emeric Crucé. Allen, Lane & Scott, Philadelphia, $4.00.

The Rights of War and Peace, 1625, Hugo Grotius (1583-1645). Old South Leaflets, Boston, 10c.

The Grand Design of Henry IV, 1635. Grotius Society Publications, Sweet & Maxwell, London, 50c.

An Essay Toward the Present and Future Peace of Europe, 1693-94, William Penn. American Peace Society, Washington, D. C., 10c.

A Project for Perpetual Peace, 1712, Abbé St. Pierre. Grotius Society Texts, Sweet & Maxwell, London, 50c.

Project of Universal Peace, Pierre André Gargaz. Originally published by Benjamin Franklin; G. S. Eddy, 2 Rector St., N. Y., $7.50.

Perpetual Peace, 1795, Immanuel Kant. American Peace Society, Washington, D. C., 20c.

A Solemn Review of the Custom of War, 1814, Noah Worcester. American Peace Society, Washington, D. C., 10c.

A Congress of Nations, 1837, William Ladd, founder of the first national peace society. Oxford University Press, N. Y., $2.00.

The Future of War, 1860, Jean de Bloch. World Peace Foundation, Boston, 65c. (One of the influences which led the Czar of Russia to call the First Hague Peace Conference.)

War Inconsistent with the Religion of Jesus, David L. Dodge, founder in 1815 of the first peace society. World Peace Foundation, Boston, 50c.

The True Grandeur of Nations, 1845, Charles Sumner. Ginn, Boston, 60c.

Solferino, 1859, Henri Dunant. John C. Winston, Philadelphia, $1.00. (As a result of a suggestion in this essay, the Red Cross Society was organized.)

VIII. FICTION ON PEACE AND WAR

Austin, F. Britten, *When the War God Walks Again.* Doubleday, Page, N. Y., 1926, $2.00.

Barbusse, Henri, *Under Fire.* Dutton, N. Y., 1917, $1.50.

Boyd, Thomas A., *Through the Wheat.* Scribner, N. Y., 1927, $3.00.

Boyd, James, *Marching On.* Scribner, N. Y., 1927, $2.50.

Brophy, John, *The Bitter End.* Dutton, N. Y., 1928, $2.50.

Caine, Hall, *The Woman of Knockaloe.* Dodd, Mead, N. Y., 1923, $1.75.

Cholmondeley, Alice, *Christine.* Grosset & Dunlap, N. Y., 1918, 75c.

Cobb, Irwin, *Paths of Glory.* Grosset & Dunlap, N. Y., 1918, 75c.

Copley, Frank Barkley, *The Impeachment of President Israels.* Macmillan, N. Y., 1913, out of print.

Dos Passos, John, *Three Soldiers.* Doran, N. Y., 1921, $2.00.

Erckmann-Chatrian, *The Conscript.* Macmillan, N. Y., 1910, $1.50.

Frenssen, Gustav, *Peter Moore's Journey to Southwest Africa.* Houghton Mifflin, Boston, 1908, $1.25.

Gibbs, A. Hamilton, *Labels.* Little, Brown, Boston, 1926, $2.00.

Gibbs, Sir Philip, *The Middle of the Road.* Grosset & Dunlap, N. Y., 1925, 75c.

Hamilton, Cicely, *Lest Ye Die.* Scribner, N. Y., 1928, $2.00.

Lawrence, D. H., *Kangaroo.* Thomas Seltzer, N. Y., 1923, $1.75.

Nason, Leonard H., *Chevrons.* Doran, N. Y., 1926, $2.00.

Noyes, Pierrepont B., *The Pallid Giant.* Revell, N. Y., 1927, $2.00.

Palmer, Frederick, *The Last Shot.* Scribner, N. Y., 1914, $1.50.

Stallings, Laurence, *Plumes.* Grosset & Dunlap, N. Y., 1926, 75c.

Suttner, Bertha von, *Lay Down Your Arms.* Longmans, Green, N. Y., 1913, 75c. (American Peace Society, Washington, D. C., 50c.)

Thompson, Edward, *These Men, Thy Friends.* Harcourt, Brace, N. Y., 1928, $2.50.

Tolstoi, Leo, *War and Peace.* John Lane Co., N. Y., 1911, $1.25.

Unruh, Fritz von, *Way of Sacrifice.* Knopf, N. Y., 1928, $2.50.

Walsh, Richard J., *When the Earth Trembled.* Carnegie Endowment for International Peace, N. Y., "*International Conciliation*" pamphlet, November, 1926, 5c. (First published in *Woman's Home Companion,* October and November, 1926.)

Wells, H. G., *In the Days of the Comet.* Doran, N. Y., 1920, $1.90.

IX. POEMS OF WAR AND PEACE (COLLECTIONS)

Gibbs, Jessie Wiseman, *Peace Sonnets*. Friends' Bookstore, 302 Arch Street, Philadelphia, 35c.

Glasier, J. Bruce (editor), *The Ministrelsy of Peace*. National Labor Press, London, 1920, 5s.

Leonard, Sterling A., *Poems of the War and the Peace*. Harcourt, Brace, N. Y., 1921, $1.35.

Leonard, R. M. (editor), *The Poetry of Peace*. Oxford University Press, N. Y., 1919, $1.60.

Sassoon, Siegfried, *The War Poems of Siegfried Sassoon*. William Heinemann, London, 1919, 3s. 6d.

Slade, William Adam, *Stardust—Sonnets*. Preston & Rounds, Providence, R. I., 1928, $1.00.

Smith, Elva S. (editor), *Peace and Patriotism*. Lothrop, Lee & Shepard, Boston, 1919, $1.50.

X. DRAMA

(These plays are listed with the idea that they will be read rather than as suggestions for amateur acting.)

Anderson, Maxwell, and Stallings, Laurence, *What Price Glory*. Harcourt, Brace, N. Y., 1926, $2.50.

Bowskill, Henry, *Which?* Daniel, London, 1924, 3s. 6d.

Brooks, George, and Lister, Walter, *Spread Eagle*. Scribner, N. Y., 1927, $1.75.

Drinkwater, John, *Abraham Lincoln*. Houghton Mifflin, Boston, 1919, $1.25.

Drinkwater, John, $X = O$ or *A Night of the Trojan War* in *The Pawns*. Houghton Mifflin, Boston, 1920, $1.50.

Euripedes, *The Trojan Women*. Oxford University Press, N. Y., 90c.

Glaspell, Susan, *Inheritors*. Small, Maynard, Boston, 1921, $1.50.

Kennedy, Charles Rann, *The Terrible Week*. Harper, N. Y., 1912, $1.00.

Millay, Edna St. Vincent, *Aria da Capo*. Harper, N. Y., 1920, $2.00.

Munroe, C. K., *The Rumour*. Knopf, N. Y., 1924, $2.00.

Mygatt, Tracy D., *The Sword of the Samurai*. Century, N. Y., 1926, 25c.

Noyes, Alfred, *Rada*. Stokes, N. Y., 1914, 60c.

Pollock, Channing, *The Enemy*. Brentano's, N. Y., 1925, $1.50.

Shaw, Bernard, *Heartbreak House*. Brentano's, N. Y., 1919, $1.75.

Stevens, Henry Bailey, *A Cry Out of the Dark*. Four Seas Co., Boston, 1919, $1.25.

Trask, Katrina, *In the Vanguard*. Macmillan, N. Y., 1913, 75c.

Wentworth, Marion Craig, *War Brides*. Century, N. Y., 1915, 75c.

Zangwill, Israel, *The War God*. Macmillan, N. Y., 1912, $1.25.

XI. Pageants and Plays

Descriptive lists of pageants and plays suitable for amateur performance can be obtained from the National Council for Prevention of War, Washington, D. C., and from the League of Nations Non-Partisan Association, New York. In writing for suggestions the number of performers and their age should be stated.

XII. Dramatic Readings

The collections of poems listed above, the dramas and several of the books of fiction, notably *The Impeachment of President Israels*, afford material for dramatic readings. Additional suggestions and short selections can be obtained from the National Council for Prevention of War, Washington, D. C.

XIII. Recitations and Declamations

Prince of Peace Declamation Contests. (Selections for the annual declamation contests.) Ohio Council of Churches, Columbus, Ohio. 2 vols., 15c each.

Peace Crusaders—Adventures in Goodwill, Anna B. Griscom. American Friends Service Committee, Philadelphia, $1.50.

XIV. Quotations on War and Peace

Selected Quotations on Peace and War. Federal Council of Churches of Christ in America, N. Y., 1915, $1.00.

Education for Peace. Foreign Missions Conference of North America, 25 Madison Ave., N. Y., 1927, 50c.

Symposium on War. John Horsch. Mennonite Publishing House, Scottdale, Penna., 1927, 10c.

The Cry for Justice. Upton Sinclair, Pasadena, Cal., 1921, $1.00, paper; $1.50, cloth. (Part XI, War.)

XV. Books of Songs

Cantate Domino. The World's Student Christian Federation, 347 Madison Ave., N. Y., 85c.

Folk Songs of Many Peoples. Woman's Press, 600 Lexington Ave., N. Y., vol. I, $2.75; vol. II, $3.50. Sections printed separately as follows, Christmas and New Year's Songs, 50c; Songs of China and Japan, of Latin America, of Poland, 75c each; Sing Around the World Songs (words only), 15c.

Laudemus. The World's Y. M. C. A. Hymnal. Y. M. C. A., 347 Madison Ave., N. Y., 50c.

Songs of Loyalty and Fraternity, Charles H. Levermore. Ginn, Boston, 50c.

PERIODICALS

The following magazines are among those which are concerned primarily with problems of world peace or with the promotion of a better understanding of international relations. Articles of importance in this field appear in many other monthly and weekly publications. A *Monthly Bibliography of International Affairs,* compiled by Mary Phillips Webster from fifty leading magazines, may be obtained from the National Council for Prevention of War, Washington, D. C. Mimeographed, $1.00 a year.

Advocate of Peace, monthly except September. The American Peace Society, Colorado Bldg., Washington, D..C., $3.00 a year.

Arbitrator, monthly. 114 E. 31st St., N. Y., 60c a year.

Asia, monthly. 461 Eighth Ave., N. Y., $400 a year.

Current History, monthly. New York Times Co., N. Y., $3.00 a year.

Foreign Affairs, quarterly. 25 W. 43rd St., N. Y., $5.00 a year.

Foreign Affairs, monthly (English). Union of Democratic Control, 34 Victoria St., London, S. W. 1, $2.00 a year.

The Herald of Peace, monthly. 210 Heinlen St., Lemoore, Calif., $2.00 a year.

The Living Age, monthly. Boston, $5.00 a year.

The Messenger of Peace, monthly. Richmond, Ind., 50c a year.

Mexican Life, monthly. Av. Uruguay, No. 3, Mexico City, $5.00 a year.

The Nation, weekly. 20 Vesey St., N. Y., $5.00 a year.

The National Graphic Magazine, monthly. Washington, D. C., $3.50 a year.

The New Era, quarterly. (Educational.) 11 Tavistock Square, London, W. C.

The New Republic, weekly. 421 West 21st St., N. Y., $5.00 a year.

The New Student, 2929 Broadway, N. Y., $1.50 a year.

BIBLIOGRAPHY

Pan American Union, monthly. Washington, D. C., $2.50 a year.

Pan Pacific Progress, monthly. Los Angeles, Cal., $2.50 a year.

The Review of Nations, monthly. Felix Valyi, Geneva, Switzerland, $10.00 a year.

Unity, weekly. Oakwood Bldg., Chicago, $3.00 a year.

The World Tomorrow, monthly. 52 Vanderbilt Ave., N. Y., $2.00 a year.

The World's Youth, monthly. Y. M. C. A., N. Y., $1.00 a year.

World Unity, monthly. 122 East 34th St., N. Y., $3.50 a year.

Youth, monthly. 421 Sentinel House, Southampton Row, London W. C. 1, 75c a year.

PUBLICATIONS OF ORGANIZATIONS

An annotated list, arranged by subjects, of the publications of organizations interested in international relations and world peace has been compiled and published by the World Peace Foundation, under the title *International Relations Publications.* It may be obtained from the World Peace Foundation, 40 Mt. Vernon Street, Boston, for 15c. Current lists of the publications of such organizations as the following will be supplied upon request and will be found very helpful: The Carnegie Endowment for International Peace; The Missionary Education Movement; the Y.W.C.A. and the Y.M.C.A.; the Foreign Policy Association, and the League of Nations Non-Partisan Association.

Among the important organization periodicals devoted chiefly to the promotion of world peace are the following:

American Foundation, N. Y. *Foreign Relations Bulletins,* occasional, free.

Carnegie Endowment for International Peace, N. Y. *In-*

ternational Conciliation, monthly, except July and August, 25c a year.

Federal Council of Churches of Christ in America, N. Y. *Bulletin*, monthly, $1.00 a year. Bi-weekly news sheet, *International Goodwill*.

Fellowship of Reconciliation, N. Y. *News Bulletin*, occasional.

Foreign Policy Association, N. Y. *Bi-weekly Information Service*, $5.00 a year. *News Bulletin*, weekly, $1.00 a year.

The Inquiry, 129 East 52nd St., N. Y. *The Inquiry*, occasional papers, free.

Institute of Pacific Relations, Honolulu. *Pacific Affairs*, monthly.

League of Nations Non-Partisan Association, N. Y. *League of Nations News*, including a digest of international affairs, monthly, $1.00 a year.

National Council for Prevention of War, Washington, D. C. *News Bulletin*, monthly, 25c a year.

Women's International League for Peace and Freedom, Washington, D. C. *Pax International*, monthly, 50c a year.

World Alliance for International Friendship through the Churches, N. Y. *News Letter*, monthly.

World Peace Foundation, Boston. *World Peace Foundation Pamphlets*, 6 issues a year.

League of Nations periodical publications distributed in the United States by the World Peace Foundation, Boston. *Monthly Summary of the League of Nations*, $1.00 a year. *International Labor Review, monthly*, $6.00 a year. *Bulletins of the International Institute of Intellectual Cooperation*, University Section, 6, $2.00 a year; Scientific Section, quarterly, $2.00 a year.

BIBLIOGRAPHY

YEAR BOOKS

The Europa Year Book, including a survey of economic and social conditions and a directory of international organizations. Europa Publishing Co., Adelphia, W. C. 2, London, 21s.

International Peace Year Book, edited by F. E. Pollard. National Council for Prevention of War, 39 Victoria St., London, S. W., 25c.

The following are publications of the League of Nations, *Armaments Year Book*, $5.00; *Handbook of International Organizations*, issued annually, $1.00; *An International Statistical Year Book*, $2.00; *Year Book of the League of Nations*, 25c. These, like other League publications, may be ordered from the World Peace Foundation.

CHILDREN'S BOOKS

I. Bibliographies Available

People of Many Lands, a list of recreational books for young people from 14 to 18 years of age. Women's Council for Promotion of Peace, Cleveland, Ohio, 1927.

Children of Many Lands, for children from 5 to 9 years old. Women's Council for Promotion of Peace, Cleveland, Ohio.

Bibliography for Children of the second, third and fourth grades. Friends' Peace Committee, 304 Arch St., Philadelphia.

International Friendship Through Children's Books, Clara W. Hunt. League of Nations Non-Partisan Association, N. Y.

A Child's Bookshelf, Miss Lilian Stevenson. Student Christian Movement, 32 Russell Square, London, W.C. 1, 3s.

Books to Read under the headings, "Story of Man's Life on Earth"; "How People Live in Other Countries"; "Heroes of Peace Times"; "The Quest for Peace and Its

Heroes." National Council for Prevention of War, Washington, D. C.

A Trip Around the World. Books of other nations arranged in the order in which they would be visited on a trip around the world, designed to be used in a school room or children's room in a library in connection with a map or globe. National Council for Prevention of War. Washington, D. C.

A World Library for Children, a collection of famous stories of all nations in illustrated paper booklets, edited by Helene Scheu-Riesz, can be ordered from the New Education Fellowship, 11 Tavistock Square, London. 34 vols., $3.75.

II. BOOKS THAT SHOW THE UNITY OF MANKIND

(The story of man's life on earth is one story and in it men everywhere are seen to have been busy trying to work out the same problems of getting food and shelter and knowledge of the earth and of themselves, and so far as these problems have been solved men of every age and every nation have helped to find the answer.)

The Child's Story of the Human Race, Ramon Coffman. Dodd, Mead, N. Y., $3.50.

Pre-Alphabet Days and *The Story of the Alphabet,* Otto F. Edge. Munder, Baltimore, $1.25 and $1.00.

The Adventure of Man, F. Crossfield Happold. Harcourt, Brace, N. Y., $2.00.

First Days of History, Frederic A. Kummer. Doran, N. Y., $2.00.

First Days of Knowledge, Frederic A. Kummer. Doran, N. Y., $2.00.

First Days of Man, Frederic A. Kummer. Doran, N. Y., $2.00.

The Young Folks' Book of Discovery, T. C. Bridges. Little, Brown, Boston, $2.00.

BIBLIOGRAPHY 551

The Story of Light, Jeanette Eaton. Harper, N. Y., $1.25.

The Story of Transportation, Jeanette Eaton. Harper, N. Y., $1.25.

The Young Folks' Book of Discovery, T. C. Bridges. tle, Brown, Boston, $2.00.

A Popular History of American Invention, W. B. Kaempffert (Scribner, N. Y., $10.00) is a thrilling stoy of invention for those of high school age or to be read by older people and adapted for children.

III. BOOKS THAT TELL OF ADVENTURES IN TIMES OF PEACE

Makers of Freedom, Sherwood Eddy and Kirby Page. Doran, N. Y., 50c.

Heroes of the Wilds, Chelsea Fraser. Crowell, N. Y., $1.75.

Work-A-Day Heroes, Chelsea Fraser. Crowell, N. Y., $1.60.

More Than Conquerors, Ariadne Gilbert. Century, N. Y., $2.00.

Stories of People Worth While, Kitty Parsons. Revell, N. Y., $1.25.

Hero Tales from History, Burnham Smith. John C. Winston, Philadelphia, 78c.

IV. BOOKS OF WORLD PEACE AND ITS HEROES

Never Again, Margaret Applegarth. Everyland Publishing Co., West Medford, Mass., $1.50.

Books of Goodwill, Florence Brewer Boeckel. National Council for Prevention of War, Washington, D. C. 2 vols., $1.00.

The Boy Who Wanted to Fly, Arthur Bunce. Harr Wagner, San Francisco, $2.00.

Friends of Ours, Elizabeth Colson. Missionary Education Movement of the United States and Canada, N. Y.

Saturday's Children, Helen Coale Crew. Friends' Bookstore, 302 Arch St., Philadelphia, $2.00.

Heroes of Peace, F. J. Gould. Harper, N. Y., 90c.

Victors of Peace, F. J. Gould. Harper, N. Y., 90c.

Peace Crusaders' Adventures in Goodwill, Anna Bassett Griscom. Lippincott, Philadelphia, $1.50.

Heroes in Friendship, Basil Mathews. Missionary Education Movement, N. Y., 85c.

Peaceway Series, short stories by various authors. Friends Book Shop, London; National Council for Prevention of War, Washington, D. C. Five booklets, $1.50.

Paths of Peace, Ross and Binyon. 2 vols. Oxford University Press, N. Y., $1.05.

The Fight for Peace (stories of the work of the League of Nations), Hebe Spaull. G. Bell & Sons, Ltd., London, 75c.

Children's Story Garden, by various authors. Lippincott, Philadelphia, $1.50.

V. BOOKS FOR LITTLE CHILDREN ABOUT OTHER NATIONS

Airplane Visits of World Children, Alexander. S. S. Board of Southern Baptist Convention, Nashville, Tenn., 25c.

Child Life in Many Lands, Blaisdell. Macmillan, N. Y., 72c.

Around the World with the Children, Frank C. Carpenter. American Book Co., N. Y., 72c.

Little Folks of Many Lands, M. O. Chance. Ginn, Boston, 64c.

Jogging Around the World, Dunham. Stokes, N. Y., $1.50.

The Books of Other Babies, Mary Entwistle. Missionary Education Movement, N. Y., 40c each.

Everyland Children, Lucy W. Peabody. A series containing so far three volumes, *Just Like You, Taro and Umé,* and *David and Susi.* Central Committee on the United Study of Foreign Missions, North Cambridge, Mass., 25c each.

BIBLIOGRAPHY

Child Life in Other Lands, H. A. Perdue. Rand McNally, Chicago, 85c.

Big People and Little People of Other Lands, Edward R. Shaw. American Book Co., N. Y., 52c.

George Washington Lincoln Goes 'Round the World, Margaret Loring Thomas. Thomas Nelson, N. Y., $1.50.

The World in a Barn, Gertrude C. Warner. Friendship Press, 150 Fifth Ave., N. Y., $1.25.

Little People Everywhere Series, McDonald and Dalrymple. Little, Brown, Boston, $1.00.

Yule-Tide in Many Lands, Pringle. Lothrop Lee, $1.50.

VI. Books of Songs and Games

Popular Folk Games and Dances. Eldridge Entertainment House, Denver, Col., 75c. (American, Danish, English, Hungarian, Italian, Lithuanian, Norwegian, Polish, Russian, Spanish, Swedish, Swiss, Welsh.)

Children at Play in Many Lands, Katharine Stanley Hall. Missionary Education Movement, N. Y., 75c.

Every Child's Folk Songs and Games. Milton Bradley Co., Springfield, Mass., $2.00 (Danish, English, French, German, Irish, Italian, Scottish, Sicilian, Swedish, Welsh.)

Folk Dances and Singing Games. G. Schirmer, N. Y., $1.50. (Bohemian, Danish, English, Hungarian, Irish, Italian, Norwegian, Russian, Scotish, Swedish.)

VII. Magazines for Children

Everyman, monthly. North Cambridge, Mass., $1.00 a year.

Junior Red Cross News, monthly (September to May). Washington, D. C., 50c a year.

The Open Road Magazine, monthly. 248 Boylston St., Boston, Mass., $1.00 a year.

Round the World with the League of Nations, monthly. League of Nations Non-Partisan Association, 6 East 39th St., N. Y., free.

APPENDIX

COVENANT OF THE LEAGUE OF NATIONS

With amendments in force September 1, 1928

THE HIGH CONTRACTING PARTIES

In order to promote international co-operation and to achieve international peace and security

by the acceptance of obligations not to resort to war,

by the prescription of open, just and honorable relations between nations,

by the firm establishment of the understandings of international law as the actual rule of conduct among Governments, and

by the maintenance of justice and a scrupulous respect for all treaty obligations in the dealings of organized peoples with one another, Agree to this Covenant of the League of Nations.

ARTICLE 1

Membership and Withdrawal

1. The original Members of the League of Nations shall be those of the Signatories which are named in the Annex to this Covenant, and also such of those other States named in the Annex as shall accede without reservation to this Covenant. Such accessions shall be effected by a declaration deposited with the Secretariat within two months of the coming into force of the Covenant. Notice thereof shall be sent to all other Members of the League.

2. Any fully self-governing State, Dominion or Colony not named in the Annex may become a Member of the League if its admission is agreed to by two-thirds of the Assembly, provided that it shall give effective guaranties of its sincere intention to observe its international obligations, and shall accept

such regulations as may be prescribed by the League in regard to its military, naval and air forces and armaments.

3. Any Member of the League may, after two years' notice of its intention so to do, withdraw from the League, provided that all its international obligations and all its obligations under this Covenant shall have been fulfilled at the time of its withdrawal.

ARTICLE 2

Executive Organs

The action of the League under this Covenant shall be effected through the instrumentality of an Assembly and of a Council, with a permanent Secretariat.

ARTICLE 3

Assembly

1. The Assembly shall consist of representatives of the Members of the League.

2. The Assembly shall meet at stated intervals and from time to time, as occasion may require, at the Seat of the League, or at such other place as may be decided upon.

3. The Assembly may deal at its meetings with any matter within the sphere of action of the League or affecting the peace of the world.

4. At meetings of the Assembly each Member of the League shall have one vote and may have not more than three Representatives.

ARTICLE 4

Council

1. The Council shall consist of representatives of the Principal Allied and Associated Powers [United States of America, the British Empire, France, Italy and Japan], together with Representatives of four [1] other Members of the

[1] The number of Members of the Council selected by the Assembly, by application of the second clause of Art. 4, par. 2, was increased from four to six on September 25, 1922, and from six to nine on September 8, 1926.

League. These four [1] Members of the League shall be selected by the Assembly from time to time in its discretion. Until the appointment of the Representatives of the four Members of the League first selected by the Assembly, Representatives of Belgium, Brazil, Greece and Spain shall be Members of the Council.

2. With the approval of the majority of the Assembly, the Council may name additional Members of the League, whose Representatives shall always be Members of the Council;[2] the Council with like approval may increase the number of Members of the League to be selected by the Assembly [2] for representation on the Council.[1]

2 bis.[3] *The Assembly shall fix by a two-thirds majority the rules dealing with the election of the non-permanent Members of the Council, and particularly such regulations as relate to their term of office and the conditions of re-eligibility.*

3. The Council shall meet from time to time as occasion may require, and at least once a year, at the Seat of the League, or at such other place as may be decided upon.

4. The Council may deal at its meetings with any matter within the sphere of action of the League or affecting the peace of the world.

5. Any Member of the League not represented on the Council shall be invited to send a Representative to sit as a Member at any meeting of the Council during the consideration of matters specially affecting the interests of that Member of the League.

6. At meetings of the Council, each Member of the League represented on the Council shall have one vote, and may have not more than one Representative.

[1] See footnote on preceding page.

[2] By application of this clause Germany was designated as a permanent Member of the Council on September 8, 1926, the appropriate action of the Council having been taken on September 4.

[3] This paragraph came into force on July 29, 1926, in accordance with Art. 26. The regulations were adopted by the Assembly on September 15.

Article 5

Voting and Procedure

1. Except where otherwise expressly provided in this Covenant, or by the terms of the present Treaty, decisions at any meeting of the Assembly or of the Council shall require the agreement of all the Members of the League represented at the meeting.

2. All matters of procedure at meetings of the Assembly or of the Council, including the appointment of Committees to investigate particular matters, shall be regulated by the Assembly or by the Council and may be decided by a majority of the Members of the League represented at the meeting.

3. The first meeting of the Assembly and the first meeting of the Council shall be summoned by the President of the United States of America.

Article 6

Secretariat and Expenses

1. The permanent Secretariat shall be established at the Seat of the League. The Secretariat shall comprise a Secretary-General and such secretaries and staff as may be required.

2. The first Secretary-General shall be the person named in the Annex; thereafter the Secretary-General shall be appointed by the Council with the approval of the majority of the Assembly.

3. The secretaries and the staff of the Secretariat shall be appointed by the Secretary-General with the approval of the Council.

4. The Secretary-General shall act in that capacity at all meetings of the Assembly and of the Council.

5. *The expenses of the League shall be borne by the Members of the League in the proportion decided by the Assembly.*[1]

[1] This paragraph came into force as an amendment on August 13, 1924, in accordance with Art. 26.

Article 7

Seat, Qualifications of Officials, Immunities

1. The Seat of the League is established at Geneva.
2. The Council may at any time decide that the Seat of the League shall be established elsewhere.
3. All positions under or in connection with the League, including the Secretariat, shall be open equally to men and women.
4. Representatives of the Members of the League and officials of the League when engaged on the business of the League shall enjoy diplomatic privileges and immunities.
5. The buildings and other property occupied by the League or its officials or by Representatives attending its meetings shall be inviolable.

Article 8

Reduction of Armaments

1. The Members of the League recognize that the maintenance of peace requires the reduction of national armaments to the lowest point consistent with national safety and the enforcement by common action of international obligations.
2. The Council, taking account of the geographical situation and circumstances of each State, shall formulate plans for such reduction for the consideration and action of the several Governments.
3. Such plans shall be subject to reconsideration and revision at least every 10 years.
4. After these plans shall have been adopted by the several Governments, the limits of armaments therein fixed shall not be exceeded without the concurrence of the Council.
5. The Members of the League agree that the manufacture by private enterprise of munitions and implements of war is open to grave objections. The Council shall advise how the evil effects attendant upon such manufacture can be prevented, due regard being had to the necessities of those Members of

the League which are not able to manufacture the munitions and implements of war necessary for their safety.

6. The Members of the League undertake to interchange full and frank information as to the scale of their armaments, their military, naval and air programs, and the condition of such of their industries as are adaptable to warlike purposes.

Article 9

Permanent Military, Naval and Air Commission

A permanent Commission shall be constituted to advise the Council on the execution of the provisions of Articles 1 and 8 and on military, naval and air questions generally.

Article 10

Guaranties Against Aggression

The Members of the League undertake to respect and preserve as against external aggression the territorial integrity and existing political independence of all Members of the League. In case of any such aggression or in case of any threat or danger of such aggression, the Council shall advise upon the means by which this obligation shall be fulfilled.

Article 11

Action in Case of War or Threat of War

1. Any war or threat of war, whether immediately affecting any of the Members of the League or not, is hereby declared a matter of concern to the whole League, and the League shall take any action that may be deemed wise and effectual to safeguard the peace of nations. In case any such emergency should arise, the Secretary-General shall, on the request of any Member of the League, forthwith summon a meeting of the Council.

2. It is also declared to be the friendly right of each Member of the League to bring to the attention of the Assembly or of the Council any circumstance whatever affecting interna-

tional relations which threatens to disturb international peace or the good understanding between nations upon which peace depends.

Article 12 [1]

1. The Members of the League agree that, if there should arise between them any dispute likely to lead to a rupture they will submit the matter either to arbitration *or judicial settlement* or to inquiry by the Council and they agree in no case to resort to war until three months after the award by the arbitrators *or the judicial decision,* or the report by the Council.

2. In any case under this Article, the award of the arbitrators *or the judicial decision* shall be made within a reasonable time, and the report of the Council shall be made within six months after the submission of the dispute.

Article 13 [1]

Arbitration or Judicial Settlement

1. The Members of the League agree that, whenever any dispute shall arise between them which they recognize to be suitable for submission to arbitration *or judicial settlement,* and which cannot be satisfactorily settled by diplomacy, they will submit the whole subject-matter to arbitration *or judicial settlement.*

2. Disputes as to the interpretation of a treaty, as to any question of international law, as to the existence of any fact which, if established, would constitute a breach of any international obligation, or as to the extent and nature of the reparation to be made for any such breach, are declared to be among those which are generally suitable for submission to arbitration *or judicial settlement.*

3. *For the consideration of any such dispute, the court to which the case is referred shall be the Permanent Court of*

[1] The text as printed came into force as an amendment on September 26, 1924, in accordance with Art. 26.

International Justice, established in accordance with Article 14, or any tribunal agreed on by the parties to the dispute or stipulated in any convention existing between them.

4. The Members of the League agree that they will carry out in full good faith any award *or decision* that may be rendered, and that they will not resort to war against a Member of the League which complies therewith. In the event of any failure to carry out such an award *or decision,* the Council shall propose what steps should be taken to give effect thereto.

ARTICLE 14

Permanent Court of International Justice

The Council shall formulate and submit to the Members of the League for adoption plans for the establishment of a Permanent Court of International Justice. The Court shall be competent to hear and determine any dispute of an international character which the parties thereto submit to it. The Court may also give an advisory opinion upon any dispute or question referred to it by the Council or by the Assembly.

ARTICLE 15

Disputes Not Submitted to Arbitration or Judicial Settlement

1.[1] If there should arise between Members of the League any dispute likely to lead to a rupture, which is not submitted to arbitration *or judicial settlement* in accordance with Article 13, the Members of the League agree that they will submit the matter to the Council. Any party to the dispute may effect such submission by giving notice of the existence of the dispute to the Secretary-General, who will make all necessary arrangements for a full investigation and consideration thereof.

2. For this purpose the parties to the dispute will communicate to the Secretary-General, as promptly as possible, statements of their case, with all the relevant facts and papers,

[1] The text of the first paragraph as printed came into force as an amendment on September 26, 1924, in accordance with Art. 26.

and the Council may forthwith direct the publication thereof.

3. The Council shall endeavor to effect a settlement of the dispute and, if such efforts are successful, a statement shall be made public giving such facts and explanations regarding the dispute and the terms of settlement thereof as the Council may deem appropriate.

4. If the dispute is not thus settled, the Council, either unanimously or by a majority vote, shall make and publish a report containing a statement of the facts of the dispute and the recommendations which are deemed just and proper in regard thereto.

5. Any Member of the League represented on the Council may make public a statement of the facts of the dispute and of its conclusions regarding the same.

6. If a report by the Council is unanimously agreed to by the Members thereof other than the Representatives of one or more of the parties to the dispute, the Members of the League agree that they will not go to war with any party to the dispute which complies with the recommendations of the report.

7. If the Council fails to reach a report which is unanimously agreed to by the members thereof, other than the Representatives of one or more of the parties to the dispute, the Members of the League reserve to themselves the right to take such action as they shall consider necessary for the maintenance of right and justice.

8. If the dispute between the parties is claimed by one of them, and is found by the Council, to arise out of a matter which by international law is solely within the domestic jurisdiction of that party, the Council shall so report, and shall make no recommendations as to its settlement.

9. The Council may in any case under this Article refer the dispute to the Assembly. The dispute shall be so referred at the request of either party to the dispute, provided that such request be made within 14 days after the submission of the dispute to the Council.

10. In any case referred to the Assembly, all the provisions

of this Article and of Article 12 relating to the action and powers of the Council shall apply to the action and powers of the Assembly, provided that a report made by the Assembly, if concurred in by the Representatives of those Members of the League represented on the Council and of a majority of the other Members of the League, exclusive in each case of the Representatives of the parties to the dispute, shall have the same force as a report by the Council concurred in by all the members thereof other than the Representatives of one or more of the parties to the dispute.

Article 16

"Sanctions"

1.[1] Should any Member of the League resort to war in dis-

[1] The Assembly has voted in favor of the following amendments to Art. 16, to replace paragraph one, and the Members are now deciding upon their ratification:

Should any Member of the League resort to war in disregard of its covenants under Articles 12, 13 or 15, it shall *ipso facto* be deemed to have committed an act of war against all other Members of the League, *which hereby undertake immediately to subject it to the severance of all trade or financial relations and to prohibit all intercourse at least between persons resident within their territories and persons resident within the territory of the covenant-breaking State and, if they deem it expedient, also between their nationals and the nationals of the covenant-breaking State, and to prevent all financial, commercial or personal intercourse at least between persons resident within the territory of that State and persons resident within the territory of any other State, whether a Member of the League or not, and, if they deem it expedient, also between the nationals of that State and the nationals of any other State whether a Member of the League or not.*

It is for the Council to give an opinion whether or not a breach of the Covenant has taken place. In deliberations on this question in the Council, the votes of Members of the League alleged to have resorted to war and of Members against whom such action was directed shall not be counted.

The Council will notify to all Members of the League the date which it recommends for the application of the economic pressure under this Article.

Nevertheless, the Council may, in the case of particular Members,

regard of its covenants under Articles 12, 13 or 15, it shall *ipso facto* be deemed to have committed an act of war against all other Members of the League, which hereby undertake immediately to subject it to the severance of all trade or financial relations, the prohibition of all intercourse between their nationals and the nationals of the covenant-breaking State, and the prevention of all financial, commercial or personal intercourse between the nationals of the covenant-breaking State and the nationals of any other State, whether a Member of the League or not.

2. It shall be the duty of the Council in such case [1] to recommend to the several Governments concerned what effective military, naval or air force the Members of the League shall severally contribute to the armed forces to be used to protect the covenants of the League.

3. The Members of the League agree, further, that they will mutually support one another in the financial and economic measures which are taken under this Article, in order to minimize the loss and inconvenience resulting from the above measures, and that they will mutually support one another in resisting any special measures aimed at one of their number by the covenant-breaking State, and that they will take the necessary steps to afford passage through their territory to the forces of any of the Members of the League which are cooperating to protect the covenants of the League.

4. Any Member of the League which has violated any covenant of the League may be declared to be no longer a Member of the League by a vote of the Council concurred in by the Representatives of all the other Members of the League represented thereon.

postpone the coming into force of any of these measures for a specified period where it is satisfied that such a postponement will facilitate the attainment of the object of the measures referred to in the preceding paragraph, or that it is necessary in order to minimize the loss and inconvenience which will be caused to such Members.

[1] The Assembly on September 21, 1925, adopted a resolution providing that the words "in such case" shall be deleted. The amendment has been submitted to Member states for ratification.

Article 17
Disputes Involving Nonmembers

1. In the event of a dispute between a Member of the League and a State which is not a Member of the League, or between States not Members of the League, the State or States not Members of the League shall be invited to accept the obligations of Membership in the League for the purposes of such dispute, upon such conditions as the Council may deem just. If such invitation is accepted, the provisions of Articles 12 to 16, inclusive, shall be applied with such modifications as may be deemed necessary by the Council.
2. Upon such invitation being given, the Council shall immediately institute an inquiry into the circumstances of the dispute and recommend such action as may seem best and most effectual in the circumstances.
3. If a State so invited shall refuse to accept the obligations of Membership in the League for the purposes of such dispute, and shall resort to war against a Member of the League, the provisions of Article 16 shall be applicable as against the State taking such action.
4. If both parties to the dispute, when so invited, refuse to accept the obligations of Membership in the League for the purposes of such dispute, the Council may take such measures and make such recommendations as will prevent hostilities and will result in the settlement of the dispute.

Article 18
Registration and Publication of Treaties

Every treaty or international engagement entered into hereafter by any Member of the League shall be forthwith registered with the Secretariat and shall as soon as possible be published by it. No such treaty or international engagement shall be binding until so registered.

Article 19
Review of Treaties

The Assembly may from time to time advise the reconsideration by Members of the League of treaties which have become inapplicable, and the consideration of international conditions whose continuance might endanger the peace of the world.

Article 20

Abrogation of Inconsistent Obligations

1. The Members of the League severally agree that this Covenant is accepted as abrogating all obligations or understandings *inter se* which are inconsistent with the terms thereof, and solemnly undertake that they will not hereafter enter into any engagements inconsistent with the terms thereof.

2. In case any Member of the League shall, before becoming a Member of the League, have undertaken any obligation inconsistent with the terms of this Covenant, it shall be the duty of such Member to take immediate steps to procure its release from such obligations.

Article 21

Engagements that Remain Valid

Nothing in this Covenant shall be deemed to affect the validity of international engagements, such as treaties of arbitration or regional understandings like the Monroe doctrine, for securing the maintenance of peace.

Article 22

Mandatory System

1. To those colonies and territories which as a consequence of the late war have ceased to be under the sovereignty of the States which formerly governed them and which are inhabited by peoples not yet able to stand by themselves under the strenuous conditions of the modern world, there should be applied the principle that the well-being and development of such peoples form a sacred trust of civilization and that securities for the performance of this trust should be embodied in this Covenant.

2. The best method of giving practical effect to this principle is that the tutelage of such peoples should be intrusted

to advanced nations who, by reason of their resources, their experience or their geographical position, can best undertake this responsibility, and who are willing to accept it, and that this tutelage should be exercised by them as Mandatories on behalf of the League.

3. The character of the mandate must differ according to the stage of the development of the people, the geographical situation of the territory, its economic conditions and other similar circumstances.

4. Certain communities formerly belonging to the Turkish Empire have reached a stage of development where their existence as independent nations can be provisionally recognized subject to the rendering of administrative advice and assistance by a Mandatory until such time as they are able to stand alone. The wishes of these communities must be a principal consideration in the selection of the Mandatory.

5. Other peoples, especially those of Central Africa, are at such a stage that the Mandatory must be responsible for the administration of the territory under conditions which will guarantee freedom of conscience and religion, subject only to the maintenance of public order and morals, the prohibition of abuses such as the slave trade, the arms traffic and the liquor traffic, and the prevention of the establishment of fortifications or military and naval bases and of military training of the natives for other than police purposes and the defense of territory, and will also secure equal opportunities for the trade and commerce of other Members of the League.

6. There are territories, such as Southwest Africa and certain of the South Pacific islands, which, owing to the sparseness of their population or their small size, or their remoteness from the centers of civilization, or their geographical contiguity to the territory of the Mandatory, and other circumstances, can be best administered under the laws of the Mandatory as integral portions of its territory, subject to the safeguards above mentioned in the interests of the indigenous population.

7. In every case of mandate, the Mandatory shall render to the Council an annual report in reference to the territory committed to its charge.

8. The degree of authority, control or administration to be exercised by the Mandatory shall, if not previously agreed upon by the Members of the League, be explicitly defined in each case by the Council.

9. A permanent Commission shall be constituted to receive and examine the annual reports of the Mandatories, and to advise the Council on all matters relating to the observance of the mandates.

Article 23

Social and Other Activities

Subject to and in accordance with the provisions of international conventions existing or hereafter to be agreed upon, the Members of the League:

(*a*) will endeavor to secure and maintain fair and humane conditions of labor for men, women, and children, both in their own countries and in all countries to which their commercial and industrial relations extend, and for that purpose will establish and maintain the necessary international organizations;

(*b*) undertake to secure just treatment of the native inhabitants of territories under their control;

(*c*) will intrust the League with the general supervision over the execution of agreements with regard to the traffic in women and children and the traffic in opium and other dangerous drugs;

(*d*) will intrust the League with the general supervision of the trade in arms and ammunition with the countries in which the control of this traffic is necessary in the common interest;

(*e*) will make provision to secure and maintain freedom of communications and of transit and equitable treatment for the commerce of all Members of the League. In this connection, the special necessities of the regions devastated during the war of 1914-1918 shall be borne in mind;

(*f*) will endeavor to take steps in matters of international concern for the prevention and control of disease.

Article 24

International Bureaus

1. There shall be placed under the direction of the League all international bureaus already established by general treaties, if the parties to such treaties consent. All such international bureaus and all commissions for the regulation of matters of international interest hereafter constituted shall be placed under the direction of the League.

2. In all matters of international interest which are regulated by general conventions but which are not placed under the control of international bureaus or commissions, the Secretariat of the League shall, subject to the consent of the Council and if desired by the parties, collect and distribute all relevant information and shall render any other assistance which may be necessary or desirable.

3. The Council may include as part of the expenses of the Secretariat the expenses of any bureau or commission which is placed under the direction of the League.

Article 25

Promotion of Red Cross and Health

The Members of the League agree to encourage and promote the establishment and co-operation of duly authorized voluntary national Red Cross organizations having as purposes the improvement of health, the prevention of disease and the mitigation of suffering throughout the world.

Article 26 [1]

Amendments

1. Amendments to this Covenant will take effect when ratified by the Members of the League whose Representatives

---

[1] The Assembly voted in favor of the following amendments to replace Art. 26, in 1921, and the Members are now deciding upon its ratification:

"Amendments to the present Covenant the text of which shall have been voted by the Assembly on a three-fourths majority, in which

APPENDIX 573

compose the Council and by a majority of the Members of the League whose Representatives compose the Assembly.

2. No such amendment shall bind any Member of the League which signifies its dissent therefrom, but in that case it shall cease to be a Member of the League.

there shall be included the votes of all the Members of the Council represented at the meeting, will take effect when ratified by the Members of the League whose Representatives composed the Council when the vote was taken and by the majority of those whose Representatives form the Assembly.

"If the required number of ratifications shall not have been obtained within twenty-two months after the vote of the Assembly, the proposed amendment shall remain without effect.

"The Secretary-General shall inform the Members of the taking of an amendment.

"Any Member of the League which has not at that time ratified the amendment is free to notify the Secretary-General within a year of its refusal to accept it, but in that case it shall cease to be a Member of the League."

TEXT OF THE MULTILATERAL TREATY FOR THE RENUNCIATION OF WAR

The President of the United States of America,
The President of the French Republic,
His Majesty the King of the Belgians,
The President of the Czechoslovak Republic,
His Majesty the King of Great Britain, Ireland and the British Dominions beyond the Seas, Emperor of India,
The President of the German Reich,
His Majesty the King of Italy,
His Majesty the Emperor of Japan,
The President of the Republic of Poland,
Deeply sensible of their solemn duty to promote the welfare of mankind;

Persuaded that the time has come when a frank renunciation of war as an instrument of national policy should be made to the end that the peaceful and friendly relations now existing between their peoples may be perpetuated;

Convinced that all changes in their relations with one another should be sought only by pacific means and be the result of a peaceful and orderly process, and that any signatory Power which shall hereafter seek to promote its national interests by resort to war should be denied the benefits furnished by this treaty;

Hopeful that, encouraged by their example, all the other nations of the world will join in this humane endeavor and by adhering to the present treaty as soon as it comes into force bring their peoples within the scope of its beneficent provisions, thus uniting the civilized nations of the world in a common renunciation of war as an instrument of their national policy;

Have decided to conclude a treaty and for that purpose have appointed as their respective Plenipotentiaries: . . . who, having communicated to one another their full powers found in good and due form have agreed upon the following articles:

Article I

The High Contracting Parties solemnly declare in the names of their respective peoples that they condemn recourse to war for the solution of international controversies, and renounce it as an instrument of national policy in their relations with one another.

Article II

The High Contracting Parties agree that the settlement or solution of all disputes or conflicts of whatever nature or of whatever origin they may be, which may arise among them, shall never be sought except by pacific means.

Article III

The present treaty shall be ratified by the High Contracting Parties named in the Preamble in accordance with their respective constitutional requirements, and shall take effect as between them as soon as all their several instruments of ratification shall have been deposited at ....

This treaty shall, when it has come into effect as prescribed in the preceding paragraph, remain open as long as may be necessary for adherence by all the other Powers of the world. Every instrument evidencing the adherence of a Power shall be deposited at ...., and the treaty shall immediately upon such deposit become effective as between the Power thus adhering and the other Powers parties hereto.

It shall be the duty of the Government of .... to furnish each Government named in the Preamble and every Government subsequently adhering to this treaty with a certified copy of the treaty and of every instrument of ratification or adherence. It shall also be the duty of the Government of .... telegraphically to notify such Governments immediately upon the deposit with it of each instrument of ratification or adherence.

In faith whereof the respective Plenipotentiaries have signed this treaty in the French and English languages both texts having equal force, and hereunto affix their seals.

INDEX

There are no citations in this Index to organizations, in so far as they are referred to in the text merely as sources of material; references are to the items of material.

Abel, J. F., quoted, 42.
Adams County Y. W. C. A., 429.
Adams, John Quincy, 286 f.
Adams, Samuel, letter to Congress, 7.
Addams, Jane, 111 ff.
Advent Christians General Conference of America, 89.
Advocate of Peace, quoted, 333.
"Aggressor" nation, 261.
Agriculture, Department of, 435, 473.
Airplanes in war, 393 ff.; protection of cities against, 394.
"*Alabama*" claims case, 111, 245; Room, 477.
All-Australian Trade Union Congress, 150.
"America First" poster, 491.
American Association of University Women, 21, 114, 115, 499.
American Council of Learned Societies, 47.
American Farm Bureau Federation, 165.
American Federation of Labor, resolutions, 152-155, 369.
American Federation of Teachers, 36-37, 115.
American Friends Service Committee, 370, 433, 434.
American Historical Association, 20.
American Home Economics Association, 115.
American Institute of International Law, 273.
American Institute of Sacred Literature, 424.

American Junior Red Cross, 446, 474.
American Legion, 166, 171-175, 176-178, 417.
American Nurses' Association, 115.
American Peace Society, 243.
"American Plan," 248.
American Schoolmaster, 462, 466, 473.
American School Citizenship League, 450, 452.
American Unitarian Association, 99.
Andrews, Mrs. Fannie Fern, 450, 474.
Andrews, Gen. Lincoln C., quoted, 400.
Angell, Norman, quoted, 128, 147.
Anglo-American relations, 385.
Anti-militarist Clergymen, International Committee of, 88.
Arbitration, 217 f., 241-264; defined, footnote, 242; resolutions of State legislatures on, 243; Congressional resolutions on, 244 ff:; in Latin America, 243, 257; "Alabama" case, 245; Conference 1928, 255; League of Nations and, 259; development of, 263 f.; bibliographies on, 515; books on, 531.
Armaments, international reduction of, 132, 210, 286-298; Congressional resolutions, 288; in League Covenant, 289; in Treaty of Versailles, 289; Washington Conference, 290; Russia's proposal, 296; bibliographies on,

515; books on, 533 (see *Munitions*).
Armistice Day, 424, 438, 474, 481, 482.
Art, galleries, 448 f.; study of, 461.
Artists, relation to peace, 448.
Ashby, Mrs. Corbett, quoted, 118.
Association for Peace Education of Chicago, 21.
Athletics, 461.
Auxiliary language, 469.

Bahá'í Church, 102 f.
Baldwin, Roger N., 306.
Bankers' Manifesto, 134 f.
Baptist Convention, Northern, 90.
Baptist Convention, Southern, 90.
Baptist World Alliance, 89.
Barker, Ernest, quoted, 66.
Barrie, Sir James, quoted, 185.
Bell High School, 478.
Bellers, John, 198.
Biblical texts, 77 f.
Billboard publicity, 442.
Biography, 462.
Black, W. W., quoted, 444.
Bliven, Bruce, quoted, 441.
Bogart, Ernest L., "Direct and Indirect Costs of the Great War," quoted, 402.
Bok, Edward, 505.
Bolivar, 243.
Borah, Senator William E., 113, 231, 235, 266; quoted, 235 f.
Botany, 463.
Bowman, Mrs. E. K., 505.
Boy Scouts, 431 f.
Brazil, Constitution of, 257.
Briand, 233.
Briand Speech Competition, 454.
British Labor Party, 150-151.
Broadcasting Organizations, International Union of, 446.
Brooks-Bright Endowment, 453.
Brooks, L. W., quoted, 37.
Bryan, William Jennings, 254.
Bryan Treaties, 254 f.
Buell, Raymond Leslie, quoted, 137.
Burns, C. Delisle, quoted, 206-207, 278.
Burton Resolution, 117, 298.

Butterfield, Dr. Kenyon L., quoted, 163 f.

Cadoux, C. J., quoted, 72.
California, University of, 50.
Calvo, Doctrine of, 351.
Canada and the U. S., 77, 286 ff.
Cancellation stamp, 332.
Candle-lighting ceremony, 487.
Capper, Senator, quoted, 158, 160.
Capper-Johnson Bill, 154.
Caravans for Peace, 434.
Carnegie Endowment for International Peace, 20, 45, 56, 441. 504.
Caribbean area, 340, 345, 348.
Carr, Wilbur, quoted, 160.
Cartels, 129.
Casares' proposal, 22.
Case, Clarence Marsh, quoted, 300.
Catholic Association for International Peace, 85 f.
Catt, Mrs. Carrie Chapman, 111 ff., 326; quoted, 113, 116.
Causey, James H., 49, 504.
Cecil, Lord Robert, quoted, 306.
Central Conference of American Rabbis, 87 f.
Central American Court of Justice, 219 f., 256.
Central American Peace Conference, 219.
Central American Tribunal, 256.
Chamberlain, J. P., quoted, 379.
Chase, Mary N., 433.
Chemical Warfare, 392 ff.; Special Committee on Chemical Warfare of League of Nations, 392-395; books on, 534.
Chicago University, 21.
Children, 478; books for, 549.
China Inland Mission, 104.
Christian Century, quoted, 71.
Christian Church, General Convention of the, 92.
Christian Science, quoted, 102.
Christianity and peace, 72 f., 77 f., 301 f.; courses on, 500 f. (See also *Church* and *Peace*.)
Christmas programs, 424, 438, 494.
Church and peace, 71-105; Church Fathers, testimony of, 72; reso-

INDEX 579

lutions on, 89-103; foreign missions, 104 f.; work through, 424; study courses on, 500 f.; books on, 536.
Church of the Brethren, 99 f.
Church Peace Union, 83-85, 504.
Churchill, Winston S., quoted, 388.
Cincinnati Peace League, 452.
Cinema Congress, International, 443 f.
Citizens' Military Training Camps, 319 f.
Civics, 464.
Clarke, E. L., courses, 51.
Clemenceau, letter to Germany, 289.
Cleveland, Ohio, schools of, 60.
Clubs, international, 487.
Codification of international law (see *International Law*).
College courses, 46 ff.
College Cruise Around the World, 40.
Collins, Ross, quoted, 317.
Columbia University, statement on foreign debt, 382.
Columbus Day, 493.
Commerce and Peace, 124-142; World Economic Conference, 130; International Chamber of Commerce, 129 f., 133; war profits, 137 ff.; treaties, commercial, 140; bibliographies on, 517; books on, 521 (see *Industry, Economic Interdependence, Imperialism*).
Committee, how to form, 416.
Committee on the Cause and Cure of War, National, 421.
Compromis, 262.
Conciliation (see *Treaties*), defined, footnote, 242.
Conferences, programs for, 421 ff.
Conference, technique of, 259.
Conference for the Control of Traffic in Arms, 297.
Conferences on the Cause and Cure of War, 115.
Congregational Churches, National Council of, 91.
Congress, power to outlaw war, 379.

Connecticut Council of International Relations, 422.
Consumers' coöperative societies, 165.
Contests, 45, 452 ff.
Convention of St. Germain, 297.
Coolidge, President, quoted, 265, 333, 482, 507.
Coolidge Naval Disarmament Conference, 294 f., 298.
Coöperation (see *International*).
Corda Fratres Association of Cosmopolitan Clubs, 56.
Cosmopolitan Club, 487.
Coudenhove-Kalergi, Count Richard N., 283.
Council of Women for Home Missions, 114 f.
County fairs, 436.
Crane, Frank, quoted, 403.
Cuba, Platt Amendment, 348; books on, 526.
Culbertson, William, 354.
Current events, 464.
Czechoslovakia, Peace education in, 30.

Daniels, Josephus, quoted, 139.
Darwin, quoted, 405.
Daughters of American Revolution, 417.
Davis-DuBois, Rachel, 59.
Dawes Plan, 387 f.; books on, 528.
Debates, 467; international, 55.
Declaration of Policy of U. S., 315-316.
Delaware, University of, 52.
Democracy and peace, 198, 242, 310 ff., 332 f.
Denver University, 49.
Dewey, John, quoted, 232, 356, 468.
Disarmament (see *Armaments, international, reduction of*).
Disciples of Christ, International Convention of, 92.
Discussion Courses (see *Study courses*), 494.
Domestic science, 465.
Dominican Republic, Constitution of, 257.
Douglas, Paul H., quoted, 143 f.
Dowling, Evaline, 474.

Downing, E. Estelle, 45, 451, 474.
Drago Doctrine, 337.
Dubois, Pierre, 197.
Dunkards, 78.
Durant School, 477.

Earlham College, 54, 56.
Economic interdependence, 124-128, 343, 458 ff., 488; bibliographies on, 517; books on, 521.
Education and peace, 15-70, 449-480; present tendencies of education, 16; studies of textbooks, 20 ff.; international organizations, 23 ff.; government encouragement of, 28; League of Nations and, 31 ff.; organizations in the United States, 33 ff.; international schools and colleges, 38 ff.; teacher training institutions, 40 ff; foreign travel for teachers, 45; exchange of teaching posts, 46; university courses and activities, 46 ff.; fellowships, 53; student tours, 54; school courses and activities, 57 ff.; international correspondence, 62; principles agreed upon, 63 ff.; cultivating world-mindedness, 63; nationalism in education, 65 ff.; teaching independence of thought, 67; bibliographies on, 515 f.; books on, 536 (see *Schools*).
Emerson, Ralph Waldo, quoted, 70.
England, Labor Party and disarmament, 9; Liberal Party and peace, 9; peace education in, 26, 30; labor in war time, 145, 149-151;; peace letter campaign, 301; peace organizations in, 509.
English, 465.
English Speaking Union, 46.
Epworth League, 427.
Erasmus, quoted, 75, 308.
Esperanto, 469.
European Student Relief Organization, 188.
Evans, Jessie C., quoted, 69.
Exchange of teaching posts, 46.
Extension Courses, 52.
Evangelical Synod of North America, 93.

Farmers and peace, 157-165; effect of war on income, 158; on prices, 158 f.; destruction of farm property in next war, 159; post-war deflation, 158, 160; National Grange, 161; United Farmers of Alberta, 161 f.; international organizations, 162 ff.
Federal Council of the Churches of Christ in America, 80-83, 424, 427, 446, 451.
Fellowships, 53 f.
Fellowship of Reconciliation, 193, 303, 424.
Fellowship of Youth for Peace, 193.
Fiction, on peace and war, 541.
Fidac, 168-171, 179, 182.
Filene, Edward A., 505.
Financial control of foreign governments, 349 ff.
Fithian, Charles Brooks, 487.
Flags, where to obtain, 481.
Foch, Marshal, quoted, 395.
Folks, Homer, quoted, 407.
Follett, Mary P., quoted, 468.
Forbes, Mrs. J. Malcolm, 112, 508.
Foreign debt, World War, Commission on, 380; amount of, 381; Columbia University statement, 382; statement of Secretary of the Treasury, 383; reparations and, 390; bibliographies on, 519; books on, 528 f.
Foreign investments, 128, 351 ff.; books on, 529.
Foreign languages, 469.
Foreign loans, State Department supervision of, 351.
Foreign Policy, courses on, 496, 501 f.; bibliographies on, 517; books on, 525.
Foreign students in America, 55.
Foreign travel, for teachers, 46; for students, 52-54; for boys, 63.
Fosdick, Harry Emerson, quoted, 179.
Fosdick, Raymond B., quoted, 48, 66, 67, 201.
Franklin, Benjamin, quoted, 8, 313, 345, 469.

INDEX

Freedom of the seas, 266, 295; books on, 526.
Friends, Society of, 78; conference of all, 101.

Games, 480; books of, 553.
Gardiner, A. G., quoted, 385.
General Federation of Women's Clubs, 114, 115, 116.
Geneva Institute of International Relations, 38.
Geneva Gas Protocol, 298.
Geneva Protocol, 261, 263, 292.
Geneva School of International Studies, 38.
Germany, education for peace, 29; entry into League of Nations, 211, 262; Treaty of Versailles and, 170, 211; World Court, optional clause signed, 223; Locarno Treaties, 262; disarmament of, 289, 290; peace letter campaign, 304; peace organizations of, 509; books on revised version of responsibility for war, 533.
Ghent, Treaty of, 242.
Girl Scouts, 431 f.
Girls' Friendly Society, 427.
Goddard, Harold C., quoted, 307.
Golden Rule, in all religions, 79.
Good Offices, defined, footnote, 242.
Goodwill Day, 429, 438, 474, 481, 486.
Goodwill teams, 434.
Green, President, of A. F. of L., quoted, 151, 155 f.
Green Acre Institute, 423.
Grotius, Hugo, 269.
Groves, Brigadier-General, 394, 396.
Guadalupe Hidalgo, Treaty of, 243.
Gulick, Sidney L., quoted, 428.

Hague Peace Conferences, The, 218 f., 270, 288; books on, 531.
Haiti, 346; books on, 526.
Hamilton, Alexander, quoted, 313, 314.
Hart, Hornell, course by, 51.

Harvard University, 49, 56.
Hawaii, 346.
Hay, John, Secretary of State, quoted, 247, 251.
Hay treaties, 248.
Hays, Will, quoted, 444.
Heraud, Marcel, quoted, 169.
Herman, Raphael, 24, 505.
Heroes of peace, 453, 463, 477, 489; books on, 551-552.
Hi-Y Clubs, 432.
Hinkle, Dr. Beatrice, quoted, 107, 108.
History, studies of textbooks, 20ff.; teaching of, 454 ff.
Hodges, Charles, quoted, 141.
Howe, Julia Ward, quoted, 106 ff.
Hrdlicka, Ales, quoted, 404.
Hudson, Manley O., quoted, 271, 273, 275.
Hughes, Charles Evans, quoted, 268, 273, 354.
Hughes, Rupert, quoted, 178.
Houghton, Alanson B., quoted, 3.
Hyde, Charles Cheney, 355.
Hygiene, 470.
Hymns, 424; books of, 545.

Ido, 469.
Immigration, 361-372; Chinese, 362; Asiatic barred zone, 364; Hindu, 366; Japanese, 363, 366 ff.; Mexican, 371; Canadian, 371; selective laws, 364 f.; bibliographies on, 516; books on, 528.
Imperialism, 342-357; books on, 532 (see *Nationalism*).
Independence Day, 490.
Independence of thought, 67-69, 480.
Indiana Council on International Relations, 422.
Individual work for peace, 155, 416, 428, 504 ff.
Industry and peace (see chapter on "*Commerce and Peace*," 124-142); and preparedness for war, 328-332; "educational orders," 329; Industrial Preparedness Committee, 328; mobilization of, 136, 328 f.; War Department

Business Council, 328; munitions battalions, 329.
Institute, 422.
Institute of International Education, 35, 36, 46, 51, 55.
Institute of Pacific Relations, 284 f.
Intellectual Coöperation, International Committee on, 22, 31-33, 39, 46; recommendations of, 63-65, 443.
Intercollegiate Peace Association, 452.
Interdependence (see *Economic*).
Interior, Department of, 435, 473.
International American Conference, 256.
International Bridge, 476, 493.
International Bureau of Education, 26, 27, 62.
International Chamber of Commerce, 124, 129, 133, 134.
International Commerce Commission, 354.
International Commission of Agriculture, 164.
International Conference on Immigration, 372.
International Coöperation, 277-285; books on, 524.
International Correspondence, 62, 432 f.
International Council of Agricultural Organizations, 164.
International Council of Religious Education, 425.
International Council of Women, 110.
International Court of Law, 219.
International Federation of Home and School, 28.
International Federation of Trade Unions, 148.
International Flag Day, 492.
International House, 55.
International Institute of Agriculture, 131, 132, 162 f.
International Institute of Teachers College, 41.
International Joint Commission, 257-259.
International Kindergarten Union, 28.

International Labor Office, 214.
International Labor Organization, 131, 132, 213 ff., 147, 358; bibliography on, 517; books on, 523.
International law, 265-276; codification defined, 265; private, 267, 270; public, 267; codification by League of Nations, 270-273; codification by Pan American Conference, 273-275; bibliographies on, 516; books on, 524.
International Mind Alcoves, 418.
International organizations (see *International Coöperation*); private, 285; bibliographies on, 516; books on, 522.
International Peoples College, 39.
International Relations Clubs, 55.
International River Commissions, 281.
International Student Hospitality Association, 54.
International Student Service, 188.
International Sugar Commission, 280.
International Union of American Republics (see *Pan American Union*).
International Woman Suffrage Alliance, 111, 118.
Interparliamentary Union, 278.
Intervention, 274, 337, 340 f., 351 ff.; books on, 526 (see chapter on "*War-making Power in United States Government*").
Intra-American Institute of Intellectual Coöperation, 33.
Iowa, University of, 56.
Irwin, Will, "The Next War," quoted, 159, 399, 406, 409.

James, William, "Moral Equivalent of War," quoted, 435.
Japan, peace education in, 26, 29; home colonization plan of, 361; "Gentlemen's Agreement," 363; radio "chair" on international relations, 447; doll messengers to, 451; International Fine Arts Society, 461; books on, 527.
Japan Chronicle, quoted, 7.
Jaszi, Oscar, course by, 51.

Jay Treaty, 242.
Jefferson, Charles E., quoted, 122, 300.
Jefferson, Thomas, quoted, 313, 314.
Johns Hopkins University, 48.
Johnson, C. W., 506.
Jordan, Dr. David Starr, 24, 505; letters to, 186.
Jouhaux, quoted, 146.
July Fourth, 490.
Junior Red Cross, American, 446, 474.
Junior Year Abroad, 52.
Jurists, Commission of, 273; International Committee of, 221.

Kant, Immanuel, 198, 199.
Kellogg, Secretary of State, quoted, 234 ff., 236 f., 255.
Kellogg, Vernon, quoted, 405.
Kellogg Treaty (see *Multilateral Treaty*).
Kent, William, quoted, 353.
Kenworthy, J. M., quoted, 395, 443.
Key, Ellen, quoted, 108, 408.
Kidd, Benjamin, quoted, 107.
Kilpatrick, William Heard, quoted, 42 f.
Knighthood of Youth, 432.
Knudsen, Sven V., 63, 433.

Labor and peace, 143-156; British Labor Party, 9, 149-151; effect of war on standards of, 145 f.; need for international organization, 147 f.; influence against war, 149-150; A. F. of L. resolutions, 152 ff.; bibliographies on, 517; books on, 538.
Ladd, William, 218.
Lägerlof, Selma, quoted, 109.
Lamont, Thomas W., quoted, 284.
Land Grant Colleges, 319.
Lantern slides, 481.
Laski, Harold J., quoted, 66, 305.
Latin America, labor resolutions dealing with, 151; relations of United States with, 345 ff.; press of, 439; courses on, 51, 502; teaching history of, 457; bibliographies on, 517; books on, 526 f.; (see chapters on *"Monroe Doctrine," "Imperialism,"* and *"War-making Power in United States Government"*).
League for Permanent Peace, 112.
League of Nations, 197-216; intellectual coöperation, 31; economic relations, 127, 130-133, 141; United States coöperation with, 204; mandates system, 203, 354, 569; methods of preserving peace, 207-213; sanctions, 209, 236, 566; "gap" in Covenant, 209; treaties for pacific settlement, 259 f.; codification of international law, 270 ff.; international coöperation, 277; armaments, 291 ff.; traffic in arms, 296 f.; private manufacture of munitions, 296 f.; teaching in history classes, 456; study courses on, 502; bibliographies on, 518; books on, 522 f.; Covenant of, 557-573.
League of Nations Non-Partisan Association, essay contest, 453.
Levermore, Charles H., 505.
Levinson, Salmon O., 231.
Libby, Frederick J., quoted, 299.
Libraries, work for peace through, 418 ff.; children's rooms, 420; extension work, 419.
Lieber, Francis, 269; quoted, 314.
Lincoln, Abraham, quoted, 310.
Lincoln's birthday, 485.
Lincoln, Charles M., quoted, 399.
Locarno, Treaties of, 262, 292.
Longstreth, Walter C., 320.
Lubin, David, 162.
Luchaire, J., quoted, 46.
Lutheran Church in America, United, 94; New York and New England Synod of, 94.

Madison, James, quoted, 311.
Mahaffy, Sir John P., quoted, 241.
Manry, James C., 18.
Maritime law, 266, 274.
Martin, Alfred W., quoted, 78.
Massachusetts, peace education in Constitution of, 30.

INDEX

Massachusetts Legislature, resolution, 243.
Mathematics, 470.
Mather, Frank Jewett, quoted, 448.
McClay, William, quoted, 312.
MacDonald, Ramsay, quoted, 150 f.
McMaster, "History of the People of the United States," quoted, 310.
Mead, Dr. and Mrs. Edwin D., 505.
Mediation, defined, footnote, 242.
Medical Women's National Association, 115.
Mellon, Secretary of the Treasury, quoted, 283, 384.
Memorial Day, 489.
Mennonites, 304; Eastern District Conference of, 78; General Conference of, 100.
Merrill, William P., quoted, 400.
Methodist Episcopal Church, General Conference of, 95.
Mexico, education in, 30; treaty with United States, 243; commission with United States proposed, 355; immigration from, 371; school friendship bags to, 451; study courses on, 500, 502; bibliography on, 518; books on, 526, 527 (see chapter on *"Monroe Doctrine"*).
Michigan State Normal School, 45.
Milgram, Joseph P., quoted, 177.
Militarism in Education, Committee on, 449.
Military policy of U. S., 309-333.
Military training, 319-323, 325-328, 449; bibliography on, 518.
Militia, 310, 317.
Miller, G. A., 493.
Milliken, Carl E., quoted, 445.
Minnesota, University of, 51.
Missionaries, 104, 105.
Missionary societies, 426.
Mobilization of industry (see *Industry*).
"Model Assemblies," of League of Nations, 56, 477.
Monroe Doctrine, 334-341; and Multilateral Treaty, 238; and Arbitration Treaties, 250 f.; announced, 335; Grant on, 336; Roosevelt on, 336, 337; defined by Hughes, 339, 340; Latin American attitude toward, 338; reference to, in Covenant of League of Nations, 339; *Baltimore Sun* quoted on, 341; study courses on, 500, 502; books on, 526.
Monroe, James, 286 f.
Montana, University of, 56.
Monuments, peace, 476.
Moon, Parker Thomas, 50, 356.
"Moral Equivalent of War," quoted, 435.
Moravian Church, 101.
Morrill Land Grant Act, 319.
Morrison, Charles Clayton, quoted, 232, 412.
Morrow, Dwight W., quoted, 267, 353.
Motion pictures, work for peace through, 442-446; war films, 442 f.; educational films, 445 f.; for programs, 481.
Mott, Lucretia, 111.
Moulton, Harold G., quoted, 390.
Multilateral Treaty, 233 ff.; French reservations, 234 f.; British reservations, 237 f.; U. S. interpretation of, 238; open to adherence, 239; signatory states, 239; text of, 574 ff.
Munitions, private manufacture of, 297; manufacturers of, 137 ff. (see *Armaments*).
Musée Pédagogique, 432.
Museums, work for peace through, 449, 477.
Music, 471.
Mutilés, march of, 391.
"My Friend Abroad," 433.
Myers, Denys P., quoted, 241, 260, 292.

National Association of Secondary School Principals, 37.
National Bureau of International Correspondence, 432.
National Child Welfare Association, 432.

National Committee of Friendly Relations among Students, 55.
National Congress of Parents and Teachers, 115.
National Council of Christian Associations, 191.
National Council of Friendly Societies in America, 115.
National Council of Jewish Women, 114, 115, 116.
National Council of Women, 114, 115.
National Council of Teachers of English, 451, 474.
National Defense, appropriation for, 410 ff.; books on, 529 (see chapters on "War Veterans and Peace," and "The Military Policy of the United States").
National Defense Act, 306, 315, 317.
National Education Association, 36, 115.
National Federation of Colored Women, 115.
National Federation of Temple Sisterhoods, 114.
National Grange, 160 f.
National Guard, 318.
National League of Women Voters, 113, 114, 115, 116, 119, 447.
National Service Star Legion, 115.
National Student Federation of America, 54, 55, 191.
National Study Conference of the Churches, 81.
National Woman's Christian Temperance Union, 114, 115, 116.
National Women's Trade Union League, 114, 116.
Nationalism, 16-18, 65; books on, 532 (see *Imperialism*).
Naturalization, 366.
Navy, program for increased, 5, 298, 315, 316, 415 f.
Navy League, 139.
Neumann, George Bradford, 16.
Neutrality, 266; course on, 502; books on, 526.
New Education Fellowship, 27.
New Republic, quoted, 386.

New York Federation of Progressive Women, 121.
New York Herald Tribune, quoted, 490.
New York Times, quoted, 193-194, 491.
New York University, 53.
Nicaragua, resolution of American Federation of Labor on, 152; member of Central American Court of Jutice, 219 f.; statistics on, 347; United States policy toward, 349, 377; bibliography on, 518; books on, 526.
Niebuhr, Reinhold, quoted, 105.
Nobel, Alfred, 111, 505; awards, 463.
Normal Schools, 40 ff., 452.
Norris, Kathleen, quoted, 123.
North Carolina, University of, 51.
Northwestern University, 49.

Oberlin College, 51.
Ogg, Frederic, quoted, 47.
Ohio Council of Churches, 427.
Oil, 344; books on, 532.
Open Road, Inc., 54.
Open Road Magazine, 433.
Oratorical contests, 433, 452.
Oregon, schools of, 61.
Organizations working for peace, in the United States, 509; in foreign countries, 509.
Organization publications, 547.
O'Ryan, Major General John F., quoted, 166, 167, 407 f., 484.
Osborn, Carter, Jr., letter to David Starr Jordan, 186.
Ottawa League of Nations Union, 484.
Outlawry of war, outline of plan, 231-240; power of Congress to outlaw war, 379; study courses on, 503; bibliographies on, 518; books on, 531.
Outlawry of War Treaty (see Multilateral Treaty for the Renunciation of War).
Overstreet, Harry A., quoted, 68, 467.

Pacific relations, College courses

on, 50; Pan Pacific Union, 284; Institute of, 284 ff.; in geography courses, 460; courses on, 500, 503, 504; bibliography on, 518; books on, 528 (see chapter on "World Population and Immigration").
Pacifism, 299-308; Christianity and, 71 ff.; bibliographies on, 515; books on, 540; absolute pacifists, conscientious objectors, 307; bibliography on conscientious objectors, 515.
Page, Kirby, quoted, 77, 180.
Pageants and Plays, 481, 543 f.
Pan American Conferences, 266, 273 ff.; codification of international law, 266, 273 ff; history of, 282 f.; and arbitration, 255 f., 341; and intervention, 275, 340 f.
Pan American Congress of Journalists, 439.
Pan American Federation of Labor, resolutions of, 1927, 151 f.
Pan American Union, 46, 51, 65, 256, 282 f.
Pan European Union, 283.
Pan Pacific Union, 284.
Panama Canal, 340, 348.
Panama, Congress of, 273.
Pasadena high schools, 60.
Pasteur, quoted, 473.
Peace classics ("famous peace documents"), 540.
Patrick, Major-General Mason M., 393.
Patriotism, 44, 66, 67; study course on, 499.
Peabody, George Foster, 326.
Peace Declamation Contests, 427, 433.
Peace Heroes Memorial Society, 489.
Peace Letter Campaign, in England, 301 f.; in Germany, 304.
Peace Movement, organized,—and political action, 4 ff.; function of, 5 f.; attack on, 417 f.; organizations in United States and other countries, 509; bibliography on, 518; books on, 535.
Peace Portal, at Blaine, 476, 492.

Peat, Harold R., quoted, 179 f.
Penn, William, 21; plan for general parliament of Europe, 198; colony in Pennsylvania, 286; "Holy Experiment," 302.
Periodicals, on world peace and international relations, 545.
Permanent Court of Arbitration, 219, 248.
Permanent Court of International Justice (see World Court).
Pershing, General, quoted, 393.
Philadelphia Yearly Meeting of Friends, 437.
Pictures, suggesting peace ideals, 479.
Pierson, William Whatley, Jr., 51.
Platoon Schools of Calais, Maine, 261.
Plays (see Pageants).
Podiebard, 198.
Poems, list of, 543.
Poison gas, treaty, 175 f.; prohibition of, 298; in modern war, 392 ff. (see Chemical warfare).
Polish school children, 19.
Political action for peace, 4, 9, 11; by women, 119; by labor, 150; in campaigns, 423.
Pomona College, 46.
Ponsonby, Arthur, quoted, 303, 305.
Population of world, 359 f.; relation of, to war, 360; bibliography on, 518.
Porter, Elliot, test by, 17.
Portugal, Constitution of, 257.
Poster campaigns, 483.
Potter, Pitman B., course by, 52, 464.
Prejudices, danger of and how to overcome, 51, 68, 467 ff., 478, 494; study courses, 497.
Preparedness for war, power to undertake, under constitution, 309; in early history of country, 312 ff.; before and since World War, 314 f.; change in program under National Defense Act, 317 ff.; military training as part of program, 318 ff.; industry's part in, 328 f.; obtaining public

support for, 329 f.; part played by motion pictures, 331; enlistment of women's interest, 131; effect of, on traditions of democratic government, 332; possibility of obtaining security through enlarged preparedness program, 333; plans for use of chemicals, flame, and disease germs in "next" war, 392 ff.; books on, 529 (see industry, and military training).
Presbyterian Church, General Assembly of, 97.
Press, 437-441; work for peace through, 437 f.; publicity material, 437; prizes offered, 438; advertisements for peace, 438; country papers, 438; relation of, to development of better international understanding, 438-441; travel fellowships for journalists, 440 f.; charged with bellicosity, 441; books on, 538 f.
Press Congress of the World, 439.
Press Experts, Conference of, 439.
Principia, school, 61.
Prizes, 45, 484, 505.
Programs, school, 57 ff., 474 f.; church, 424; Sunday schools, 425 f.; women's clubs, 428 f.; young people's, 429 f.; Armistice Day, 424, 482; Lincoln's Birthday, 485; Washington's Birthday, 485 f.; Goodwill Day, 424, 486 ff.; Memorial Day, 489 f.; Independence Day, 490 ff.; International Flag Day, 492 f.; Columbus Day, 493 f.; Christmas, 424, 494; flags for, 481; lantern slides for, 481; candle-lighting ceremony, 487.
Progressive Education Association, 28.
Projects, for school classes, 475.
Protestant Episcopal Church, Convention of the, 93.
Protocol for Pacific Settlement, 261, 263.
Public International Unions (see chapter "International Coöperation," 277-285).

Public meetings, 420 ff.; fliers, for, 423.
Public opinion and the peace movement, 5, 10, 11, 12, 206, 231 f., 240, 267, 276; books on, 521.
Putney, Albert H., 373 ff.

Quaker principles, 101, 302, 305 (see Friends).
Quinn, John R., quoted, 167 f.
Quotations, books of, 545.

Racial problems, 358 ff.; race statistics, 360; courses on, 457 f., 497, 503; books on, 532 (see chapter on "World Population and Immigration").
Radio, international organization, 446; work for peace through, 446; programs, 447; radio teas, 447.
Raw materials, government control of, 135-136 (see Economic interdependence, and chapter on "Imperialism").
Recitations, books of, 545.
"Reconciliation Trips," 488.
Red Cross, American, preparations for protection against gas attacks, 396 (see Junior).
Redfield, William C., quoted, 125.
Reformed Church in the United States of America, Eastern Synod of, 97.
Reinsch, Paul, "Public International Unions," quoted, 164, 277, 285.
Religious Education Association, 427.
"Remember Again" (poem), 181.
Reparations, 387-390, 211; bibliographies on, 518; books on, 528.
Repudiated state debts, 251.
Reserve Officers' Association, 330 f.
Reserve Officers' Training Corps, 318 ff.
R. O. T. C., 321-324.
Revisionist theory, books on, 533.
Rhoades, Mrs. Theodora, 449.

Riverside Council, California, 452.
Robinson, James Harvey, quoted, 47.
Rock Springs Lyons Club, 487.
Roosevelt, Theodore, quoted on, arbitration treaties, 248, 250 f.; Monroe Doctrine, 336, 337; intervention, 376; Pacific region, 460.
Root, Elihu, 221, 270; quoted, 212.
Root Treaties, 249.
Rotary International, 140 f.
Rowe, Leo S., quoted, 493.
Rural groups, work for peace through, 436.
Rush, Richard, 286.
Rush-Bagot Treaty, 288.

Saint Pierre, 198.
Saleeby, Caleb W., quoted, 404.
Salter, Sir Arthur, quoted, 6.
Salvador, 350.
Santiago, Treaty of, 256.
Santo Domingo, 336, 346, 377; books on, 527.
Saturday Evening Post, quoted, 10, 146.
Sayre, Francis B., 326.
Senate, resolutions supporting methods of pacific settlement, 244, 246; reservations to arbitration treaties, 249 ff.; insistence upon constitutional power, 250; reservations to World Court, 224 ff.
Schools, what schools are doing, 57-63; work for peace through, 449-478; suggestions for classwork in history, geography, art, athletics, botany, civics, current events, domestic science, English, debates, foreign languages, hygiene, mathematics, music, science, 454-472; projects, 473; school programs, 474; material for teachers, where to obtain, 451 (see Education and Peace).
School World Friendship League, 59.
Schreiner, Olive, quoted, 120.
Science, 472.

Scientific attitude of mind, 472.
Scott, James Brown, quoted, 217 f., 275.
Seabury, prizes, 45, 452, 505.
Security, 233, 261, 299.
Service Civile, 434.
Seventh Day Baptist Church, General Conference of, 98.
Sewall, Mrs. May Wright, 110.
Shotwell, James T., 259.
Smith College, 53.
Smith, H. L., suggestions for teachers, 43.
Smith, J. Russell, 457.
Social Research, 47.
Social Studies, 34 (see civics, history, etc.).
Soldiers and Peace (see War veterans and peace).
Songs, 471; books of, 545, 553.
South Philadelphia High School for Girls, 60.
Southern California, University of, 50.
Sportsmanship Brotherhood, 432.
Stanford University, International Club, 56.
Stresemann, quoted, 210 f.
Student Conference on Limitation of Armaments, 190.
Study courses, 496 (see also discussion courses, 494; and reading courses, 504).
Summer camps, 430, 433.
Summer schools, 423.
Sunday schools, 425, 426.
Suttner, Baroness Bertha von, 111.
Syracuse University, 52, 57.

Taft, quoted, 249.
Taft Treaties, 249 f.
Tariffs, action on, by World Economic Conference, 132 ff.; action on by International Chamber of Commerce, 133; United States attitude toward, 133 f.; bankers' manifesto, 134; free trade between states of United States, 135 f.; bibliographies on, 518; books on, 521.
Tavenner, Clyde H., quoted, 138-139.

INDEX

Tests of attitudes on international problems, 16 ff.
Textbooks, studies of, 20 ff.; World Federation of Education Associations Committee on, 248; resolution on, 25; in Japan, 29; resolution by French teachers, 29 f.; in England, 30; resolution on by United Farmers of Alberta, 161 f.; resolutions by American Legion, 174.
Theosophical Society, 103.
Thomas, Dr. Augustus O., 23; quoted, 34, 77.
Tigert, John J., quoted, 34, 35.
Trades and Labor Congress of Canada, 150.
Traffic in arms, 296 f.
Treaties, Kellogg Multilateral Treaty for the Renunciation of War, 234 ff.; Jay Treaty, 242; of Ghent, 242; treaty-making power of U. S. Government, footnote, 246; Root, 249; Taft, 249; Bryan, 254 f.; of conciliation, 259 f.; arbitration, conciliation and disarmament, 261; Locarno, 262; for pacific settlement, 261, 263; not "supreme law," 363.
"Truce of God," 74.
Trueblood, Benjamin F., 241 f.

Union of American Hebrew Congregations, 86-87.
United Farmers of Alberta, 161.
United States Bureau of Education, 34, 41.
United States and World Peace, efforts of Founders to promote, 7 ff., 199 ff., 242 ff.; education and peace, 33 ff.; World Court proposals, 218 ff.; outlawry of war proposal, 239; promotion of arbitration, 242 ff.; with Latin America, 257; with Canada, 282, 286; Washington Conference on Limitation of Armaments, 290; policy of, 314, 315 f.; study courses on, 495, 499; books on, 525, 535.
Universal Postal Union, 279 f.

Universal Religious Peace Conference, 78.
Universalist General Convention, 98.
University Afloat, 40.
University Institute of Higher International Studies in Geneva, 39.

Vacation Bible Schools, 425.
Venezuela, Constitution of, 257.
Vermont, legislature, resolution of, 243.
Versailles, Treaty of, protest of women against, 113; attitude of Germans toward, 170, 211; and League of Nations, 211; provisions for disarmament of Germany, 289.

Wales, radio message of children of, 489; course in history, 45.
Walter Hines Page School of International Relations, 48.
War, profits, 298; character of modern, 122, 180, 181, 391-400; property losses in next, 399; cost of, 401-412; in money, 402; in lives, 403; to the race, 404 f.; in health, 407; in character, 407 f.; in constructive work, 408; in taxes, 409; in social progress, 412; and human nature, 3, 4, 19 f., 456, 534; not always existed, 456; teaching history of, 456 ff.; bibliographies on, 519; books on, 529, 530, 534.
War Debts (see Foreign Debt, World War).
War-making Power in the U. S. Government, 309; executive assumption of, 373-379; books on, 525, 526.
"War to end war," 166-168.
War Veterans and Peace, 166-182; purpose in World War, 166 ff.; international organization for peace, 168 ff.; peace resolutions of American Legion, 172 ff.; resolution on education, 173; resolution on press, 174; resolution

on military training, 175; responsibility of American Legion in present effort to abolish war, 176; soldiers' special contribution to peace movement, 179.
Washington Conference on the Limitation of Armaments, 113, 190, 290 ff.
Washington, George, quoted, 8, 313, 344; programs for Birthday, 485.
Washington Naval Treaty, 290.
Washington, University of, 50.
Watkins, Arthur Charles, 454.
Watson, Goodwin B., tests by, 18.
Wells, H. G., quoted, 121, 397, 507.
Wentworth, Lydia G., 506.
Wesleyan University, 52.
West, Roscoe L., 464.
West Virginia, schools, 62.
Weyl, Mrs. Carrie S., 447.
Wickersham, George W., 271, 273; quoted, 229.
Willard, Frances E., 111.
William and Mary, College of, 53.
Williams, Mary Wilhelmine, 457.
Williamstown Institute of Politics, 422.
Wilson, Mrs. Alice, 57.
Wilson, Woodrow, 200, 202; quoted, on necessity for peace, 6; on labor standards, 145 f.; reduction of armaments called for in Fourteen Points, 289.
Wirt, Lincoln, 424.
Wisconsin, University of, 52, 320.
Wise, James Waterman, quoted, 189, 190.
Wise, Stephen S., 326.
Woman's Boards of Foreign Missions of North America, Federation of, 116.
Woman's Christian Temperance Union, National, 111.
Woman's Home Companion, quoted, 123.
Woman's Missionary Union of Friends in America, 114.
Woman's Peace Party, 111 ff.
Women, and Peace, 106-123; statements of psychologists, 107 ff.; organized effort for peace, 110 ff.; political activities for peace, 119 f.; peace movement and woman's movement, 120 ff.; effect of war propaganda on, 121; in a "next" war, 120, 406.
Women's Clubs, work for peace through, 428 f.
Women's Committee for World Disarmament, 113.
Women's Council for Promotion of Peace, 429.
Women's International League for Peace and Freedom, 112-113, 114, 119-120, 353, 423; Pennsylvania Branch, 421.
Women's Peace Society, 114, 302.
Women's Peace Union, 114; constitutional amendment to prevent war, 115, 302.
Women's World Court Committee, 115.
Wood, Richard R., quoted, 307.
Woodbury High School, program, 59.
Woodcraft League of America, 432.
Woods, Erville B., quoted, 144.
Woolf, Leonard S., quoted, 280.
Woolley, Mary E., 326.
World Agricultural Society, 163.
World Alliance for International Friendship Through the Churches, 78, 84-85.
World Christian Endeavor Society, 427.
World Court, 217-230; organization of, 220 ff.; protocol of, 221; Statute of, 221; decisions of, 222 f.; method of electing judges, 222; sessions, 222; optional clause, 223; reservations to U. S. resolution of adherence, 224 ff.; advisory opinions, 229; Gillett Resolution, 230; study courses on, 502; bibliographies on, 519; books on, 523.
World Economic Conference, 127, 130-133, 159, 164.
World Federation of Education Associations, 21, 23-26, 43, 46.
World League of International Education Associations, 58.

INDEX

World Population, 358 ff.
World Population Conference, 358.
World Student Christian Federation, 187, 191-192.
World Union of Women, 110.
World Unity, quoted, 78.
World Unity, 65, 455; bibliographies on, 519; books on, 520.
World War Foreign Debt Commission, 380.
World War Guilt, 170, 211; books on, 533.
World-Y tours, 430.
World Youth Peace Congress, 184.

Young, Owen D., quoted, 49, 133.
Young Men's Christian Association, 430, 432.
Young Women's Christian Association, National Board of, 115, 116; activities of, 424, 430.
Youth Peace Contest, 433.
Young People's Societies, 427.
Young people and peace, 183-194; attitude on international problems, 16 ff.; experience in war, 183, 185 f.; international organization, 184; effect on European youth, 188-190; in American Universities, 190 f.; religious groups, 191 f.; hope of older generation in, 193 f.; peace work in organizations of young people, 429-436; vote on participation in war, 191 f.; study courses on, 496; bibliographies on, 519; books on, 539.

Zimmern, Alfred E., quoted, 38.